# 3rd Workshop on Cognitive Aspects of the Lexicon

# (CogALex-III)



**Held at the 24th International Conference on Computational Linguistics (COLING 2012)**

## Mumbai, India
## 15 December 2012

**Editors:**

**Michael Zock**
**Reinhard Rapp**

ISBN: 978-1-62748-352-0

**Printed from e-media with permission by:**

Curran Associates, Inc.
57 Morehouse Lane
Red Hook, NY 12571

**Some format issues inherent in the e-media version may also appear in this print version.**



Printed by Curran Associates, Inc. (2013)



Association for Computational Linguistics
209 N. Eighth Street
Stroudsburg, Pennsylvania 18360

Phone: 1-570-476-8006
Fax: 1-570-476-0860

acl@aclweb.org

**Additional copies of this publication are available from:**

Curran Associates, Inc.
57 Morehouse Lane
Red Hook, NY 12571 USA
Phone: 845-758-0400
Fax: 845-758-2634
Email: curran@proceedings.com
Web: www.proceedings.com

COLING 2012

# 24th International Conference on Computational Linguistics

# Proceedings of the 3rd Workshop on Cognitive Aspects of the Lexicon (CogALex-III)

Workshop chairs:
Michael Zock and Reinhard Rapp

15 December 2012
Mumbai, India

## Diamond sponsors

Tata Consultancy Services
Linguistic Data Consortium for Indian Languages (LDC-IL)

## Gold Sponsors

Microsoft Research
Beijing Baidu Netcon Science Technology Co. Ltd.

## Silver sponsors

IBM, India Private Limited
Crimson Interactive Pvt. Ltd.
Yahoo
Easy Transcription & Software Pvt. Ltd.

# Introduction to the 3rd Workshop on Cognitive Aspects of the Lexicon (CogALex-III)

Encouraged by the enthusiasm and interest expressed by the participants of COGALEX-I (co-located with COLING 2008 in Manchester)[1] and COGALEX-II (co-located with COLING 2010 in Beijing)[2] it was natural to come up with a follow-up workshop. As with the preceding events (including the workshop "*Enhancing and Using Electronic Dictionaries*" held in conjunction with COLING 2004 in Geneva),[3] our aim was to provide a forum for computational lexicographers, researchers in NLP, and industrial practitioners to share their knowledge concerning the construction, organisation and use of a lexicon by people (lexical access) and machines (NLP, IR, data-mining). However, given the progress in various fields outside of linguistics (biology, psycholinguistics, neuro-sciences, network sciences, etc.) we decided to broaden the scope by inviting researchers from other domains, as we believe their work to be relevant.

Dictionaries store knowledge concerning words. Obviously, they should be comprehensive and complete enough to reveal the meaning of words (analysis), their form or other related information relevant for language producers (speakers, writers). Yet, the quality of a dictionary depends not only on *coverage*, but also on *accessibility* of information. Access strategies vary with the task (text understanding vs. text production) and the knowledge available at the moment of consultation (words, concepts, speech sounds). Unlike readers who look for meanings, writers start from them, searching for the corresponding words. While paper dictionaries are static, permitting only limited strategies for accessing information, their electronic counterparts promise dynamic, proactive search via multiple criteria (meaning, sound, related words) and via diverse access routes. Navigation takes place in a huge conceptual lexical space, and the results are displayable in a multitude of forms (e.g. as trees, as lists, as graphs, or sorted alphabetically, by topic, by frequency).

The way we look at dictionaries (their creation and use) has changed dramatically over the past 30 years. While being considered as an appendix to grammar in the past, they have in the meantime moved to centre stage. Indeed, there is hardly any task in NLP which can be conducted without them. Also, rather than being static entities (data-base view), dictionaries are now viewed as graphs, whose nodes and links (connection strengths) may change over time. Interestingly, properties concerning topology, clustering and evolution known from other disciplines (society, economy, human brain) also apply to dictionaries: everything is linked, hence accessible, and everything is evolving. Given these similarities, one may wonder what we can learn from these disciplines. In the 3rd edition of the CogALex workshop we therefore intended to also invite scientists working in these fields, our goals being to broaden the picture, i.e. to gain a better understanding concerning the mental lexicon and to integrate these findings into our dictionaries in order to support navigation. Given recent advances in neurosciences, it appears timely to seek inspiration from neuroscientists studying the human brain. There is also a lot to be learned from other fields studying graphs and networks, even if their object of study is something else than language, for example biology, economy or society.

---

[1] Workshop proceedings (in ACL anthology): http://www.aclweb.org/anthology/W/W08/#1900
[2] Workshop proceedings (in ACL anthology): http://aclweb.org/anthology-new/W/W10/#3400
[3] Workshop proceedings (in ACL anthology): http://aclweb.org/anthology-new/W/W04/#2100

We agree with van Deemter and colleagues[4] when they write "... computational and psycholinguistic approaches to reference production can benefit from closer interaction, and this is likely to result in the construction of algorithms that differ markedly from the ones currently known in the computational literature.". One might add that the same is true for many areas of NLP, including the lexicon. This is in line with Krahmer's[5] inspirational paper 'What computational linguists can learn from psychologists (and vice versa)' which was published in the Computational Linguistics journal.

This workshop is about possible enhancements of existing electronic dictionaries. To perform the groundwork for the next generation of electronic dictionaries we invited researchers involved in the building of such dictionaries. The idea is to discuss modifications of existing resources by taking the users' needs and knowledge states into account, and to capitalize on the advantages of the digital media. For this workshop we invited papers including but not limited to the following topics which can be considered from various points of view: linguistics, neuro- or psycholinguistics (tip of the tongue problem, associations), network related sciences (sociology, economy, biology), mathematics (vector-based approaches, graph theory, small-world problem), etc.

Analysis of the conceptual input of a dictionary user

- What does a language producer start from (bag of words)?
- What is in the authors' minds when they are generating a message and looking for a word?
- What does it take to bridge the gap between this input and the desired output (target word)?

The meaning of words

- Lexical representation (holistic, decomposed)
- Meaning representation (concept based, primitives)
- Revelation of hidden information (vector-based approaches: LSA/HAL)
- Neural models, neurosemantics, neurocomputational theories of content representation.

Structure of the lexicon

- Discovering structures in the lexicon: formal and semantic point of view (clustering, topical structure)
- Creative ways of getting access to and using word associations
- Evolution, i.e. dynamic aspects of the lexicon (changes of weights)
- Neural models of the mental lexicon (distribution of information concerning words, organisation of words)

Methods for crafting dictionaries or indexes

- Manual, automatic or collaborative building of dictionaries and indexes (distributional semantics, crowd-sourcing, serious games, etc.)
- Impact and use of social networks (Facebook, Twitter) for building dictionaries, for organizing and indexing the data (clustering of words), and for allowing to track navigational strategies, etc.
- (Semi-) automatic induction of the link type (e.g. synonym, hypernym, meronym, association, collocation, ...)

---

[4] van Deemter, K., Gatt, A., van Gompel, R. & Krahmer, E. (2012). Towards a computational psycholinguistics of reference production. *Topics in Cognitive Science*, 4 (2), 166–183.

[5] Krahmer, E. (2010). What computational linguists can learn from psychologists (and vice versa). *Computational Linguistics*, 36 (2), 285–294.

- Use of corpora and patterns (data-mining) for getting access to words, their uses, combinations and associations

Dictionary access (navigation and search strategies), interface issues

- Semantic-based search
- Search (simple query vs multiple words)
- Context-dependent search (modification of users' goals during search)
- Recovery
- Navigation (frequent navigational patterns or search strategies used by people)
- Interface problems, data-visualisation

We received 22 submissions, of which ten were accepted as full papers, while six were chosen for poster presentation. While we did not get papers on all the issues mentioned in our call, we did get a quite rich panel of topics including cognitive approaches to lexical access, considerations on word meaning and ontologies, manual and automatic approaches for constructing lexicons, as well as pragmatic aspects.

It was also interesting to see the variety of languages in which these issues are addressed. The proposals range from European languages such as Bulgarian, Dutch, English, French, German, Italian, Polish, Romanian, Russian, and Spanish to Asian languages including Assamese, Bangla, Bodo, Chinese, Hindi and Japanese. In sum, the community working on dictionaries is dynamic, and there seems to be a growing awareness of the importance of some of the problems presented in our call for papers.

We would like to thank Alain Polguère for having accepted to be our invited speaker, and the COLING organizers, in particular publication chair Roger Evans, for providing the framework and for their support. We would also like to express our sincerest thanks to all the members of the Programme Committee whose expertise was invaluable to assure a good selection of papers, despite the very tight schedule. Their reviews were helpful not only for us to make the decisions, but also for the authors, helping them to improve their work. In the hope that the results will inspire you, provoke fruitful discussions and result in future collaborations.

*Michael Zock* and *Reinhard Rapp*

## Organizers:

Michael Zock (LIF-CNRS, Marseille, France)
Reinhard Rapp (LIF, Marseille, France & University of Mainz, Germany)

## Invited Speaker:

Alain Polguère (Université de Lorraine, ATILF, France)

## Programme Committee:

Eduard Barbu (Universidad de Jaén, Spain)
Alain Barrat (Centre de physique théorique, CNRS & Aix-Marseille Université, France)
Gemma Bel-Enguix (LIF, Aix-Marseille Université, France)
Pierrette Bouillon (TIM, Faculty of Translation and Interpretating, Geneva, Switzerland)
Paul Cook (The University of Melbourne, Australia)
Dan Cristea (University of Iasi, Romania)
Cedrick Fairon (CENTAL, Université catholique de Louvain, Belgium)
Afsaneh Fazly (University of Toronto, Canada)
Christiane Fellbaum (University of Princeton, USA)
Olivier Ferret (CEA LIST, Palaiseau, France)
Thierry Fontenelle (Translation Centre for the Bodies of the European Union, Luxemburg)
Sylviane Granger (Université Catholique de Louvain, Belgium)
Gregory Grefenstette (3DS Exalead, Paris, France)
Silvia Hansen-Schirra (University of Mainz, FTSK, Germany)
Ulrich Heid (University of Hildesheim, Germany)
Graeme Hirst (University of Toronto, Canada)
Ed Hovy (ISI, Los Angeles, USA)
Terry Joyce (Tama University, Kanagawa-ken, Japan)
Olivia Kwong (City University of Hong Kong, China)
Marie Claude L'Homme (OLST, University of Montreal, Canada)
Guy Lapalme (RALI, University of Montreal, Canada)
Verginica Mititelu (RACAI, Bucharest, Romania)
Vito Pirrelli (ILC, Pisa, Italy)
Alain Polguère (Université de Lorraine, ATILF, France)
Reinhard Rapp (LIF Marseille, France & University of Mainz, Germany)
Tom Ruette (KU Leuven, Belgium)
Didier Schwab (LIG, Grenoble, France)
Gilles Sérasset (IMAG, Grenoble, France)
Serge Sharoff (University of Leeds, UK)
Anna Sinopalnikova (FIT, BUT, Brno, Czech Republic)
John Sowa (VivoMind Research, LLC, USA)
Carole Tiberius (Institute for Dutch Lexicology, The Netherlands)
Takenobu Tokunaga (TITECH, Tokyo, Japan)
Dan Tufis (RACAI, Bucharest, Romania)
Alessandro Valitutti (University of Helsinki and HIIT, Finland)
Piek Vossen (Vrije Universiteit, Amsterdam, The Netherlands)
Eric Wehrli (LATL, University of Geneva, Switzerland)
Michael Zock (LIF, CNRS & Aix-Marseille Université, France)
Pierre Zweigenbaum (LIMSI-CNRS, Orsay & ERTIM-INALCO, Paris, France)

# Table of Contents

# 3rd Workshop on Cognitive Aspects of the Lexicon
## Program

**Saturday, 15 December 2012**

| | |
|---|---|
| 09:00–0905 | **Opening Remarks** |
| 09:05–1000 | **Invited Presentation**<br>*Like a Lexicographer Weaving Her Lexical Network*<br>Alain Polguère |
| 10:00-11:30 | **Session 1: Cognitive Approaches** |
| 10:00–10:30 | *Long Tail in Weighted Lexical Networks*<br>Mathieu Lafourcade and Alain Joubert |
| 10:30–11:00 | *On discriminating fMRI representations of abstract WordNet taxonomic categories*<br>Andrew Anderson, Tao Yuan, Brian Murphy and Massimo Poesio |
| 11:00–11:30 | *Automatic index creation to support navigation in lexical graphs encoding part_of relations*<br>Michael Zock and Debela Tesfaye |
| 11:30–12:00 | Tea break |
| 12:00-13:30 | **Session 2: Word Meaning and Ontological Considerations** |
| 12:00–12:30 | *Modeling Word Meaning: Distributional Semantics and the Corpus Quality-Quantity Trade-Off*<br>Seshadri Sridharan and Brian Murphy |
| 12:30–13:00 | *Verb interpretation for basic action types: annotation, ontology induction and creation of prototypical scenes*<br>Francesca Frontini, Irene de Felice, Fahad Khan, Irene Russo, Monica Monachini, Gloria Gagliardi and Alessandro Panunzi |
| 13:00–13:30 | *Dictionary-ontology cross-enrichment*<br>Emmanuel Eckard, Lucie Barque, Alexis Nasr and Benoît Sagot |
| 13:30–14:30 | Lunch |

**Saturday, 15 December 2012 (continued)**

14:30–15:30 **Session 3: Crafting Lexicons, Manual and Automatic Approaches**

14:30–15:00 *Automatic Construction of a MultiWord Expressions Bilingual Lexicon: A Statistical Machine Translation Evaluation Perspective*
Dhouha Bouamor, Nasredine Semmar and Pierre Zweigenbaum

15:00–15:30 *Hand-Crafting a Lexical Network With a Knowledge-Based Graph Editor*
Nabil Gader, Veronika Lux-Pogodalla and Alain Polguère

15:30–16:30 **Session 4: Posters with Booster Session**

15:30–15:35 *A Procedural DTD Project for Dictionary Entry Parsing Described with Parameterized Grammars*
Neculai Curteanu and Mihai Alex Moruz

15:35–15:40 *Automatic Generation of the Universal Word Explanation from UNL Ontology*
Khan Md Anwarus Salam, Hiroshi Uchida and Tetsuro Nishino

15:40–15:45 *Towards merging common and technical lexicon wordnets*
Raquel Amaro and Sara Mendes

15:45–15:50 *Building Multilingual Lexical Resources using Wordnets: Structure, Design and Implementation*
Shikhar Kr. Sarma, Dibyajyoti Sarmah, Biswajit Brahma, Himadri Bharali, Mayashree Mahanta and Utpal Saikia

15:50–15:55 *A New Semantic Lexicon and Similarity Measure in Bangla*
Manjira Sinha, Abhik Jana, Tirthankar Dasgupta and Anupam Basu

15:55–16:00 *Where's the meeting that was cancelled? existential implications of transitive verbs*
Patricia Amaral, Valeria de Paiva, Cleo Condoravdi and Annie Zaenen

16:30-17:00 Tea break

17:00–1800 **Session 5: Pragmatic Aspects**

17:00–17:30 *SEJFEK - a Lexicon and a Shallow Grammar of Polish Economic Multi-Word Units*
Agata Savary, Bartosz Zaborowski, Aleksandra Krawczyk-Wieczorek and Filip Makowiecki

17:30–18:00 *The Compreno Semantic Model as Integral Framework for Multilingual Lexical Database*
Ekaterina Manicheva, Maria Petrova, Elena Kozlova and Tatiana Popova

18:00–18:15 **Session 6: Wrap-up Discussion and Closing Address**

18:15 **End of the Workshop**

# Like a Lexicographer Weaving Her Lexical Network*

Alain POLGUÈRE
Université de Lorraine, ATILF, UMR 7118, Nancy, F-54000, FRANCE
Alain.Polguere@univ-lorraine.fr

## The spider attitude

The title of our talk—an implicit reference to the English cliché *like a spider weaving her web*—intends to attract one's attention to the metaphor that can be drawn between the dance of a spider weaving her web and a new *lexicographic gesture* that is gradually emerging from the work on Net-like lexical resources (Fellbaum, 1998; Baker et al., 2003; Gader et al., 2012). Our claim is that the inherent graph structure of natural language lexicons not only determine vocabulary acquisition and use (Wolter, 2006), but also lexicographic activity. In that respect, reflecting on new ways to implement the task of building lexical resources is essential for lexicographers themselves, but also for anyone interested is lexicons as mental structures. After all, lexicographers and language learners are those who have the most direct contact with lexical structures, through closely related activities: describing a natural phenomenon is a form of learning through explicit conceptualization. Lexicographers often experience the fact that by completing the description of a word they achieve a form of understanding and mastering of this word. They do not merely transcribe word knowledge and observations made on word behavior in speech and texts: they "acquire" the word. This makes them feel good and this explains why lexicography is indeed extremely addictive.

Our talk title is also an implicit reference to the English collocation *web of words*, that is so often used to refer to natural language lexicons as messy and too big to be embraced entities —cf. (Murray, 1977), entitled *Caught in the web of words: James A. H. Murray and the Oxford English dictionary*. Of course, webs can be seen as being essentially traps that one gets caught in. This is so to speak the fly or innocent bug perspective. However, lexicographers ought not be caught in the web: they can behave as spiders weaving the web. This is possible if the model they are constructing is indeed a diagrammatic representation—in a semiotic sense (Farias and Queiroz, 2006)—of the natural language lexicon that is being scrutinized. It is when lexicographers run on pages, writing dictionary articles, like flies walking on a glass window, that they have the most chance to get caught in the web of words. This is why lexicographers have long ago introduced systems of cards and records to help them compile data on lexical units. Lexicographic records helped lexicographers free themselves from the two-dimensional prison of the dictionary. Their knowledge about words occupied a "volume," that of filing cabinets, which is more in line with the three-dimensional nature of the lexicons they had to describe. Later, with the advent of computational lexicography, relational databases replaced filing cabinets as convenient tools... and metaphors.

* Extended abstract for CogALex III invited lecture.

## Towards a lexicography of virtual dictionaries

New data structures for lexical resources should come together with new ways of building lexical models, and this is the main topic we are dealing with here. In order to propose an alternate perspective on lexicography, one that in our opinion is more cognition-compatible in nature, it is necessary to first eradicate a rather widespread misconception related to the construction of lexical models. According to common perception, lexicography is all about writing dictionaries and, therefore, any activity that targets the construction of other types of lexical models, freed from the two-dimensional (textual) dictionary, is not "true" lexicography. This misconception, very common among laypersons and endorsed by many natural language researchers, originates mainly for the sheer fact that, for centuries, lexicographers had no better medium of encoding than the text and no better physical support for their description than sheets of paper bound together to make dictionaries. However, the dictionary—whether in paper or electronic format—is just one among many possible incarnations of lexical models. What is truly necessary and sufficient for a task to be termed *lexicography* is that:

- it targets the description of lexical units of one or more natural languages in terms of sense, forms and all other relevant linguistic properties;
- it uses a well-defined frame of analysis that allows for a coherent and uniform description of all lexical units;
- it is essentially a hand-made task, but with no limitation to the amount and diversity of tools and external data that can be used to perform this task;
- it "sees big:" the greater the coverage and depth of description for each lexical unit, the more lexicographic the task will be.

This last point is more important than it may appear: when it comes to the lexicon—its description, as well as learning, mastering, etc.—size does matter. To take an extreme case, a person whose only experience in the field is the description of just one or a couple of lexical units can simply not be considered a lexicographer and the task accomplished is all but an exercise in lexicography. By contrast, someone who has achieved the description of tens of thousands of lexical units is no doubt an experienced lexicographer. Somewhere in between, there is the transition from being an apprentice to being an actual lexicographer.

Notice that no mention of the formal nature of lexical models is made in the above characterization of lexicography. In fact, when the construction of a totally new, graph-based model of lexical knowledge was proposed by WordNet initiators (Miller et al., 1990), no claim was made on the advent of a new discipline. On the contrary, lexicography remained the reference, with work performed by individuals called *lexicographers*, who were constructing datasets called *lexicographer files*. And this is entirely justified as, precisely, lexicography is not about writing dictionaries *per se*. This fact has already been pointed at by some dictionary-makers; (Atkins, 1996), for instance, adopts a rather visionary perspective and goes as far as to consider that bilingual lexicography should be aiming at *virtual dictionaries*—cf. S. Atkins' proposal for "real databases, real links and virtual dictionaries" (section 2.2.1 of her paper).

## From writing dictionaries to weaving lexical networks

In our talk, we take the above observations as given, including the fact that lexicography should indeed be targeting virtual dictionaries, generated from non-textual lexical models

(Polguère, 2012). We illustrate how the lexicographic process of building graph-based lexical models can benefit from tools that allow lexicographers to wade through the lexical web, following paradigmatic and syntagmatic paths, while **simultaneously** weaving new links and incrementing the lexical description. Work performed on the *French Lexical Network* (Gader et al., 2012) will serve to demonstrate how the lexicographic process can be made closer to actual navigation through lexical knowledge by the speaker. The main theoretical and descriptive tool that makes such navigation possible is the system of lexical functions proposed by the Meaning-Text linguistic approach (Mel'čuk, 1996). It induces the multidimensional and non-hierarchical graph structure of the FLN that, we believe, is far better suited for designing lexical resources than hyperonymy-based structures.

Computational aspects of the work on the French Lexical Network are dealt with in (Gader et al., 2012). In our presentation, we focus on the actual process of weaving lexical relations.

## References


Atkins, B. T. S. (1996). Bilingual Dictionaries: Past, Present and Future. In Gellerstam, M., Järborg, J., Malmgren, S.-G., Norén, K., Rogström, L., and Papmehl, C. R., editors, *Euralex'96 Proceedings*, pages 515–590, Gothenburg. Gothenburg University, Department of Swedish.

Baker, C. F., Fillmore, C. J., and Cronin, B. (2003). The Structure of the FrameNet Database. *International Journal of Lexicography*, 16(3):281–296.

Farias, P. and Queiroz, J. (2006). Images, diagrams, and metaphors: Hypoicons in the context of Peirce's sixty-six-fold classification of signs. *Semiotica*, 162(1/4):287–307.

Fellbaum, C., editor (1998). *WordNet: An Electronic Lexical Database*. The MIT Press, Cambridge MA.

Gader, N., Lux-Pogodalla, V., and Polguère, A. (2012). Hand-Crafting a Lexical Network With a Knowledge-Based Graph Editor. In *Proceedings of the Third Workshop on Cognitive Aspects of the Lexicon. Enhancing the Structure and Look-up Mechanisms of Electronic Dictionaries (CogALex III)*, Mumbai.

Mel'čuk, I. (1996). Lexical Functions: A Tool for the Description of Lexical Relations in the Lexicon. In Wanner, L., editor, *Lexical Functions in Lexicography and Natural Language Processing*, volume 31 of *Language Companion Series*, pages 37–102. John Benjamins, Amsterdam/Philadelphia.

Miller, G. A., Beckwith, R., Fellbaum, C., Gross, D., and Miller, K. J. (1990). Introduction to WordNet: An On-line Lexical Database. *International Journal of Lexicography*, 3(4):235–244.

Murray, K. M. E. (1977). *Caught in the web of words: James A. H. Murray and the Oxford English dictionary*. Yale University Press, New Haven.

Polguère, A. (2012). Lexicographie des dictionnaires virtuels. In Apresjan, Y., Boguslavsky, I., L'Homme, M.-C., Iomdin, L., Milićević, J., Polguère, A., and Wanner, L., editors, *Meanings, Texts, and Other Exciting Things. A Festschrift to Commemorate the 80$^{th}$ Anniversary of Professor Igor Alexandrovič Mel'čuk*, Studia Philologica, pages 509–523. Jazyki slavjanskoj kultury Publishers, Moscow.

Wolter, B. (2006). Lexical Network Structures and L2 Vocabulary Acquisition: The Role of L1 Lexical/Conceptual Knowledge. *Applied Linguistics*, 27(4):741–747.

# Long Tail in Weighted Lexical Networks

*Mathieu Lafourcade Alain Joubert*
LIRMM, Montpellier, France
mathieu.lafourcade@lirmm.fr, alain.joubert@lirmm.fr

ABSTRACT

Lexical networks can be used with benefit for semantic analysis of texts, word sense disambiguation (WSD) and in general for graph-based Natural Language Processing. Usually strong relations between terms (e.g.: cat --> animal) are sufficient to help for the task, but quite often, weak relations (e.g.: cat --> ball of wool) are necessary. Our purpose here is to acquire such relations by means of online serious games as other classical approaches seems impractical. Indeed, it is difficult to ask the users (non experts) to define a proper weighting for the relations they propose, and then we decided to relate weights with the frequency of their propositions. It allows us to acquire first the strongest relations, but also to populate the long tail of an already existing network. Furthermore, trying to get an estimation of our network by the very users thanks to a tip of the tongue (TOT) software, we realized that they rather tend to favor the relations of the long tail and thus promote their emergence. Developing the long tail of a lexical network with standard and non-standard relations of low weight can be of advantage for tasks such that words retrieval from clues or WSD in texts.

KEYWORDS : LEXICAL NETWORK, LONG TAIL, GAME WITH A PURPOSE, TIP OF THE TONGUE SOFTWARE, TYPED RELATIONS, WEIGHTED RELATIONS, WSD

## Introduction

Lexical/semantic networks are very precious resources for NLP applications in general and for Word Sense Disambiguation (WSD) in particular. Their construction is delicate as automated approaches from corpora may have various shortcomings (mainly high noise level and/or low recall) and a manual approach may be long, tedious, costly and of unsatisfactory quality or coverage. A way of handling the building of such resources can be direct crowdsourcing (as contributive approaches) or indirect crowdsourcing through for instance serious games.

What is a long tail in a lexical network?

A lexical/semantic network (thereafter dubbed JDM) for French is under construction with methods based on popular consensus by means of games with a purpose named JeuxDeMots (Lafourcade 2007). Thus, in 5 years, a high number of players lead to the construction a large scale lexical network for the French language (currently more than 240 000 terms with around 1.4 million semantic relations) representing a common general knowledge but also including word senses referred as *word usages* (Lafourcade and Joubert, 2010). The relations of the lexical networks created this way are directed and typed, with classical ontological relations (like hypernym, hyponyms, part-of, whole, material/substance, ...), lexical relations (synonyms, antonyms, lexical family, ...);

semantic roles (agent, patient, instrument, ...) and less standard relations (typical location and time, cause, consequence, ...). Furthermore, relation occurrences are weighted which constitutes a quite original aspect in the lexical network domain exemplified by (for example) WordNet (Miller, 1990). The interpretation of a weight might by difficult but can be related to the *strength* of the relation as collectively perceived by speakers/players. The weight computation is done by emergence along with the gaming activity. Obviously by intuition, the relation *cat--> animal* is stronger than *cat --> ball of wool,* none withstanding their types.

The lexical network has been made available (at http://jeuxdemots.org) and free to use by their authors, giving the research community a resource to play with. The question of the evaluation of its quality, usability in WSD and word recollection (Tip of the Tongue problem), and distributional properties are the main subjects of this article. One specific question is whether low weight but still important relations can be captured by some similar approaches and to which extend they are useful.

We observed that many (if not most) relations in JDM are "frontal/direct/obvious" relations (e.g.: *chat-->-feline*), but some others are more farfetched/indirect. We wish to evaluate but also find practical ways to *densify* the network increasing the number of "indirect" relations (e.g.: *chat --> allergy*) belonging to the long tail. To do so, we use a TOT tool in a *taboo mode,* that is, refraining from using the strongest relations.

In a first section, we will briefly remind to the reader the principles of *long tail* and the link with the network construction. Then, we introduce our TOT (tip of the tongue) tool, named AKI and we will explain the taboo mode, and show how it leads to *densifying* the JDM network. An evaluation of the long tailed network obtained is done for AKI and for a simplified WSD task.

## 1 Long tailed lexical networks

Lexical networks, either general or specialized, are quite well known, especially with the advent of WordNet (Fellbaum, 1998). But relations in those lexical networks are not weighted, that is to say relations between terms are just enumerated and being viewed as equivalent in their influence (not considering their type). Introducing weights to relations to discriminate between *strong* and *loose* relations seems interesting but leads to also critical issues like: *how it could be done in practice and how to evaluate the obtained lexical network relatively to weights?* Propagation algorithms in WSD can take advantage of weighted relations, and especially in case of loose but numerous connexions between words of the text.

In (Sigman and Cecchi, 2002), a study of the organisation of the WordNet lexicon showed that the statistical distribution of the relation shows long tail behaviour, although they are not weighted. In fact, the study focused on the relations distribution amongst terms of WordNet, not of the distribution of the relations weights. Gaume (2008) studied various lexical networks and particularly graph of synonyms, and showed that they are "Small worlds graphs", and as such amongst other properties, having a long tail in the relation distribution relatively to terms. But again, such long tail doesn't relate to the strength of the relations by themselves, even they are highly applicable between synonyms.

Some works aim at introducing weights in lexical network and especially WordNet. generally weights are added to synsets (and not relations betweens synsets) for handling default cases in WSD tasks. Such approaches relate generally to term frequency or various evaluation of terms pairs computed in the basis of the network itself. For instance (Boyd-Graber , 2006) and (Budanitsky & Hirst, 2001) amongst others, added numerically evaluated WordNet relations, weights being computed from various similarity measures. Weights are generally added either by asking people to evaluate the strength of term pairs, or 3-uples (when a relation type is added, like hypernym, synonymy, cause, consequence, etc) by giving a value on a closed scale (between 0 and 100, for example), or automatically by counting occurrences of such pairs from corpora.

## 1.1 Which Tail to Look at in Weighted and Typed Lexical Network?

The concept of *long tail* has been first popularized by (Zipf, 1965) for word occurrences in texts. Also in different domains, (Anderson, 2004) actually coined the phrase *long tail* about selling strategies of providing a large number of unique items in small quantities of each, usually combined to selling less popular items in large quantities. More precisely in our context, a long tail is a statistical property that a large share of a population belong to the tail of a probability distribution (larger than a normal "Gaussian" distribution) usually related to a power-law distribution.

The tail in a weighted lexical network is

the lower part of the distribution of relation weights for a given term

It is not the distribution of relations amongst terms, nor the distribution of term weights (if there is any). The tail can be considered with advantage separately for incoming or outgoing relations, as relations or even free associations are seldom symmetric. A question arises as when does the tail start in the distribution? The answer to this question is highly debatable and falls outside the scope of this paper. A simple (if not simplistic) approach is to consider that the tail starts at the point where

the cumulated weight of the relations of the tail **equals**
the cumulated weights of the relations which do not belong to the tail.

For example, in figure 1 is shown the distribution of outgoing relation weights for the term *chat* (eng. *cat*) in the JDM network. The pike (at around 45 on the x-axis, around 9,5% of the relation number) is an indication of the limit where the surface below the curve at the left of the pike is equal to the surface below the curve at the right. In this case, the first 45 relations have together the same importance than the rest of 405 relations.

However, in WSD we generally consider than the strongest relations (those on the left of the pike, in what is called the *belly* zone) are able to disambiguate around 70-75% on the ambiguity. The 25-30% could be solved with relations of the long tail, of course only if they are available in the knowledge base. None withstanding these figures (some literature would rather refer to the 20/80 rule), capturing the long tail is not only a challenge but a requirement to increase resolution percentage of WSD.

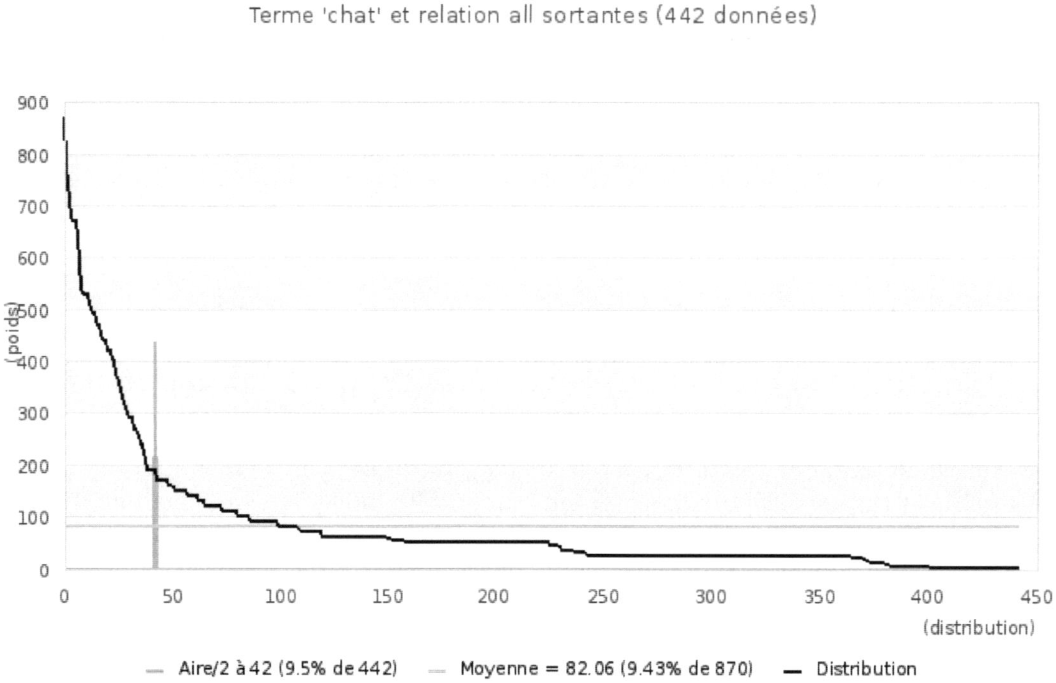


Figure 1a: distribution of outgoing relations for the term *chat* (eng. *cat*) The x-axis is the rank of the relations, the y-axis if the strength (weight). The frontier between *belly* and the *tail* of the curve is indicated by the pike. On the left, the belly part of the curve stops after the first 9.5% of strongest relations. The tail in this case covers the 90.5% weakest relations.

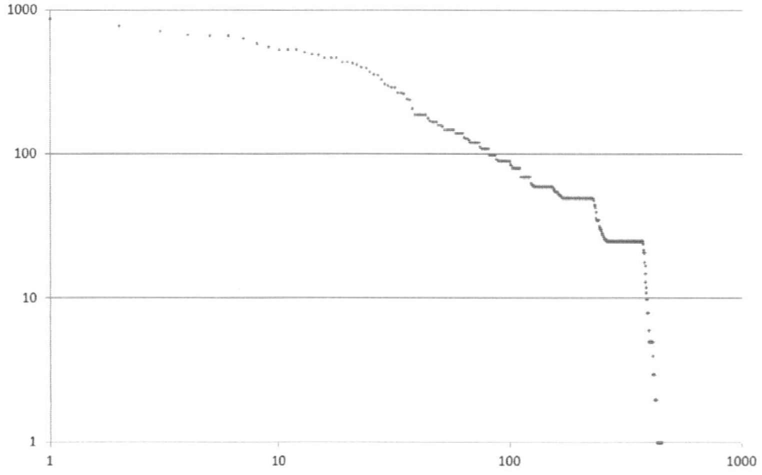


Figure 1b : the log-log version of the Figure 1a.

Put another way, Figure 1 can be interpreted, that the descriptive impact (in terms of weights) of the remaining 90.5% of the relations is equivalent that that of the first 9.5%. The curve reminds a zipfian power law (and is usually presented under a doubly-logarithmic scale, but the issue here is to pinpoint the frontier pike between the belly and the tail) or perhaps more precisely a Mandelbrot law of the form : $K/(a+bn)^c$ . However, we should stress this is not because such a curve is zipfian in shape that the data are actually related to a power law. Moreover, knowing the actual distribution law of the relations is by no mean any help in either the construction of the lexical network nor its use in lexical assistance or WSD. The question of lexical assistance have been largely presented in (Zock et al., 2010) as a difficult problem by itself. Indeed, it is not that a word is contained in such a resource that it is *de facto* easy to retrieve either by a speaker native of not, nor by any automated process.

## 1.2 Long Tailed Lexical Network Construction

The basic principles of JeuxDeMots (thereafter JDM) software, the game design, as well as the incremental construction of the lexical network, have already been described in (Lafourcade and Joubert, 2010). A game takes place between two players, in an asynchronous way. For the same target term[1] T and a same instruction (synonyms, domains, free associations ...), the answers common to both players are recorded. Validations are thus made by concordance of the propositions between pairs of players.

This validating process is similar to the one used by (von Ahn and Dabbish, 2004) to index images and by (Liberman et al., 2007) to collect *common sense knowledge*. As far as we know, this is the first time it is done for lexical/semantic networks. However, using games for collecting resources of use in NLP is nowhere new, as (Chamberlain et al.) used it for anaphora annotations and (Mihalcea and Chklovski, 2003) for annotating corpora, to name a few.

The structure of the lexical network built in JDM relies on the nodes and relations between nodes, as it was initially introduced by (Collins and Quillian, 1969) and more recently explicited by (Polguère, 2006). More precisely, JDM game leads to the construction of a lexical network connecting terms by typed and weighted relations[2], some of them being quite non-classical. These relations are labelled by the instruction given to the players and they are weighted according to the number of pairs of players who proposed them. Also similar at first sight, this a strong departure from collecting concurrences (typed or not) form corpora. Indeed, there is less guarantee, if any, that term associations extracted from corpora faithfully reflect what people have in their mind than asking them directly.

In a similar way to JDM, a PtiClic game (Zampa and Lafourcade, 2009) takes place in an asynchronous way between two players. A target term T, origin of relations, as well as a cluster of words resulting from terms connected with T in the lexical network produced by JDM are proposed to a first player. Several instructions corresponding to types of relations are also displayed. The player associates words of the cluster with instructions he thinks correspond by a drag and drop. The same term T, as well as the same cluster of words and the same instructions, are also proposed to a second player. According to a

---

[1] A term can be a compound word (for example: *Christmas tree*)

[2] A relation can be thus considered as a quadruplet: origin term, destination term, type and weight of the relation. Between two same terms, several relations of different types can exist.

principle similar to that set up for JDM, only the propositions common to both players are taken into account, thus strengthening the relations of the lexical network. Contrary to JDM, the players of PtiClic cannot suggest new terms, but are forced to choose among those proposed. This design choice should allow to reduce the noise due to misspelt terms or to meaning confusion. There are at least two aims to this game: 1) to make the weights of the relation more reliable, and 2) to cast freely associated terms to more specific relations when possible. The first one is crucial as it counterbalances a strong bias in JDM: people tend to *over propose* terms to be associated.

It is generally assumed that when a relation holds between two terms, it is of only one type. However this should be mitigated as polysemy comes into play. For example, *café* can be located in a *café* (the *beverage* and the *place,* respectively), *café* can be made of *café* (*beverage* and the *plant/grain*). Some relation might not always be clearly distinct : is a *seat* part of a *car* or located in a *car*, or both? For semantic roles, it is quite common that an agent can also be the patient of a predicate (an *animal* can kill or be killed).

With the help of more than 3000 players, relations between pairs of terms have been collected, most of them being spontaneous, and thus "frontal" ones. Other "indirect" relations, are more uncommon, which seems quite logical considering the network creating mode (consensus filtered by player pairs). More formally, a clue can be said to as frontal for a target term if it belong to the belly of the distribution curve of that target.

Finally, looking at actual weight values isolated is of little significance. Instead comparing at least two values, for the same term and the same relation is of interest and may have meaning. Some terms are more played than others for various reasons (popularity, funniness, etc.), and tend to have higher strength values. The more played a term, the more reliable are the distribution of its relations and their *relative* values.

## 2 A Tip of the Tongue System: AKI

The questions we answer are the following: for a given term are its relations with other terms able to characterize it in a unique way? When it is the case, is it useful for a Tip of the Tongue Software? Such a tool aimed at helping someone retrieving a word that is "on the tip of the tongue" by the help of clue words. As the user is supposedly unable to retrieve the target word, he can only provide words that are related. Those words are the clues given to the system.

If the answer to the first question is positive, any term may be found via one or several reduced sets of typed clues. A tool helping the resolution of "word on the tip of the tongue" is a way to undertake the evaluation of the lexical network. Through such a tool made available on the web, the evaluation can thus be made permanent in time and rely on a large number of evaluators (not necessarily knowing that they are part of a global evaluation process).

The system we developed (named AKI) is a tool for helping retrieving some word on the tip of the tongue. Alternatively, it can be viewed as a game, whose goal is to make the system find a given word through clue, or to trick it.

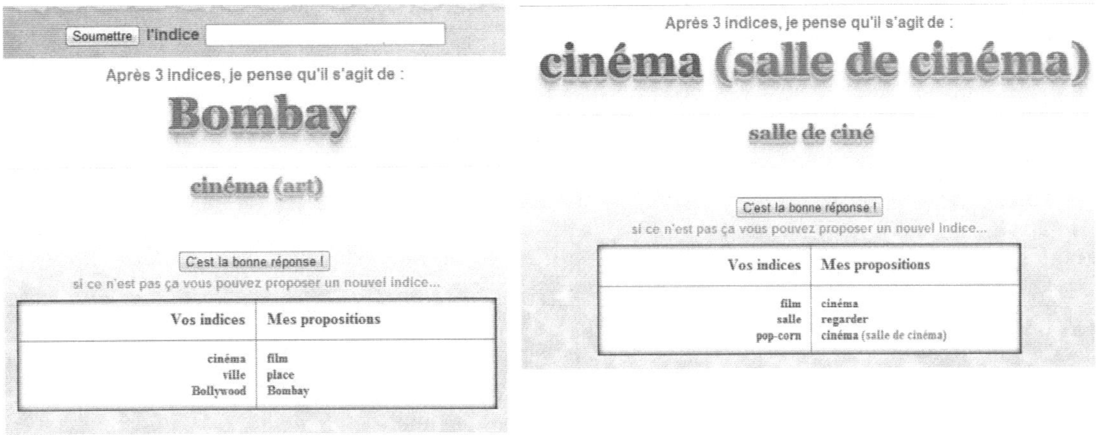


Figure 2 (a and b): examples of AKI plays. In the first play (on the left), the clues given are *cinéma (movie), ville (town)* and *Bollywood*, leading the system to propose in turn *film, place* and finally *Bombay*. In the second play (on the right), the clues are *film, salle (room),* and *pop-corn* leading in the end to *cinéma (as movie theater).*

Figures 2 are typical AKI games. At the stages displayed, the player, can either click on the button "C'est la bonne réponse" (Eng. *This is the proper answer*) if the proposition made by the system is the target term, or introduce another clue to get another proposition. The second plays, lead to a specific meaning of the word *cinéma* which may relate in French to *movie* or *theater*.

Players can introduce typed clues. A type relates to the king of relation holding between the clue and the target word. For example, a clue of the form *:isa town*, indicates that the target word is a town. When the clues are not typed (as in the above plays), they are assumed to be related to the target no considering any specific relation type. The available relations types that can be chosen by players are as follows:

| | |
|---|---|
| :isa | Hypernym, *:isa dog* means the target word is a *dog* |
| :hypo | Hyponym, *:hypo eagle*, means that the target word is an hypernym of *eagle* |
| :syn | Synonym, the target word and *clue* are synonyms. |
| :anto | Antonym, the target word is antonym of *clue*. For example, *:anto cold* |
| :subst | The target word has *clue* as substance. For example, *:subst silver* |
| :loc | The target word can be found in *clue*. For example, *:loc garden, :loc desert* |
| :locfor | The target word is a location for *clue*. For example, *:locfor money* |
| :carac | The target word has *clue* as a property. For example, *:carac cold* |
| :part | The target word has *clue* as part. For example, *:part wheel* |
| :partof | The target word is a part of *clue*. For example, *:partof car* |
| :do | The target word can do *clue*. For example, *:do roar* |
| :patientof | The target word can be an patient of *clue*. For example, *:* patientof *paint* |
| :cause | The target word can cause *clue*. For example, *:cause disease.* |
| :hascause | The target word is a consequence of clue. For example, *:* hascause *virus* |

The reader can refer for example to (Morris and Hirst, 2004) for a discussion of non-classical semantic relations and their relevance for NLP.

## 2.1 Principle and General Algorithm

When viewing AKI as a game, the user tries consciously to make the computer guess a term, supplying, one by one, a succession of typed clues. After each clue, AKI makes the most probable proposition. If it corresponds to the searched term, the user confirms the proposition as the proper one; otherwise he introduces a new clue. This dialogue goes on, until either AKI finds the target term, or gives up asking the user to supply the solution. The algorithm relies both on the intersection of sets of terms activated by the clues and the fuzzy set of concepts linked to the clues.

The algorithm is based on manipulating sets of weighted words (named thereafter *lexical signatures*). We call a *clue* a term proposed by the user for the system to guess what could be the term to be found (called thereafter *target term*). Finally, we call a *proposition*, a term returned by the system from a set of clues.

From the first clue $i_1$, a lexical signature is computed on the basis of what can be found in the lexical network: $S(i_1) = S_1 = t_1, t_2, \ldots$ where the $t_i$ are the terms related to the clue and sorted by descending activation (weight). By default, we consider all terms in the lexical network to be eligible as propositions and potential target terms. Put another way, $t_1$ is the term for which the sum of all relations related to the clue $i_1$ is the strongest. The first proposition made by AKI, $p_1$ is this term. The player is supposed to acknowledge it, if it is the target term, otherwise he/she is invited to propose another clue. In this case, the clue and the proposition is removed from the signature : $S'_1 = S_1 - \{p_1, i_1\}$.

With the second clue $i_2$, the next lexical signature is computed : $S_2 = (S'_1 \cap S(i_2)) - i_2$. The generalized formula at stage n is :

$$S_n = (S'_{n-1} \cap S(i_n)) - i_n \quad \text{and} \quad S'_n = S_n - p_n$$

where $i_n$ is the n-th clue given by the user and $p_n$ the n-th proposition returned by AKI. With such a process, the size of signatures steadily diminishes as clues are added. The weight of each term of the signature is then the geometric mean of the weight of this term in the previous signatures.

If the signature becomes empty, the system has not found the target term. We could stop the process at this stage, but it is more valuable to set a recovering procedure which will try a simple heuristic. In this case, a boolean union of signatures are made instead of intersections:

$$S_n = (S'_{n-1} + S(i_n)) - i_n \quad \text{and} \quad S'_n = S_n - p_n$$

The weight if a term is the signature is then the sum of its occurrences in the previous signatures. This is a form of majority vote, where the proposal with the most votes is returned by AKI. This recovery induce a form of learning for the system as if the target term is found this way, as unlinked clues are added in the lexical network. We have found that using the recovering procedure two times before making AKI giving up, leads to satisfactory results. Be more lenient then the system tends to propose very general and too loosely related terms, be more strict the system tend to learn less or not at all.

About ¼ of the games concern common words and are played with “indirect” clues. The other games concern non common words, often connected to the current events, and are played with "frontal" clues. Thus, as with JDM, most of the created relations are "frontal" ones.

## 2.2 AKI in Taboo Mode

As we find out, the JDM network contains mainly "frontal" relations, and we wish to extend it by creating or reinforcing "indirect" ones. In other words, we would like to increase the population of the long tail.

The aim of this work is to make the system guess a target term, without using clue terms which are the most strongly connected with the target term in the lexical network. We generally limit this list of *forbidden* (or *taboo*) terms to the first 20. It means clues given by the user cannot be any of these terms, and thus the user has to give other clues, less strong connected with the target term and belonging to the long tail. Using this network extension, it increases the recall of the system.

How to play in the taboo mode? In AKI, players has access to a list of recently played words, guessed or not. They can then choose one of these terms to make AKI guess it, avoiding as clues the terms indicated as taboos (forbidden by the system). These are in fact the terms in the *belly* in the lexical network. Alternatively, the player can send by email a term of its choice to be played to another person. *Tabooing* allows either to create new relations, or to strengthen already existing but relatively weak relations.

Figure 3 (a and b) shows a typical game under taboo mode. The target term along with the forbidden clues is first presented to the user. The player succeeded in making the system find the term *Bollywood* not using the forbidden clues.

How the taboo approach affect the relation frequency (or strength)? We can wonder that explicitly excluding the most common terms we might as well influence the *natural strength* in an artificial way. In the experiments we conducted, it has been observed that people *do not only* play in taboo mode, and that strongest and most immediate relations have their weight increased as well. The distribution curve (as exemplified in Figure 1) is globally pushed upward, revealing new more distant and low weight relations.

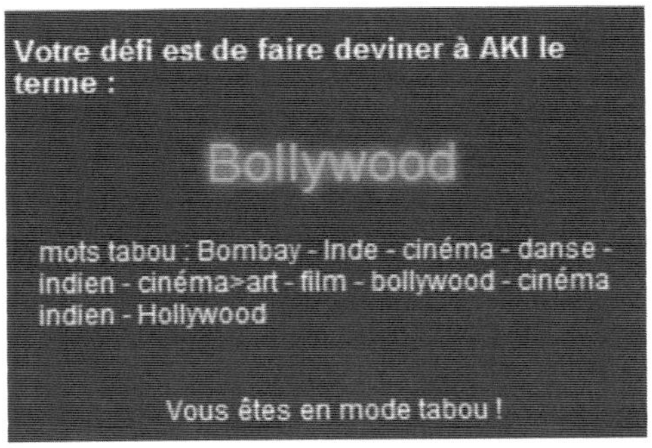

Figure 3 (a and b): AKI play with taboo words. On the left, the target term is Bollywood and the forbidden clues are *Bombay, Inde (India), cinéma (movie), danse, indien (indian), cinéma>art (cinema as art), film, bollywood* (no upercase) *cinéma indien (indian movies)* and *Hollywod.* On the right, the user made the system find the target term without using those forbidden clues, but with *acteur (actor), hindi* and *Mumbai.*

# 3 Evaluation for the long Tailed Network

With AKI, more 15000 games were played creating more than original 80000 relations that were not part of the network beforehand. Also, around 1500 new terms have been introduced. We evaluated the impact of long tail relations in two contexts: 1) the evolution over time of the retrieving capability of AKI and 2) under a WSD task.

## 3.1 Performances as a Tip of the Tongue Tool

The performance of the AKI tool in properly guessing terms is found to be around 75% with an evaluation undertaken during around 18 months. That is to say 11545 out of the 15895 game sessions played ended by AKI successfully guessing the target term of the player. On a smaller scale (3000 games) , we proposed the very same games where people were supposed to replace AKI in order to try to find target terms from clues. The global performance of people was only 48%. This is very interesting especially considering that the clues given to people, were exactly those given by people to AKI. It can be interpreted that the system is better at guessing from clues given by people, than people to guess their own clues. The question that remains is to know if achieving 75% success rate is enough for a useful Tip of the Tongue Tool?

In fact, when used as a tool, people tend to give frontal (more straightforward) clues and were not willingly trying to tick the system. I this case, actual performances are much higher than 75%. Nevertheless, these facts have been collected from people that were using AKI as a TOT tool and a large scale planned experiment might be quite difficult to set up.

Another question, left open, is whether 75% of success rate is by itself a limit. Certainly, we cannot expect to achieve a 100% rate, considering new incoming words over time.

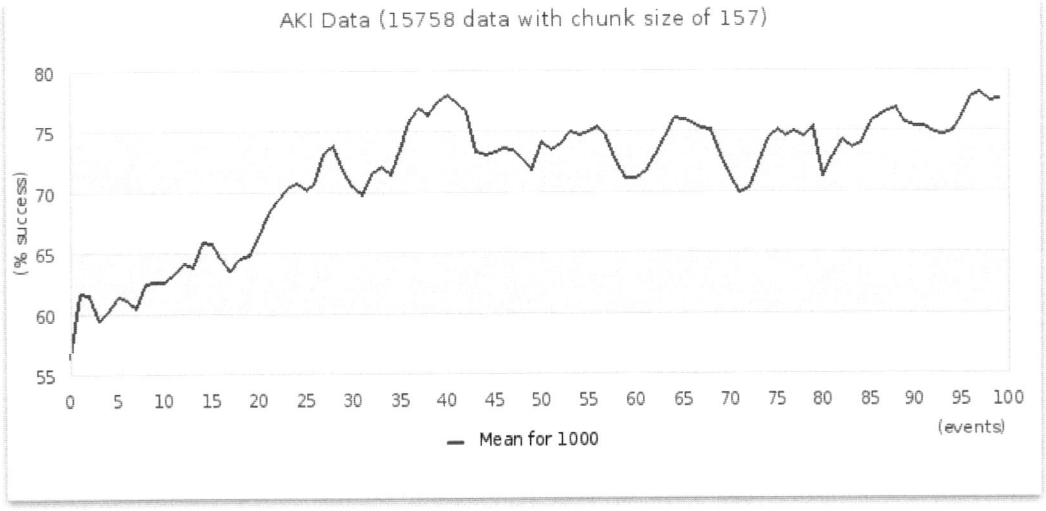


Figure 4: Evolution of AKI success over time. The x-axis is the number of games (by segment of 157 games). The curve shows the success rate at guessing the proper term that a user has in mind from the clues he/she giving to the system.

## 3.2 Performances for WSD

The purpose of the evaluation on WSD was to access the impact of the network in the case of WSD when viewing this task as a guessing problem almost identical to the guessing game presented above. A full presentation of various WSD techniques is beyond the scope of this paper, the interested reader can refer to (Navigli, 2009) and for a more general account of graph-based NLP to (Mihalcea and Radev, 2011).

We selected, from the French version of Wikipedia, a set of 250 sentences containing polysemous words (restricted to common nouns) that are going to be used as target words to be disambiguated. The number of different target nouns was 48 (there was 5.20 sentence per target word has a mean). Not all meanings for each target word were represented, but we ensure that at least two meanings were proposed for each of them. We then asked to French native speakers to be volunteers for enumerating typed clues that seemed relevant for guessing the proper usage of the polysemous target words.

For example, the word *mine* in French has, amongst others, the meanings of: *appearance*, *explosive device*, *mineral exploitation (coalmine, gold mine)*, and the *graphite part of a pencil*. In the following sentences, they have been asked to select the proper meaning above all to produce clues (as given in below). The figures correspond to the number of time this clues has been given by volunteers.

*(1) La première* ***mine*** *antipersonnel, hautement explosive et dotée d'un détonateur mécanique moderne fut employée par les troupes confédérés. (Eng. The first antipersonnel mine, highly explosive and provided with a mechanical detonator was used by confederate troops.)*

Target term : *mine > charge explosive (mine as explosive)*

| | | |
|---|---|---|
| :carac antipersonnel (4)<br>bataille (2) | :carac explosive (4)<br>:patientof employer | :part détonateur (3)<br>:part détonateur mécanique |

*(2) Une **mine** est un gisement exploité de matériaux. (Eng. A mine is a field exploited for materials.)*

Target term : *mine > gisement (mine as field)*

| | | |
|---|---|---|
| :isa gisement (3) | :carac exploité (2)<br>exploité | :locof matériaux (3)<br>matériaux(2) |

*(3) On trouve la trace dès la très haute antiquité de l'exploitation des **mines** d'argent du Laurion. (Eng. We find evidence since antiquity of exploitation of the Laurion silver mines.)*

Target term : *mine > gisement (mine as field)*

| | | |
|---|---|---|
| exploitation (5) | argent (3)<br>:locof argent | Laurion (2)<br>:loc Laurion |

*(4) La **mine** noire est réalisée à partir d'un mélange de graphite en poudre combiné à un mélange de kaolin et de bentonite. (Eng. The black mine is realized from a mixture of graphite powder combined to a mixture of kaolin and bentonite.)*

Target term : *mine > dessiner (mine as drawing/pencil)*

| | | |
|---|---|---|
| :carac noire (3)<br>noire (2) noir (2) | graphite (4)<br>:subst graphite | kaolin (3)<br>bentonite |

First, some few remarks are worthy. The annotators were free to choose their clues (and the type if any) but only from the words present in the sentences. They were not asked the type of the clues to follow any syntactic/semantic constraints present in the sentence. This last point could be discussed, but this constraint was felt as too complicated to the majority of volunteers. The clues could be given in the form occurring in the text or in a lemmatized version (like *noire/noir*). Terms of clues could be given several time with different types. Multiword terms could be used as long they are present in the text and known to the system, that is to say, existing in the lexical network).

Prior to the experiment, we made a large number of people to plays with AKI in taboo mode for the target words. Those players were not those who volunteering for producing clues, and they were not aware of the global experiment nor the sentences we would be using as test corpus.

The evaluation experiment was conducted has follow. For a given target word, the *initial lexical signature* was composed of its word senses (usages) with an equal weight equal to 1. The learning mechanism (adding new relations to the network) was disabled. All clues were given at the same time, reading the proposal made by the system only after.

The obtained figures are the following when considering all clues (typed or not) :

| | Random | | Belly only no weight | | Belly + tail no weight | | Belly only | | Belly + tail | |
|---|---|---|---|---|---|---|---|---|---|---|
| | count | % | count | % | count | % | count | % | count | % |
| OK | 69 | 27,6 | 158 | *63* | 176 | *70* | 195 | *78* | 245 | *98* |
| NOK | 181 | 72,4 | 92 | *37* | 74 | *30* | 29,6 | *12* | 5 | *2* |

The *OK* line refers to when the system has found the proper meaning/usage, and the *NOK* when the system proposed any other inadequate usage. The *Random* column refers to a totally random choice amongst senses. Columns with the mention *belly only* refers to when only relations concerning the target terms and belonging to the belly are considered. In that case, we ignore all relations of the tail. Column with *no weight* means that weights are ignored (they are all equal to 1). The mention of *belly + tail* means that all relations in the lexical network are taken into account.

We made also a comparison of the performances with ignoring the type of the clue. For example, the set of clues of sentence (1) given above is reduced to :

| | | |
|---|---|---|
| antipersonnel (4)<br>bataille (2) | explosive (4)<br>employer | détonateur (3)<br>détonateur mécanique |

The obtained figures are the following when clue types are ignored :

| | belly only no type | | Belly + tail no type | |
|---|---|---|---|---|
| | count | % | count | % |
| OK | 165 | 66 | 223 | 89,2 |
| NOK | 85 | 34 | 27 | 10,8 |

As we said earlier, this experiment doesn't mean to prove anything as a new WSD approach but rather to assess the impact of the contents of the lexical network with a very simple approach. The experiment, although slightly reminiscent of (Véronis and Ide, 1990), is by itself far too limited (a very small set of terms and sentences and only limited to nouns) to pretend to have any insight in general large scope WSD. Nevertheless, the obtained results seem to show that relations belonging to the tail have a positive effect in guessing what could be the proper meaning in the context of a sentence. Moreover, the explicit use of strength (weights) for relations does improve the overall performance. Ignoring types for clues does reduce performance but to a less extend than ignoring weights. This can be explained by the large proportion of specific relations that are also existing as associated ideas (the basic relations without particular type in JDM).

A large scale experiment would be desirable, especially including verbs. A fully automatic handling of the process, that is to say not asking people to produce the clues, is also certainly a way to go, but at this stage the lack of a French analyzer able to produce the proper typed clues remains an obstacle. In any case, asking people to produce clues for WSD is by itself interesting for assessing the relative usefulness of the various relation types. Annotating this way a large collection of sentences may be worth the effort.

## Conclusion

The lexical network (JDM) created under the JeuxDeMots project is large scaled and has a wide coverage. From this network, we have conceived a prototype that can be viewed both as a game and as a Tip of the Tongue (TOT) tool, and whose purpose is to increase the number of low weight relations, thus making the JDM lexical network *long tailed*. We have in this paper considered the long tail property as a global property of the edge weights, and not the frequency distribution of terms nor the distribution of relation number linking terms. Globally, for a given term the cumulated weight of the first 20% stronger relations is equivalent to the 80% remaining. Depending on terms and of their lexical richness and usage, the long tail can start in a range from 10% to 30% of the cumulated relation weight. Under the game process with intersection by pairs, the construction of dense long tail can be slow (in an inverse quadratic way), because they are not "frontal" ones and users do not spontaneously think to them. We saw in this paper how a TOT game, used in a taboo mode, can help create such "indirect" relations in a more efficient way, while retaining the principle of typed and weighted relations. Beside presenting the approach for increasing the long tail, the second objective of this paper was to try to assess if this work had any usefulness. We evaluated the impact of the long tail in two different contexts. First, it does help the retrieval process of a TOT software as evaluated in a quite large number of occurrences (more than 15000 plays) over more than a year time span. Secondly, the long tailed of typed and weighed relations seems to have a positive effect on a WSD task.

## References


von Ahn L., Dabbish L. (2004). *Labelling Images with a Computer Game.* ACM Conference on Human Factors in Computing Systems (CHI). pp. 319-326.

von Ahn L., Dabbish L. (2008) *Designing Games With a Purpose.* Communication of the ACM, 51(8):58–67 August 2008.

Anderson, Ch. (2004) *The Long Tail.* Wired 12:10, October 2004.

Boyd-Graber J., Fellbaum C., Osherson D., and Schapire R. (2006) *Adding Dense, Weighted Connections to WordNet.* In *Proceedings of the Thirds International WordNet Conference.* Masaryk University Brno, 2006, 9 p.

Budanitsky A., Hirst G. (2001) *Semantic distance in WordNet: an Experimental, Applicationoriented Evaluation of Five Measures.* Proceedings Workshop WordNet and Other Lexical Resources. The North American Chapter of the Association for Computation Linguistics (NAACL), Pittsburgh, PA, 2001.

Chamberlain, J., Poesio, M., and Kruschwitz, U. (2008). *Phrase Detectives: A Web-based Collaborative Annotation Game.* In Proceedings of the International Conference on Semantic Systems (I-Semantics'08), Graz.

Chklovski, T. and Gil, Y. (2005) *Improving the design of intelligent acquisition interfaces for collecting world knowledge from web contributors*. In Proceedings of K-CAP '05, pages 35–42.

Collins A, Quillian M.R. (1969). *Retrieval time from semantic memory.* Journal of verbal learning and verbal behaviour, 8(2), pp. 240-248.

Fellbaum C. (ed.): *WordNet, an Electronic Lexical Database*, MIT Press, (1998)

Gaume, B. (2008) *Maping the form of meaning in Small Worlds.* in Journal of Intelligent Systems, 15 p.

Lafourcade M., (2007) *Making people play for Lexical Acquisition.* In Proc. SNLP 2007, 7th Symposium on Natural Language Processing. Pattaya, Thailande, 13-15 December 2007, 8 p.

Lafourcade M., Joubert A. (2010). *Computing trees of named word usages from a crowdsourced lexical network.* Investigationes Linguisticae, volume XXI, pp. 39-56.

Lenat D. (1995) *CYC: A large-scale investment in knowledge infrastructure.* Communications of the ACM, 38(11):33–38, 1995.

Lieberman H., Smith D.A., Teeters A. (2007). *Common Consensus: a web-based game for collecting commonsense goals.* International Conference on Intelligent User Interfaces (IUI'07). Hawaï, USA.

Mihalcea, R. and Chklovski, T. (2003). *Open MindWord Expert: Creating large annotated data collections with web users help.* In Proceedings of the EACL 2003, Workshop on Linguistically Annotated Corpora (LINC 2003).

Mihalcea R. and Radev D. (2011), *Graph-based Natural Language Processing and Information Retrieval* , Cambridge University Press, 2011.

Miller G.A., Beckwith R., Fellbaum C., Gross D. and Miller K.J. (1990). *Introduction to WordNet: an on-line lexical database* , International Journal of Lexicography, 3 (4), pp. 235-244.

Morris J., Hirst G. (2004) *Non-classical lexical semantic relations* Proceedings of the HLT-NAACL Workshop on Computational Lexical Semantics, 46-51, 2004.

Navigli R. (2009) *Word Sense Disambiguation: a Survey.* ACM Computing Surveys, 41(2), ACM Press, 2009, pp. 1-69.

Navigli R., Ponzetto S. (2010) *BabelNet: Building a very large multilingual semantic network.* In Proceedings of the 48th Annual Meeting of the Association for Computational Linguistics, Uppsala, Sweden, 11-16 July 2010, pp. 216-225.

Polguère A. (2006). *Structural properties of Lexical Systems : Monolingual and Multilingual Perspectives.* Proceedings of the Workshop on Multilingual Language Resources and Interoperability (Coling/ACL), Sydney, pp. 50-59.

Sagot B. et Fiser D. (2008) *Construction d'un WordNet libre du français à partir de ressources multilingues.* Dans les actes de TALN 2008, Avignon, France, 2008.

Sigman M, Cecchi GA. (2002) *Global organization of the WordNet lexicon.* Proc Natl Acad Sci USA. 2002;99:1742–1747.

Véronis J., & Ide N. (1990). *Word Sense Disambiguation with Very Large Neural Networks Extracted from Machine Readable Dictionaries.* In Proceedings of 13th International Conference on Computational Linguistics (COLING'90), vol. 2, pp. 389-394. Helsinki.

Lafourcade, M., Zampa, V. (2009) *PtiClic : a game for vocabulary assessment combining JeuxDeMots and LSA.* In proc of CICLing (Conference on Intelligent text processing and Comptational Linguistics). Mexico : Marsh 1-7 , 10 p.

Zesch, T.& I. Gurevych, I. (2009) *Wisdom of crowds versus wisdom of linguists measuring the semantic relatedness of words.* Natural Language Engineering, Cambridge University Press, pp 25–59, 2009.

Zipf G K. (1965) *The Psycho-Biology of Language.* Cambridge, MA: MIT Press; 1965.

Zock M., Ferret O. and Schwab D. (2010), *Deliberate word access : an intuition, a roadmap and some preliminary empirical results,* in International Journal of Speech Technology, Volume 13, Number 4, December 2010, Springer Verlag.

# On Discriminating fMRI Representations of Abstract WordNet Taxonomic Categories

*Andrew James ANDERSON*[1], *Yuan TAO*[1], *Brian MURPHY*[2], *Massimo POESIO*[1,3]
(1) Centro Interdipartimentale Mente e Cervello (CIMeC), University of Trento, Italy
(2) Machine Learning Department, School of Computer Science, Carnegie Mellon University, USA
(3) School of Computer Science and Electronic Engineering, University of Essex, UK
andrew.anderson@unitn.it, yuan.tao@unitn.it, brianmurphy@cmu.edu, massimo.poesio@unitn.it

ABSTRACT

How abstract knowledge is organised is a key question in cognitive science, and has clear repercussions for the design of artifical lexical resources, but is poorly understood. We present fMRI results for an experiment where participants imagined situations associated with abstract words, when cued with a visual word stimulus. We use a multivariate-pattern analysis procedure to demonstrate that 7 WordNet style Taxonomic categories (e.g. 'Attribute', 'Event', 'Social-Role'), can be decoded from neural data at a level better than chance. This demonstrates that category distinctions in artificial lexical resources have some explanatory value for neural organisation.

Secondly, we tested for similarity in the interrelationship of the taxonomic categories in our fMRI data and the associated interrelations in popular distributed semantic models (LSA,HAL,COALS). Although distributed models have been successfully applied to predict concrete noun fMRI data (e.g. Mitchell et al., 2008), no evidence of association was found for our abstract concepts. This suggests that development of new models/experimental strategies may be necessary to elucidate the organisation of abstract knowledge.

KEYWORDS : fMRI, Concept Representation, Abstract, MVPA, WordNet

## 1 Introduction

Data about the organization of conceptual knowledge in the brain coming from patients with semantic deficits (e.g. Warrington & Shallice, 1984, Caramazza & Shelton, 1998) or collected from healthy patients using functional Magnetic Resonance Imaging[1] (fMRI) (e.g. Martin & Chao, 2001) have proven an essential source of evidence for our understanding of conceptual representations, particularly when analyzed using machine learning methods (e.g. Haxby et al 2001, Mitchell et al., 2008). Most of this work has focused on a fairly narrow range of conceptual categories, primarily concrete concepts such as animals, plants, tools, etc., which represent only a small percentage of the range of conceptual categories that are part of human knowledge. Until recently only a few studies studied the representation in the brain of abstract concepts such as law

[1]functional Magnetic Resonance Imaging measures blood flow in the brain, which reflects neural cells' energy consumption which in turn is generally regarded to relate to neural activity. Comparative to other popular neuroimaging techniques (e.g. EEG, MEG) fMRI offers relatively high spatial resolution (data is measured as a 3D volume built from rectangular cuboids known as voxels, of side 1-5 mm, over the entire brain) at relatively low sampling frequency (commonly ≥ 1Hz).

or freedom (Binder et al, 2005; Friederici et al, 2002; Grossman et al, 2002). Some recent studies have shown that fMRI data contain sufficient information to discriminate between concrete and abstract concepts (Binder et al, 2005; Wang et al, 2012) but meta-analyses such as (Wang et al, 2010) also showed that fairly different results are obtained depending on the types of abstract concepts under study, and that the range of abstract concepts considered tends to be fairly narrow.

This type of analysis is complicated by the fact that the representation and organization of human knowledge about abstract conceptual categories is much less understood than for concrete concepts. Human intuitions about abstract concepts are not very sharp: e.g., studies asking subjects to specify the defining characteristics of abstract concepts find that this task is much harder than for concrete ones (Hampton 1981, McRae & Cree, 2002, Wiemer-Hastings & Xu, 2005). On the theoretical side, as well, there is not much agreement on abstract concepts among psychologists, (computational) linguists, philosophers and other cognitive scientists who have proposed theories about the organization of conceptual knowledge. Just about the only point of agreement among such proposals is that there is no such thing as an 'abstract concept' –human conceptual knowledge includes a great variety of abstract categories of varying degrees of abstractness ranging from knowledge about space and time (e.g., day, country) to knowledge about actions and events (e.g., solo, robbery) to knowledge about inner states including emotions (fear) and cognitive states (belief), to purely abstract concepts (e.g., art, jazz, law). It is also known that many of these categories have their own distinct representation in memory (Binder & Desai, 2009). But there is a lot of disagreement among exactly which categories these different types of abstract concepts belong to, e.g., which category does the concept law belong to. These disagreements are clearly in evidence in the significant differences between the representation of such categories in the large-scale repositories of conceptual knowledge that have been developed in the last twenty years, such as WordNet (Fellbaum, 1998), CYC (Lenat, & Guha, 1990) and DOLCE (Gangemi et al, 2002). In WordNet, the top category 'abstract concept' covers attributes, events and actions, temporal entities, and highly abstract concepts such as law both in the sense of 'collection of all laws' and in the sense of 'area of study', whereas locations are considered concrete concepts. In DOLCE, actions and events, attributes, and highly abstract concepts such as propositions are treated as completely unrelated conceptual categories, whereas both temporal and spatial locations are included in the quality category.

It follows that there is joint motivation from cognitive science and computational linguistics to extend our understanding of abstract knowledge representation. The objectives of the present work are two fold, (1) to broaden the range of abstract concepts studied using neuroimaging; (2) to examine whether artificial knowledge representation strategies can be used to interpret fMRI data.

We adopt an fMRI paradigm, where stimuli were presented in the form of words on the screen and participants were required to imagine a situation associated with the word. We used as stimuli concepts belonging to seven distinct WordNet style taxonomic categories, ranging from concrete to more abstract (tool, location, social role, event, communication, attribute, and a category we called urabstract of highly abstract words) and two different domains (music and law). Domain membership is not important to this paper and will be addressed in future work (this point is returned to in section 4). Firstly a Multivariate Pattern Analysis (MVPA) procedure was used to test whether single stimulus trials could be classified by their taxonomic class. On demonstrating that classifications can indeed be made at a level better than chance (section 3.1), we further examined whether there are similarities between concept representations in the fMRI data and popular distributed semantic models used in computational linguistics (section 3.2).

Three semantic models were selected: Hyperspace Analogue to Language (HAL) (Burgess, 1998), Correlated Occurrence Analogue to Lexical Semantics (COALS) (Rohde, et al., 2005) which is a refinement of HAL and Latent Semantic Analysis (LSA) (Landauer et al, 1998). All three models express meaning in terms of a multidimensional statistical model of a word's context. HAL models meaning as a function of the number of times a word occurs in close proximity to a each of a large set of feature words, within a large body of text. LSA counts the occurrences of words in individual documents and subsequently reduces the dimensionality (in documents) through singular value decomposition. COALS incorporates a number of algorithmic modifications to the HAL, including data reduction by singular value decomposition. The important conceptual difference is that LSA attempts to bind words to topic (assumed to be derived from the general themes of the documents), whereas HAL and COALS captures meaning through word inter-relations. All models have been applied with success in one way or other to interpret human cognition in a variety of semantic tasks and psychological experiments, including synonym test, word relatedness judgment, semantic priming, semantic categorization, (Lund & Burgess, 1996; Burgess, 1998; Landauer et al., 1997, 1998; Rohde et al., 2005). Despite their success in explaining behavioural tasks, by using representational dissimilarity analysis (section 3.3) we found that none of the models provide a good general match for the structure of the abstract fMRI data.

# 2 Methods

## 2.1 Participants

Seven right handed native Italian speakers (3 female), aged between 19 and 38, were recruited to take part in the study. All had normal or corrected-to-normal vision. Participants received compensation of €15 per hour. The studies were conducted under the approval of the ethics committee of the host University, and participants gave informed consent.

## 2.2 Data Acquisition

fMRI images were recorded on a 4T Bruker MedSpec MRI. An EPI pulse sequence with TR=1000ms, TE=33ms, and 26° flip angle was used. A 64 * 64 acquisition matrix was used and seventeen slices were imaged with a between slice gap of 1mm. Voxels had dimensions 3mm * 3mm * 5mm.

## 2.3 Experimental Paradigm

The names of 70 concepts were presented to participants in the form of written words on the screen. The stimuli were displayed using bold Arial-Black size 20 font on a grey background. Each stimulus was presented five times, for a total of 350 trials, split in five blocks with the order of presentation being randomized in each block. Participants had the opportunity to pause between blocks and the overall task time did not exceed 60 minutes. Each trial began with the presentation of a blank screen for 0.5s, followed by the stimulus word of dark grey on a light grey background for 3s, and a fixation cross for 6.5s. Participants were asked to keep still during the task and during breaks.

With concrete concepts, participants are often asked to think actively about the properties of the object named (see, e.g., Mitchell et al, 2008) but eliciting properties is not so easy for abstract concepts. On the other hand, participants to studies such as (Hampton, 1981; McRae & Cree, 2002; Wiemer-Hastings & Xu, 2005) appeared able to produce situation-related objects. Our participants were therefore instructed to "think about situations that exemplify the object the word refers to".

The list of concept words were supplied to participants in advance of the experiment, so that they could prepare appropriate situations to simulate consistently.

## 2.4 Materials

Our objective was to obtain a list of words representative of the full range of non-concrete concepts. The list of categories was produced by associating WordNet (Fellbaum, 1998) categories to the terms with highest abstractness ranking in an abstractness norm for Italian. We identified the 6 WordNet categories that occurred most frequently in the norms. Finally, WordNet Domains (Pianta et al, 2002) was used to select 70 words whose unique or most preferred sense belonged to these categories.

More in detail, our starting point was the set of behavioural norms by Barca et al (2002) listing Italian words ranked by perceived abstractness. These words were next looked up in the Italian WordNet contained in MultiWordNet (Pianta et al, 2002) to determine the taxonomic category of their dominant sense(s). The authors edited this list down to a set of six taxonomic categories of concepts found in Barca et al's norms plus a category of concrete concepts, *tool*, for comparison purposes. The six non-concrete categories are:

*Locations*, including concepts such as court, jail and theatre. *Locations* are considered as concrete objects in WordNet but belong to the separate category `qualities' in DOLCE, and could therefore be considered concepts in between concrete and abstract.

Four non-concrete categories of arguably increasing levels of abstractness: *event*, *communication* (covering concepts such as accusation or symphony), *attribute*, and *urabstract* (our term for concepts such as law or jazz which are fairly common in abstractness norms, are classified as abstract in WordNet, but do not belong to a clear subcategory of abstract such as event or attribute)

Finally, the category *social-role*, containing concepts such as judge or tenor which are fairly common in abstractness norms and are typically associated with scenarios but whose status as concrete or abstract is not very clear. The complete word list including English translations of the Italian stimuli is in TABLE 1.

## 2.5 Preprocessing

Preprocessing was undertaken using the Statistical Parametric Mapping software (SPM99, Wellcome Department of Cognitive Neurology, London, UK). Data were corrected for head motion, unwarped (to compensate for geometric distortions in the image interacting with motion) and spatially normalised to the MNI template image and resampled at 3mm * 3mm * 6mm. Only voxels estimated to be grey matter were included in the subsequent analysis. For each participant the data, per voxel, in each session (presentation cycle of 70 words) was corrected for linear trend and transformed to z-scores.

A single volume was computed to represent each stimulus word, by taking the voxel-wise mean of the four seconds of data offset by four seconds from the stimulus onset (to account for hemodynamic response).

| | | | | |
|---|---|---|---|---|
| tool | manette | handcuffs | violino | violin |
| | toga | robe | tamburo | drum |
| | manganello | truncheon | tromba | trumpet |
| | cappio | noose | metronomo | metronome |
| | grimaldello | skeleton key | radio | radio |
| location | tribunale | court/tribunal | palco | stage |
| | carcere | prison | auditorium | auditorium |
| | questura | police station | discoteca | disco |
| | penitenziario | penitentiary | conservatorio | conservatory |
| | patibolo | gallows | teatro | theatre |
| social-role | giudice | judge | musicista | musician |
| | ladro | thief | cantante | singer |
| | imputato | defendant | compositore | composer |
| | testimone | witness | chitarrista | guitarist |
| | avvocato | lawyer | tenore | tenor |
| event | arresto | arrest | concerto | concert |
| | processo | trial | recital | recital |
| | reato | crime | assolo | solo |
| | furto | theft | festival | festival |
| | assoluzione | acquittal | spettacolo | show |
| communication | divieto | prohibition | canzone | song |
| | verdetto | verdict | pentagramma | stave |
| | ordinanza | decree | ballata | ballad |
| | addebito | accusation | ritornello | refrain |
| | ingiunzione | injunction | sinfonia | symphony |
| attribute | giurisdizione | jurisdiction | sonorita' | sonority |
| | cittadinanza | citizenship | ritmo | rhythm |
| | impunita' | impunity | melodia | melody |
| | legalita' | legality | tonalita' | tonality |
| | illegalita' | illegality | intonazione | pitch |
| urabstracts | giustizia | justice | musica | music |
| | liberta' | liberty | blues | blues |
| | legge | law | jazz | jazz |
| | corruzione | corruption | canto | singing |
| | refurtiva | loot | punk | punk |

TABLE 1. Italian stimuli words and English translations, Taxonomic category is indicated in the left column. Taxonomic categories are ordered in terms of increasing abstractness.

## 2.6 Cross validation analysis procedure

Broadly the same cross-validation procedure was followed for each analyses. Input and target data pairs were partitioned into training and testing sets (using a leave-n-out approach) to support a number of cross validation iterations. Target patterns were binary vectors with a single field set to one to uniquely specify the category. Input was a masked version of the fMRI grey-matter data, retaining the 1000 most stable voxels in the training set according to the following procedure, similar to that used by Mitchell et al. (2008). For each voxel, the set of 70 words from each unique pair of scanning sessions in the training set were correlated, and the mean of the six resulting correlations (from 4 scanning sets) was taken as the measure of stability. The 1000 voxels with highest mean correlations were selected for analysis.

Pattern classification used a single layer neural network with logistic activation functions (MATLAB 2009B, Mathworks, Neural Network toolbox). Weights and biases were initialized using the Nguyen-Widrow algorithm and training used conjugate gradient decent, continued until convergence, with performance evaluated using mean square error, with a goal of $10^{-4}$ or completion of 2000 training epochs. In each cross-validation iteration the network was trained using the masked fMRI data and binary target codes in the training set and subsequently tested on the previously unseen masked fMRI data. The Euclidean distance between the network output vectors and target codes was computed, and the target code with the minimum distance selected as the network output.

# 3 Results

Leave-out-session cross validation analyses were undertaken for each participant to recognize taxonomic distinctions from the fMRI data. There were 5 scanning sessions, therefore training in each of the five cross-validation iterations was on 280 words (4 replicates of each of the 70 stimulus words) and testing was on the remaining 70 words. Figure 1 shows a confusion matrix averaging results across all 7 participants (and cross-validation iterations within participant).

## 3.1 Can taxonomic distinctions be recognized within participant?

Mean classification accuracy for the 7-way taxonomic distinctions was ~0.3 with chance level at 0.143. Accuracy is greatest for location, tool and attributes and there is a visible diagonal in Figure 1, suggesting all classes can be discriminated. This claim is however statistically unsubstantiated, and indeed until recently the question of how to rigorously interpret the classification performance of multiway classifiers had not been directly addressed. Binomial tests are often applied to test whether a classifier is predicting randomly, however in the multi-class case this leaves many questions unanswered. For instance, here there were 730/2450 correct classifications, and the probability of achieving this by chance is $p=2.2*10^{-16}$ (2-tailed Binomial test), however this does not answer whether the classifier capable of distinguishing between all test categories, or just between subsets of categories. Motivated by these concerns, and drawing from the statistical literature of contingency tables, Olivetti et al (2012) developed a test exploiting Bayesian hypothesis testing to evaluate the posterior probability of each possible partitioning of distinguishable subsets of test classes. For example taking three classes, possible distinguishable test class partitions are [1][2][3]; [1,2][3]; [1,3][2]; [1][2,3]; [1,2,3], and each of these would be assigned a posterior probability, where as a general rule of thumb a probability in excess of 1/K, where K is the number of hypotheses, (i.e., 5 in the 3 class example) would be seen as informative evidence. (Olivetti pers. comm.)

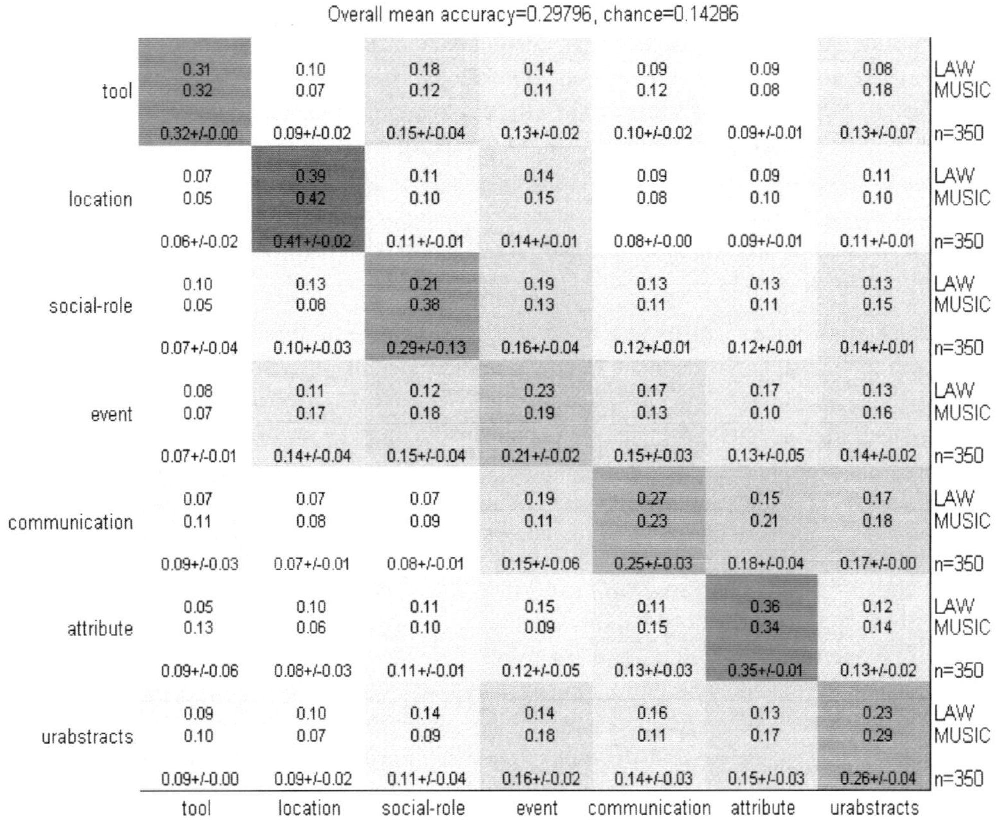


FIGURE 1. Leave-out-one-session Taxonomic category classification confusion matrix. Rows are the target labels and columns are predictions. Numbers overlaid on each cell indicate the proportion of predictions per law and music respectively (as indicated on the right y-axis) for that row, averaging over 7 participants. The numbers on the bottom line of each cell are the mean and standard deviation of predictions. Cell shading is scaled to the range 0 to 0.41 (0.41 is the maximum mean accuracy per cell displayed).

Applying Olivetti et al.s' (2012) test to the taxonomic confusion matrix in Figure 1 and sorting all subset partitions in descending order of posterior probability, finds the top ranking partition (posterior probability=0.93) to be that all test classes are discriminable. The highest ranked three partitions are below (posterior probabilities rapidly diminish in the remaining 874 partitions that are not displayed).

[1=tool][2=location][3=social-role][4=event][5=communication][6=attribute][7=urabstracts]

Partition: [[1][2][3][4][5][6][7]], postP: 0.93

Partition: [[1][2][3][4 5][6][7]], postP: 0.04

Partition: [[1][2][3][4 7][5][6]], postP: 0.02

Tool, Location and Attribute are most clearly distinguished, whereas prediction of taxonomic category is weakest for categories toward the middle of the concreteness scale (Event and Communication) and in the second partition of Olivetti et al.s' (2012) analysis these categories aggregate (although the posterior probability for this partition at 0.04 is much lower than the first).

### 3.2 Representational dissimilarity analysis between fMRI data and distributed semantic models

Representational dissimilarity analyses (Kriegeskorte, 2008) between the fMRI data and the three distributed semantic models (LSA, HAL, COALS) identified in the introduction were run to test for association in inter-representations of taxonomic classes between modalities. Each semantic model was built using the corpus itWaC. This corpus is from WaCky, a collection of very large (>1 billion words) corpora built by web crawling, and annotated with Part-of-Speech tagging and lemmatisation. itWaC is the largest publicly documented Italian language resource (Baroni *et al.*, 2008).

Representational dissimilarity analysis was as follows. For each participant, all fMRI representations within each of the seven taxonomic categories were voxel-wise averaged. Then the pairwise difference between each unique taxonomic category pairing was computed (n=21) using 1-rho as a distance metric, where rho is Spearman's rank correlation coefficient. Likewise, for LSA, HAL and COALS, semantic representations of all word models within each taxonomic category were averaged, and pairwise differences between all unique category pairs taken. The list of respective category pair differences for imaging data and each of the semantic models were correlated using Spearman's rank correlation to give a correlation coefficient for each. Following this the 7 per participant lists of 21 category pair differences were collapsed (by averaging) and the resulting list of average differences correlated with the 3 semantic models. Significance was tested using a permutation test as follows. The seven taxonomic condition labels were shuffled in every possible way to construct a null distribution that the two dissimilarity lists are not correlated. The p-value is calculated as the proportion of random correlation coefficients that are greater than or equal to the observed coefficient. Results are in Table 2.

Although there are two participants who show signs of a correlation with the HAL, HAL/COALS models, it is clear that this is not a general pattern across participants. Correlations range from positive to negative, and if p-values are corrected for multiple comparisons using Bonferroni correction (where the conventional significance threshold becomes $p=0.05/21$), results that individually are significant disappear. There is additionally no correlation between the fMRI dissimilarity matrices averaged over participants and the three semantic models.

## 4 Discussion

We have collected evidence that fMRI recordings contain sufficient information to discriminate between all Taxonomic categories that we tested. In other words, the distinctions between types of non-concrete concepts proposed in state-of-the-art models of conceptual knowledge such as WordNet are supported to a certain extent by brain data.

| Participant | | HAL | COALS | LSA |
|---|---|---|---|---|
| **19730713** | **rho** | **0.3571** | **0.1416** | **-0.1649** |
| | P-value | 0.0206 | 0.2061 | 0.7502 |
| **19820508** | **rho** | **0.0662** | **-0.0896** | **0.0156** |
| | P-value | 0.346 | 0.6987 | 0.4465 |
| **19830625** | **rho** | **0.5455** | **0.5312** | **-0.1091** |
| | P-value | 0.0347 | 0.0407 | 0.6909 |
| **19850913** | **rho** | **0.0364** | **-0.1169** | **0.2169** |
| | P-value | 0.4083 | 0.7744 | 0.17 |
| **19861211** | **rho** | **-0.2494** | **-0.2649** | **-0.1805** |
| | P-value | 0.9288 | 0.9683 | 0.7756 |
| **19891011** | **rho** | **-0.2338** | **-0.0805** | **-0.039** |
| | P-value | 0.8931 | 0.6568 | 0.5299 |
| **19920102** | **rho** | **0.1273** | **0.1051** | **0.0156** |
| | P-value | 0.2581 | 0.2767 | 0.4469 |
| **Collapsed dissimilarity** | **rho** | **0.2455** | **0.1481** | **-0.013** |
| **matrix correlation** | P-value | 0.1351 | 0.2437 | 0.5281 |

TABLE 2. Representational dissimilarity analysis between neural data and semantic models.

Whereas a number of studies have demonstrated a connection between distributional semantic models and neuroimaging data for concrete concepts (e.g. Mitchell et al, 2008; Murphy et al. 2009; Murphy et al., 2011; Chang et al., 2011), representational similarity analysis failed to find a systematic association between the inter-relationship of categories in the fMRI data and the inter-relationship of categories in distributional semantic models. There could be a number of reasons for this. Firstly, it may be that the neural organisation of abstract knowledge is in fact entirely different to the distributed semantic representations in common usage. Given that the semantic models show some explanatory power for human behavioural data, it would be unwise to discount them too quickly. Alternatively it could be that the experimental/fMRI protocol used is unfit for the challenge. As concerns the experimental protocol, abstract concepts generally speaking are more difficult to imagine than concrete objects, and the richness of the neural representations invoked in our experiment may consequently be comparatively weak. Additionally we have no guarantee that participants were compliant with the task (the only gauge on this being the ability to detect systematic patterns in a participants data). It will be valuable to consider modifying the task and if/where possible, to develop tasks that require mental manipulation of the concept in a more realistic context, where the performance of the participant can be evaluated. As concerns fMRI, it is possible that abstract concepts may be represented on a smaller spatial scale than concrete concepts, especially if they are not grounded in sensorimotor mechanisms and associated neural maps (as frequently thought to be the case for concrete concepts). Thus our whole brain analysis using large voxels may overlook pertinent features. However given the success of taxonomic category classification with the current fMRI setup, it should not be dismissed to quickly either.

This paper has thus far not directly addressed an important competing theory of concept organisation. Gentner (1981), Hampton (1981), and others found that unlike concrete concepts, abstract concepts are mostly characterized in terms of relations to other entities present in a situation. Wiemer-Hastings & Xu (2005) provided further support for this finding and proposed that abstract concepts are "anchored in situations" (Wiemer-Hastings & Xu 2005, p. 731); in a similar fashion, Barsalou (1999) argued that the representation of abstract concepts is 'framed by abstract event sequences'. This suggests a scenario-based organization for non-concrete concepts. In this type of organization, non-concrete concepts are defined in terms of their role with respect to a scenario: e.g., *law* is defined with respect to the *court* scenario, whereas *jazz* is defined with relation to a *music* scenario. In fact our experimental data set was carefully selected to allow us to begin to target this question (50% of our words are associated with Law and 50% with Music). Our preliminary analyses suggest that law and music scenarios can also be successfully decoded from the neural data. Complete results will be presented in future work.

## Conclusion

Conclusions are: (1) WordNet style taxonomic categories for abstract concepts, are at least cognitively relevant in that they can be distinguished from neural data; (2) In contrast to previous findings for concrete concepts, we were unable to detect a relationship between inter-representation of abstract concept categories in fMRI data and inter-representations in popular distributed semantic models.

The question of how abstract knowledge organised remains murky, however given the taxonomic classification success we are optimistic that advances are possible with current technology and methods.

## References


Barca, L., Burani, C., Arduino, S., (2002). Word naming times and psycholinguistic norms for Italian nouns. *Behavior Research Methods*, 34(3): 424-434.

Baroni, M., Bernardini, S., Ferraresi, A., Zanchetta, E., (2008). The WaCky Wide Web: A collection of very large linguistically processed web-crawled corpora. *Language Resources and Evaluation,* 43:209-226.

Barsalou, L.W., (1999). Perceptual Symbol systems. *Behavioral and Brain Sciences,* 22: 577-660.

Bentivogli, L., Forner, P., Magnini, B., Pianta, E. (2004). Revising WordNet Domains Hierarchy: Semantics, Coverage, and Balancing. In Proceedings of COLING 2004 Workshop on "Multilingual Linguistic Resources", Geneva, Switzerland, August 28, 2004, 101-108.

Binder, J.R., Desai, R.H., Graves, W.W., Conant, L.L., (2009). Where is the semantic system? A critical review and meta-analysis of 120 functional neuroimaging studies. *Cerebral Cortex*, bhp055.

Binder, J.R., Westbury, C.F., McKiernan, K.A. Possing, E.T., Medler, D.A., (2005). Distinct brain systems for processing concrete and abstract concepts. *Journal of Cognitive Neuroscience*. 17:905-917.

Burgess, C. (1998). From simple associations to the building blocks of language: Modeling meaning in memory with the HAL model. *Behavior Research Methods, Instruments, &*

*Computers, 30,* 188-198.

Chang, K. M., Mitchell, T., Just, M. A. (2011). Quantitative modeling of the neural representation of objects: How semantic feature norms can account for fMRI activation, *NeuroImage* 56 (2011) 716–727.

Fellbaum, C., (1998, ed.). WordNet: An Electronic Lexical Database. Cambridge, MA: MIT Press.

Friederici, A.D., Ruschemeyer S-A, Hahne A., Fiebach, C.J., (2003). The role of left inferior frontal gyrus and superior temporal cortex in sentence comprehension: localizing syntactic and semantic processes. *Cereb Cortex, 13:170-177.*

Gangemi, A., Guarino, N., Masolo, C., Oltramari, A., Schneider, L., (2002). Sweetening Ontologies with DOLCE. In A. Gómez-Pérez, V.R. Benjamins (eds.) Knowledge Engineering and Knowledge Management. Ontologies and the Semantic Web, 13th International Conference, EKAW 2002, Siguenza, Spain, October 1-4, 2002, Springer Verlag, pp. 166-181

Gentner, D., (1981). Why nouns are learned before verbs: Linguistic relativity versus natural partitioning. *In S. A. Kuczaj, editor, Language development:* 2:301-334. Erlbaum, Hillsdale, NJ.

Grossman, M., Koenig, P., DeVita, C., Glosser, G., Alsop, D., Detre, J., (2002). The neural basis for category specific knowledge: An fMRI study. *Neuroimage*, 16:936-948.

Hampton, J., (1981). An investigation of the nature of abstract concepts. *Memory & Cognition,* 9(2):149-156.

Haxby, J.V., Gobbini, M.I., Furey, M.L, Ishai, A., Schouten, J.L., Pietrini, P., (2001). Distributed and overlapping representations of faces and objects in ventral temporal cortex. *Science*, 293:2425-2430.

Kriegeskorte, N., Mur. M., Bandettini, P., (2008). Representational similarity analysis - connecting the branches of systems neuroscience. *Frontiers in Systems Neuroscience*, 2:4.

Landauer, T.K., Dumais, S.T., (1997). A solution to Plato's problem: The latent semantic analysis, theory of acquisition, induction, and representation of knowledge. *Psychological Review*, 104(2):211-240.

Landauer, T.K., Foltz, P.W., Laham, D., (1998). An introduction to latent semantic analysis. *Discourse Processes*, 27:303-310.

Lenat, D. and Guha, R. V., (1990). Building large Knowledge-based systems: Representation and inference in the Cyc Project. *Addision-Weslely.*

Lund, K., Burgess, C., (1996). Producing high-dimensional semantic spaces from lexical co-occurrence. *Behavior Research Methods, Instrumentation and Computers*, 28: 203-208.

McRae, K., Cree, G.S., Seidenberg, M.S., McNorgan, C., (2005). Semantic feature production norms for a large set of living and nonliving things. *Behavior Research Methods, Instruments, and computers*, 37(4):547-559.

Mitchell, T. M., Shinkareva, S. V., Carlson, A., Chang, K.M., Malave, V. L., Mason R. A., and Just., M. A. (2008). Predicting Human Brain Activity Associated with the Meanings of Nouns, *Science*, 320, 1191-1195. DOI: 10.1126/science.1152876

Murphy, B., Baroni, M., Poesio, M. (2009). EEG Responds to Conceptual Stimuli and Corpus Semantics. Proceedings of ACL/EMNLP 2009.

Murphy, B., Poesio. M, Bovolo, F., Bruzzone, L., Dalponte, M., Lakany, H. (2011). EEG decoding of semantic category reveals distributed representations for single concepts. *Brain and Language*, 117, 12-22.

Olivetti, E., Greiner, S., & Avesani, P. (2012). Testing multiclass pattern discrimination. In IEEE International Workshop on Pattern Recognition in NeuroImaging (PRNI). 57-60 DOI:10.1109/PRNI.2012.14

Pianta, E., Bentivogli, L., Girardi., C., (2002). MultiWordNet: developing an aligned multilingual database" pdf document. In Proceedings of the First International Conference on Global WordNet, Mysore, India, January 21-25, 2002.

Wang, J., Conder, J.A., Blitzer, D.N., Shinkareva, S.V. (2010). Neural representation of abstract and concrete concepts: A meta-analysis of neuroimaging studies. *Human Brain Mapping*, 31:1459-1468.

Wang, J., Baucom, L.B., Shinkareva, S.V. (2012). Decoding abstract and concrete concept representations based on single-trial fMRI data. *Human Brain Mapping*, DOI: 10.1002/hbm.21498

Warrington, E.K. & Shallice, T., (1984). Category specific semantic impairments. *Brain,* 107(3):829-853.

Wiemer-Hastings, K., Xu, X. (2005). Content differences for abstract and concrete concepts. *Cognitive Science*, 29:719-736.

# Automatic index creation to support navigation in lexical graphs encoding *part_of* relations

*Michael Zock*[1] *Debela Tesfaye*[2]
(1) LIF-CNRS, 163 Avenue de Luminy, 13288 Marseille, France
(2) ITPHD PROGRAM, Addis Ababa University, Addis Ababa, Ethiopia
michael.zock@lif.univ-mrs.fr, dabookoo@yahoo.com

ABSTRACT

We describe here the principles underlying the automatic creation of a semantic map to support navigation in a lexicon, our target group being authors (speakers, writers) rather than readers. While machines can generally access information that it has stored, this does not always hold for people. A speaker may very well know a word, yet still be (occasionally) unable to access it.

To help authors to overcome word-finding problems one could add to an existing electronic resource an index based on the (age-old) notion of association. Since ideas or their expressive forms (words) are related, they may evoke each other (lemon-yellow), but the likelihood for doing so varies over time and with the context. For example, the word 'piano' may prime 'instrument' or 'weight', but which of the two gets evoked depends on the context: 'concert' vs. 'house moving'. Given this dynamic aspect of the human brain, we should build the index automatically, computing the relation of terms and their weights on the fly. This dynamic creation of the index could be done via a corpus. This latter representing ideally the dictionary users' world knowledge, and the way how the prominence of words and ideas varies over time.

Another important point are link-names, i.e. the type of relationship holding between two associates: [(rose) <--color (red)]. Given the fact that any query (e.g. 'India') may yield many hits, hits whose weights may be misleading, it makes sense to group the output according to some (other) category, for example, link names (color, city_of, instrument, ...). Yet, important as they may be, links or relations are hard to extract and to name. This is why we have decided to start with a very small sub-set, meronymic-, i.e. part-of relations (x is *part of* y, x *has* y, etc.).

KEYWORDS : Lexical access, navigation, word association, lexical graphs, semantic maps, automatic index creation, dynamic index, link extraction, link-names, part-of relations.

## 1 Introduction

One of the most vexing problems in speaking or writing is the fact that one has memorized, i.e. stored a given word, yet one fails to access it when needed. This kind of search failure known as *dysnomia* or *Tip of the Tongue-problem* (TOT),[1] occurs not only in language, but also in other activities of everyday life. It is basically a search- and index problem which we are reminded of when we look for something that exists in real world or our mind (keys, glasses, people's names), but which we are unable to locate, access or retrieve in time.

[1] The TOT-problem is characterized by the fact that the author (speaker/writer) has only partial access to the word s/he is looking for. The typically lacking parts are phonological (syllables, phonemes). Since all information except this last one seems to be available, and since this is the one preceding articulation, we say: the word is stuck on the *tip of the tongue*.

Word finding problems are generally dealt with via a lexicon. Obviously, readers and writers have different behaviors and expectations concerning input and output (target information). While the *decoder* (listener/reader) provides the word s/he wants additional information for — (say, what is the meaning of 'rug', or what are its synonymes?),— the *encoder* (speaker/writer) provides the meaning, or meaning-related elements (for example, 'typical british sport') of the word for which s/he lacks the corresponding form (=> cricket).

Our concern here is more with the language producer, *i.e.* lexical access in language production, a task often neglected in lexicographical work. Language producers typically start from meanings (concepts) or lexical items related to the target word: associations (strong + black + bitter + beverage + made_from beans => coffee). Eventhough empirically well founded, *concept-based search* or access via associations (Deese, 1965; Schvaneveldt, 1989) is not well supported in current electronic dictionaries. Actually, there are several problems to be addressed, let us mention only two: (a) the problem of *input*: how (i.e. in what terms) shall the user specify the meaning of the word whose form he is looking for? —(say, 'name of the beverage the British fancy to take in the afternoon'),— and (b) the problem of *navigation*. How do you get from some input (*source word*), —say, 'huge animal, gray, trunk, ivory, Africa',— to the *target word* (elephant)? Note that studies concerning the TOT-problem have shown over and over that people being in this state know a lot concerning the target word —meaning, origin, gender, number of syllables, etc.,— even if they cannot access its form (Brown,1991; Brown and Mc Neill, 1966 ).

## 2 Creation of an association-based index

To support word finding, i.e. navigation/word access in electronic dictionaries, Zock and colleagues proposed to add to an existing electronic resource a corpus-derived index based on the notion of association (Zock et al., 2010). Dictionary entries (headwords), say 'rose' or 'book', are indexed in terms of the words they evoke: rose => red or flower; book => bible or library, .... This kind of information can be gleaned via various methods, including corpus analysis, i.e. collocation-extraction (Ferret and Zock, 2006). Words co-occurring in a given text —the window being generally a sentence or a paragraph at the most— can be considered as associates. They tend to evoke each other. Note that associations can be bi-directional, though their strength and link-type are hardly ever the same. The list of co-occurrences can be represented in various ways, lists, graphs, etc. They can be seen as a special kind of semantic network (Sowa, 1992). Indeed, the links are hardly ever deep-case roles (agent, beneficiary, etc.), but rather associations, i.e. binary relations.

The fact that the index is a network has various interesting features. It provides agents (people, robots) with a powerful search tool, while offering a lot of freedom, i.e. flexibility. Since all words are connected, any of them can be the source (prime, potential starting point) or the target (probe). Search can start at any point, i.e. all words can be reached from anywhere, regardless of their distance (indirect neighborhood). Even if search has been initiated from a remotely related word, one may still be able to find the target word. One just has to use (recursively) one of the query's associates (direct neighbour) as new starting point. Since all words can act as retrieval cue, all of them trigger at least one related word, and if they trigger more, that is, a list of words (they usually do), it may contain the target word, and if not, a word indirectly related to it.

The idea of association is of course not new. It was known already to the Greek philosophers and it has a quite a long tradition in psychology (Aitchison, 2003; Galton, 1880) More recently it has been used in computational linguistics (vector-based approaches: Landauer and Dumais, 1997 ; Lund and Burgess, 1996) and computational lexicography, lexical graphs like WordNet (Miller, 1990). It should be noted though that many lexical graphs lack a vital piece of information, the link type (synonyms, hypernym, etc.). Yet this is vital information, as we will see (section 3.3) at the interface level for human users. Concerning WordNet (WN)[2], it should be pointed out that links are all hand-coded (see section 5), and the resource is not corpus-based, hence it lacks many of the needed links, mostly syntagmatic associations. WN suffers from the well-known 'tennis-problem': words typically occurring together, hence naturally associated (tennis, umpire, racket, court, backhand), are not always linked in WN. Before discussing this last point, the core of the paper, let us describe briefly the method used for building the index and some of the problems.

## 3 Building the resource

Creating a dictionary involves typically the following decisions: (a) which words to include (this raises the problem of what a word is); (b) what *information* to *associate* with each one of them (definition, grammatical information, ...); (c) how to organize the lexicon, i.e. lexical entries (alphabetically, topically). Of course, all these decisions depend to a large extent on the subsequent usage of the resource (reading, writing).

The resource we have started to build is a kind of semantic map, with words being connected, and the links (or connections) being typed (categorized, labeled) and weighted. Of course, there are various methods to build such a map. One way is to ask people to get lists of associations (Deese, 1965). This has been the main strategy of psychologists trying to define word association norms (Nelson et.al., 1998). Another way is to use games (Lafourcade, 2007). Still another approach is to use corpora and to extract collocations. This is the route we are taking. Yet, in order to teach our goal several problems need to be addressed:

### 3.1 Building a representative corpus:

Since we start from the assumption that peoples' associations are based on specific- and on general knowlege (episodic- and encyclopedic knowledge), we must make sure that this kind of information is also contained in the sources upon which we draw in order to build our lexical map (association lists). Put differently, our sources (in our case corpora) must be representative. To this end we need a well balanced corpus, that is a corpus containing general information (for example, London, capital of England, etc) as well as information concerning a specific person, place or event.

### 3.2 Indexing:

In order to find the words a dictionary contains, we must organize them. Put differently, the resource must be structured, i.e. it must contain an index or a semantic map. Words can be organized according various criteria or viewpoints, *formal*-syntactic (spelling, part-of-speech, morphemes), pragmatic-*semantic*, etc. In this latter case one may consider (a) the word's components, i.e. the elements occuring in a word's definition (bag of word: Dutoit et al. 2002; Bilac et al. 2004; El-Khalout et al. 2004), (b) its recurring elements (semantic primitives (Schank,

[2] http://wordnet.princeton.edu

1975; Wierbicka, 1996) or (c) its role in discourse: words are grouped by domain, (see Roget's Thesaurus, Roget, 1852).

Unlike linguists, psychologists are more interested in word relations.Gathering typically related terms (x evoking y) they've built association lists (Deese, 1965; Schvaneveldt, 1989). Such lists are nowadays freely available in different languages : Dutch,[3] English ([4],[5]), French[6], German,[7] Japanese,[8] and Russian.[9] The Edinburgh Associative Thesaurus is particularly interesting, in as it shows not only the words evoked ('red', 'flower', etc.) in response to a given stimulus ('rose'), but also the causes (primes) of this input. For example, 'thorn', 'petal', 'flower', etc. in response to the prime 'rose'. Put differently, we get bi-directional, i.e., incoming and outgoing links. While such resources are extremely useful for many tasks (pratical applications, research), they nevertheless do have certain shortcomings. For example, they are fairly static. Hence, they cannot take topic changes into account. Yet, associations are sensitive to such variations. Think of the word 'piano' in the context of moving from one place to another. Also, most of these resources lack the link type, yet this is an important feature to reduce search time by clustering information pertaining to the same link type. This last comment does not apply to WN or JeuxdeMots. They both contain a small set of link types[10] which is very useful for navigation.[11]

### 3.3 Ranking:

Words occur with a certain frequency. The same holds true for their combination, that is, words and their relations do have a certain weight. While one should not overestimate the notion of weight with respect to word access, it may nevertheless be useful for word order (priorization of words in the list of candidates) and for deciding where to draw the line (cut-off point in case that the list gets long), that is which words to display and which to hide. Ideally, the weight is (re-) computed on the fly, taking into account contextual variations. As mentionned already in our piano example, a word may give prominence to quite different associations depending on the context. Likewise, the word 'Java' may evoke in people's mind quite different concepts ('island' or 'programming language') depending on whether we are talking about holidays, geography or computers.

### 3.4 Identification and 'typing' the links:

Associations must not only be identified, they must also be labeled. Qualifying, i.e. typing the links is the hardest task, yet it is vital for navigation. Frequency alone is not only of limited use

---

[3] http://www. kuleuven.be/semlab/interface/index.php

[4] Edinburgh Associative Thesaurus : http://www.eat.rl.ac.uk/

[5] University of South Florida Word Association: http://w3.usf.edu/FreeAssociation/

[6] JeuxdeMots: (www.lirmm.fr/~lafourcade/jeuxdemots/diko.php)

[7] http://www.coli.uni-saarland.de/projects/nag/, http://www.schulteimwalde.de/resources/assoc-norms.html

[8] http://www.valdes.titech.ac.jp/~terry/jwad.html

[9] http://wordassociations.ru

[10] JeuxdeMots contains the following links (isa, hyponyme, syonyme, antonyme, domain, substance, location, caracteristics, part_of, meronym, quantifier, do, cause, consequence) plus a 'link' called: 'free association'.

[11] AKI: http://www.jeuxdemots.org//AKI.php

(people cannot interpret properly numerical values in a context like this),— it can even be misleading. Two terms of very similar weight, say, ‘mouse’ and ‘PC’, may belong to entirely different categories: 'computer device' vs. 'type of computer'. Hence choosing one instead of the other may decrease the chances of finding the desired target-word. In the same vein, BLACK(x) may be strongly associated with WHITE(x), DARK(x) and COFFEE(x), eventhough its relationship may be quite different in each case: 'opposite', 'similar to' and 'color'. Last, but not least, 'right' may be strongly associated with 'write', 'light', 'left' or 'wrong' which, of course, does not imply that the relationship is the same.

Note, that weights are a main feature in the programs written by psychologists where they try to mimick the performance of the human brain, or, the mental lexicon. The goal is to mimick *precision* (correct output, or similar errors to the ones produced by people) and *access time* (word access in real-time). This work is generally done within the connectionist framework (Dell, 1996; Levelt et al., 1999). Impressive as these simulations are, this approach cannot be used here for several reasons: (a) the information encoded in these networks is not interpretable by human user. Actually, the information contributing to the 'building' of a word,—words are synthesized rather than stored,— is distributed across various layers[12]; (b) the weights are tuned by the system builders (psychologists) who know the final output (target word). This does not hold for the user of our future resource, since target word is precisely the item s/he is looking for, and if s/he knew it, the problem were solved.

## 4 Some justifications for making explicit the link-type

As mentioned already, a lexical graph composed of words only is of little use for navigation, if one does not know the kind of link holding between two adjacent nodes (direct neighbors, i.e. associated words). Indeed, every node, i.e. every word may have a great many associates, some being linked via the same type of association —(imagine all the days subsumed under the label 'weekdays' or 'colors'),— others being connected via a link of a different type (*week*-month; *week*-weak, *week*-geek, etc.).

Obviously, the greater the number of words associated with a term, and the more numerous the type of links, the more complex the graph will be. This reduces considerably the value of graphs as adequate representation at the interface level in order to support navigation. There are at least three potential problems challenging readability:

- **High connectivity** (i.e. the great number of possible links). These links can be of different types, bi-directional (incoming and outgoing), asymmetric and of different weights.
- **Distribution** (i.e. non-adjacency, of conceptually related nodes, that is, nodes activated by the same kind of association (e.g. synonyms), but not being displayed next to each other.
- **The possible crossing of links** in the case of indirect association (see A1 – B2 or A2 – B1 in Figure 1, next page).[13]

[12] For a detailed description, see Zock et al., 2010.

[13] Note, that the crossing of lines can be avoided in the immediate neighborhood (distance 1, i.e direct associations), but not at the next level. If two sets of words, say A1 + A3 and A2 + A4, have both B1 + B2 as associates at the next level, then the links are bound to cross.suppo Also, bear in mind that the scope is the entire graph and not only the next adjacent level (i.e. direct neighbors). Note also, that this crossing of links is a side-effect of mapping an n-dimensional graph on two dimensions.

All these factors may leed to confusion. Also, the role of frequencies must be relativized or defined more precisely. Indeed, many researchers believe that frequencies or weights are the crucial element for guiding search. Yet, taken alone they are too poor to guide the user, helping him to decide on the direction to go (see section 3.4).

In sum, lexical graphs can become complex, not only because of the number of nodes (words they contain), but also because of the number of possible connection types (associates). Hence, lexical graphs devoid of this kind of information are like maps that omit showing 'how' cities are connected (road, railway, airplane). Hence, they are not sufficiently good representations of the territory (semantic map) to be used as orientational guides or navigational aids.

To overcome these problems, we suggest to display by category (clusters) all the words linked by the same kind of association to the source word. Hence, rather than displaying all the connected words as a flat list, we suggest to present them in chunks to allow for categorical search. Having chosen a category, the user will be presented a list of words or categories from which he must choose. If the target word is in the category chosen by the user —(suppose he looked for a hyperonym, hence he checked the is_a bag),— search stops, otherwise it goes on. The user could choose either another category, or a word in the current list, either of which becoming then the new starting point.

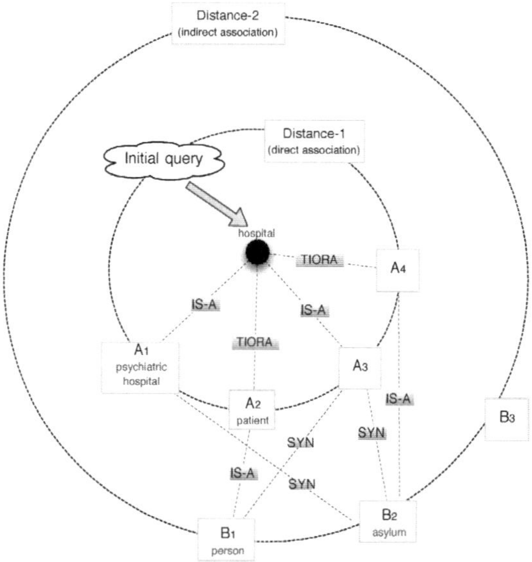


FIGURE 1-Potential problems with graphs:
crossing links with indirect neighbors.[14]

In the next section we will present some initial results of how to infer automatically the type of link for a small subset of links: part_of relations.

[14] IS-A (subtype); SYN (synonym); TIORA ('Typically Involved Object, Relation or Actor', for example, tools, employees, ...).

## 5 Initial results for inferring automatically the type of link

Suppose that you wanted to express the following concept: '*superior dark coffee made of beans from Arabia*', and that neither 'espresso' nor 'cappuccino' are the desired target words. In this case there are three kinds of relations likely to help the language producer find the target word 'mocha'. Indeed, the mentioned seed words (superior, dark, coffee, made of, beans, from Arabia) express different kind of relations: an *attribute* relation (superior, coffee; dark, coffee), a *resulting* relationship (coffee made of beans) and a *source* relation (from Arabia). Aggregating them and using them as retrieval cues might help the language producer to narrow down the search space, zooming into a small set of words possibly containing the target word. To allow for this, we need, of course, something like a semantic map. This latter specifies the form of the major words and the way how they are related to their direct neighbors. Such a map can reveal many things: list of available words, distance between two words, type of relations, relative density, i.e. tightly populated parts of the network, hubs, i.e. number of incoming and outcoming links, etc.

Starting from such a set of seed- or source words, Zock and colleagues (Zock et al., 2009) have used LSA and the Tf-idf measure values to identify the target word. LSA is quite successful with respect to identifying the relative similarity between concepts. Actually, it achieves similar scores as non-natives do: 64% vs. 64,5% (Landauer and Dumais, 1997). While this is surely impressive, LSA cannot provide us with the kind of information we care for: the name of the relationship holding between two concepts or words. Actually, our problem is a bit different from the one addressed by LSA. Our goal does not consist in finding synonyms of the source- or target-word, our goal is to help people to *find* the *target word*, bottom-line. In other words, we need a different approach. For example, our system should be able to draw on any information available at the onset of search. Hence, search should be possible by entering the graph at any point. Also, our associations must not only be identified as in LSA or lexical graphs in general, they must also be labeled in terms of their type. As mentioned already, this is a prerequisite if we want to help humans to navigate in the semantic space for which we try to build a map.

To achieve this goal we will draw on the idea described in section 2. The problem of developing such a semantic space is enormous as there are many kinds of relations needed, for example: Cause-Effect (laugh-wrinkles), Product-Producer (honey-bee), Content-Container (wine-bottle), Part-Whole (tip-tongue), Instrument-Agency (laser-printer), etc. We will focus here only on one of them, Part-Whole relations (PT-WHRs) and their automatic extraction from corpora to build the semantic map or space. Several scholars have proposed taxonomies of PT-WHRs (Winston et al., 1987; Vieu and Aurnague, 2007). We will follow Winston's classical proposal:

| | | |
|---|---|---|
| 1. | component – integral object | handle – cup |
| 2. | member – collection | tree – forest |
| 3. | portion – mass | grain – salt |
| 4. | stuff – object | steel – bike |
| 5. | feature – activity | paying – shopping |
| 6. | place – area | oasis – desert |

- *Integral objects* have a structure; their components can be torn apart, and their elements have a functional relation with respect to the whole. For example, 'kitchen–apartment' or 'aria–opera.
- 'Tree-forest' and 'chairman-committee' are typical representatives of Member-Collection relations.

- Portion-Mass captures the relations between portions, masses, objects and physical dimensions. For example: 'meter-kilometer'.
- The Stuff-Object category encodes the relations between an object and the stuff of which it is made of. For example, 'steel-car' or 'snow-snowball'.
- Place-Area captures the relation between an area and a sub-area like 'Ethiopia-Addis Ababa'.

Meronymic relations can also be categorized as typical or accidental. The former are always true (roof-house), while the latter are episodic (cucumber-sandwich), they have happened only at some point in time. We focus here only on the first type.

To capture the meaning of words we relied on the intuition that meanings depend to some extent on a word's neighbourhood, be it direct (black coffee) or indirect (the color of coffee is generally black). Words occurring in similar contexts tend to have similar meanings (Harshman, 1970). This idea, known as the 'distributional hypothesis,'[15] has been proposed by various scholars (Harris, 1954; Firth, 1957; Wittgenstein, 1922). It implies that word meanings are context sensitive. A word's meaning cannot be fully grasped unless one takes the context into account. Meaning and context can be captured in terms of (more or less direct) neighbourhood, i.e. words co-occurring within a defined window (phrase, sentence, paragraph).

## 5.1 Description of our approach

Since we try to capture meaning via word similarity, the question arises of how to operationalize this notion. One way of doing so is to create a vector space composed of the target word and its neighbours (Lund and Burgess, 1996). This approach, known as vector space model (VSM) has been developed by Salton and colleagues (Salton et al., 1975) for information retrieval. Their idea was to represent all documents of a collection as points in a space, i.e. a vector in a vector space. Semantic similarity is expressed via the distance of two points: closely related points express similarity, while distant points signal unrelated ideas, or remotely related words. We are concerned here with word similarity rather than document similarity. The meaning of a word is represented as a vector based on the n-gram value of all co-occurring words. The use of the VSM to extract PT-WHRs has two advantages: it requires little man power (human effort) and few resources (corpora), at least far less than Girju's approach (Girju et al., 2005) which relies heavily on annotated corpora and WN.

The underlying idea is that the type of relation holding between two concepts/words can be inferred from data (for example, corpora containing co-occurrences), by using the similarity values and n-gram information for clustering the relevant terms. The similarity value allows us to extract part_of relations, while clustering is used to group similar words. The similarity value can be obtained in different ways, and it may depend on the type of relation to be identified. Put differently, the vectors used for encoding, say, a part-whole relation are different from those encoding hyponyms. The n-gram information used to extract the vectors is also specific to the type of semantic relation to be encoded.

---

[15] http://en.wikipedia.org/wiki/Distributional_hypothesis

We devised a weakly supervised method for automatic extraction of meronymic relations (component–integral object; part-whole).[16] Indeed, our method hardly depends on language and it is completely domain-independent. However, we do need a 'Part of Speech Tagger' or a 'part-of-speech tagged corpus'. In this respect our work differs quite a bit from other people's work as it does not require a resource like WN. Hence, our approach can be used even for under-resourced languages, or languages lacking a resource like WN. In other words, the methods is sufficiently general to be applicable to other languages than the one for which it has been initially designed.

Since word-meaning is represented as a vector based on the n-gram value of all co-occurring words we need a corpus. To build the required vectors we used the 'Corpus of Historial American English' (COHA) which contains 400 million words. COHA is an n-gram corpus tagged for parts of speech (Mark, 2011). For languages lacking this kind of (tagged) corpus, plain text can be used, as the system is able to identify the concepts' n-gram value in the corpus. This feature is very convenient for under-resourced languages, as it makes their preparation (pre-processing) easier than if one had to annotate the corpus manually.

## 5.2 Related works

Previous works attempting to identify semantic information are somewhere on a scale, ranging from exclusively hand-crafted patterns (Hearst, 1998) and rules to probabilistic methods. For example, Finin (1980) relied exclusively on manually built rules. Girju (2005) and Beamer (2008) used a knowledge intensive approaches by drawing on huge resources like WordNet. Hage's (2006) and Harshman's work (1970) is domain dependent, while the proposals of (Girju, 2005; Matthew & Charniak, 1999) rely on syntactic structures, hence they are language specific.

Resource intensive approaches (like the ones relying on WordNet) are not suitable for languages lacking such a resource, for example, under resourced languages. Resource intensive approaches use texts, tagged with WordNet information, for example, senses. However, this kind of approach cannot be applied to applications relying on real world data, real world texts are hardly ever tagged with WordNet information (senses, type of link, etc.). In addition, most of the above mentioned approaches are highly language dependent. The classification features used to build the rules are extracted from a specific language. For example, Hearst (1998) uses syntactic features that occur frequently in sentences and in many kinds of texts. However, such syntactic structures are rare, their coverage is small and their effectiveness greatly depends on the type of semantic relation extracted. Indeed, Hearst (1998) reported better results for *hyponyms* than for *meronyms* which may be due to the fact that syntactic structures encoding this latter kind of relation tend to be ambiguous. This being so we may need to take a different approach.

We decided to use a Vector Space Model (VSM) which was highly successful for various applications, including question-answering. For instance, using this kind of approach for representing word meaning Rapp [38] achieved a score of 92.5% on multiple-choice synonym questions from the TOEFL Test (the test foreigners have to take to evaluation their level of English before entering an american university[17]), whereas the average human score for non-

[16] *Supervised* learning means that the examples on the basis of which the system learns are *labeled*, i.e. they specify explicitly which forms are correct and which are not. In *unsupervised* learning examples are not *labeled*, the system clusters data into classes, giving the latter some arbitrary name.

[17] http://www.ets.org/toefl

native speakers was 64.5%. Motivated by this success we decided to try this approach for automatically extracting part_of relations.

## 5.3 Our approach in more detail

As explained in section 3, four problems need to be solved for building the resource. We need to get a representative corpus, index lexical entries in terms of associations (i.e. build an association matrix), rank the terms and label the links.

To address the first task we used the Brown corpus, though, other corpora are probably needed. Next, we developed a system, i.e. a pipeline of 6 stages or components (see figure 2) to address the remaining problems. The process works as follows. Starting with the first word in the corpus, the system extracts all associated words expressing a PT-WHR to continue then with the next word until it has reached the end. Actually, the system performs the following six operations:

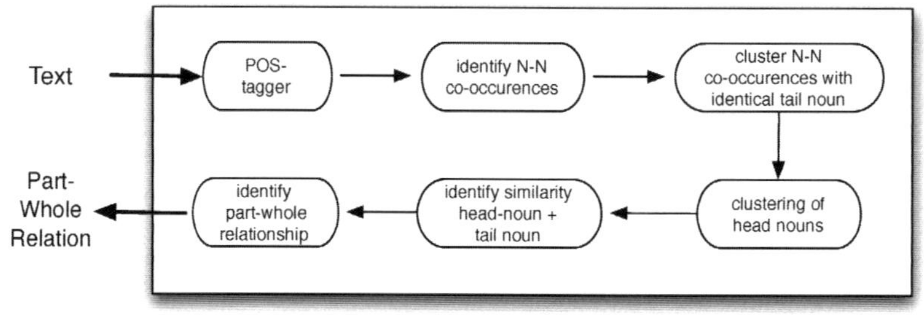


FIGURE 2- System information flow

- *Step 1*: This component identifies the part of speech of the sentence elements. Since *part-whole relations* connect only nouns, the system requires only a tagger able to identify nouns. As mentioned already, we used the 'Corpus of Historical American English' (COHA) (Mark, 2011). This is an n-gram corpus whose elements are tagged in terms of part of speech.
- *Step 2*: The next component extracts Noun-Noun co-occurrences (N-N sequences) from the tagged corpus. For example, 'corolla car', 'door of car', 'car engine', 'engine of car', 'car design', 'network design', 'airplane engine', 'search engine' etc. Noun phrases are not included in our current version. There are two types of co-occurrences: nouns occurring directly together, that is, in adjacent position (NN) and nouns whose co-occurrence is mediated via another type of word occurring in between them (possibly a preposition, adjective, verbs). Both types need to be identified. Nouns can be easily extracted, regardless of their distance to each other and regardless of the type and the number of words in between them, provided that none of them is a noun. The procedure works as follows: starting from the current noun, we increase the window size to the point to include the next noun. Having two nouns (car-engine; engine of car), we signal their respective functions via names, calling the first one the *head* and the second the *tail*. 'Car' and 'engine' are respectively the *head* and the *tail* in the 'car-engine' co-occurrence, while they are the reverse in the 'engine-car' example. Hence, cases where the *part* appears both before and after the *whole object* will be retrieved. Since the conclusion that a noun assumes the role of the part or whole may be incorrect, we have decided to delay this decision until the very end.

- *Step 3*: N-N co-occurrences with an identical tail noun take N-N co-occurrences from the preceding step to cluster them on the basis of their tail noun. For example, 'corolla car' and 'door of car' belong to one cluster, both of them having the same *tail* noun: 'car', while 'car design' and 'network design' belong to another cluster. The same holds true for 'airplane engine,' 'search engine' and 'car engine'.

  car [corolla, door],
  design [car, network],
  engine [airplane, search, car]

- *Step 4*: the noun pairs of the clusters created in step three are clustered again, but this time on the basis of the similarity value of their head nouns.

  car { [corolla] [door] }
  design { [car] [network] }
  engine {[airplane, car] [search]}

  The similarity value is calculated by taking the cosine value of the vectors of the head nouns. The vectors are created by taking every word co-occurring with the noun (n-gram). This component and the next one require n-gram information. We got this from COHA[18]. All words are represented as a vector of their bi-gram value. Hence, each word has an n-gram value, represented as a vector. In order to calculate the similarity between the *head* nouns we used the cosine value of the vectors of the *head* noun. *Head* nouns whose cosine values are above a certain threshold are clustered together.
- *Step 5*: This component computes the similarity between the head and tail noun. In this module two types of similarity values are calculated. We call them $S_1$ and $S_2$. Note that the vector used to create $S_1$ in this module is different from the one used in the preceding step. The vector for $S_1$ is built here only on the basis of words co-occurring with the tail noun. If ever a word co-occurs both with the tail and the head noun, its n-gram value is recorded in both vectors, otherwise their respective vector values will be 1 for the tail noun and zero for the head noun. Words co-occurring only with the head noun will not be included in the vector. Hence, the size of the vector is equal to the size of the number of words co-occurring with the tail noun. However, in order to create a vector for $S_2$, we will also consider words co-occurring with the head noun also. The similarity value for $S_1$ and $S_2$ is again derived from the distance between the vectors i.e. their cosine value. The basic idea is that the *tail* nouns of the noun pairs presenting the 'Component-Integral object' or a 'Part-Whole relation' have a strong similarity value with their head nouns in their clusters. Hence, words like 'airplane' and 'car' have a strong similarity value with respect to 'engine', while 'search' has only a small one in the cluster: airplane-engine, 'search-engine', 'car-engine'.

- *Step 6*: the last module identifies whether two nouns are linked via an integral component Part-Whole relation or not (PT-WHR). To do so, the system draws on information provided by the above-mentioned modules. Given some cluster(s) (built in step 3 and 4) and a set of similarity values (identified in the training corpus, step 5), the system extracts automatically a production rule: if <condition> then <action>. This latter is used to decide whether two words are linked via an integral component PT-WHR or not. In order to achieve this goal, we took a corpus and tagged as "T" nouns pairs exhibiting a part-of

[18] http://www.ngrams.info

relationship and as "F" in the remaining cases. The system counts then the similarity values exhibited by the majority of noun pairs in the training set. The range of these values are learned automatically. The system calculates two similarity values ($S_1$, $S_2$) for every noun co-occurrence in the training set and takes then the range of values exhibited by the majority of part-of noun co-occurrences in the corpus. In order to determine this range, we calculated an error rate for all possible similarity ranges obtained for all NN co-occurrences in the corpus and selected the one with the lowest error rate. For example, suppose your corpus contained six NN occurrences (the first three being negative, the remaining being positive examples). Suppose further that the nouns having respectively the following values for $S_1$ (0.2, 0.3, 0.6, 0.8, 0.85, 0.9) and $S_2$ (0.1,0.3,0.4,0.45,0.5,0.55). This would yield the following result:

| Range | % of negative relations retrieved | % of positive relations excluded |
|---|---|---|
| $S_1 < 0.2$ and $S_2 < 0.1$ | 0% | 100% |
| $S_1 < 0.2$ and $S_2 > 0.1$ | 0% | 100% |
| $S_1 < 0.2$ and $0.3 > S_2 > 0.1$ | 0% | 100% |
| $S_1 < 0.2$ and $S_2 < 0.3$ | 0% | 100% |
| $S_1 < 0.2$ and $S_2 > 0.3$ | 0% | 100% |
| $S_1 < 0.2$ and $0.4 > S_2 < 0.3$ | 0% | 100% |
| ... | ... | ... |
| $S_1 > 0.2$ and $S_2 < 0.4$ | 100% | 0% |
| ... | ... | ... |
| $S_1 > 0.8$ and $S_2 > 0.4$ | 0% | 0% (best range) |

Table 1: samples of the possible ranges of similarity values generated and their error rate

We assume in the example above that the values of $S_1$ and $S_2$ of the first three lines are based on negative examples, while the remainder are positive, i.e. they contain a part of relation. In our case, most of the similarity values exceed 0.4 for $S_1$ and 0.8 for $S_2$. Here below is a subset of the algorithm: Given a pair of nouns as described in the steps 3 and 4 here above.

```
If the similarity value S2 > 0.4 && if the similarity value S1 > 0.8
   If the noun pairs occurred at least once as compound noun
   Then the head noun refers to the whole and the tail to the part
Else
   If the average similarity value (C) between the noun and the other nouns in the
     cluster > 0.4
   If one of the nouns in the cluster has S2> 0.4 and S1 > 0.8
      If the noun pairs occurred at least once as compound noun
      Then the head noun refers to the whole and the tail to the part
   Else
      The relationship between the nouns is other than a whole-part relation
```

The rule stipulating that 'noun pairs occurring at least once as compound noun', does not imply that the noun referring to the 'part' is always the second noun, and the 'whole' the first. Indeed, the two may be separated by words of another type, for example, a preposition. In this case the arguments will swap position, the 'part' preceding the 'whole'. Both cases will be handled as discussed in step 2. Having extracting the nouns for both cases, we can find the pairs as a compound noun at least once in a well-balanced corpus. For example, 'engine of car' can be extracted as explained already in step 2, and the system will then interpret the pair as 'part-whole' if it exists as 'car engine', which is always the case in a well-balanced English corpus.

We managed to extract the specific semantic similarity patterns for NN co-occurrences exhibiting a part of relation. We also showed that different types of similarity measures ($S_1$, $S_2$) can be extracted from n-gram information. For example, for part_of relations we have extracted two types of similarity values ($S_1$, $S_2$) with their respective range of values. N-N co-occurrences that do not fall within the defined range are filtered out. They do not express part_of relations. Note that, unlike other approaches including LSA, we do not simply measure the similarity values of the two noun pairs, but we build two types of vectors to determine two similarity values ($S_1$ and $S_2$) and check them then according to a set of rules. Note also, that our similarity measures filter only part of relations, hence different measures will be required if we want to deal with other types of semantic relations.

The vectors used by us for identifying the similarity values are built automatically by the system. However, the way of developing a specific vector for encoding part-of relations is not based on learning from a training set, it is based on a set of observations and assumptions.

Words co-occurring with *parts*, say 'engine', will very frequently be the very object of which they are part ("car-engine, airplane-engine".), but not vice versa. The two sets are quite different. While a 'car' may contain many parts ('tyre', 'steering-wheel', 'gear box', etc.)', it may nevertheless be linked to many concepts playing another role than being a *part* : 'driver', 'accident', 'race', etc. Put differently, the link can be other than 'part_of'. Nevertheless, objects expressing a part are nearly always connected to the entity of which they are part of.

The example here below illustrates the functioning of the algorithm: at step 2 the algorithm lists N-N occurrences like car-engine, train-engine, airplane-engine, benzine-engine, gasoline-engine, and search-engine. N-N occurrences are put in the same cluster as they have the same tail noun : engine (step 3). In step 4 the cluster is further classified in to three sub-clusters: cluster $_1$, cluster $_2$ and cluster $_3$:

*Cluster 1*: VEHICLES [car-engine, train-engine, airplane-engine]

Comment: We have an integral component Part-Whole relation, as 'engine' is part of a holistic entity: VEHICLES (car, train, and airplane).

*Cluster 2*: OIL [benzine-engine, gasoline-engine]

Comment: 'Engine' is not part of 'oil' (benzine or gasoline).

*Cluster 3*: SEARCH-ENGINE

The two clusters here above are created within a cluster having engine as tail noun. The clusters are identified on the basis of the similarity value of the head nouns. Since 'car', 'train', and 'airplane' have a strong similarity value they are put in the same cluster. Likewise, 'benzine' and 'gasoline' are put into some cluster and so does 'search'. At step 6 the system separates the cluster

1 from the rest, as the vector similarity of 'engine' and 'oil' on one hand and 'search' on the other is below a given threshold value, while the one of 'engine' and 'vehicle' is above it.

### 5.3.1 A walkthrough

Let us explain our approach in more detail via an example. Suppose the following input :

> The Japanese government decided to raise taxes for the export of Toyota cars. This is not the only problem Toyota had to face during the last few months. Indeed, the motors of their new car models having problems, the company decided to revise for free all the recently cars sold......

The POS tagger identifies in step-1 the part of the speech of the words

> The Japanese government decided to raise taxes for the export of Toyota/$NP_1$ cars/NN. This is not the only problem Toyota/$NP_1$ had to face recently. Indeed, the motors/NN of their new car/NN models/$NN_2$ having problems, the company/NN decided to revise for free all the recently cars/NN sold......

At the next step we extract NN co-occurences: `Toyota-car; motors-car, car-models`, etc. At step-3 we cluster these co-occurences according to their tail noun :{[Toyota-car, motors-car], car models]]} At step-4, the head nouns are clustered according to their similarity value. This latter is based on the distance between the vectors of the head nouns (the nouns appearing first). This yields the following results: `Toyota`, `motors` and `car`. We also calculate at step-4 the dot product (similarity of the vectors of the head nouns).To create the vectors we use the N-gram information contained in the COHA corpus, that is, we take all words co-occuring with nouns. Words with similar vectors will be grouped in the same cluster. At step-5, we identify the similarity values ($S_1$ and $S_2$) for the head and the tail noun as shown in the table below:

| NN co-ocurrence | $S_1$ for head | $S_1$ for tail | $S_2$ |
|---|---|---|---|
| Toyota-car | 0.73521462209380772 | 0.1348399724926484 | 0.099136319419321925 |
| Motor-car | 0.82118460785425675 | 0.519575448720232 | 0.40259135545057436 |

This is the way how vectors are built:

- The vector value is 1 for words co-occuring with 'Toyota' and 0 for words that, while not co-occuring with 'Toyota', do occur with 'car'. This allows us to create the vector $S_1$ for 'Toyota'. The $S_1$ similarity value for 'Toyota' is calculated by taking the distance (dot product) between the $S_1$ vector of 'Toyota' and a vector built on the basis of words co-occuring with both nouns (the intersection of 'Toyota' and 'car'). Put differently, the vector is built by taking words whose similarity value is 1 in both vectors, for example, 'Toyota' and 'car'.
- Likewise, the vector value is 1 for words co-occuring with 'car' and 0 for words, that while not co-occuring with 'car' do co-occur with 'Toyota'. This allows us to build the $S_1$ for 'car'. The $S_1$ similarity values for 'car' are calculated by taking the distance (dot product) between the $S_1$ vector for 'car' and a vector built on the basis of words co-occuring with

both nouns (the intersection of 'Toyota' and 'car'). As here above, the vector is built by taking words whose similarity value is 1 in both vectors (again, 'Toyota' and 'car').

- The $S_2$ similarity value is calculated by taking the dot product between the $S_1$ vectors of 'Toyota' and 'car'.

How do we decide wheter a relationship is of the kind 'part_whole' (step-6)?

The rules use the similarity values of the table here above in order to decide whether there is a meronymic relation between the two nouns, and what respective roles of the nouns are (which is the 'whole' and which is the 'part'). This is how the rule works. $S_1$ is 0.73521462209380772 for 'Toyota' and 0.1348399724926484 for 'car', $S_2$ being 0.099136319419321925. Likewise, $S_1$ is 0.82118460785425675 for 'motor' and 0.519575448720232 for 'car', the value of $S_2$ being 0.40259135545057436.

Assume that $N_1$ and $N_2$ are respectively the first and the second noun. Hence, $N_1$ $S_1$ and $N_2$ $S_1$ are the respective $S_1$ similarity values of the first and the second noun, $S_2$ being identical for both nouns. The production rule checks now the similarity values against the treshold learned from the training set, the thresholds being the ranges of the similarity values exhibited by most of the meronyms in the training set.

if ($N_1S_1$ > = 0.8 and $S_2$ > = 0.4) then print: $N_1$ <part>; $N_2$ <whole>

if ($N_2$ $S_2$> = 0.8 and $S_2$ > = 0.4) then print: $N_2$ <part>; $N_1$ <whole>

In the 'Toyota-car' co-occurrence, 'Toyota' and 'car' are respectively $N_1$ and $N_2$. $N_1S_1$ is $S_1$ for 'Toyota', while $N_2S_2$ is $S_1$ for 'car'. Substituting the values in the rule would yield:

if (0.735 > = 0.8 and 0.099 > = 0.4) then print ('Toyota' is <part> and 'car' is <whole>)

if(0.135 > = 0.8 and 0.099 > = 0.4) then print ('car' is the <part> and 'Toyota' is the <whole>)

Since none of the above apply, the relationship between the nouns is other than a meronymic one. Let's do the same for 'motor-car':

if (0.821 > = 0.8 and 0.402 > = 0.4) then print ('motor' is the <part> and 'car' is the <whole>)

The condition stated in the rule is satisfied by the similarity value of the noun pairs. Hence, we do have a meronymic relationship with 'motor' being the <part> and 'car' being the <whole>.

if (0.51 > = 0.8 and 0.402 > = 0.4) then print ('car' is the <part> and 'motor' is the <whole>), which is false.

The steps just described are performed for all NN co-occurences in the paragraph.

### 5.3.2 Identification of the links senses

The concepts and the links holding between them are thus extracted from the corpus as explained above. However, there is one other problem that needs to be addressed. A word may express several meanings. For example, the word-form (lemma) 'mouse' may stand for a 'rodent' (animal) or a 'computer device'.

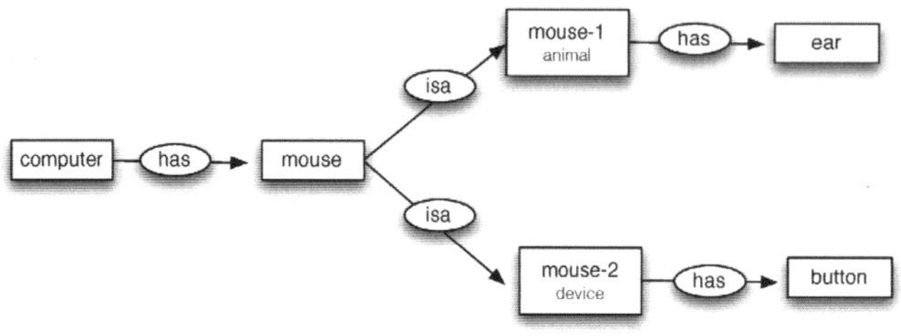


FIGURE 3- Sample of the semantic map for two senses

Likewise, the noun ‘table’ has various senses. WN[19] lists among others the following four:

- S1 (n) table, tabular array (a set of data arranged in rows and columns). Example: 'mathematical table'
- S2 (n) table (a piece of furniture having a smooth flat top that is usually supported by one or more vertical legs). Example : 'it was a sturdy table'
- S3 (n) table (a piece of furniture with tableware for a meal laid out on it). Example: '''I reserved a table at my favorite restaurant'
- S4 (n) table (a company of people assembled at a table for a meal or game). Example: 'he entertained the whole table with his witty remarks'

Of course, we have to identify (possibly automatically) which one of them applies in our case, as different senses, say 'array' rather than 'kitchen table', encode different semantic relations and arguments (['row' and 'column'] vs. ['leg', 'tabletop', 'meal' and 'tableware']).

In order to identify the senses, we start by listing all the parts of the concepts and cluster then the extracted parts on the basis of the cosine value between their vectors constructed from their n-gram. Polysemous words, that is concepts/words with several senses, will have several clusters. The links/associations holding between the concepts are marked on the basis of their senses. Hence, the link between two concepts encodes two types of information: the nature of the semantic relationship and the sense. In our current version we have only one type of relation i.e. meronym and the senses are not labelled semantically.

The senses are learned from the number of clusters built on the basis of the parts of the concepts. Example, 'table has parts: column, row, leg, tabletop and tableware'. The cosine value of each part is compared with all other parts to identify the clusters. To this end we used the k-means clustering technique[20]. In our 'table' example, 'column and row' and 'leg, tabletop and tableware' are grouped together given their respective vectors.

To identify senses we use like (Rapp, 2004; Diab & Resnik, 2002; Kaji, 2003; Pinto et al., 2007) a clustering method. However, our task is narrower in that the clusters are formed only from a small set of words associated with a given word at a time. Also we have considered meronymic word senses only i.e. senses that affect PT-WHRs.

The extracted wholes and their parts are organized into a network. Concepts are organized hierarchically i.e. going from the whole to its parts. For example 'tooth' is part of 'gear' which is part of an 'engine' which is part of a 'car'. In this case, 'car' is the root. Concepts which are parts of

---

[19] http://poets.notredame.ac.jp/cgi-bin/wn

[20] http://en.wikipedia.org/wiki/K-means_clustering

several concepts are connected via several links. For example, 'engine' being part both of 'car' and 'train' it has two incoming links (see figure 4)

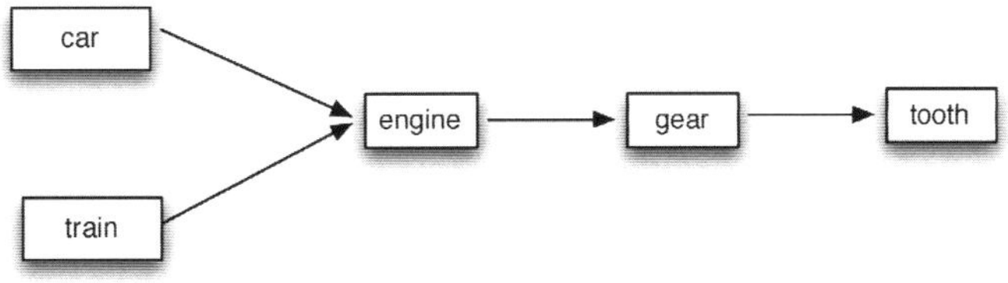


FIGURE 4-Sample of the semantic map showing multiple links

## 5.4 Evaluation

We have tested our system for its ability to extract PT-WHRs by using the text collection of SemEval (Girju et al. 2007). The test corpus is POS-tagged and annotated in terms of WN senses. The corpus has positive and negative semantic relations. The corpus has positive and negative semantic relations. The part–whole relations extracted by the system were validated by comparing them with the valid relations labeled in the test set answer key. The format of the test set is described in the sample here below:

> "Some sophisticated <e2>tables</e2> have three <e1>legs</e1>."
> WordNet(e1) = "n3", WordNet(e2)="n2"; Part-Whole(e1, e2) = "true"

This format has been defined by Girju et al (Girju et al. 2007). Since this does not correspond to a real text format, we have changed the corpus accordingly, to obtain the following text: "Some sophisticated tables have three legs". To evaluate the performance of our system we defined precision, recall, and F-measure metrics in the following way:

| | |
|---|---|
| Recall | $\frac{\text{Number of correctly retrieved relations}}{\text{Number of correct relations}}$ |
| Precision | $\frac{\text{Number of correctly retrieved relations}}{\text{Number of relations retrieved}}$ |
| F-measure | $\frac{2}{\frac{1}{precision} + \frac{1}{recall}}$ |

Our system identified almost all (19/20) of the *present Component-Integral object part-whole* relation pairs of the SemEval test set. Since these relations are both present and non-present in the Semeval training set and test set, we considered the present relations to evaluate the performance of our approach.

As the number of concepts having parts in different senses is very small in the SemEval test set, we have added some concepts from WN. The resulting number of relation pairs accounts now for 20% of our test set. 80 % of this set contains negative examples coming either from the SemEval test set (all of them) or from our own. We defined 'recall' as the percentage of correctly retrieved relations out of the correct relations available in the test set, while 'precision' is defined as the percentage of correctly retrieved relation out of retrieved relations. We obtained 95,2% for precision, 95% for recall and 95,1% for the F-measure. The PT-WHRs extracted by the system were validated by comparing them with the valid relations labeled in the test set answer key. The test set has answer key, so we manually counted correctly retrieved relations. Table 2 is a sample of correctly retrieved relations: Arm wrist, man head, hand finger, car engine. The following table shows the similarity values of some noun pairs taken from the program :

| The noun pairs | $S_1$ similarity values | $S_2$ similarity value | interpretation |
|---|---|---|---|
| 'car', 'engine' | 0.8788321167883211 | 0.4524886877828054 | part_of |
| 'search', 'engine' | 0.5040650406504065 | 0.3229166666666667 | other |
| 'chemistry', 'laboratory' | 0.6666666666666666 | 0.28426395939086296 | other |
| 'laboratory', 'hand' | 0.5238095238095238 | 0.06063947078280044 | other |
| 'hand', 'finger' | 0.8631840796019901 | 0.49118457300275482 | part_of |
| 'arm wrist' | 0.8911223341267891 | 0.59118958311003478 | part_of |
| 'man head' | 0.8234512378001223 | 0.43407700124560945 | part_of |

Table 2: the similarity values of selected noun pairs

All the encountered errors are hyponyms ('car' and 'vehicle'). However, this does not imply that all the hyponyms in the test are incorrectly retrieved as part-whole relation. Actually, only 12% of the hyponyms in the test set are incorrectly retrieved as part-whole relation. It should also be noted that the majority (80%) of our test set relations are not *part-whole relations.* Therefore, the probability of randomly selecting *part-whole relation* is 20/80 (0.25), showing the effectiveness of this approach for discriminating such relations.

We have also evaluated the performance of the system in determining the senses of a concept. To do so we used the clustering technique described above. Word forms expressing several senses have several clusters. We evaluated the results against the gold standard of meronymic word senses taken from WN (Miller, 1990).

Our clustering is based on the distance between the vectors of the parts of a given concept. We defined precision as the percentage of words assigned to their actual WN meronymic senses out of total words assigned to output clusters. Recall is the ratio of words assigned to their actual WN meronymic senses' correct relations available in the test set. We have achieved 89% for precision, 86% for recall and 87, 47 % for the F-measure.

## 6 Conclusion

We have started this paper by arguing that relational information is important for many tasks. We were concerned here mainly with lexical access, a very important task in language production (speaking, writing). Noting that current dictionaries do not support authors as well as needed, —a criticism that holds even for electronic dictionaries despite the recent progress,— we suggested to add to an existing electronic resource an index based on the notion of associations, i.e associated words to a prime (source word) and relations holding between the two associated words.

Since this index is based on the co-occurences of words in a corpus, —the latter representing ideally the user's world-knowledge, and since this knowledge changes frequently, it is desirable to allow for updating the index dynamically by taking into account the changes of the corpus. Hence, the idea to extract the links or associations automatically. As this is a very complex problem, we decided to study its feasibility only for a small subset, meronymic relations.

Despite certain shortcomings (this is work in progress), the results obtained are quite promising. This is all the more encouraging as we used very few resources compared to similar works. We believe that this approach can be generalized, allowing us to extract other types of semantic relations. But of course, much more work is needed to substantiate this latter claim.

## References


Aitchison, J. (2003). Words in the Mind: *an Introduction to the Mental Lexicon.* Oxford, Blackwell.

Beamer, B., Rozovskaya, A. and Girju, A. (2008). *Automatic Semantic Relation Extraction with Multiple Boundary Generation.* Association for the Advancement of Artificial Intelligence.

Bilac, S., Watanabe, W., Hashimoto, T., Tokunaga, T. and Tanaka, H. (2004). *Dictionary search based on the target word description.* In: Proc. of the Tenth Annual Meeting of The Association for Natural Language Processing (NLP2004), pages 556-559.

Brown A.S. (1991). *The tip of the tongue experience A review and evaluation.* Psychological Bulletin, 10, 204-223

Brown, R and Mc Neill, D. (1966). *The tip of the tongue phenomenon.* In: Journal of Verbal Learning and Verbal Behaviour, 5:325-337.

Deese, J. 1965. *The structure of associations in language and thought.* Johns Hopkins Press. Baltimore.

Dell, G. and Juliano, C. (1996). Computational models of phonological encoding. T. Dijkstra et K. De Smedt (Eds.), Computational Psycholinguistics. London: Taylor & Francis, 328-359

Diab, M. and Resnik, P. (2002). *An unsupervised method for word sense tagging using parallel corpora.* In Proc. of ACL.

Dutoit, D. and P. Nugues (2002): *A lexical network and an algorithm to find words from definitions.* In Frank van Harmelen (ed.): ECAI2002, Proceedings of the 15th European Conference on Artificial Intelligence, Lyon, pp.450-454, IOS Press, Amsterdam.

El-Kahlout I. D. and K. Oflazer. (2004). *Use of Wordnet for Retrieving Words from Their Meanings.* 2nd Global WordNet Conference, Brno Roget, P. (1852) *Thesaurus of English Words and Phrases*, Longman, London

Ferret, O. and Zock, M. (2006). *Enhancing Electronic Dictionaries with an Index Based on Associations.* 21st Intern. Conference on Computational Linguistics, Sidney

Finin, T. (1980). *The semantic interpretation of compound nominals.* Ph.D. Dissertation, University of Illinois at Urbana-Champaign.

Firth, J.R. (1957). *A synopsis of linguistic theory* 1930-1955. In Studies in Linguistic Analysis, pp. 1-32. Oxford: Philological Society.

Galton, F. (1880). *Psychometric experiments.* Brain, 2, 149-162.

Girju R., Moldovan D., Tatu, M. and Antohe, D. (2005). *Automatic Discovery of Part–Whole Relations.* ACM 32(1)

Girju, R., Hearst, M., Nakov, P., Nastase, V., Szpakowicz; S., Turney, P. and Yuret D. (2007). *Classification of semantic Relations between Nominals: Dataset for Task 4 in SemEval*, 4th International Workshop on Semantic Evaluations, Prague, Czech Republic.

Hage, W., Kolb, H. and Schreiber, G. (2006). *A Method for Learning Part-Whole Relations.* TNO Science & Industry Delft, Vrije Universiteit Amsterdam.

Harris, Z. (1954). *Distributional structure.* Word 10 (23), 46–162.

Harshman, R. (1970). *Foundations of the parafac procedure: Models and conditions for an "explanatory" multi-modal factor analysis.* UCLA Working Papers in Phonetics, 16.

Hearst M. A. (1998). *Automated Discovery of WordNet Relations.* In Fellbaum, C. (Ed.) WordNet: An Electronic Lexical Database and Some of its Applications, MIT Press. pp. 131-151

Kaji, H. (2003). *Word sense acquisition from bilingual comparable corpora.* In Proceedings of NAACL.

Lafourcade, M. (2007). *Making people play for Lexical Acquisition with the JeuxDeMots prototype.* In 7th International Symposium on Natural Language Processing, Pattaya, Chonburi, Thailand.

Landauer, T.K., & Dumais, S. (1997). *A Solution to Plato's Problem: The latent semantic analysis theory of acquisition, induction and representation of knowledge.* Psychological Review, 104, 211-240.

Levelt W., Roelofs A. et Meyer, A. (1999). *A theory of lexical access in speech production.* Behavioral and Brain Sciences, 22, 1-75

Lund, K. and Burgess, C. (1996). *Producing high-dimensional semantic spaces from lexical co-occurrence.* Behavior Research Methods, Instruments, and Computers, 28(2), 203–208.

Mark, D. (2011). *N-grams and word frequency data from the Corpus of Historical American English (COHA).*

Matthew, B. and Charniak, E. (1999). *Finding parts in very large corpora.* In Proceedings of the 37th Annual Meeting of the Association for Computational Linguistics, pp. 57–64, University of Maryland.

Miller, G. (ed.) (1990). *WordNet: An On-Line Lexical Data-base.* International Journal of Lexicography, 3(4), 235-312.

Nelson, D. L., McEvoy, C. L., & Schreiber, T. A. (1998). *The University of South Florida word association, rhyme, and word fragment norms.* http://www.usf.edu/FreeAssociation/

Pinto, D., Rosso, P. and Jimenez-Salazar, H. (2007). *Word sense induction using self-term expansion.* In Proceedings of the 4th International Workshop on Semantic Evaluations (SemEval-2007), 430–433.

Rapp, R. (2003). *Word sense discovery based on sense descriptor dissimilarity.* In: Proceedings of the Ninth Machine Translation Summit, New Orleans, pp. 315–322.

Rapp, R. (2004). *A practical solution to the problem of automatic word sense induction.* In proceedings of the ACL 2004 on Interactive poster and demonstration sessions.

Salton, G., Wong, A. and Yang, C.-S. (1975). *A vector space model for automatic indexing.* Communications of the ACM, 18(11), 613–620.

Schank, R. (ed.) (1975). *Conceptual Information Processing*, New York, American Elsevier.

Schvaneveldt, R. editor. (1989). *Pathfinder Associative Networks: studies in knowledge organization.* Norwood. N.J.

Sowa, J. (1992) *Semantic networks.* In 'Encyclopedia of Artificial Intelligence', edited by S. C. Shapiro, Wiley, New York

Vieu, L. and Aurnague, M. (2007). *Part-of relations, functionality and dependence.* In Aurnague, M., Hickmann, M. and Vieu, L. (eds.), The Categorization of Spatial Entities in Language and Cognition, pp. 307–336. J. Benjamins, Amsterdam

Wierzbicka, A. (1996). *Semantics: Primes and Universals.* Oxford University Press, Oxford.

Winston, M., Chaffin, R. and Hermann, D. (1987). *Taxonomy of part-whole relations.* Cognitive Science, 11(4), 417–444.

Wittgenstein, L. (1922). *Tractatus Logico-Philosophicus.* London: Routledge & Kegan Paul

Zock, M., Ferret, O. and D. Schwab, (2010). *Deliberate word access : an intuition, a roadmap and some preliminary empirical results.* In International Journal of Speech Technology, 13(4), pp. 107-117, 2010. Springer Verlag

Zock, M., Wandmacher, T. and Ovchinnikova, E. (2009). *Are vector-based approaches a feasible solution to the 'tip-of-the-tongue' problem*? Granger S. & Paquot, M. (Eds.) eLexicography in the 21st century: New challenges, new applications, Louvain-la-Neuve. pp. 355-366

# Modeling Word Meaning: Distributional Semantics and the Corpus Quality-Quantity Trade-Off

*Seshadri Sridharan*[1] *Brian Murphy*[2]
(1) Language Technologies Institute, Carnegie Mellon University, Pittsburgh, USA
(2) Machine Learning Department, Carnegie Mellon University, Pittsburgh, USA
seshadrs@cs.cmu.edu, brianmurphy@cmu.edu

ABSTRACT

Dictionaries constructed using distributional models of lexical semantics have a wide range of applications in NLP and in the modeling of linguistic cognition. However when constructing such a model, we are faced with range of corpora to choose from. Often there is a choice between small carefully constructed corpora of well-edited text, and very large heterogeneous collections harvested automatically from the web. There may also be differences in the distribution of genres and registers in such corpora. In this paper we examine these trade-offs by constructing a simple SVD-reduced word-collocate model, using four English corpora: the Google Web 5-gram collection, the Google Book 5-gram collection, the English Wikipedia, and collection of short social messages harvested from Twitter. Since these models need to encode semantics in a way that approximates the mental lexicon, we evaluate the felicity of the resulting semantic representations using a set of behavioral and neural-activity benchmarks that depend on word-similarity. We find that the quality of the input text has a very strong effect on the performance of the output model, and that a corpus of high quality at a small size can outperform a corpus of poor quality that is many orders of magnitude larger. We also explore the semantic closeness of the models using their mutual information overlap to interpret the similarity of corpus texts.

KEYWORDS : VECTOR SPACE MODELS, DISTRIBUTIONAL SEMANTICS, CORPUS SIZE, CORPUS GENRE, CORPUS QUALITY, NEUROSEMANTICS, WORD SIMILARITY

## 1 Introduction

Distributional semantic models (DSM) or distributional similarity models (Landauer, 1997) are unsupervised models based on the assertion that the meaning of a word can be inferred to some extent based on its distribution in the text. They are high dimensional vector space representations that encode the semantics of words learnt from a statistical analysis of the context they appear in. Word level dictionaries constructed using DSMs find use in many computational linguistics and cognitive science applications (Leacock, 1993; Bellegarda, 2000; Mitchell, 2008). To build these models in a given language, there is typically a choice among several source corpora. Often there is a choice between small well-curated text of good composition, and very large easy to collect text that is of inferior composition. In addition, there are choices along the dimensions of language style, genre and register. What kind of a corpus is most representative of a person's language experience? Is colloquial text more preferable than the formal variety? How does corpus size affect the model learnt? In this paper we attempt to identify the trade-off between source corpus size and quality, measured based on their performance in modeling the mental lexicon. Multiple behavioural and neurosemantic tests are used for this evaluation. As additional explorations, we study the effects of dimensionality on model performance, and the mutual similarity by word categories among models derived from various corpora.

There is ample literature analysing the effects of feature types, normalization, dimensionality, pruning, among other factors, on distributional semantics (Bullinaria and Levy 2007; Murphy, 2012). Quantitative and qualitative comparison of corpora based on the surface text has been performed as well (Kilgariff 2001, 2012). But, to our knowledge, there is not any systematic analysis of the effect of the corpus quality on distributional semantics. Authors have expressed that it is not adequate to explore the effects of size on model quality, it is important to analyse the effects of corpus quality as well (Bullinaria and Levy 2007; Lindsey, 2007). Although a wide range of corpora have been used to build DSMs, variation in modeling parameters, processing techniques and evaluation metrics used by the authors makes a direct comparison of corpus quality unfeasible.

In this paper, we build simple SVD-reduced word-collocate models using four English corpora that differ considerably in quality, size and composition. We employ simple word co-occurrence based models rather than the more complex ones (such as dependency or document models) because it is possible to build word-collocate models for most languages and corpora that are available. More importantly, the goal of the paper is to arrive at general reliable performance trends to address the quality-quantity trade off, and not to obtain the very best performance possible. Thus, we employ more generic, commonly used methods and evaluation metrics in our experiments. We find that the quality of the input text has a very strong effect on the performance of the output model, and that a corpus of high quality at a small size can outperform a corpus of poor quality that is many orders of magnitude larger. And, we also explore the reasons for the relative performance of different corpora, in terms of the mutual similarity of the semantic spaces described by their corresponding models.

## 1.1 Characterestics of a Textual Corpus

Textual corpora vary along many dimensions. Microblogs are colloquial, abbreviated, have varied grammar, misspellings, and emoticons. Duplication of messages propagated by the social network (virality) is a phenomenon specific to this domain. On the other hand, books and news text are extremely formal, diligently edited content with superior use of the language. They are practically devoid of any spelling errors, adhere to conventional grammar and discuss a broad range of topics. Encyclopaedic sources contain factual accounts of entities in the world that go through the highest scrutiny by authors. They are well edited, and the use of language within an article is constrained to the subject of discussion, with pockets of rare terms within articles rather than a more even distribution across documents. Webpage characteristics generally are a mixture of all of the above. Content on the Internet is also skewed in its representation of topic and genre – for example computing topics may be over-represented.

The most desirable corpus to learn a cognitively plausible semantic model would be the one that is representative of the language experience of a native speaker. But, every corpus in some way is an idiosyncratic sample of the language, with biases of grammar, style and vocabulary, which may affect the semantic model that can be derived from it. For our experiments we consider four widely used research corpora that represent the major characteristics described above. They are available in many languages and in considerable sizes. We use Twitter messages (or tweets), Google Web n-grams, Google Books n-grams and Wikipedia articles. Tweets are short snippets of microblog text exchanged within a social network. The content tends to be biased towards the most trending news events and personal conversations. Webpages are online documents that are intended to be information resources. They are composed of heterogeneous data sources ranging from product pages to blog posts to news articles etc. Books are works of literature that are carefully created by authors and typically edited by reviewers. The high quality text spans multitude of genres, topics and writing styles. The rest of the paper is structured as such: Section 2 describes the acquisition and pre-processing of corpora, process of building the semantic models and evaluating them. Section 3 details the experiments that vary the SVD dimensions and corpus sizes. Section 4 interprets those findings.

## 2 Methods

### 2.1 Collecting and Preprocessing Corpora

The Google Web corpus (Web) (Brants, 2006) contains *n*-grams of length up to 5 generated from publicly accessible Web pages. The Google Books dataset (Books) containing *n*-grams up to length 5 is extracted from a combination of dialects and genres, including American and British English, and both fiction and non-fiction. The Wikipedia corpus (Wiki) is a recent version, the July 2012 dump of the English encyclopaedia. Only running article text was extracted for use, with editing records, navigational text and other meta-data removed. The tweets corpus (Twitter) is a collection of 207 million public tweets collected from the twitter firehose over a 16-month period ranging from May 2009 to August 2010, a subset of the corpus collected by O'Connor et al., (2010). Among these, only tweets with five or more standard English words were retained, to discard non-standard utterances (e.g. telegraphic speech), and messages in other languages. The English word list used to filter the tweets contains the top 100K words in the American National Corpus (ANC) .To avoid biases that reposting of messages may cause, duplicate posts were also discarded. All web links in the tweets were replaced with the token "[LINK]", all usernames were replaced with "[PERSON]" and all hash-tags were stripped off the '#' character and treated as normal tokens. After tokenizing the running text based on whitespaces, the tokens in all corpora were converted to lower case and only tokens composed solely of letters and internal punctuation were considered. No stemming or spelling correction was performed in the interest of impartiality towards all corpora.

| | WIKIPEDIA | TWITTER | BOOKS | WEB |
|---|---|---|---|---|
| SIZE (ratios) | 1 X | ~1.2 X | ~100 X | ~200 X |
| LEXICAL DIVERSITY | 483 k | 736 k | 135 k | 206 k |
| CURATION | Very High, Peer Reviewed, Updated Frequently | None. High rate of typos and non standard language | Professionally edited. | Mix |
| REGISTER | Very Formal, Reporting Fashion | Very Informal, Colloquial | Formal, Narrative style | Mix |
| OBJECTIVITY | Completely Factual | More Opinions | More Fictional | More factual |

TABLE 1 – Corpus facts and characteristics

After pre-processing, we found the Web, Books, Twitter and Wikipedia corpora to have 353.4 billion, 199.4 billion, 2.1 billion and 1.7 billion tokens respectively (see Table 1 for the same sizes expressed as ratios). Since the Google Books and Web corpora are available only as *n*-grams with a maximum sequence length of five, all other corpora were also reduced to five grams. Hence, all textual statistics were gathered from a fixed text window of 4 lower-case tokens either side of the target word of interest, which is in the mid-range of optimal values found by various authors (Lund and Burgess, 1996; Rapp, 2003; Sahlgren, 2006). Since the corpora are substantially different from each other, it is not feasible to use a common word-list as the vocabulary that would be equally suitable for all. As a result, we compiled a vocabulary specific to each corpus, taking all frequency-sorted tokens to achieve 99% token-coverage of that corpus (Table 1 shows the vocabulary size as lexical diversity).

## 2.2 Models of Semantics

All the models described here were subjected to a common pre-processing pipeline. Raw lower-case word co-occurrences were extracted in the +- 4-word window. In the case of *n*-gram models that include a pre-applied frequency cut-off for rare tuples, a smoothing strategy was used to approximately reconstruct these missing counts. The 99% token-coverage vocabulary, and a subsequent 99% co-occurrence cut-off discarded low-frequency noisy counts before frequency normalization with PPMI (positive pointwise-mutual-information). The dimensionality of each word/collocate matrix was then reduced with singular value decomposition (SVD), taking the resulting left-singular vector as the vector-space representation for each word in the vocabulary.

$$\mathrm{PPMI}_{wf} = \begin{cases} \mathrm{PMI}_{wf} & \text{if } \mathrm{PMI}_{wf} > 0 \\ 0 & \text{otherwise} \end{cases} \quad (1)$$

$$\mathrm{PMI}_{wf} = log\left(\frac{p(w,f)}{p(w)p(f)}\right) \quad (2)$$

Positive Pointwise-mutual-information (1,2) is used as an association measure to normalize the observed word co-occurrence frequency $p(w,f)$ for the varying frequency of the target word $p(w)$ and its features $p(f)$. PPMI up-weights co-occurrences between rare words, yielding positive values for collocations that are more common than would be expected by chance, and discards negative values that represent patterns of co-occurrences that are rarer than one would expect by chance (i.e. if word distributions were independent). PPMI has been shown to perform well for a range of model types (Bullinaria and Levy, 2007; Turney and Pantel, 2010; Murphy, Talukdar and Mitchell, 2012). To filter out the noisy low frequency co-occurrences, we consider only those types that yield a 99% co-occurrence token coverage over all co-occurrence tokens. Filtering this Zipfian distribution also reduces the data to a manageable size.

The *n*-grams found in the Web and Books corpora were pre-filtered to different extents based on their counts. We observed that the lower the n-gram order, the lower the cut-off counts. So, to get a more accurate estimate of the co-occurrences in the original unfiltered corpus, we calculate the co-occurrence count using *n*-grams of all orders (two to five) rather than using only the five-grams. For a particular co-occurrence *ab* (where *a* and *b* are the co-occurring words), we calculate its scaled count $c_{ab}$ (3) using $NG_{ab}$, the set of all n-grams that contain words *a* and *b*. $o(x)$ is the order of the n-gram $x$ and $d(x,a,b)$ is the distance between words *a* and *b* in the n-gram. This scaled value is an approximation of the actual count a co-occurrence type would have when counted within five-grams from the original unfiltered corpus. This scaled count better approximates the original count than the pre-filtered counts in the corpus five-grams. Preliminary evaluations on these corpora and the tests described later suggest that using these scaled counts to calculate the PPMI scores yields a better performance.

$$c_{ab} = \Sigma_{x \in NG_{ab}} \frac{5 - d(x,a,b)}{o(x) - d(x,a,b)} \quad (3)$$

Once the PPMI scores are obtained for all co-occurrences, every word has an associated vector containing the PPMI scores of that word with every word in the vocabulary. A singular value decomposition (SVD) is applied on the PPMI matrix to identify the *k* dimensions within each model with the greatest explanatory power, which also has the effect of combining similar dimensions (such as synonyms and inflectional variants) into common components, and discarding more noisy dimensions in the data. This gives us a vector of length *k* for every word in the vocabulary. We use these vector space models of word semantics (the word level dictionaries) produced by the SVD to perform behavioral tests and brain tests where we explore performance of models by varying the number of dimensions and the corpus size, one at a time.

## 2.3 Evaluating the Semantic Models

### 2.3.1 Neurolinguistic Decoding

Since neurosemantic tests require models to test directly on the brain activity associated with language, we believe they are a good approach to test models of the lexicon. The dataset used here is that reported in Mitchell et al., (2008) and released publicly as part of the First Workshop on Computational Neurolinguistics (Murphy et al., 2010). The functional MRI (fMRI) data had been recorded from 9 participants while they performed a property generation task. The stimuli were line-drawings, accompanied by their text label, of 60 everyday concrete concepts such as *ant, apartment, car, lettuce, hand, glass*. Each participant's data contained a time-course for each of approximately 20 thousand voxels (three-dimensional pixels, or neural data points), and multiple presentations of the same concept had been averaged to yield a single brain image for each concept. Following the analytical paradigm of (Mitchell et al., 2008), we use a linear model to predict the brain activity for a particular concept (4). For each participant and selected voxel, we train a model where the level of activation of the latter in response to different concepts is approximated by a regularized linear combination of their semantic features where $f$ is the vector of activations of a specific fMRI feature for different concepts, the matrix $C$ contains the values of the semantic features for the same concepts, $\beta$ is the weight for each of those (corpus-derived) features, and $\lambda$ tunes the degree of regularization.

$$f = \mathbf{C}\beta + \lambda||\beta||^2 \quad (4)$$

The linear model is estimated with a least squared errors method and *L2* regularization, selecting $\lambda$ over the range 0.0001 to 5000 using Generalized Cross-Validation (see Hastie et al., 2011, p.244). The activation of each fMRI voxel in response to a concept unseen during training is then predicted by the weighted sum of the values on each semantic dimension, building a picture of expected neural activity response for an arbitrary concept. We use the leave-2-out paradigm as used by Mitchell et al. (2008), in which a linear model for each neural feature is trained in turn on all concepts minus 2, having selected the 500 most stable voxels in the training set. For each of the 2 left-out concepts, we try to match the predicted and observed activations, using the cosine distance between the model-generated estimate of fMRI activity and that observed in the experiment. The score reported is the classification accuracy over the 1770 comparisons (60 select 2) by 9 participants.

### 2.3.2 Behavioral Measures

Since behavioral tests of language semantics capture human judgments based on their language experience, we believe they are a reasonable way to benchmark the different word dictionaries we generate. We apply commonly used behavioral tests of semantic knowledge (see e.g. Bullinaria and Levy 2007, Baroni et al 2010) to measure the quality of the corpus-derived models. Figure 1 depicts the distribution of the test vocabularies across the four corpora. All these tests involve pairwise comparison between two vectors, either corresponding to a pair of words, or between a word vector and a cluster centroid. We use the commonly used cosine geometric measure (Landauer and Dumais, 1997; Levy and Bullinara 2007) to calculate the distance between two vectors in the model's vector space, independent of scaling. The distance measure is one minus the cosine of the angle between the two vectors *t* and *e* (5).

$$cosine\_similarity(t,e) = 1 - \frac{\sum_{i=1}^{n} \mathbf{t}_i \mathbf{e}_i}{\sqrt{\sum_{i=1}^{n} (\mathbf{t}_i)^2}\sqrt{\sum_{i=1}^{n} (\mathbf{e}_i)^2}} \quad (5)$$

The TOEFL test, initially introduced by Landauer and Dumais (1997) consists of eighty multiple choice questions from the synonym portion of the TOEFL test. The test vocabulary consists of 203 adjectives, 96 abstract nouns and 82 verbs. The questions consist of a target word and four other word choices, including a synonym, and three distracters. (e.g. 'Which of the following is closest in meaning to *prominent*: *battered, ancient, mysterious* or *conspicuous*?'). To evaluate a semantic model, we choose the word with the smallest cosine distance as the answer. The score reported is the answer-accuracy over all 80 questions.

The Rubenstein Goodenough (Rubenstein et al., 1965) and the WordSim (Finkelstein et al., 2002) datasets are comprised of word-pairs with corresponding a semantic-similarity score. R&G has 65 concrete noun pairs and WordSim has a mix of 203 nouns (concrete and abstract) and adjectives. The similarity scores for the word pairs (e.g. gem - jewel, 3.940) are values averaged over similarity judgments provided by multiple human judges. Modeled similarity scores for each word pair are generated using the cosine distance between the vectors in the semantic space. The test scores reported are Spearman correlation coefficients $\rho$ between the similarity estimates $x$ generated by the model and the gold standard similarity measures $y$ (7).

$$\rho = \frac{\sum_i (x_i - \bar{x})(y_i - \bar{y})}{\sqrt{\sum_i (x_i - \bar{x})^2 \sum_i (y_i - \bar{y})^2}}. \quad (6)$$

The Battig (Battig and Montague, 1969) and AAMP (Almuhareb and Poesio, 2004) tests have pairs of a word and its immediate superordinate category (e.g. aeroplane – vehicle, anger – feeling). The Battig dataset is composed of 82 concrete words and AAMP has a mix of 402 concrete and abstract words. The CLUTO clustering toolkit (Karypis 2003) is used to cluster the word vectors using cosine distance and the toolkit's default parameters to obtain as many clusters as there are word-categories in the test. The score reported is the overall cluster purity *P*, the sum of the purities of individual clusters ($P_r$) calculated (8). The purity of a cluster is the fraction of its members that belong to the most representative (i.e. plurality) category *c*.

$$P = \sum_{r=1}^{k} \frac{n_r}{n} P_r \quad (7) \qquad P_r = \frac{1}{n_r} \max_c \left( n_r^c \right) \quad (8)$$

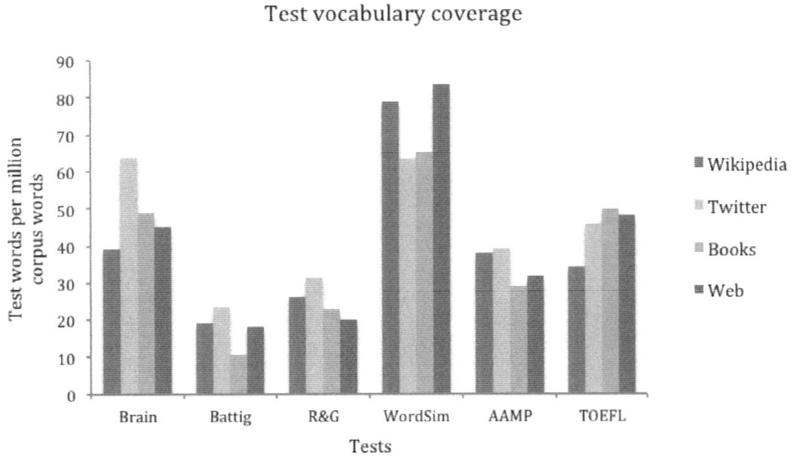


FIGURE 1 – Coverage per test-word as average word count per million corpus tokens (wpm)

## 3 Results

Our goal is to compare the performance of the models learnt from the four corpora in an impartial manner. Hence, we learn models on the corpora subsampled at the same size, at a particular dimensionality that is suitable to all corpora. To determine the appropriate number of SVD dimensions for the corpora, we compile test scores for the corpus models at the original sizes, varying the number of SVD dimensions (Section 3.1). This helps us study the impact of extra dimensions on the corpus model performance, and the top performance obtainable when the dimensionality is adapted to the corpus (Section 3.2). By looking at the trend of these performance curves, we determine the widely stable and well performing dimensionality. Once the optimal dimensionality is found, we compile test scores for the models with the optimal dimension count, varying the size of the corpus subsets (Section 3.3). This helps us quantify the corpus quantity-quality trade off in terms of the test performances.

### 3.1 Effect of Dimensionality

To explore the number of dimensions that is optimal for the different corpora and tasks, we run the behavioural and brain tests at different dimensionalities. We vary the number of SVD dimensions for the behavioural tests in steps of 25 over the range 25 to 1250 and we considered the SVD dimensions 75, 125, 250, 375, 500, 750 and 1000 for the neurosemantic decoding test (this less exhaustive search is due to the increased computational complexity of this task). Figure 2 shows the performance plots for the corpora across all six tests.

From Figure 2, we notice a general trend that all behavioural tests tend to improve as the number of dimensions increases. But, most of these tests flatten out after a particular point. In some case, at higher dimensions, we notice that the curve dips, presumably as noisy or irrelevant SVD dimensions are encountered. We find that the TOEFL test follows a very strong linear trend for most corpora. Extra dimensions seem to aid performance in this test. Books seems to have a substantial advantage in this test.

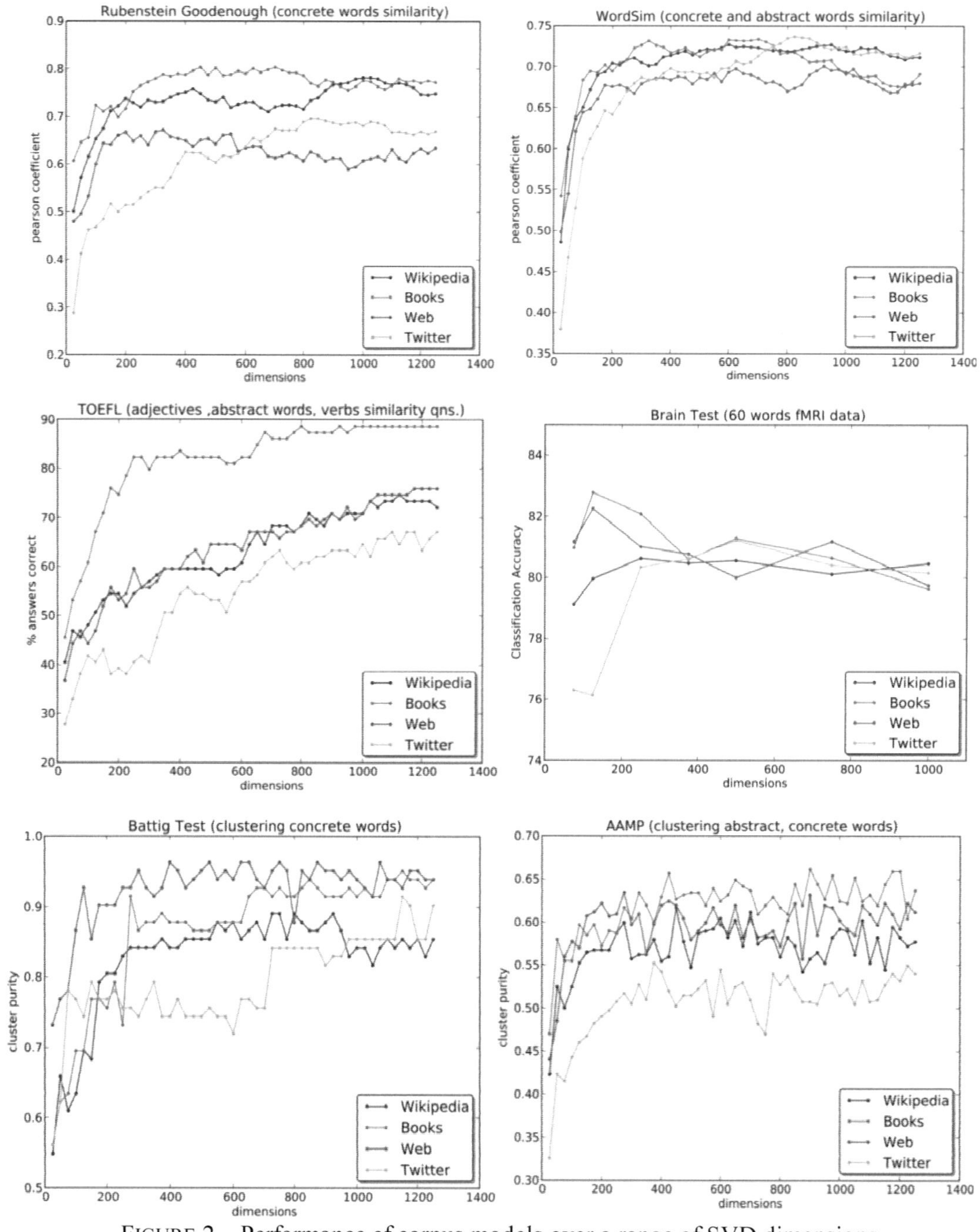


FIGURE 2 – Performance of corpus models over a range of SVD dimensions

The stability of the Twitter curves is lower than the others irrespective of the test. From the behavioural tests involving concrete nouns (Battig, R&G and WordSim), we notice that Twitter requires more SVD dimensions to attain peak performance, or reach a more stable score. The tests based on clustering (Battig and AAMP) appear to have unstable curves relative to the similarity and classification based tests. This has more to do with the nature of the tests than the corpus behaviour. The word clusters tend to vary greatly with dimensionality.

The Brain test is discriminating only at lower dimensions. Contrasting to the behavioural tests, extra dimensions do not affect the performance of the models noticeably. At lower dimensions, we find Books to perform best, and Twitter the worst. Model performances above 375 dimensions are all comparable. It is interesting that the Brain test peaks at such low dimensionality while tests like TOEFL and AAMP need a lot more dimensions. This could be because the top few SVD dimensions are more likely to be the important ones that encode the more common attributes (such as 'living' or 'non-living'), which can help distinguish concrete nouns. On the other hand, a lot more dimensions are required to distinguish the more subtle differences between the TOEFL choices.

## 3.2 Peak Performances for Whole Corpora

As we saw in Figure 2, model performance is somewhat unstable, and varies in value and trend for different tests. To estimate the peak performance that is possible with each model, we aggregate over the top few points in the plots, reporting the average of the top 3 values rather than the very best value (Table 2). These results represent peak performances when dimensionality is tailored to each model/test pair. The best score among the corpora is highlighted in bold.

| | Wikipedia | Twitter | Books | Web |
|---|---|---|---|---|
| Brain | 0.81 | 0.81 | **0.82** | 0.82 |
| Battig | 0.89 | 0.94 | 0.94 | **0.96** |
| R&G | 0.78 | 0.69 | **0.80** | 0.66 |
| WordSim | 0.72 | **0.73** | **0.73** | 0.69 |
| AAMP | 0.61 | 0.54 | **0.66** | 0.63 |
| TOEFL | 0.74 | 0.67 | **0.89** | 0.76 |

TABLE 2 – Average of the top three scores over a range of dimensions

Overall, we find the performance of Books to be superior to the other corpora. It scores higher than the others in everything but the Battig test on which it is very close to the higher value achieved by the Web corpus. The Books model also has a substantial lead in the TOEFL and AAMP tests. This may be due to an advantage in capturing the meaning of adjectives, abstract nouns and verbs better. We explore the reasons for this performance gap later (Section 4). On the other hand, the Twitter model seems to perform very poorly over these two tests. Although the performances in the Brain test are very much similar, they exhibit the general performance trend observed in the other tests. As noted by Levy and Bullinara (2012) and Murphy et al (2012), the Brain test appears to have a performance ceiling, possibly due to noisiness in data. On close inspection of the Table, a trend emerges that Books is the best corpus model, followed by Web and Wikipedia, followed closely by Twitter.

### 3.3 Effect of Corpus Size

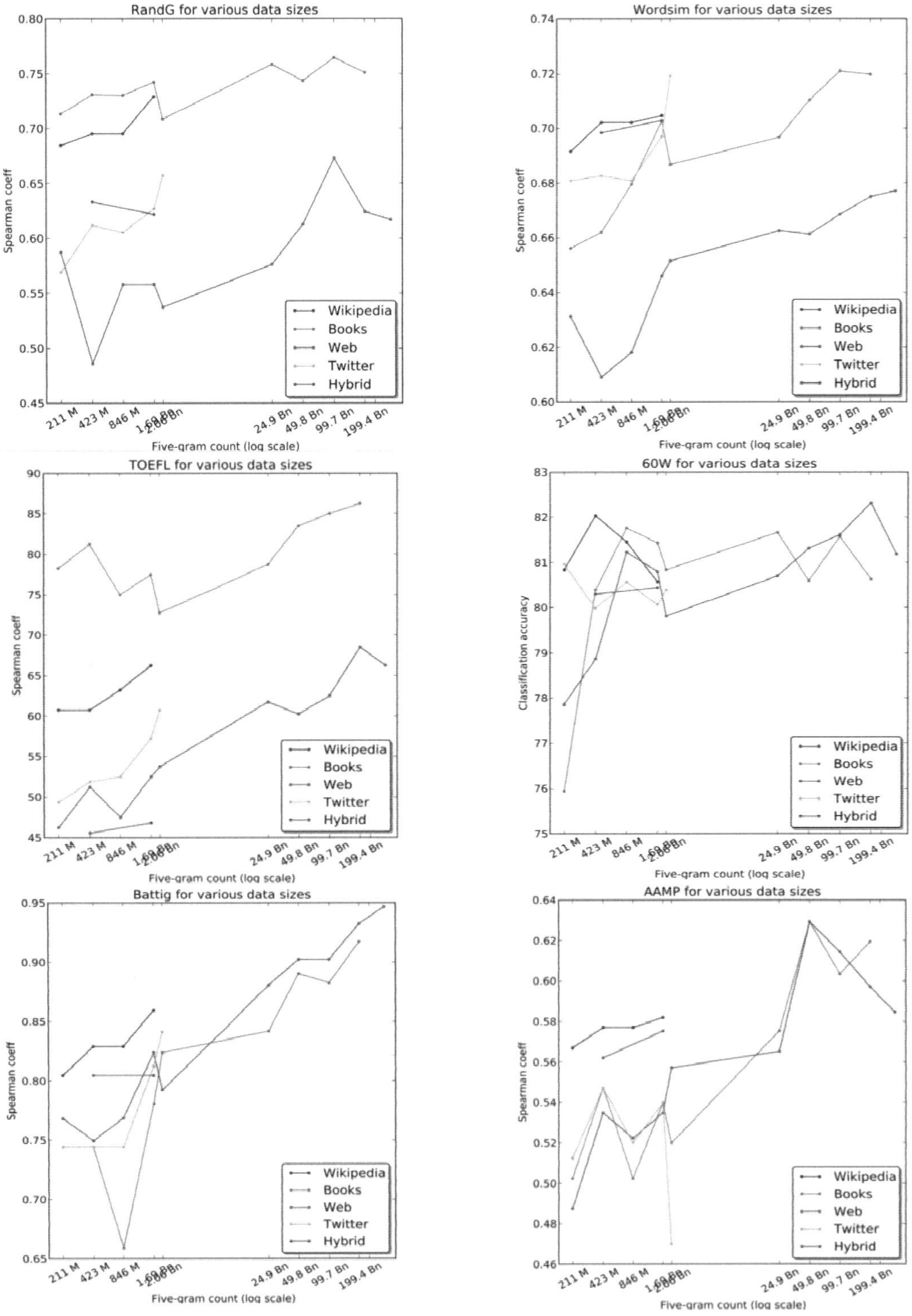


FIGURE 3 – Performance of corpus models over a range of data sizes

The corpus models analysed in the previous sections are on corpora of different sizes. Although it helps us establish trends in peak performance, this is not a fair comparison of the corpus types, given that there is enormous disparity in their original sizes (Table 1). To be able to compare the quality of the semantic models across corpora, we need to build them from corpora of similar sizes, at a dimensionality that is favourable to all these corpus types. From Figure 2 we notice that the performance for all corpora are stable and close to their peak values at 750 SVD dimensions. Although 750 dimensions may not be the most optimal dimensionality for these corpus models at different corpus sizes, we keep the dimensionality constant at 750, and vary the data sizes the models are learnt from. We under-sample (by random selection) the four different corpora to the 5-gram sizes of 12.5% Wiki, 25% Wiki, 50% Wiki, 100% Wiki, 100% Twitter, 12.5% Books, 50% Books and 100% Books. Also, at the sizes 50% Wiki and 100% Wiki we generate Hybrid corpora that have equal proportions of the randomly sampled five-grams from Wikipedia, Books, Web and Twitter. Figure 3 contains the performance plots of the corpus types across the above-mentioned data sizes, at 750 SVD dimensions. These new models are built similar to the old ones, as described in Section 2.2.

In many cases, we find an approximately log-linear trend in the performance with the corpus size for the behavioral test. We find models at smaller data sizes to be less stable, with more deviations from log-linearity. Although averaging scores over multiple randomly drawn samples may give a better approximation, it is extremely expensive and does not guarantee any bounds on the approximation. Regardless, all the original corpora considered are random samples of text of that nature to begin with. For this reason, we believe this approach is satisfactory to draw broad conclusions on the effects of corpus size, even if there exist local deviations from linearity.

In the behavioral tests, we notice that at smaller sizes, the Books and Web models generally have a considerable drop in performance. Wiki outperforms the others or achieves competitive scores at data sizes within 1.7 billion tokens. We notice that Books still retains its advantage in the TOEFL test at all data sizes. A similar advantage is observed to some extent for the Web corpus in the Battig test. The performance curves for Wiki are the most stable across all behavioral tests. The Brain test, unlike the behavioral tests does not seem to be affected by the sizes above 423 million five-grams. The curves stay flat across larger data sizes, with little increase in accuracies. Performance of the Hybrid set varies relative to the component corpora from which it is assembled. In some cases it is close to peak performance, but in others it underperforms considerably. This suggests that there is not beneficial complementarity among the corpora.

# 4 Discussion

## 4.1 What is the quality-size trade off?

Although we can see in detail how the corpus models perform in the six tests at different data sizes, we are primarily interested in how the corpora compare against each other. To understand the general quality of the corpus types, which is some function of the performances in the six tests, we compare them by their performances at a particular data size. We assign a rank to every result in the plot for a particular test, based on the score. Once this is done for all the tests, we compile the average rank for a corpus across all tests scores for a particular corpus size, which serves as a summarization of the 6 plots in Figure 3. Figure 4 shows the ranked model plots we obtain over different corpus sizes.

Corpus quality does have a considerable impact on the model performance. Although we see that the more the data, the better the performance, we clearly see that a corpus of high quality at a small size can perform better than a corpus of poor quality that is many orders of magnitude larger. At all corpus sizes up to 1.7 billion five-grams, Wikipedia is the best choice. The next best option in this size range is Books. Performance of Twitter and Web is comparable, although at very small sizes, Twitter performs better. The Hybrid corpus does not give us any advantage over the models that can be built from the constituent corpora. Above 2 billion five-grams, Books is the best choice, followed by Web.

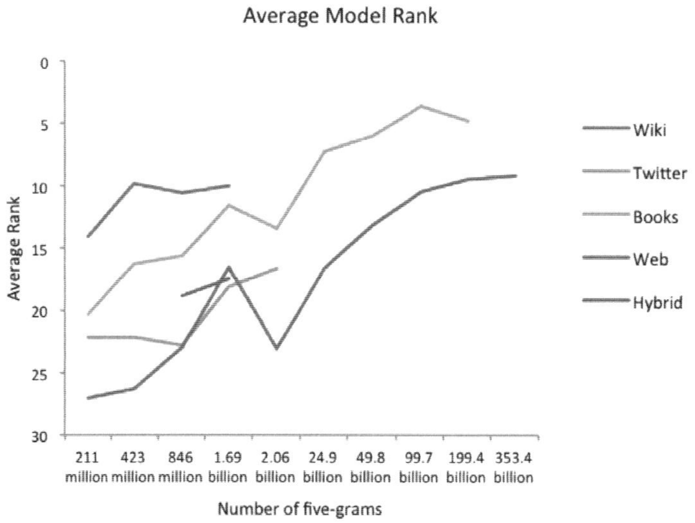


FIGURE 4 – Average rank over corpus size (in five-grams)

## 4.2 What is the quality-dimensionality trade off?

Working with a large number of dimensions can be expensive in certain applications. To determine the optimal number of dimensions for the corpora, we plot average corpus ranks across SVD dimensionalities (Figure 5) for the models built from the original corpus sizes. The response to dimensionality is not considerably different among these corpora. All of them perform better with extra dimensions up till a point after which they either fall in performance or flatten out. Although, Twitter in particular needs more dimensions than the other corpora to reach a similar rank. Also, Wikipedia tends to benefit more from extra dimensions than Web does.

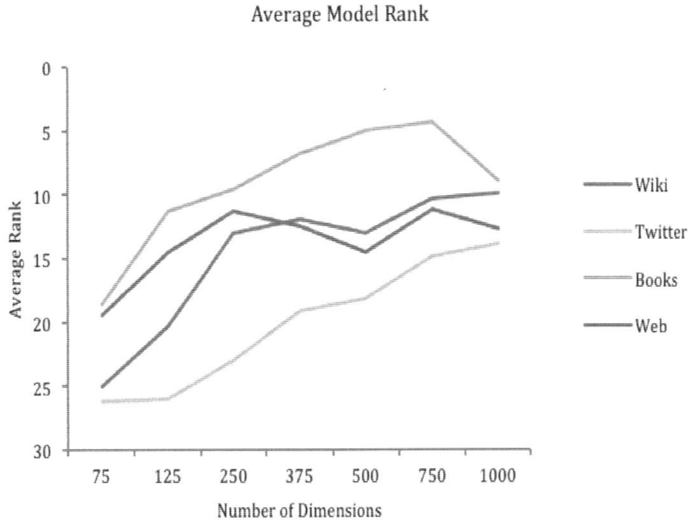


FIGURE 5 – Average rank across SVD dimensions

## 4.3 How different are the corpus models ?

To try to explain why we see these differences, we can explore whether the information encoded in the semantic models are in fact substantially different. Here we perform a follow-on analysis that measures the informational overlap between the corpus-derived models. We use the method introduced by Murphy et al (2012) to measure how much a model can explain the information contained by another model with the same vocabulary. We use the semantic models of 750 dimensions learnt from the full sized corpora. Besides analyzing the overlap for the common vocabulary among the corpus models, we also perform analyses for selected concrete nouns, abstract nouns, adjectives and verbs. From the MRC Psycholinguistic Norms (Coltheart.M, 1981), we first select nouns with the top 1000 concreteness score for the concrete-nouns list and those with the least 1000 concreteness scores for the abstract nouns list. From the American National Corpus (ANC) (Macleod et al. 2002) we include the top 1000 words that are adjectives 80% or more of the times into the adjectives list. We include the top 600 ANC words that are verbs 40% or more of the times into the verbs list. After calculating the information overlap values, we create a cosine similarity based isomap of the corpus-types for the five word groups by reducing the 4 dimensions of information overlap (with every corpus-type) down to 2 dimensions (Figure 6). In these corpus maps, the lesser the distance between two corpora, the more the common-information that is present, the more their semantic similarity.

As a general pattern, we notice that Twitter is the most semantically dissimilar among all corpora. This might be explained by its minimal lexical overlap and distinct language use. In the common-words and abstract-nouns plots, Web is equidistant from the other corpora. This is interesting since we assume the general-coverage Web to have a mix of the characteristics of the others. We find that the semantic information contained by the corpora for verb vectors has very high similarity. i.e. all corpora model verbs in a similar way. There is far lesser information overlap for adjectives, with Books and Twitter containing very different information compared to Wiki and Web. Books encodes very dissimilar information for abstract nouns as well. This could explain its differentiating performance in the TOEFL test.

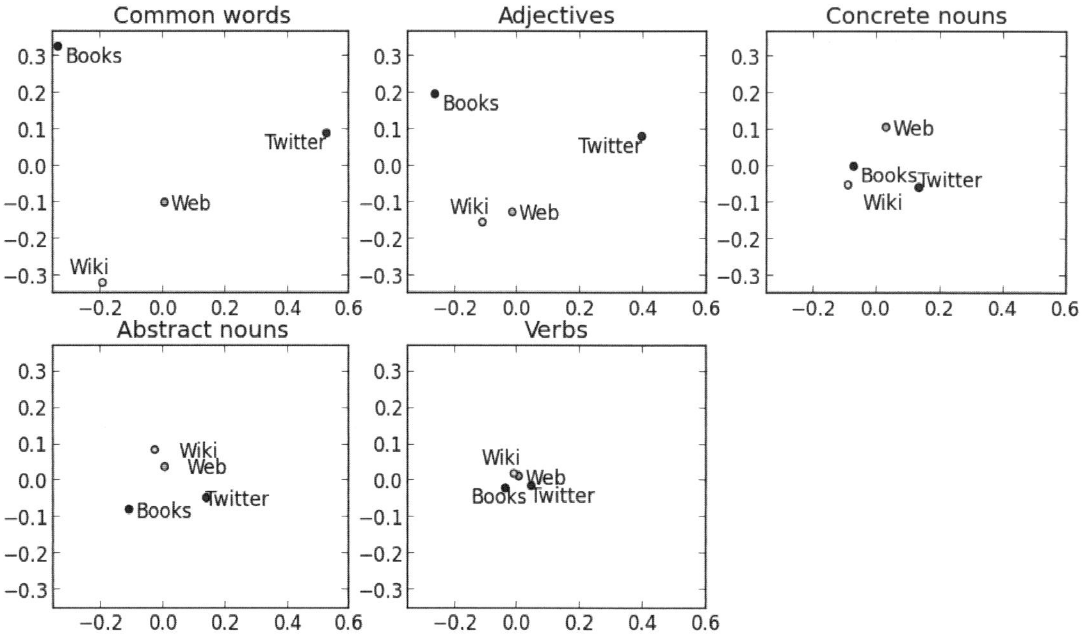


FIGURE 6 – Isomapped Corpora for different word-groups

## 4.4 Conclusions and future work

Given the wide array of corpus choices to build dictionaries based on distributional semantics, and their ubiquity, it is important to understand the contribution of corpus size and quality. From our experiments, it is evident that corpus choice does matter. Massive quantity is required to match the quality advantage. It is clear that Wikipedia is the corpus of choice for the data size in which it is available. The next most competitive corpus, Google-Books, must be an order of magnitude larger than Wikipedia before it can provide superior performance; and Google-Web must be two order of magnitude larger to match Wikipedia.

We speculate that the impressive performance of Wikipedia can be attributed to the balance in topics and cleanliness. While Books, a corpus roughly half the size of Web, is not as carefully balanced by topics, it presumably draws its advantage from its cleanliness and superior use of the language. On the other hand, the Twitter and Web do not exhibit any of these characteristics. Although the tweets have been heavily pre-filtered for our experiments, they probably still suffer from the colloquial nature of text, imbalance in topics and high rate of lexical errors. Web text also suffers from formatting errors, informal language use and imbalance in topics. These characteristics may have hampered their performance.

The advantage of quality over quantity for modeling word meaning, and the distinguishing performance of Wikipedia is a very interesting since the open-source encyclopedia is available in many languages at considerable sizes. As a next phase of this research, we plan to perform this analysis on similar corpora of other languages to study the generalizability of these results. We also plan to study the impact of different model types (directional, part of speech, dependency etc.) on corpus-derived model performance.

## References


Almuhareb, A., Poesio, M., (2004), Attribute-based and value-based clustering: an evaluation. In *Proceedings of the Conference on Empirical Methods in Natural Language Processing*, Barcelona, Spain.

Battig, W.F., Montague, W.E. (1969). Category norms for verbal items in 56 categories: A replication and extension of the Connecticut category norms. In *Journal of Experimental Psychology* Monograph, 80:1-45.

Bellegarda, J.R. (2000). Large vocabulary speech recognition with multispan statistical language models. In *Proceedings of the IEEE Transactions on Speech and Audio Processing*, Jan 2000

Brants, T., Franz, A.(2006). Web 1T 5-gram Version 1. In *Linguistic Data Consortium*, Philadelphia, PA, USA.

Bullinaria, J.A. and Levy, J.P. (2007). Extracting semantic representations from word co-occurrence statistics: A computational study. In *Journal of Behavior Research Methods*, 2007.

Coltheart, M. (1981b). The MRC Psycholinguistic Database. In *Quarterly Journal of Experimental Psychology*, 33A, 497-505.

Finkelstein, L., Gabrilovich, E., Matias, Y., Rivlin, E., Solan, Z., Wolfman, G., and Ruppin, E. (2002). Placing Search in Context: The Concept Revisited, In *Proceedings of the ACM Transactions on Information Systems*, 20(1):116-131.

Hastie, T., Tibshirani, R., and Friedman, J. (2011). The Elements of Statistical Learning. In *Volume 18 of Springer Series in Statistics. Springer*, 5th edition.

Karypis, G. (2002). CLUTO: a software package for clustering high Dimensional data sets. *University of Minnesota, Dept. of Computer Science*.

Kilgariff, A. (2001). Comparing Corpora. *International Journal of Corpus Linguistics*, 97-233.

Kilgariff, A. (2012). Getting To Know Your Corpus. *Lecture Notes In Computer Science*, Sojka, P., Horak, A., Kopecek, I., Pala, K. (eds). Springer.

Landauer, Thomas, K. and Dumais, Susan T. (1997) A solution to Plato's problem: The latent semantic analysis theory of acquisition, induction and representation of knowledge. *Psychological Review*, 104(2):211-240.

Leacock C., Towell, G., Voorhees, E. (1993) Corpus-based statistical sense resolution, In *Proceedings of the Workshop on Human Language Technology*, Pages 260—265.

Levy, J.P., & Bullinaria, J.A. (2012). Using enriched semantic representations in predictions of human brain activity. In *Proceedings of Connectionist Models of Neurocognition and Emergent Behavior: From Theory to Applications, 292-308. Singapore: World Scientific, 2012.*

Lin, D., Pantel, P. (2001). DIRT – discovery of inference rules from text. *Proceedings of the seventh ACM SIGKDD-International Conference on Knowledge Discovery and Data Mining*, San Francisco, California, USA.

Robert L., Vladislav, D.V., Alex, G., Wayne D. G. (2007) Be Wary of What Your Computer Reads: The Effects of Corpus Selection on Measuring Semantic Relatedness. In *Proceedigns of the Eighth International Conference on Cognitive Modeling* 279–284.

Rubenstein, H., Goodenough, J. (1965). Contextual correlates of synonymy. In *Journal Commun. ACM* 8(10): 627-633.

Lund, K. and Burgess, C. (1996). Producing high-dimensional semantic spaces from lexical co-occurrence. In *Journal Behavior Research Methods, Instruments, and Computers*, 28:203–208.

Macleod, C., Grishman, R. (2002). The American National Corpus: Standardized Resources for American English. *In Proceedings of 2nd Language Resources and Evaluation Conference (LREC)*, Athens, Greece.

Mitchell, T. M., Shinkareva, S. V., Carlson, A., Chang, K.-M., Malave, V. L., Mason, R. A., and Just, M. A. (2008). Predicting Human Brain Activity Associated with the Meanings of Nouns. *Science*, 320:1191–1195.

Murphy, B., Korhonen, A., Chang, K. K.-M., editors (2010). In *Proceedings of the Workshop on Computational Neurolinguistics, NAACL-HLT,* Los Angeles, CA, USA.

Murphy, B., Talukdar, P., and Mitchell, T. (2012). Selecting corpus-semantic models for neurolinguistic decoding. In *Proceedings of the First Joint Conference on Lexical and Computational Semantics* (*SEM), Montreal, QC, Canada.

O'Connor, B., Balasubramanyan, R., Routledge, B. R. and Smith, N. A. (2010). From Tweets to Polls: Linking Text Sentiment to Public Opinion Time Series. *In Proceedings of the International AAAI Conference on Weblogs and Social Media (ICWSM)*, Washington, DC, USA.

Rapp, R. (2003). Word Sense Discovery Based on Sense Descriptor Dissimilarity. *In Proceedings of the Ninth Machine Translation Summit*, New Orleans, USA.

Sahlgren, M. (2006). The Word-Space Model: Using distributional analysis to represent syntagmatic and paradigmatic relations between words in high-dimensional vector spaces. *PhD dissertation, Department of Linguistics, Stockholm University.*

# Verb Interpretation for Basic Action Types: Annotation, Ontology Induction and Creation of Prototypical Scenes

*Francesca Frontini, Irene De Felice, Fahad Khan, Irene Russo, Monica Monachini*[1] *Gloria Gagliardi, Alessandro Panunzi*[2]
(1) ILC CNR Pisa, {francesca.frontini, irene.defelice, fahad.khan, irene.russo, monica.monachini} @ilc.cnr.it
(2) University of Florence, gloria.gagliardi@unifi.it

ABSTRACT

In the last 20 years dictionaries and lexicographic resources such as WordNet have started to be enriched with multimodal content. Short videos depicting basic actions support the user's need (especially in second language acquisition) to fully understand the range of applicability of verbs. The IMAGACT project has among its results a repository of action verbs ontologically organised around prototypical action scenes in the form of both video recordings and 3D animations. The creation of the IMAGACT ontology, which consists in deriving action types from corpus instances of action verbs, intra and cross linguistically validating them and producing the prototypical scenes thereof, is the preliminary step for the creation of a resouce that users can browse by verb, learning how to match different action prototypes with the correct verbs in the target language. The mapping of IMAGACT types onto WordNet synsets allows for a mutual enrichment of both resources.

# Interpretazione dei verbi per tipi azionali di base: annotazione, induzione di ontologia e creazione di scene prototipiche

Negli ultimi venti anni dizionari e risorse lessicografiche come WordNet sono stati arricchiti con contenuto multimediale. Brevi video in grado di rappresentare azioni di base supportano i bisogni degli utenti (in particolar modo per quanto riguarda l' acquisizione della seconda lingua) nel comprendere l' ambito di applicabilità dei verbi. Il progetto IMAGACT ha tra i suoi risultati una base di dati di verbi d'azione ontologicamente organizzati e raffiguranti scene che riproducono azioni prototipiche sottoforma di registrazioni video e animazioni 3D. La creazione dell' ontologia IMAGACT che consiste nella derivazione di tipi azionali da istanze di verbi d'azione estratte da un corpus, nella loro validazione intra e crosslinguisticamente e nella conseguente produzione di scene prototipiche, è il passaggio preliminare per la creazione di una risorsa che gli utenti possono consultare partendo dal verbo, imparando come alllineare differenti prototipi d'azione con il verbo corretto nella lingua da apprendere. Il *mapping* dei tipi di IMAGACT sui *synsets* di WordNet consente un arricchimento reciproco di entrambe le risorse.

---

KEYWORDS : ontology of actions, lexical resource, 3D animations
KEYWORDS IN ITALIAN : ontologia di azioni, risorse lessicali, animazioni 3D

---

# 1 Introduction

In the last 20 years dictionaries and lexicographic resources such as WordNet have started to be enriched with multimodal content (e.g. pictorial illustrations, animations, videos, audio files). Pictures are effective in conveying the meaning of denotative words such as concrete nouns, while for abstract relations (instantiated by prepositional meanings) schematic illustrations can depict several semantic properties. Conveying the meaning of verbs with static representations is not possible; for such cases the use of animations and videos has been proposed (see Stein 1991 cited in Lew 2010). Short videos depicting basic actions support the user's need (especially in second language acquisition) to fully understand the range of applicability of verbs i.e. to start with a mental image of an action and from this image find out the L2 verb(s) that can be used to predicate that action. This process involves semantic and pragmatic comparisons that occur in the mind of the learner, with considerations respecting the type of movement involved, the instrument/tool that can be used, the duration, the strength of the movement etc.

In this paper we introduce the IMAGACT project and its results: a repository of action verbs ontologically organised around prototypical action scenes in the form of both video recordings and 3D animations. The focus of IMAGACT is on action verbs, because in all language modalities they bear basic information that should be processed in order to make sense of a sentence. Especially in speech, they are the most frequent structuring elements (Moneglia and Panunzi, 2007), but unfortunately no one-to-one correspondence can be established between an action verb, conceived as a lexical entry, and an action type, conceived as an ontological entity.

In order to bridge this gap 500 English and Italian action verbs have been analysed in their different contexts of use in corpora and grouped into action types according to their internal variation. Types representing the same prototypical actions are then gathered together under the same scene and represented in 3D animations, generated ad hoc which thus illustrate the different uses of action verbs across languages (see Figure 1).

For instance, the English verb *to roll* can refer to qualitatively different actions. In some uses the agent changes the form of the object (B and 1), in some other uses the agent moves himself in space (C and 2), and in other cases, the agent moves the object in space, applying a force to it (D and 3):

(1) John rolls the poster into a tube.
(2) John rolls onto his side.
(3) John rolls the barrel.

In short, different action types occur in the above examples. This judgment is confirmed by the productivity of each action type. Despite the fact that the predicate is applied to different objects, humans are able to judge whether the same action is performed or not by reading a set of sentences:

(1a) John rolls the poster / his sleeve/ the pants up.
(2a) John /Mary / the horse rolls.
(3a) John rolls the barrel / the cylinder.

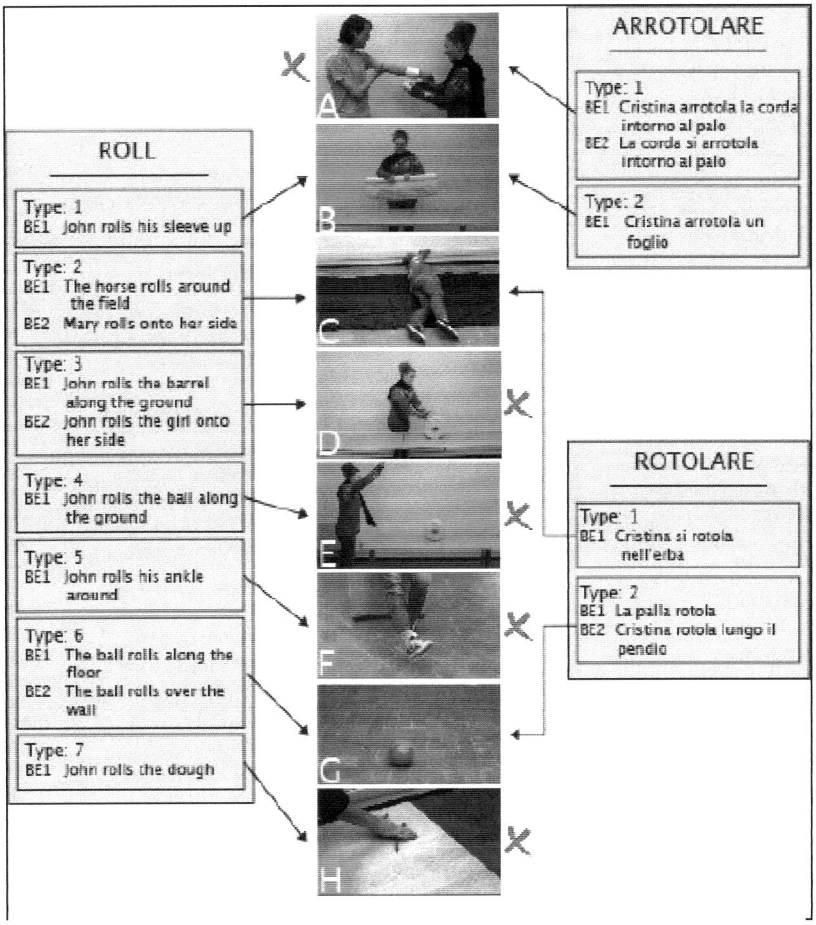


FIGURE 1 - Cross-linguistic gallery of scenes representing the variation of *to roll, arrotolare* and *rotolare*

In other words, *to roll* has several interpretations corresponding to the different action types, and none of these types can be considered more appropriate than the others in characterizing the meaning of the verb. Each one could be a prototypic instance of the verb (Givon, 1986).

We call general verbs all natural language action verbs that share this property. In the case of general verbs, ordinary language does not mirror the ontology of action and the lemma does not specify the referred ontological entity. As shown by Figure 1, the different types of a general verb may map onto different verbs in other languages. This causes huge problems for second language acquisition since each language categorises the space of action in its own way. Figure 1 is an example of the relation of English and Italian verbal entries with respect to the same *continuum*.

The targets of the IMAGACT resource are L2 learners of the supported languages (focus on Italian) who can browse the resource by verb, learning how to match different action prototypes with the correct verbs in the target language.

In the following paragraphs we shall describe the procedure for the creation of the IMAGACT ontology, which consists in deriving action types from corpus instances of action verbs, intra and cross linguistically validating them and producing the prototypical scenes thereof. Criteria applied for the creation of prototypical scenes will also be investigated. Finally, the possibility of mapping of IMAGACT types onto WordNet synsets, thus allowing for a mutual enrichment of both resources. We will end with conclusions and ideas for future work.

## 2 Related Works

The importance of providing visual support for lexical and ontological resources is becoming more and more evident. Ontologies like SUMO[1] provide links to pictures from external sources (often Wikimedia) to add a visual illustration of many of its concepts. DBpedia also contains links to pictures, which are already part of the information derived from each Wikipedia entry. Image-net[2] goes even further, presenting itself as a veritable image database organised according to the WordNet hierarchy.

In traditional dictionaries words are explained with words, using a definition or an equivalent word (for bilingual dictionaries); definitions as paraphrases of lexical units through syntactic construction (with or without examples) are common also in lexical resources such as WordNet. In electronic dictionaries a wide usage of other means (such as pictorial illustrations, pictures, animations, videos, audio files) is possible and paves the way for multimodal lexicographic resources. If pictorial illustrations are effective for nouns (in particular for plants, animals and common objects), their utility for complex actions and the abstract or figurative meaning of words is less predictable. Adamska-Sałaciak (2008) (working on lexicography from a cognitive linguistics perspective) suggests that the inclusion of schematic graphs to represent the meaning of prepositions in dictionaries is useful. Animated illustrations are effective because they provide user-friendly representation of stages or the progression of an action and, together with videos, constitute the better modality for presenting verbal meanings, even if this is still an underinvestigated issue. Video sequences can convey information about situational contexts but are rather costly in terms of storage space and their realization is not easy (i.e. several semiotic principles should be followed for their realization).

Yet in all these resources entries are linguistically or conceptually motivated. Images are linked to concepts, synsets or lexical entries, which provide the hierarchical structure to the resource. None has, to our knowledge, attempted to do the inverse; that is to build a veritable visual ontology, where the types are visually represented, and semantic and lexical information is dependent to visual types. In the IMAGACT ontology each type is represented by a prototypical scene, specifically one produced with 3D animation techniques in order to describe in a salient way one prototypical action.

## 3 The IMAGACT project

The IMAGACT project uses both corpus-based and competence-based methodologies for simultaneous extraction of a language independent action inventory from spontaneous speech corpora of different languages.

The IMAGACT infrastructure faces key issues in ontology building. It grounds productive translation relations since it distinguishes the primary usage of verbs from their metaphorical or

---

[1]sigma.ontologyportal.org:4010/sigma/Browse.jsp?lang=EnglishLanguage&flang=SUO-KIF&kb=SUMO&term=Pump

[2] www.image-net.org

phraseological extensions; it allows easy identification of types in the variation, it is cross-linguistic in nature, it derives from the actual use of language but it can be freely extended to other languages through competence-based judgments and it is therefore suitable for filling gaps in lexical resources.

The IMAGACT database focuses on high frequency action verbs, which can provide sufficient variation in spoken corpora; i.e. roughly 500 verbs referring to actions which represent the full basic action oriented verbal lexicon. In order to maximize the probability of occurrence of relevant action types, IMAGACT identifies the variation of this set in parallel on two spoken corpora:

- a 2 million word English corpus, taken from the British National Corpus;
- a collection of spoken Italian corpora with 1.6 million words in total (LABLITA corpus, Cresti and Moneglia, 2005; LIP, De Mauro et al., 1993; CLIPS corpus).

## 3.1 The IMAGACT annotation framework

The annotation procedure is structured into two main steps, standardization & clustering of occurrences and types annotation & assessment, accomplished by annotators with the assistance of a supervisor. The first task is to examine and interpret verb occurrences in the oral context, which is frequently fragmented and may not provide enough semantic evidence for an immediate interpretation. To this end the infrastructure allows the annotator to read the larger context of the verbal occurrence in order to grasp the meaning (Figure 2 presents two of the occurrences of *to roll* in the corpus). The annotator represents the referred action with a simple sentence in a standard form for easy processing. This sentence must be in the positive form, in the third person, present tense, active voice and must fill the essential argument positions of the verb (possible specifiers that are useful in grasping the meaning are placed in square brackets). Basic level expressions (Rosch 1978) are preferred or otherwise a proper name is used and word order in sentences must be linear, with no embedding and/or distance relationships.

Crucially, along with the standardization, the annotator assigns each occurrence to a "variation class" thus determining whether or not it conveys the verb's meaning. This is what we mean by a PRIMARY occurrence. This task is accomplished through a synthetic judgment which exploits the semantic competence of the annotator (Cresswell 1978) and is given in conjunction with Wittgenstein's hypothesis on how word extensions can be learned (Wittgenstein 1953). The occurrence is judged PRIMARY according to two main operational criteria: a) it refers to a physical action; b) it can be presented to somebody who does not know the meaning of the verb V, by asserting that "the referred action and similar events are what we intend with V".

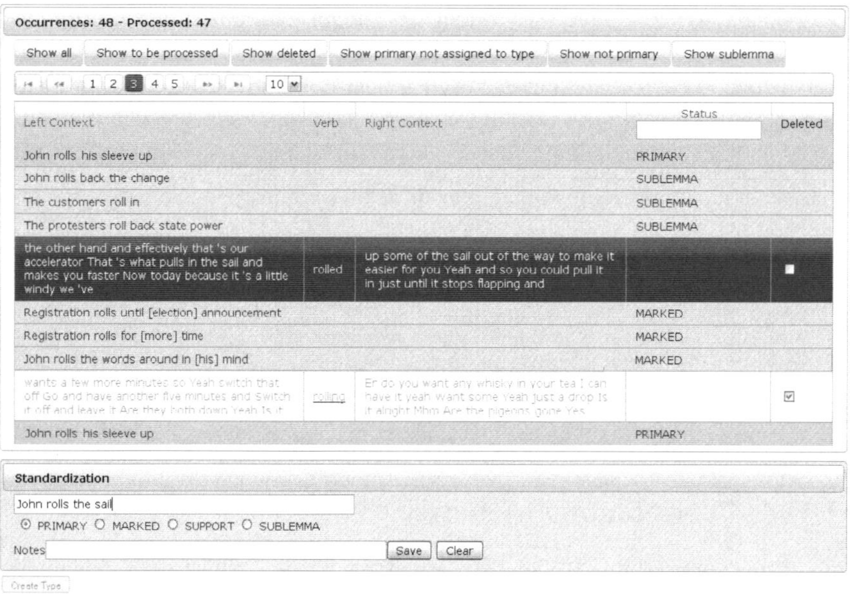


FIGURE 2 - Verb occurrence and Standardization box

The occurrence is judged MARKED otherwise, as with "John rolls the words in his mind".

Only occurrences assigned to the PRIMARY variation class make up the set of Action Types stored in the ontology. To this end they must be clustered into families which constitute the productive variation of the verb predicate. The workflow thus requires the examination of the full set of standardized primary occurrences recorded in the corpus, whose meaning is now clear.

The infrastructure is designed to allow the annotator to create types ensuring both cognitive similarity among their events and pragmatic differences between them. The overall criterion for type creation is to keep granularity to its minimal level, assigning instances to the same type as long as they fit with one "best example". Clustered sentences should be similar as regards:

- the possibility to extend the occurrence by way of similarity with the virtual image provided by the best example (Cognitive Constraint);
- "equivalent verbs applied in their proper meaning" i.e. the synset (Fellbaum 1998) (Linguistic Constraints);
- involved Action schema.

Among the occurrences the annotator chooses the most representative as best examples of the recorded variation, creates types headed by one (or more) best example(s), and assigns each individual standardization to a type by dragging and dropping. The infrastructure assists the annotator in the task by showing the types that have been created so far and the equivalent verbs used to differentiate them.

The assigned instances can be shown by type and best example according to the annotator's needs. The infrastructure also provides functionality for making easy revisions to hypotheses (by showing instances not yet assigned, showing all instances, the verification of Marked variation, editing/merging/splitting types etc.).

The approach underlying the annotation strategy does not require a priori any inter-annotator agreement in this core task, which is strongly underdetermined, and rather relies on a supervised process of revision.

Once all occurrences have been processed, negotiation with a supervisor leads to a consensus on the minimal granularity of the action types extended by the verb in its corpus occurrences. The verification criteria are practical: the supervisor verifies for each type that it cannot be referred to as an instance of another without losing internal cohesion. The operational test checks if it is understandable that the native speaker is referring to the event by pointing to the prototype. The supervisor considers the pragmatic relevance of these judgments and keeps the granularity accordingly.

The relation to images of prototypical scenes provides a challenging question in restricting granularity to a minimal family resemblance set: "can you specify the action referred to by one type as something like the best example of another?". Granularity is kept when this is not reasonable.

Once types are verified the infrastructure presents the annotator with the "Types Annotation & Assessment" interface. Conversely, in this task the annotator assesses that all instances gathered within each type can indeed be extensions of its best example(s), thus validating its consistency. Those that aren't are assigned to other types.

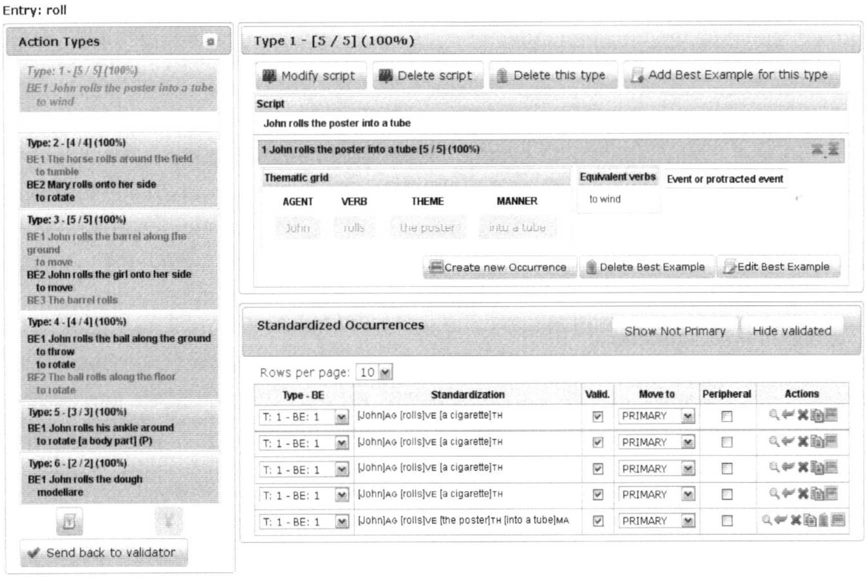


FIGURE 3 - Types Annotation and Assessment

The assessment runs in parallel with the annotation of the main linguistic features of a type. More best examples can be added in order to represent all the thematic structures of a verb which satisfies that interpretation. As shown in Figure 3 the thematic grid must be filled, by writing each argument in a separate cell and selecting a role-label from the adjacent combo-box. The tagset for thematic role annotation is constituted by a restricted set of labels derived from current practices in computational lexicons. We are using Palmer's Tagset in VerbNet with adaptations.

Each best example is also annotated with an aspectual class which is assigned by means of the Imperfective Paradox Test (Dowty, 1979). Aspect can assume three values: event, process or state. Sentences that are judged peripheral instances of the type can be marked, thus identifying fuzziness in pragmatic boundaries. The annotation procedure ends when all proper occurrences of a verb have been assessed. The annotator produces a "script" for each type and delivers the verb annotation to the supervisor for cross-linguistic mapping.

### 3.1.1 Description of the methodology of interlinguistic validation

The direct representation of actions through scenes that can be interpreted independently of language allows the mapping of lexicons from different languages onto the same cross-linguistic ontology.

Working with data coming from more than one language corpus, IMAGACT must produce a language independent type inventory. For instance, in the case of *to roll* action types must be consistent with those extended by the Italian verb *rotolare/arrolotolare*, which in principle could be roughly equivalent. Therefore the supervisor will face two lists of types independently derived from corpora annotation. In this scenario, setting the cross-linguistic relations among verbal entries relies on the identification of a strict similarity between the Types that have been identified (and not through the active writing of a definition). The task is mapping similar types onto one prototypic scene that they can be an instance of.

Figure 1 roughly sketches the main types derived from the annotation of *to roll* and *rotolare / arrotolare* and their mapping onto scenes. The supervisor should recognize for instance, that type 2 of *to roll* and type 1 of *rotolare* are instances of the same prototype. The supervisor will accordingly produce a scene (scene C here). Cross-linguistic mapping allows us to predict relevant information which does not emerge from simple corpus annotation. For instance some types of *rotolare* may never occur in the English corpus, but native English speakers can recognize from the scene that they too are a possible extension of *to roll*. The mapping of the verb onto that type will therefore be established, providing competence based information. Mappings are not always possible: in this case the native speaker recognizes that T1 of *to roll* cannot be extended by *rotolare* while *arrotolare* is applicable. In other words the infrastructure and the methodology embodied in it allow the identification of the pragmatic universe of action and of how different languages parse it. This result is obtained in a Wittgenstein-like scenario without the comparison of definitions. The use of prototypic images bypasses this complex problem and permits the identification of the focal pragmatic variation of general verbs and their differentials in different languages.

Notice that this first mapping is performed on the basis of Types only. Its productivity must be then validated at the level of each single instance. A second step of interlinguistic validation consists in asking mother tongue informants what verb(s) should be applied in their language to each scene and whether the verb(s) is applicable to the set of English/Italian sentences headed by that scene.

Crucially, the informant will verify whether or not the choice is correct for all arguments retrieved from the corpus and assigned to that type and in doing so will verify to which extent the pragmatic concepts stored in the ontology are productive i.e. they permit generalizations at a cross-linguistic level. This means that in IMAGACT a concept is valid for cross-linguistic reference to action if, independently of the language, the verb that is applied to the prototypic instance can also be applied to all sentences gathered in it.

The cross linguistic validation is performed in parallel on English and Italian sentences gathered within each entry and it generates a data set of parallel sentences. A competence based extension to other languages (Spanish and Chinese Mandarin) is also in progress, and consists in identifying a verb in the target language for each type of the source language and verifying the applicability to all instances in the target language, without actually producing sentences in the target language.

The interlinguistic validation of types is a very crucial phase of the IMAGACT project. Distinguishing families of usages of general verbs from the granular variations allows us to discover productive cross-linguistic relations, thus validating the ontology entries in the real world.

## 4 From words to videos: methodology

Once types of actions referred to by action verbs have been identified and the scripts have been produced for the best examples, with cross-linguistic equivalences established, the supervisor produces a prototypical scene.

Actors perform the action described in the script or an equivalent action. The scene is recorded according to the following requirements, which are intended to reduce ambiguity and to trigger the preferred interpretation:

- Use of real-world objects instead of abstract/generic forms
- Minimal, necessary background information
- The scene is produced as an uninterrupted shot ("long take")
- The action is performed with its usual temporal span (no slow-motion)
- The sequence is edited to focus on the sole relevant nucleus of the performed action (3-7 seconds)

The semiotic relevance of each scene and its capacity to elicit the appropriate verb is scrutinized by more than three experts before storage in the database.

Subsequently a 3D animation is created from the videos, in order to make the scene even less ambiguous. The animation software used for the production of 3D videos is Autodesk MAYA[3].

An animation must be equivalent to the real scene for what concerns its possible interpretation, but not necessarily equivalent with respect to the used objects.

## 5 Mapping IMAGACT onto WordNet

We are currently dealing with another task, that is to establish a link between IMAGACT and WordNet.

[3] The output format is H.264/mpeg-4, with framesize 1024*576.

WordNet is one of the best-known lexical resources and it contains one of the most complete verbal ontologies of any lexical resource, not only in terms of lexical entries, but also for the number of relations among verbs (hyponymy/hypernymy, troponymy, entailment). It is therefore very useful to investigate how IMAGACT maps onto WordNet. A mapping of both resources would lead to a reciprocal enrichment of several aspects: for instance IMAGACT does not show semantic relations among verbs, nor does it use definitions/glosses to define actions or action types, while WordNet does; on the other side WordNet does not distinguish between primary and marked senses, often confusing proper uses with metaphorical or idiomatical ones. Furthermore, WordNet defines horizontal relations among senses (synsets) with glosses, while IMAGACT uses scenes to represent the event type which different verbs can refer to in similar contexts (equivalent verb classes). So in case of perfect matching between an action type and a synset, IMAGACT videos would be enriched by WN glosses, and WN glosses could be more intuitively understood if visually represented.

It is also important to stress that WordNets have been now produced for many languages (and sometimes connected one to another: see for example EuroWordNet, GlobalWordNet projects). This would allow in the future the extension of the mapping to new languages, once they have been implemented in IMAGACT. Furthermore, we can imagine that if different WordNet ontologies are mapped onto the same IMAGACT interlinguistical ontology, they will be automatically linked one to another, and this will be of great benefit to the multilingual projects cited above.

As we said above the ontology of action types has already been completed by extracting data from Italian corpus annotation, therefore a first mapping of Italian action types onto ItalWordNet senses has been attempted. For every IMAGACT action verb, we compared the action types with the senses of the corresponding ItalWordNet lexical entry and with their related synsets.

We have already mapped about 150 Italian action types onto ItalWordNet. In some cases, especially when the verb refers to a very specific action (e.g. *stirare, to iron*) or it has a strong prototypical meaning (e.g. *camminare, to walk*), as often happens with activity verbs, the verb has only one IMAGACT action type and only one (or very few) ItalWordNet senses. On many occasions it is possible to map a type onto a sense only excluding WordNet senses clearly referring to marked uses (metaphorical, idiomatic, etc.). With general verbs some difficulties emerge: sometimes an action type perfectly matches a WordNet sense or synset, but sometimes synsets are more generic than action types (and a best match may be found with hyponyms, if present). So the relations linking IMAGACT action types and ItalWordNet senses are the following: semantic equivalence, when a type perfectly matches a sense (ItalWordNet gloss perfectly describes the content of the video); otherwise, imperfect match, when the relation is one of subsumption (one type subsuming two or more senses, or two or more types being subsumed by one sense). We cannot exclude, a priori, the null relation (when a type cannot be related to any sense), but far we have not run into this.

Part of our future work will be to complete the mapping and to implement in IMAGACT, for each action type, an ItalWordNet direct link. We will also apply the same metodology to map English action types onto WordNet.

## 6 Conclusions and future work

The key innovation of IMAGACT is to provide a methodology which exploits the language independent capacity to appreciate similarities among scenes, distinguishing the identification of action types from their definition. By focusing its attention on action verbs, IMAGACT provides an interesting modality of presentation for their basic meaning distinctions; the navigation and search strategies are particularly promising for access to verbal meaning.

After its first delivery the IMAGACT infrastructure will grow freely as a function of its competence-based implementation in an open set of languages. The Interlinguistic Action Ontology DB will be available through the Internet as a web resource. The annotation infrastructure will be open source. We foresee that the infrastructure will have to cope with three main scenarios. The user may ask for:

a) the set of verbs of a target language that can be applied to a given action (language independent scenario);

b) the differential between the actions referred to by one verb in his own language and the actions referred to by a target verb in another language (distinguish the lexical properties of the target language in L2 acquisition);

c) the set of action types referred to by one or more action verbs in a given language (focusing on the lexical properties of action verbs).

The main NLP use foreseen for IMAGACT annotated data is word sense disambiguation. The resource will be tested in language acquisition and assisted translation scenarios; it will also be the starting point for the development of neuropsychological test batteries for the assessment of semantic knowledge[4]. Moreover the Ontology contains a large amount of information on actions potentially useful for ambient intelligence and for the modeling of artificial systems aimed at interacting in the natural environment on the basis of natural language instructions.

## Acknowledgments

The IMAGACT project has been funded in Italy within the PAR/FAS program of the Tuscan Region and it is undertaken by the University of Florence, ILC-CNR, Pisa, and the University of Siena.

## References

British National Corpus, version 3 (BNC XML Edition). 2007. Distributed by Oxford University Computing Services URL: http://www.natcorp.ox.ac.uk/

CLIPS Corpus. URL: http://www.clips.unina.it

C-ORALROM http://catalog.elra.info/product_info.php?products_id=757

Adamska-Sałaciak, A. 2008. Prepositions in Dictionaries for Foreign Learners: A Cognitive Linguistic Look. Bernal, E. and J. DeCesaris (Eds.). 2008: 1477-1485.

Cresswell M. F. 1978 Semantic Competence in F. Guenthner, M. Guenthner-Reutter, Meaning and translation. NY University Press: New York, 9-28

[4] There is a PhD thesis to be written on this topic.

De Mauro T., Mancini F., Vedovelli M., Voghera M. 1993. Lessico di frequenza dell'italiano parlato (LIP). Milano: ETASLIBRI.

Fellbaum, Ch. (ed.) 1998. WordNet: An Electronic Lexical Database. Cambridge: MIT Press.

Lew, Robert. 2010. 'New ways of indicating meaning in electronic dictionaries: hope or hype?' In: Zhang, Yihua (ed.), Learner's Lexicography and Second Language Teaching Shanghai: Shanghai Foreign Language Education Press. 387-404.

Rosch, E. 1978. Principles of Categorization. In E. Rosch & B.B. Lloyd (eds), Cognition and Categorization. Hillsdale: Lawrence Erlbaum, 27–48.

Wittgenstein, L. 1953. Philosophical Investigations. Oxford: Blackwell.

# Dictionary-Ontology Cross-Enrichment
# Using TLFi and WOLF to enrich one another

*Emmanuel ECKARD*[1] *Lucie BARQUE*[2] *Alexis NASR*[1] *Benoît SAGOT*[3]
(1) Laboratoire d'Informatique Fondamentale de Marseille, UMR 7279 - CNRS, Université Aix Marseille
(2) LDI, UMR 7187- CNRS, Université Paris 13, France
(3) Alpage, INRIA Paris-Rocquencourt & Université Paris 7, France
`Emmanuel.Eckard@a3.epfl.ch, lucie.barque@univ-paris13.fr, benoit.sagot@inria.fr, Alexis.Nasr@lif.univ-mrs.fr`

## ABSTRACT

It has been known since Ide and Veronis [6] that it is impossible to automatically extract an ontology structure from a dictionary, because that information is simply not present. We attempt to extract structure elements from a dictionary using clues taken from a formal ontology, and use these elements to match dictionary definitions to ontology synsets; this allows us to enrich the ontology with dictionary definitions, assign ontological structure to the dictionary, and disambiguate elements of definitions and synsets.

KEYWORDS: Dictionaries, ontologies, WordNet.

## 1 Introduction

It has been known since Ide and Veronis [6] that it is impossible to extract an ontology structure from a dictionary, because this information is simply not present in the dictionnary as it is in the ontology, not even implicitly. Human intuition that dictionary definitions contain an ontology-like structure stems from the world knowledge that we uncounsciously also take into consideration as context when we read them; since this world knowledge is not available to computers, automated extraction fails. For instance, one of the Wiktionary definitions for "lock" is "A segment of a canal or other waterway enclosed by gates, used for raising and lowering boats between levels". The term "canal" here is polysemous, defined either as "An artificial waterway, often connecting one body of water with another" or "A tubular channel within the body". A computer has no straightforward[1] way to tell which of the senses is relevant, while a human, linking "waterway", "boats" and "body of water" to a common semantic field through their experience of the world, will easily choose the boating sense over the anatomic one.

Since the closest thing to a world knowledge available to computers is precisely ontologies, it seems appealing to design an ontology-powered automated process to identify elements of ontological structure present in the dictionary. Clearly, the ontology information that we inject into the process should not excessively constrain it, lest we find that very information. Instead, the process should trigger a virtuous circle where clues from the ontology permit structuring the dictionary, which in turn enriches the ontology with dictionary information. Only under these conditions can the process be both practical and useful. The approach of nurturing

[1]Recognising a common semantic field for two segments of text that share few or no common words goes beyond mere co-occurrence count; it is feasible, but requires sophisticated strategies such as latent semantics, for instance, and is difficult on small samples.

interpretation of dictionary definition with ontology information can be considered from two points of view: a minima, as relaxing the strong hypotheses of "dictionary information only", under which Ide and Veronis showed extraction to be impossible[2]; a maxima, as injecting information into the process to mimick Human understanding of definitions through world knowledge.

Resources containing world knowledge can provide their information in different formats: for instance, dictionaries provide a number of definitions for each given word, with a distinct definition for each sense, and possibly hierarchies of sub-meanings; ontologies also provide short definitions, but mostly provide a structured set of relationships between senses, such as hypernymy, meronymy, etc. Although a wealth of resources exists in computer-readable form, resources become scarcer when we consider languages other than English. For instance, the general ontologies WordNet and FrameNet in English are hand-built, quite complete and available under a Free software-like licence [3, 4]. In French, on the other hand, the most notable alternatives are Euro Wordnet, which is quite complete and hand-built but only available under a commercial licence [13], and WOLF, which is available under a Free licence but is computer-generated from WordNet and incompletely translated. WOLF particularly suffers from the difficulty to adequately identify and translate polysemous words [12].

Since it provides a great deal of information while leaving room for improvement, WOLF constitutes both a resource and a testing bed for new algorithms and heuristics. As a resource, we can use it to generate clues for our heuristic; as a testing bed, contribute improvements to it. In this work, we attempt to enrich WOLF with dictionary definitions taken from the TLFi (*Trésor de la Langue française informatisé*). Practically, this comes down to assigning a dictionary definition to ontology synset elements, or to match ontology synsets with precise senses of a word in the dictionary. To achieve this result, we will explore the ambiguous graph structure implicitly formed by TLFi definitions. The heuristic attempts to connect two words $h$ and $H$ through a hypernymy relation by recursively roaming the definitions of words contained in a definition, concentrating on a hypernym; when successful, it stores the list of elementary segments that connect $h$ to $H$. For instance, WOLF predicts that *établissement* (establishment) is a hypernym of *académie* (academy); indeed, in TLFi, these words are connected through certain senses of *école* (school): we find

$$\text{académie} \rightarrow \text{école} \rightarrow \text{établissement}$$

The word *école* is contained in the definition of *académie* and its own definition in turn contains *établissement*. Hence, *académie* leads to *établissement* as predicted by the clue provided by WOLF. Each of the words visited by the heuristic yields a number of different senses, each with its own definition which is examined separately. Hence, the hierarchy actually detects

$$\text{académie-6} \rightarrow \text{école-1} \rightarrow \text{établissement}$$

After a successful connection attempt, the pairs of unique senses immediately connected to each other (like académie-6 → école-1) are recorded and a frequentation counter associated with the sense pair is incremented. The result of the process allows us to tell which sense of *école* is expressed in the definition of *académie* that we considered.

[2]Several studies proposed automatic or semi-automatic methods to develop lexical hierarchies from dictionary data, e.g. [2, 10].

## 2 Resources

## 2.1 TLFi

The *Trésor de la Langue française informatisé* (TLFi) [11] is the digital version of the *Trésor de la Langue française*, a large reference dictionary for French. The two main reasons why we have chosen the TLFi is that it is available in electronic form for research purpose and that most of its definitions belong to so-called *definitions by genus and differentiæ* allowing us to extract genus (or hypernym of the defined unit). The TLFi has also a wide coverage with around 270,000 definitions. This study is restricted to nouns, for which the TLFi provide 100,493 definitions describing the meaning(s) of 35,498 nominal entries.

The senses of a lexical entry in TLFi are subdivised into a hierarchy of senses and subsenses, each complete with a unique identification number and a definition; for instance, the word *bois* (wood) comprises the following senses[3]:

> 1.1.1 Ensemble d'arbres croissant sur un terrain d'étendue moyenne; ce terrain même.
> 2.1.1.1 Matière (racines, tronc, branches) qui constitue l'arbre (à l'exception du feuillage).

### 2.1.1 Identification of definitions genus

In the framework of the *Definiens* project, TLFi definitions of nouns were POS-tagged and processed to determine the *genus* of a given definition, that is, the noun or noun phrase that corresponds to the hypernym of the defined noun [1]. The Definiens heuristic relies on lexico-syntactic patterns that recognise nouns or noun phrases as possible genus candidates. More precisely, around fifty rules have been manually elaborated to identify geni in the TLFi definitions. Represented as finite-state transducers, the rules have been run on definitions previously labeled with part of speech tags by the NLP tool suite MACAON [8]. The rule presented in figure 1 identifies nominal definitions that begin with a common noun (nc for *nom commun* in French), followed by a preposition and then another noun (left hand side of the rule). The right hand side of the rule proposes two possible geni for this kind definition: the first noun or a more specific phrasal genus constituted by the three elements (noun, preposition, noun) detected in the left hand side of the rule. This rule matches for example the definition of JODHPURS presented below since it begins with a noun (*pantalon*) followed by a preposition (*de*) followed by a noun (*équitation*). The right hand side of the rule thus indicates two possible geni for this definition : *pantalon* (trousers) and *pantalon d'équitation* (horse riding trousers).

> JODHPURS = Pantalon d'équitation importé des Indes par les officiers anglais, ajusté du genou à la cheville et qui se porte sans bottes (Horse riding trousers imported from India by English officers, tight from knee to ankle and that is worn without boots.) ⇒ **genus 1**: pantalon, **genus 2**: pantalon d'équitation

The rule presented in figure 1 also matches the definiton of BOIS-1.1.1 given above. Nevertheless, geni like "ensemble de N" have to be treated in a particular way. Thus, the rules can also include lexical elements, as illustrated below in figure 2: when a definition matches the

[3]"Wood" 1.1.1 Set of trees growing on a medium-sized area of land; said terrain.
2.1.1.1 Matter (roots, trunk, branches) that constitute a tree (except the
foliage). This particular case is provided here to examplify definition numbering, without prejudice of further questions, like whether the "said terrain" metonymy should ideally be numbered separately. In the Princeton Wordnet, only the first half of this definition appears at all.

```
<rule>
  <lhs>
    <elt cat="nc"/>
    <elt cat="prep"/>
    <elt cat="nc"/>
  </lhs>
  <rhs>
    <genus><elt num="1"/></genus>
    <rhs>
       <genus>
         <elt num="1"/>
         <elt num="2"/>
         <elt num="3"/>
       </genus>
    </rhs>
  </rhs>
</rule>
```

Figure 1: Example of a syntactic genus extraction rule

sequence *ensemble de/d' + nc* (set of), the selected genus is not *ensemble* but the common noun that follows the preposition. The noun is moreover applied to the function "set of".

```
<regle>
  <lhs>
    <elt lex="ensemble"/>
    <elt cat="prep"/>
    <elt cat="nc"/>
  </lhs>
  <rhs>
    <function><elt num="1"/></function>
    <genus><elt num="3"/></genus>
  </rhs>
</regle>
```

Figure 2: Example of a lexico-syntactic genus extraction rule

When the rules propose multiple geni for a given word sense, as in the rule presented in figure 1 above, the genus that is selected is the most specific one, provided that this most specific genus is classifying (*i. e.* appears as a genus in at least another definition). In other words, the genus that is nor too specific nor too general is assumed to represent the most accurate genus. In the JODHPURS example, the genus *pantalon d'équitation* (horse riding trousers) is more specific than *pantalon* (trousers) but the processing of the whole corpus tells us that *pantalon d'équitation* appears only once, in the definition of JODHPURS, whereas *pantalon* appears in the definition of eighteen word senses (BLUE-JEAN, SAROUAL, ...) in the TLFi.

This automatic process, that consists in counting every possible geni of every definitions through the corpus, allows us to obtain the data described in table 1 below. As shown in

| | |
|---|---|
| **Nominal words** | 35,498 |
| **Nominal word senses** | 100,493 |
| **Distinct geni** | 17,204 |
| **Classifying geni** : | 13,924 |
| Simple nouns | 5,578 |
| Phrasal nouns | 8,346 |

Table 1: Geni extracted from the TLFi

this table, the 13,924 classifying geni are composed of 5,578 simple nouns (*e.g.* `conifère` (conifer), `formule` (formula), ...) and 8,346 phrasal nouns (*e.g.* `conifère de grande taille` (tall conifer), `courte formule` (short formula); ...). Let's recall that phrasal geni are very interesting in that they "naturally" disambiguate ambiguous forms (cf. `carte` *vs* `carte géographique` (map) and `carte à jouer` (playing card)). The 8,346 phrasal geni that have been yet detected are based on only 1,754 distinct nominal heads and more than 90 percent of them are included in the simple nouns set. The total number of words to disambiguate is therefore equal to 5,578 simple nouns plus 175 heads of complex nouns that are not already included in the simple geni set. Most of these geni are ambiguous, for an average of 4 senses per genus.

### 2.1.2 Adaptation of the sense hierarchy to limit ambiguity

The number of distinct senses can be high, and the differences between some of them can be quite subtle. For instance, the verb "to dive" distinguishes the senses "move briskly and rapidly downwards" and "being directed downwards". TLFi also records unusual or archaic senses of words: for instance, the term *fourchette* ("fork") lists the chess configuration, which might not be the first to spring to mind, as well as an archaic vernacular word for "bayonet".

In TLFi, the different senses of a word are organised in a hierarchy of sense numbers, such as "1", "2.3.1", etc. Senses with more decimals in their sense number are children of the parent sense, i.e. variants of the parent sense in a particular framework. Senses with 4 or more decimals in their sense number tend to be very specific senses, with long definitions. To avoid hyper-correction, we deem it adequate to trim this sense hierarchy, as the fine granularity achieved by human lexicographers is not a realistic goal for our automatic system [7]. We devise two simple schemes to this purpose: the "cut" scheme simply ignores all definitions whose sense number bears more than a given number of decimals; and the "merge" scheme deletes all definitions whose sense number bears more than a given number of decimals, but concatenates their definition to that of their direct parent. For instance, "cut 2" will retain senses "1", "2.1" and "3.1", but will eliminate senses "1.2.1", "2.1.1", "3.1.2.1", etc.; and "merge 1" will retain senses "1" and "2", and will eliminate sense "2.1" and "2.3.1.1" after concatenating their definition to the definition of sense "2". In cases where definitions are merged, their geni are stored in a vector, which allows us to take them into consideration one by one.

## 2.2 WOLF

WOLF (*WOrdNet Libre du Français*)[4] is a French-language ontology, automatically built from the Princeton WordNet (PWN) and various other resources [12]. Monosemous literals in the PWN 2.0 were translated using a bilingual French-English lexicon built from various multilingual resources. Polysemous PWN literals were handled by an alignment approach based on a multilingual parallel corpus. The synsets obtained from both approaches were then merged. The resulting resource, WOLF, preserves the hierarchy and structure of PWN 2.0 and contains the definitions and usage examples provided in PWN for each synset. Although new approaches are currently being used for increasing its coverage [5], WOLF is rather sparse, as information was not found for all PWN synsets by these automatic methods. Indeed, one of the difficulties in completing WOLF is to disambiguate the words contained in its synsets as to

[4] `http://alpage.inria.fr/~sagot/wolf.html`

allow a correct translation, since the level of polysemy is high.

In this work, we used the version 0.2.0 of the WOLF, in which 46,449 out of the 115,424 PWN 2.0 synsets are filled with at least one French literal. WOLF 0.2.0 contains 50,968 unique literals which take part in 86,235 (literal, synset) pairs, i.e., lexical entries (to be compared with the 145,627 such pairs in the PWN 2.0). Approximately half of these pairs are nouns, i.e., belong to nominal synsets.

Since the WOLF was created automatically using several distinct techniques, each (literal, synset) pair is associated with the set of techniques that suggested its creation, together with a technique-specific confidence measure. This information is used for filtering out (literal, synset) pairs with the lowest confidence scores. We defined two filters: a medium filter, which retain more candidates, and a strong filter, which retain only the most reliable candidates (cf. figures in the next section).

## 3 Using hypernymic paths for synset–definition matching

Our aim is to enrich WOLF and TLFi with one another, entailing that we need to assign specific definitions to given WOLF synsets. These synsets, or sets of synonyms, contain words that share a same meaning, but this meaning is yet not explicitly determined. As such, these words are ambiguous with respect to TLFi, and it is not straightforward to decide which of the TLFi definitions should be associated with them, if any. To solve this issue, we propose to use the two resources and compound them with a heuristic.

The heuristic attempts to connect two words with a hypernymy relation, and stores the senses through which the connection goes in case of success. At each step, a definition is associated with hypernym candidate words — typically the head of the genus of the TLFi definition, provided by a pre-processing of TLFi (see section 2.1.1 ; the senses of this word are explored recursively in a breadth-first search until the goal is reached.

The WOLF hypernymy hierarchy provides us with numerous hyponym–hypernym couples, including measures of confidence for these couples. The heuristic processes all these couples, storing the elementary steps that constitute successful hypernymy paths, and keeping track of their frequentation.

The nature of dictionary definitions — short bursts of text completely independent from one another — prevents us from using machine learning techniques. Instead, we take advantage of the graph structures that are explicitly expressed in the ontology, and to some extent implicitly in the dictionary. Given a word $h$ and a hypernym $H$ of $h$, we use a graph exploration technique to connect senses of $h$ and $H$. We then record pairs to constitute the path between $h$ and $H$. This provides us with a set of word sense pairs that TLFi puts in direct hypernymy relation. We can then use these pairs to populate WOLF: if two words $w$ and $W$ are deemed to have definitions $d$ and $D$ in direct hypernymy according to TLFi, and belong to synsets $s$ and $S$ in WOLF, these synsets also being in the hypernymy relation, then we can safely identify $d$ to $s$ and $D$ to $S$.

To disambiguate the hyponyms of an ($h$, $H$) pair, we explore the graph by *hypernymic ascent*: we consider the different senses $h_1, \ldots, h_n$ that TLFi provides for $h$, and attempt to connect each of them to any of the senses of $H$. Inspired by [9], we propose a connection scheme whereby we jump from one word to a word of its definition, iteratively, until we reach the target $H$. In our implementation of the hypernymic ascent scheme, we select the *genus* of the

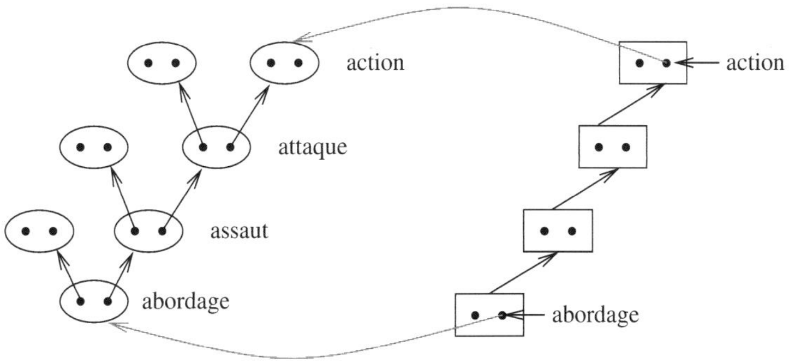


Figure 3: TLFi ambiguous structure (left) WOLF structure (right)

definition of a word (that can also be considered as its hypernym) to carry on the next iteration step, taking advantage of the preprocessing performed in the Definiens project [1].

This process is illustrated in figure 3. In the left hand part of the figure, we have represented the TLFi ambiguous structure. In this figure, the dots represent word senses while ellipses represent words. An ellipse that contains two dots therefore represent a polysemous word that has two possible different senses. An arrow linking a sense $s$ (a dot) to an ellipse $w$ (a word) indicates that the $w$ is a hypernym of $s$. The problem, of course, is that we do not know which sense of $w$ is actually the hypernym of $s$.

The right hand side of the figure represents the WOLF synset structure. Synsets are represented as rectangles while dots represent word senses. It must be noted that, in WOLF, word senses are not associated with definitions. In case of a polysemous word such that one of its senses is part of a synset, we do not actually know which sense it is. The arrows between rectangles represent the hypernymic relation.

In our example, we can extract from the WOLF subgraph that one sense of *abordage* has as a hypernym one sense of *action* although we do not know which sense of *abordage* nor which sense of *action* are linked by this relation. This is where the hypernymic ascent comes into play by looking, in the TLFi graph, for a path that links one sense of *abordage* with one sense of *action*.

The result of the hypernymic ascent is represented in figure 3. A path relating one sense of *abordage* to the word *action* has been discovered, it goes through a given sense of *assaut* (assault) as well as a given sense of *attaque* (attack). The number that labels the arcs between two senses corresponds to the number of paths that go through this arc.

Hypernymic ascent described can fail for several reasons. The main ones are described below:

1. Either the hypernym of the hyponym in an $(h, H)$ pair extracted from the WOLF is absent from the TLFi. When used with the medium filter, a total number of $86,636$ $(h, H)$ couples are extracted from the WOLF. For $49,908$ of them, both the hyponym and the hypernym are present in the TLFi. When the strong filter is used, $47,858$ couples are extracted out of which $24,443$ have both their hyponym and hypernym present in the TLFi.

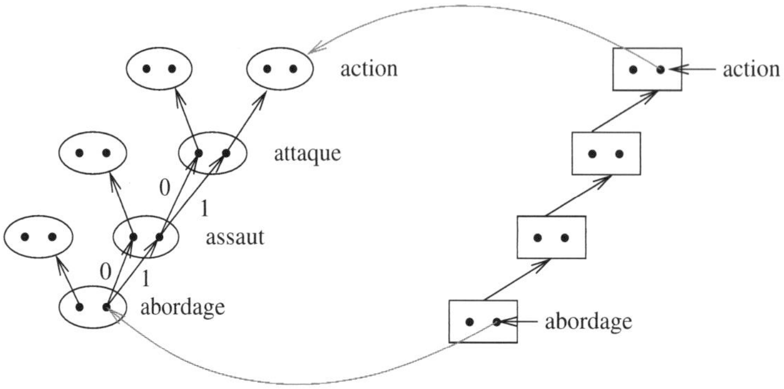


Figure 4: Result of the hypernymic ascent

2. Both $h$ and $H$ appear in the TLFi but no path was found that links them. This situation can have several causes :

   (a) Pre-processing errors. The preprocessing of the TLFi definition is made of several steps, each of which is error-prone. These steps are word segmentation of the definition, part of speech tagging and lemmatization.

   (b) Non standard definition. Although TLFi definitions generally follow a genus differentia schema some of them do not, some senses are defined, for example, by means of synonyms. In such cases the identification of the genus in the definition fails.

3. The $(h, H)$ pair extracted from WOLF is incorrect. In such a case, a path can be found which contains at least one incorrect arc.

When the process actually succeeds, it can be the case that several paths are found that link $h$ to $H$. A crude but quite effective way to deal with this situation is to select the shortest paths.

With the strong filter on WOLF hypernym couples (supposedly the most reliable set of ($h$, $H$) pairs given as clues), the success rate for connections is 21%; this falls to 18% with the medium filter (more details in table 2: for the strong and medium filters on WOLF (strong is the strictest and produces the most reliable couples), we give the number of words to explore, the number of senses yielded by the words, the number of successful connections, and the success rate of the connection attempts.).

| | words | senses | success | success rate |
|---|---|---|---|---|
| medium | 48,188 | 109,306 | 8,787 | 18.23% |
| strong | 23,291 | 52,408 | 4,916 | 21.11% |

Table 2: Connection attempts through hypernyms between two given words in hypernymic relationship.

The low success rate is ultimately neither a surprise, since a successful connection on one particular hyponym-hypernym pair is subject to many imponderables, nor a severe hindrance to our endeavour, since it is the accumulation of the elementary components yielded by the successful connections that constitutes our result. Therefore, success rates around 20% are both well explained, and quite fit for our purpose.

It is worth noting that the scheme described above does not generalise as to disambiguate the hypernym in the $(h, H)$ couple as well. This is ultimately due to a fundamental asymetry between the definitions of $h$ and $H$: though the hyponym is often defined in terms that ultimately lead to the hypernym (either directly or through other definitions), the converse is not true since the hypernym $H$ contains no information leading to the hyponym $h$. For example, a clue tells us that "snake" is the ultimate hypernym of "naja". The direct hypernym of "naja" is "cobra", which has several senses; only one of these senses has "snake" for hypernym, allowing us to discard cars and helicopters as candidate semantic fields. However, we have no way to determine which sense of "snake" is relevant (see figure 5).

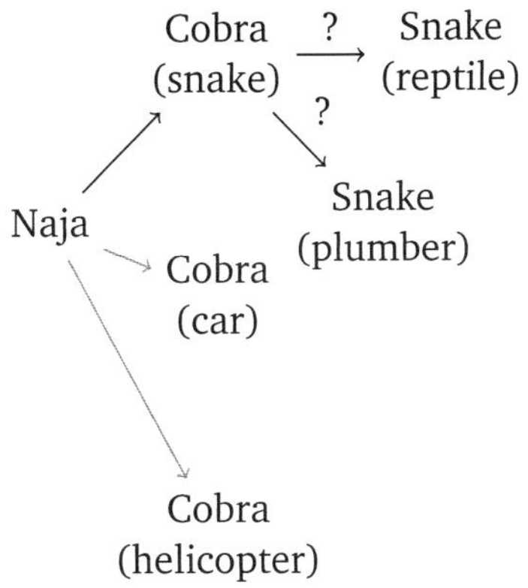


Figure 5: Ambiguous hypernym

One could attempt to reverse the hypernymic ascent into a hyponymic descent. However, this cannot be done simply by backtracking the path found during the hypernymic ascent, since the path is then completely determined. Hyponymic relationships linking TLFi dictionary definitions together should be available independently from the previously performed hypernymic ascent, for the hyponymic descent scheme to be viable. Unfortunately, this information is not present in TLFi. It is not possible to efficiently recreate this information by an exploratory preprocessing. For instance, envision a couple of direct hyponym-hypernym $(w, W)$, such as one of the $w_i$ is defined as being a kind of $W$; a pre-exploration of these relations would accurately detect that $w_i$ is a hyponym of one of the $W_1, \ldots, W_n$, but it would have no direct way to tell the relevant $W_i$. In consequence, it is impossible to tell one $W_i$ from another with this method, making hyponymic descent impractical with TLFi alone.

In summary, existence of quasi-hypernymic information in the form of geni of definitions featured in TLFi makes hypernymic ascent possible; absence of similar hyponymic data in definitions (like examples would partially provide) makes it impossible in practice to reverse the scheme.

# 4 Experiments

In order to measure the performances of the method, we ran it over two samples of 48,188 and 23,291 clues respectively (see table 2). After completion of the task, we randomly choose one hundred of the elementary hyponym-hypernym pairs and manually checked whether the chosen senses for the hyponym and the hypernym are relevant *i.e.* we answer the question : "is H an appropriate hypernym of h?". The answer is yes for the "homme-10 / mâle-1" pair given below and no for the "verbe-4 / expression-1" pair :

- homme-10 = **Mâle** adulte de l'espèce humaine (adult male human) / mâle-1 = Individu appartenant au sexe qui possède le pouvoir de fécondation
- verbe-4 = **Expression** verbale de la pensée (à l'oral ou par écrit) (verbal expression of the thought) / expression-1 = Action d'extraire d'un corps le liquide qu'il contient (extraction of liquid from a substance)

We find a 45% accuracy in the tested sample. Given the average polysemy of 4.03 for Central Components in our sample, a random baseline will yield performance in the order of 25%; with our 45% accuracy, we are therefore significantly higher than the baseline.

The frequency of a segment (the number of times a segment appear in a successful path) did not correlate with the correctness of the segment. Instead, they tend to correlate with how high the segment is in the ontology, and thus to how general or abstract a segment is: many hypernymic paths tend to feature them as they climb towards the root of the ontology. Using them as an indicator for the correctness of a segment will need some kind of normalization with respect to the abstractness of the segment.

In order to get a better understanding of what happens during the hypernymic ascent, we present below a few examples of partially successful or failed paths.

**academy – establishment, an unexpected and convoluted connection:** We have seen a correct connection of "academy" to "establishment", through an adequate meaning of "school". Nevertheless, "academy" has no less than 15 meanings in TLFi. Notably, académie-18 is defined as "house of gaming or pleasure"[5]. This triggers a search through the heavily polysemic word *maison* (28 definitions) which eventually leads to "establishment" through

$$\text{académie-18} \rightarrow \text{maison-41} \rightarrow \text{bâtiment-11} \rightarrow \text{grange-4} \rightarrow \text{établissement}$$

Interestingly, all of the segments yielded by this search are actually valid. This is a good illustration of the fact that the connection of the terms of the WOLF clue is a mere pretext to the research of elementary segments: it does not matter much that the connection has taken a detour, as long as the elementary segments are valid – it can in fact yield more segments to enrich our collection.

**baboon – animal, a connection through irrelevant definitions:** WOLF predicts that *animal* (animal) is a hypernym of *babouin* (baboon); indeed, in TLFi, these words are connected through certain senses of *singe* (monkey) and *voyageur* (traveller): we find

$$\text{babouin-1} \rightarrow \text{singe-24} \rightarrow \text{voyageur-14} \rightarrow \text{animal}$$

By examining the definitions of these senses, we see there that the word *voyageur* ("traveller"), perhaps surprising at a first glance, is in fact taken in its acceptation of "moving animal"[6]; on

[5] *maison de jeu ou de plaisir*

[6] The definition for voyageur-14 gives "Animal roaming its natural habitat (air, sea, ground), particularly migratory birds" (*Animal se déplaçant dans son milieu naturel (air, mer, terre); en particulier, oiseau migrateur.*)

the other hand, the word *singe* ("monkey" or "ape") is taken in its unusual and little-known acceptation of "surnumerary passenger"[7], which is clearly not relevant in the context[8]. This case has successfully connected "baboon" to "animal", yet it yields two segments, babouin-1 → singe-24 and singe-24 → voyageur-14, that are both incorrect.

Similarly WOLF predicts that *adonis* (adonis) is a hyponym of *mâle* (male). One of the connections found is

adonis-7 → papillon-3 → personne-1 → individu-11 → homme-10 → male

Starting with the entomological sense of "adonis" (a *Lycaena* butterfly), we jump to "butterfly", but in the sense of "socialite"; from there, we follow a foreseeable path through "person", "individual", "man" and eventually "male". Here, the segment adonis-7 → papillon-3 is false, though the others are correct. Obviously, the overall path connecting the terms of the WOLF clue makes little sense to the Human eye, but this is less problematic than incorrect segments. The overall path is merely a pretext to the research of elementary segments. By contrast, another path found for the same clue is

adonis-8 → nom-30 → partie-31 → individu-11 → homme-10 → male

which makes more sense, but does not yield more correct elementary segments than the previous example.

**steal mill – factory, a trivial connection:** WOLF predicts that *aciérie* (steal mill) is a hyponym of *usine* (factory); indeed, in TLFi, the first and only definition of *aciérie* is "factory where steal is manufactured"[9], entailing that the connection is direct and trivial. Since the term *usine* has seven different definitions on TLFi, and since our heuristic leaves the ultimate hypernym ambiguous, it is impossible to select which sense of *usine* is relevant. Thus, in spite of a successful connection, this path yields no useful segment.

**poster – worker, an erroneous WOLF clue:** WOLF predicts that *affiche* (poster) is a hypernym of *ouvrier* (worker), a rather counter-intuitive pair; our heuristic manages to find a convoluted path that connects these two words, but it is clear that integrity of the semantic field has been lost en route. The connection path goes

affiche-8 → action-2 → mise-72 → investissement-1 → manœuvre-1 → ouvrier

The word *mise* is here taken as "stakes in a gamble", leading to "investment" taken in its economic sense; the sense of "investment" then switches to the military term for "surrounding an enemy", yielding the word *manœuvre* ("manoeuver"); *manœuvre* then switches to its meaning of "unqualified worker", eventually completing the connection. Yet, the segments mise-72 → investissement-1 and investissement-1 → manœuvre-1 are incorrect.

[7]The definition for singe-24 gives "Traveller installed on the upper floor out of a lack of space in the inside of a public car" (*Voyageur installé sur l'impériale faute de place à l'intérieur d'une voiture publique.*)

[8]One set of experiments considered ignoring archaic meanings, as well as all specialised meaning marked by a domain tag in TLFi, to aleviate ambiguity somewhat; this did not yield significant improvement in performance.

[9]*Usine où se fabrique l'acier*

## 5 Conclusions

We have described an exploration scheme of how the hypotheses of Ide and Veronis can be relaxed as to make it possible to automatically align a dictionary and an ontology. We use "clues" extracted from an ontology to search consistent paths in the dictionary linking a hyponym to a hypernym, recording the intermediary steps that form the overall path. We attempted this using WOLF and TLFi, taking advantage of the TLFi dataset that was made available to us.

This "hypernymic ascent" scheme yields a high rate of connection failures, which is not in itself a problem as these connections are a pretext to recording the elementary segments that form the connection. Nevertheless, this indicates that relying on Central Components to climb in the hypernymy chain is not very efficient in the context of a natural language dictionary. We could envision better performances using more rigidely formatted dictionaries and less naive approximations for the hypernym of a definition than merely using its Central Component.

Another issue is that words close to the root of the ontology tend to be very fundamental and highly polysemic. Therefore, a connection that passes through them is likely to have lost its semantic integrity. The yields semantically inconsistant segments, thereby generating noise.

In spite of the many difficulties that we encounter with the data and the naive nature of some elements of our system, we still managed to obtain a 45% accuracy on a randomly selected sample, significantly above the random baseline. This makes our system suitable as a weak classifier as it is, and leaves much room for improvement using more rigidely formatted and self-consistent data, better management of word inflexions, and refined selection of definition features beyond mere central components.

## Acknowledgments

This work has been funded by the French Agence Nationale pour la Recherche, through the project EDYLEX (ANR-08-CORD-009).

## References

[1] L. Barque, A. Nasr, and A. Polguère. From the definitions of the trésor de la langue française to a semantic database of the french language. In *European Association for Lexicography International Congress (EURALEX)*, Leeuwarden, Pays Bas, 2010.

[2] M. Chodorow, R. Byrd, and G. Heidorn. Extracting semantic hierarchies from a large on-line dictionary. In *ACL*, pages 299–304, 1985.

[3] C. Fellbaum. *WordNet: An Electronic Lexical Database*. MIT Press, Cambridge, Mass, 1998.

[4] C. Fillmore, C. Johnson, and M. Petruck. Background to Framenet. *International Journal of Lexicography*, 16:235–250, 2003.

[5] V. Hanoka and B. Sagot. Wordnet creation and extension made simple: A multilingual lexicon-based approach using wiki resources. In *Proc. of the 8th international conference on Language Resources and Evaluation (LREC)*, page 6, Istanbul, Turquie, 2012.

[6] N. Ide and J. Veronis. Extracting knowledge-bases from machine-readable dictionaries: Have we wasted our time? In *Proc KB&KB'93 Workshop*, 1993.

[7] N. Ide and Y. Wilks. Making sense about sense. In *Text, Speech and Language Technology*, volume 33, pages 47–73, 2006.

[8] A. Nasr, F. Béchet, J.-F. Rey, B. Favre, and J. Le Roux. Macaon: An nlp tool suite for processing word lattices. In *The 49th Annual Meeting of the Association for Computational Linguistics*, 2011.

[9] R. Navigli. Using cycles and quasi-cycles to disambiguate dictionary glosses. In *Proceedings of the 12th Conference of the European Chapter of the Association for Computational Linguistics*, EACL '09, pages 594–602, Athens, Greece, 2009.

[10] R. Navigli and P. Velardi. From glossaries to ontologies: Extracting semantic structure from textual definitions. In *Ontology Learning and Population: Bridging the Gap between Text and Knowledge*, pages 71–87, 2008.

[11] J. M. Pierrel. Le Trésor de la Langue Française Informatisé : un dictionnaire de référence accessible à tous. *AMOPA*, (174):25–28, 2006.

[12] B. Sagot and D. Fišer. Automatic Extension of WOLF. In *GWC2012 - 6th International Global Wordnet Conference*, Matsue, Japon, January 2012. PHC PROTEUS 22718UC.

[13] P. Vossen. *EuroWordNet : a multilingual database with lexical semantic networks for European Languages*. Kluwer, Dordrecht, 1999.

# Automatic Construction of a MultiWord Expressions Bilingual Lexicon: A Statistical Machine Translation Evaluation Perspective

*Dhouha Bouamor*[1,2] *Nasredine Semmar*[1] *Pierre Zweigenbeaum*[2]
(1) CEA-LIST, Vision and Content Engineering Laboratory 91191 Gif-sur-Yvette Cedex, France
(2) LIMSI-CNRS, F-91403 Orsay, France
dhouha.bouamor@cea.fr, nasredine.semmar@cea.fr, pz@limsi.fr

ABSTRACT
Identifying and translating MultiWord Expressions (MWEs) in a text represent a key issue for numerous applications of Natural Language Processing (NLP), especially for Machine Translation (MT). In this paper, we present a method aiming to construct a bilingual lexicon of MWEs from a French-English parallel corpus. In order to assess the quality of the mined lexicon, a Statistical Machine Translation (SMT) task-based evaluation is conducted. We investigate the performance of three dynamic strategies and of one static strategy to integrate the mined bilingual MWEs lexicon in a SMT system. Experimental results shows that such a lexicon improves the quality of translation.

## Construction Automatique d'un Lexique Bilingue d'Expressions Multi-Mots: Une Perspective d'Évaluation par un Système de Traduction Statistique

Identifier et traduire correctement les Expressions Multi-Mots (EMMs) dans un texte constituent un défi majeur pour différentes applications du Traitement Automatique des Langues Naturelles, et surtout en Traduction Automatique. Ce présent travail présente une méthode permettant de construire un lexique bilingue d'EMMs à partir d'un corpus parallèle Français-Anglais. Afin d'évaluer la qualité du lexique acquis, une évaluation axée sur la tâche de Traduction Automatique Statistique (TAS) est menée. Nous étudions les performances de trois stratégies dynamiques et d'une stratégie statique pour intégrer le lexique bilingue d'EMMs dans un système de TAS. Les expériences menées dans ce cadre montrent que ces unités améliorent la qualité de traduction.

KEYWORDS: MultiWord Expressions, Bilingual Alignment, Statistical Machine Translation.

KEYWORDS IN FRENCH: Expressions Multi-Mots, Alignement Bilingue, Traduction Automatique Statistique.

# 1 Introduction

A MultiWord Expression (MWE) can be defined as a combination of words for which syntactic or semantic properties of the whole expression cannot be obtained from its parts (Sag et al., 2002). Such units are made up of collocations (*"cordon bleu"*), frozen expressions (*"kick the bucket"*), named entities (*"New York"*) etc. (Sag et al., 2002; Constant et al., 2011). These units are numerous and constitute a significant portion of the lexicon of any natural language. (Jackendoff, 1997) claims that the frequency of MWEs in a speaker's lexicon is almost equivalent to the frequency of single words. While easily mastered by native speakers, their interpretation poses a major challenge for Natural Language Processing (NLP) applications, especially for those addressing semantic aspects of language.

For Statistical Machine Translation (SMT) systems, various improvements of translation quality were achieved with the emergence of phrase based approaches (Koehn et al., 2003). Phrases are usually defined as simply arbitrary n-grams with no sophisticated linguistic motivation consistently translated in a parallel corpus. In such systems, the lack of an adequate processing of MWEs could affect the translation quality. In fact, the literal translation of an unrecognized expression is the source of an erroneous and incomprehensible translation. For example, these systems would suggest *"way of iron"* as a translation of *"chemin de fer"* instead of *"railway"*. It is therefore important to use a lexicon in which MWEs are handled. But such a resource is not readily available in all languages, and if it exists, as described by (Sagot et al., 2005), it does not cover all MWEs of a given language.

In this paper, we propose a method aiming to acquire a bilingual lexicon of MWEs from a French-English parallel corpus. We consider any compositional and non-compositional contiguous sequence, belonging to one of the three classes defined by (Luka et al., 2006), as a MWE. Classes of MWEs were distinguished on the basis of their categorical properties and their syntactic and semantic fixedness degrees and consist of *compounds*, *idiomatic expressions* and *collocations*. Intuitively, bilingual MWEs are useful to improve the performance of SMT. However, further research is still needed to find the best way to bring such external knowledge to the decoder. In this study, we view SMT as an extrinsic evaluation of the usefulness of MWEs and explore strategies for integrating such textual units in an SMT system. Given a constructed bilingual MWEs lexicon, we propose (1) three *dynamic integration* strategies in which we attempt to change the translation model in several ways to handle MWEs and (2) a *static integration* strategy in which we would like to plug these translations into the decoder without changing the model.

This paper is organized as follows: the next section (section 2) describes in some details previous works addressing the task of bilingual extraction of MWEs and its applications. In section 3, we present the method we used to build the bilingual lexicon of MWEs and then introduce in section 4 four strategies aiming to integrate MWEs in an SMT system. In section 5, we report and discuss the obtained results. We finally conclude and present our future work in section 6.

# 2 Related Work

In recent years, a number of techniques have been introduced to tackle the task of bilingual MWEs extraction from parallel corpora. Most works start by identifying monolingual MWE candidates then, apply different alignment methods to acquire bilingual correspondences. Monolingual extraction of MWEs techniques revolve around three approaches: (1) symbolic methods relying on morphosyntactic patterns (Okita et al., 2010; Dagan and Church, 1994); (2) statistical methods which use association measures to rank MWE candidates (Vintar and Fisier, 2008) and (3) Hybrid approaches combining (1) and (2) (Wu and Chang, 2004; Seretan and Wehrli, 2007; Daille, 2001; Boulaknadel et al., 2008). Each approach shows several limitations. It is, for example, difficult to apply symbolic methods to data without syntactic annotations. Furthermore, due to corpus size, statistical measures have mostly been applied to bigrams and trigrams, and it becomes more problematic to extract MWEs of more than three words. Concerning the alignment task, numerous approaches have already been introduced to deal with this issue. Some works make use of simple-word alignment tools (Dagan and Church, 1994; Lefever et al., 2009). Others rely on machine learning algorithms such as the *Expectation Maximisation (EM)* algorithm (Kupiec, 1993; Okita et al., 2010). In another direction, (Tufis and Ion, 2007; Seretan and Wehrli, 2007) introduce a linguistic approach in which they claim that MWEs keep in most cases the same morphosyntactic structure in the source and target language, which is not universal. For example the French MWE *"insulaire en développement"*, aligned with the English MWE *"small island developing"* do not share the same morphosyntactic structure.

Most of the methods described above aims at identifying MWEs in a corpus to construct or extend a bilingual lexicon without any application perspective. However, few works have focused on the extraction of bilingual MWEs lexicons in order to improve the performance of MT systems by reporting improved BLEU (Papineni et al., 2002) scores. This measure calculates the n-grams precision against a reference translation. In (Lambert and Banchs, 2005), authors introduce a method in which a bilingual MWEs lexicon was used to modify the word alignment in order to improve the translation quality. In their work, bilingual MWEs were grouped as one unique token before training alignment models. They showed on a small corpus, that both alignment quality and translation accuracy were improved. However, in a further study, a lower BLEU score is reported after grouping MWEs by part-of-speech on a large corpus (Lambert and Banchs, 2006). Some works have however focused on automatically learning translations of very specific MWEs categories, such as, for instance, idiomatic four character expressions in Chinese (Bai et al., 2009) or domain specific MWEs (Ren et al., 2009). (Carpuat and Diab, 2010) introduced a framework of two complementary integration strategies for monolingual MWEs in SMT. The first strategy segments training and test sentences according to the monolingual MWEs vocabulary of *Wordnet*. In the second strategy, they add a new MWE-based feature in SMT translation lexicons representing the number of MWEs in the source sentence. More recently, In (Bouamor et al., 2011), we proposed a method to enrich an SMT system's phrase table by a bilingual lexicon handling MWEs. On a small corpus (10*k* sentences), this method yeilds an improvement of 0.24 points in BLEU score. This study is an extention of the approach we presented in (Bouamor et al., 2011). We propose a method aiming to extract and align such units and study different strategies to integrate them into MOSES (Koehn, 2005), the state-of-the art SMT system.

## 3 Bilingual MWEs lexicon

In this section, we describe the approach we used to mine the bilingual lexicon of MWEs from a sentence aligned French-English parallel corpus. This approach is conducted in two steps. We first extract monolingual MWEs from each part of the parallel corpus. The second step consists in acquiring bilingual correspondences of MWEs.

| Pattern | English/ French MWEs |
|---|---|
| Adj-Noun | Plenary meeting / Libre circulation |
| Noun-Adj | ... / Parlement européen |
| Noun-Noun | Member state / Etat membre |
| Past_Participle -Noun | Developped country/ ... |
| Noun-Past_Participle | Parliament adopted/ Pays developpé |
| Adj-Adj-Noun | European public prosecutor /... |
| Adj-Noun-Adj | Social market economy / Bon conduite administratif |
| Adj-Noun-Noun | Renewable energy source / ... |
| Noun-Noun-Adj | ... / Industrie automobile allemand |
| Noun-Adj-Adj | ... / Ministère public européen |
| Adj-Noun-Adj | ... / Important débat politique |
| Noun-Prep-Noun | Point of view / Chemin de fer |
| Noun-Prep-Adj-Noun | Court of first instance/ Court de première instance |
| Noun-Prep-Noun-Adj | .../ Source d'énergie renouvelable |
| Adj-Noun-Prep-Noun | European court of justice/ ... |
| Noun-Adj-Prep-Noun | .../ Politique européen de concurrence |

Table 1: French and English MWE's morphosyntactic patterns

## 3.1 Monolingual Extraction of MWEs

The method we propose to identify monolingual MWEs in a text is based on a symbolic approach. This method is quite similar to the one used by (Okita et al., 2010). If they define patterns to handle only noun phrases, our approach takes into account both noun phrases, fixed expressions and named entities. Relatively simple, it does not use additional correlations statistics such as Mutual Information or Log Likelihood Ratio and attempts to find translations for all extracted MWEs (both highly and weakly correlated MWEs), to our knowledge, none of other approaches can make this claim. This method involves only a full morphosyntactic analysis of source and target texts. This morphosyntactic analysis is achieved using the CEA LIST Multilingual Analysis platform (LIMA) (Besançon et al., 2010) which produces a set of part of speech tagged normalized lemmas. Our algorithm operates on lemmas instead of surface forms which can draw on richer statistics and overcome the data sparseness problems. Since most MWEs consist of noun, adjectives and prepositions, we adopted a linguistic filter keeping only n-gram units ($2 \leq n \leq 4$) which match a list of 16 hand created morphosyntactic patterns. Such a process is used to keep only specific *strings* and filter out undesirable ones such as candidates composed mainly of stop words (*"of a, is a, that was"*). In Table 1 we give an example of MWE produced for each pattern. There exists extraction patterns (or configuration) for which no MWE has been generated (i.e. Noun-Adj).

Some of the fixed expressions such as (*in particular, in the light of, as regards...*) and named entities (*Midle East, South Africa, El-Salvador...*) recognized by the morphosyntactic analyzer are added to the candidate list. Then, all extracted MWEs are stored with their total frequency of occurrence. To avoid an over-generation of MWEs and remove irrelevant candidates from the process, a redundancy cleaning approach is introduced. In this approach, if a MWE is nested in another, and they both have the same frequency, we discard the smaller one. Otherwise we keep them both. Additionally, if a MWE occurs in a high number of longer terms, we discard all such longer terms.

| French | → | English |
|---|---|---|
| parlement européen | → | european parliament |
| état par état | → | amount of state |
| coup d'état | → | military coup |
| zone non fumeur | → | no smoking area |
| insulaire en développement | → | small island developing |
| de bonne foi | → | good faith |
| politique de concurrence | → | competition policy |
| chemin de fer | → | railway sector |
| en ce qui concerne | → | in regard to |
| en ce qui concerne | → | as regards |
| en ce qui concerne | → | with reference to |
| en ce qui concerne | → | with respect to |
| coupe forestier | → | cut in forestation |

Table 2: Sample of aligned MWEs

## 3.2 Bilingual Alignment

Bilingual alignment is achieved by a method which consists in finding for each MWE in a source language its adequate translation in the target language. Traditionally, this task was handled through the use of external linguistic resources such as bilingual dictionaries or simple-word alignment tools. We propose a *resource-independant* method which simply requires a parallel corpus and a list of input MWE candidates to translate. Our approach is based on aspects of distributional semantics (Harris, 1954), where a specific representation is associated to each expression (source and target). We associate to each MWE an $N$ sized vector, where $N$ is the number of sentences in the corpus, indicating whether or not it occurs in each sentence of the corpus. Our algorithm is based on the Vector Space Model (VSM). VSM (Salton et al., 1975) is a well-known algebraic model used in information retrieval, indexing and relevance ranking. This *vector space representation* will serve, eventually, as a basis to establish a translation relation between each pair of MWEs. To extract translation pairs of MWEs, we propose an iterative, greedy alignment algorithm which operates as follows:

1. Find the most frequent MWE $exp$ in each source sentence.
2. Extract all target translation candidates, occurring in all sentences parallel to those containing $exp$.
3. Compute a confidence value $V_{Conf}$ for each translation relation between $exp$ and each target translation candidate.
4. Consider that the target MWE maximizing $V_{Conf}$ is the best translation.
5. Discard the translation pair from the process and go back to 1.

The confidence value $V_{Conf}$ is computed on the basis of the *Jaccard Index* (1).

$$Jaccard = \frac{I_{st}}{V_s + V_t + I_{st}} \tag{1}$$

This measure is based on the number $I_{st}$ of sentences shared by each target and a source MWE. This is normalized by the sum of the number of sentences where the source and target MWEs appear independently of each other ($V_s$ and $V_t$) increased by $I_{st}$. In table 2, a sample of MWEs aligned by means of the algorithm described above.

From observing some pairs, we notice that our method presents several advantages: In order to find the adequate translation of a MWE and contrary to most previous works (Dagan and Church, 1994; Ren et al., 2009) using simple-word alignment tools to establish word-to-word alignment relations, our method captures the semantic equivalence between expressions such as *"insulaire en dévelopement"* and *"small island developing"* without any prior information about word alignment. It also permits the alignment of idioms such as *à nouveau* $\rightarrow$ *once more* or even *état par état* $\rightarrow$ *amount of state* and works for MWEs for which multiple correct target MWEs exist. For instance it captures that the *MWE "en ce qui concerne"* could be translated by *"in regard to", "with reference to", "with respect to"* and even by *"as regards"*.

## 4 Integration strategies

In the previous section, we described the approach we followed to mine the bilingual lexicon of MWEs. In order to assess the lexicon's quality, we carried out in a previous work (Bouamor et al., 2011) an intrinsic evaluation in which we compared the obtained pairs of bilingual MWEs to a manual alignment reference. On a small set of 100 French-English parallel sentences derived from the Europarl corpus, our approach yielded a precision of 63, 93% , a recall of 62, 46% and an F-measure of 63, 19%. As it lacks a common benchmark data set for evaluation in MWE extraction and alignment researches, we carry out an extrinsic evaluation based on an SMT application and use MOSES (Koehn, 2005) as our BASELINE system. However, as we mentioned in section 1, the difficulty lies in how to integrate MWEs into such systems. To do so, we propose three dynamic integration strategies in which the translation model is amended in severals ways, and a static integration strategy in which we plug MWEs into the decoder without changing the model. We compare their performance in section 5.

### 4.1 Dynamic integration strategies

#### 4.1.1 New Translation model with MWEs

Phrase tables are the main knowledge source for the machine translation decoder. The decoder consults these tables to figure out how to translate an input candidate in a source language into the target one. However, due to the errors in automatic word alignment, extracted phrases might be meaningless. To alleviate this problem, we add the extracted bilingual MWE as a parallel corpus and retrain the translation model. In this method (TRAIN), we expect that by increasing the occurrences of bilingual MWEs, considered as good phrases, a modification of the alignment and the translation probability will be noticed.

#### 4.1.2 Extention of the phrase table

In this method, we attempt to extend the BASELINE system's phrase table by integrating the found bilingual MWEs candidates. We use the Jaccard Index (proposed for each pair of MWEs) to define the translation probabilities in the two directions and set the lexical probabilities to 1 for simplicity. So, for each phrase in a given input sentence, the decoder will take into account bilingual MWEs when searching for all candidate translation phrases. This method is denoted TABLE in the remaining part of this paper.

### 4.1.3 New feature for MWEs

(Lopez and Resnik, 2006) pointed out that better feature mining can lead to substantial gain in translation quality. We followed this claim and extended TABLE by adding a new feature indicating whether a phrase is a MWE or not. The aim of this method (FEAT) is to guide the system to choose bilingual MWEs returned by our aligner instead of the BASELINE's system phrases.

## 4.2 Static Integration strategy

In this method, noted FORCED, we want to bring the bilingual MWEs lexicon to the decoder without changing the translation model. For this claim, we used the *forced decoding mode* of the Moses system. The decoder has an *XML markup scheme* that allows the specification of translations for parts of the sentence. In its simplest form, we can indicate to the decoder what to use to translate certain words or phrases in the sentence. So we represented each MWE occuring in the test set by its adequate XML markup scheme, using the translation pair of the lexicon. Bclow is an example of representing the MWE *à nouveau* in the test set.

. . . sembler être **à nouveau** mis en accusation, le ministère public . . .

⇓

. . . sembler être < ***mwe* translation=*"once more"*** >**à nouveau**< /***mwe***> mis en accusation, le ministère public . . .

# 5 Experiments

## 5.1 Data and tools

We used the French-English Europarl (Koehn, 2005) corpus of parliamentary debates as a source of the parallel corpus. To train the BASELINE system's translation model, we extracted 100000 pairs of sentences from the corpus. First, we tokenized, cleaned up the training corpus and kept only sentences containing at most 50 words. We mined the bilingual lexicon of MWEs from the same training corpus. Because the lexicon contains only lemmas of MWEs and the forced decoding mode of Moses is not currently compatible with factored models, the translation model was trained on lemmas instead of their surface forms. Training data were annotated with lemmas by means of the TreeTagger Toolkit[1]. Next, word-alignment for all the sentences in the parallel training corpus is established and uses the same methodology as in phrase-based models (symmetrized GIZA++ alignments) to create the phrase table. We also specified a language model using the IRST Language Modeling Toolkit [2] to train a lemma based tri-gram model on the total size of the Europarl corpus (1.8*M* sentences). Afterwards, we applied the above-described integration strategies.

The features used in the BASELINE system include: (1) four translation probability features, (2) one language model and (3) word penalty. For the "TRAIN" method, bilingual MWEs are added into the training corpus, as results, new alignments and phrase table are obtained. For the "TABLE" method, bilingual units are incorporated into the BASELINE system's phrase table. In "FEAT", an additional 1/0 feature is introduced for each entry of the phrase table. Concerning the FORCED method, it keeps the same models as BASELINE. Afterwards, the obtained models

[1]http://www.ims.uni-stuttgart.de/projekte/corplex/TreeTagger/

[2]http://hlt.fbk.eu/en/irstlm

| Method | BLEU | | TER | |
|---|---|---|---|---|
| | *All_Test* | *MWEs_Test* | *All_Test* | *MWEs_Test* |
| BASELINE | 28.85 | 30.83 | 55.44 | 53.59 |
| ***Dynamic*** | | | | |
| TRAIN | **28.87** | **31.06** | **55.38** | **53.32** |
| TABLE | 28.82 | **30.88** | **55.42** | **53.46** |
| FEAT | **28.95** | **31.06** | 55.48 | **53.56** |
| ***Static*** | | | | |
| FORCED | 28.20 | 29.19 | 56.01 | 55.05 |

Table 3: Translation results in term of BLEU and TER

were tuned by Minimum Error Rate Training (Och, 2003) on a development set of 4000 pairs of sentences.

## 5.2 Results and discussion

We conducted two test experiments: *All_Test* and *MWEs_Test*. For this, we *randomly* extracted 1000 parallel sentences from the corpus described above to construct the *All_Test* test corpus. In order to measure the real contribution of bilingual MWEs handled by different translation models, we constituted the *MWEs_Test* corpus, in which we kept only sentences of the *All_Test* corpus containing at least one MWE of the lexicon. This corpus contains 323 pairs of sentences. We evaluate the translation quality of the described dynamic and static strategies on the two test sets with respect to BLEU (Papineni et al., 2002) score, which is based on *n-gram* precision, and Translation Error Rate (TER) (Snover et al., 2006), which generalizes edit distance beyond single-word edits. For this evaluation, we consider one reference per sentence. Table 3 reports the obtained results.

The first substantial observation, as can be seen, is related to the BLEU scores which vary according to the test set type. Concerning the *All_test* corpus, the best improvement is achieved by the FEAT dynamic strategy, in which we add a new feature indicating wether a phrase in the phrase table is a MWE or not. Compared to the BASELINE, this method reports a gain of +0.1 point in BLEU score. The first translation example in Table 4 points out the contribution of the introduced feature to the performance of the translation approach. Contrary to the BASELINE system, which translates the unit *"initiative communautaire"* as simply *"initiative"*, the FEAT strategy adequately translates both the MWE *"initiative communautaire"*→*"community initiative"* and its immediate right context(*"for africa"*). Lower BLEU scores are achieved by TABLE and FORCED wrt. the BASELINE system. For the *MWEs_Test* corpus, which considers only sentences containing MWEs of the lexicon, we notice that all dynamic integration strategies report increased BLEU scores compared to the BASELINE and the static integration strategy (FORCED). The FEAT and TRAIN methods achieve a gain of +0.23 BLEU points over the BASELINE system. The TABLE strategy comes next with a slighly improved BLEU score showing a gain of +0.05 BLEU points. However, the FORCED static strategy reports lower scores on both *All_Test* and *MWEs_Test* test corpora. This can certainly be explained as follows: while forcing the decoder to translate a MWE with a given MWE candidate, even if it is a good translation, it fails to adequately translate the immediate left or right context of the MWEs which consequently lowers the BLEU score. For example, in the second example of Table 4, both systems suggest a correct translation for the MWE *"aide international"* but FORCED fails to adequately translate the

| | |
|---|---|
| SOURCE SENTENCE | je entendre en effet lancer un initiative communautaire pour le afrique en étendre le ligne nepad ... |
| REFERENCE | indeed , i intend to launch a *community initiative* **for africa** , develop the nepad line... |
| BASELINE | i hear be indeed launch an *initiative* **for the eu africa** by extend the nepad line ... |
| FEAT | i hear in fact launch a *community initiative* **for africa** by extend the nepad line ... |
| SOURCE SENTENCE | le deuxième groupe de problème relever de le aide international et du prochain engagement de johannesburg. |
| REFERENCE | another series of problem **mention be a matter of** *international aid* and the forthcoming johannesburg summit. |
| BASELINE | the second group of the problem **be a matter of** *international aid* and the forthcoming johannesburg commitment. |
| FORCED | the second group of the problem **relate to the** *international aid* and the forthcoming johannesburg commitment. |

Table 4: Translation examples. Note that the text is lemmatized. We underline MWEs and put in bold different suggestion of immediate left or right context.

| Method | *p-value* (95%*CI*) | |
|---|---|---|
| | *All_Test* | *MWE_Test* |
| BASELINE | - | - |
| TRAIN | 0.1 | 0.05 |
| TABLE | - | 0.3 |
| FEAT | 0.01 | 0.01 |

Table 5: Statistical significance test of BLEU improvements in term of *p-value*

phrase *"relever de"*. It is important to note that this translation could be supported if we have for each source sentence multiple references. In an earlier study, (Ren et al., 2009) proposed a strategy quite similar to the FEAT method in which they indicate for each entry in the phrase table wether a phrase contains a *domain specific bilingual* MWE. For the medical domain, their method gained +0.17 of BLEU score compared to the baseline system, a lower improvement than the one reported by the FEAT method. The question that arises based on these different results is: Is it possible to claim that the system having the best score is the best one? In other words, are the obtained results for the different experimental settings statistically significant?

In order to assess statistical significance of previously obtained test results, we use the *paired bootstrap resampling* method (Koehn, 2004). This method estimates the probability (*p-value*) that a measured difference in BLEU scores arose by chance by repeatedly (10 times) creating new virtual test sets by drawing sentences with replacement from a given collection of translated sentences. If there is no significant difference between the systems (*i.e., the null hypothesis is true*), then this shuffling should not change the computed metric score. We carry out experiments using this method to compare each of the methods TRAIN, TABLE and FEAT, yielding improvements in BLEU scores (Table 3) over the BASELINE system on the two test set results *All_Test* and *MWE_Test*.

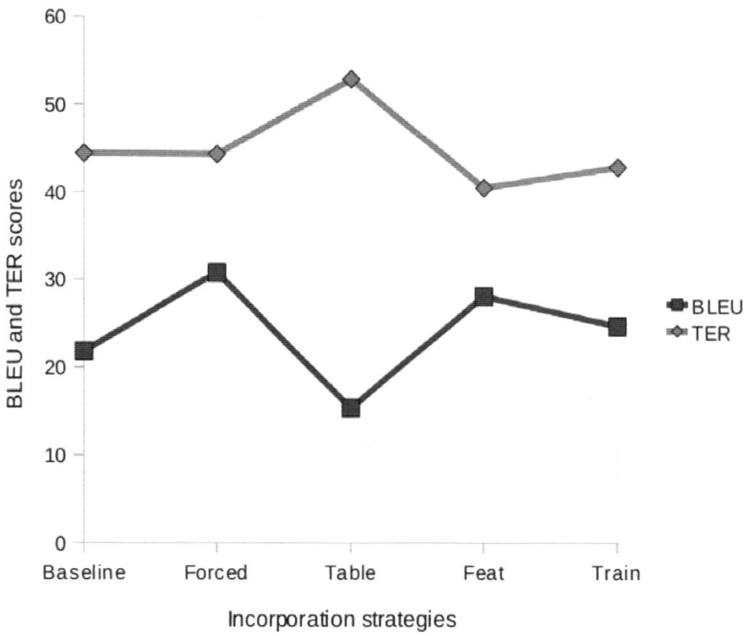


Figure 1: Lexical evaluation of MWEs in term of BLEU and TER

Table 5 displays reported *p-values* at the edge of the 95% *confidence interval* (CI). As can be observed, the results vary from insignificant (at $p > 0.05$) to highly significant. On both test set results, we notice that improvements achieved by the FEAT integration startegy are statistically significant. However, the small improvement of BLEU score yielded by the TABLE method (having a $p$-value of 0.3) is non significant. The reason being that we used the *Jaccard Index*, a measure defined for comparing similarity and diversity of sample sets, to define a translation probability. This could be adjusted by transforming obtained Jaccard Index for each pair of MWE to a translation probability in order to ensure the uniformity and consistency of translation probabilities in the phrase table.

The BLEU metric reports only global improvements and does not show significant differences that can be revealed by human evaluation. This observation motivated us to set up a fine-grained *lexical evaluation* of MWEs in the *MWEs_test* corpus. We kept only MWEs on the test corpus and manually created the gold standard from the reference. We translated the new test corpus according to dynamic and static integration strategies and computed BLEU and TER scores. Figure 1 illustrates obtained results. As one can note, a gain of almost +9.8 BLEU, −0.2 TER points are achieved by the FORCED strategy. This confirms that the worsening of BLEU scores in previous experiments are not affected by the quality of the bilingual MWEs lexicon. We notice also that both TRAIN and FEAT strategies report higher scores (respectively 24.67 and 28.06 points BLEU) compared to the BASELINE which comes with 21.84 points BLEU.

## 6 Conclusion

We proposed in this paper a hybrid approach to identify and find bilingual MWEs correspondences in a French-English parallel corpus. The alignment algorithm we propose works only on many to many correspondences and deals with highly and weakly correlated MWEs in a given sentence pair. In order to assess the lexicon's quality, we investigated the performance of three dynamic strategies and of one static strategy to integrate the mined bilingual MWE lexicon in the MOSES SMT system. We showed that the FEAT method, in which we add a new feature indicating whether a phrase is a MWE or not, brings a small but statistically significant improvement to the translation quality of the test sets. We also introduced a lexical evaluation of MWEs units based on the measure of BLEU score.

Although our initial experiments are positive, we believe that they can be improved in a number of ways. We first plan to set up a large scale evaluation by enlarging the size of the training corpus. In all experiments, we trained a translation model on lemmas instead of surface forms. We will make use of a generation model to generate adequate surface forms from lemmas. In addition to their application in a phrase based SMT system, we plan to evaluate the impact of the mined lexicon on the relevance of a cross-language search engine results. We also expect to extract such textual units from more available but less parallel data sources: *comparable corpora*.

## References


Bai, M., Y., J.-M., C., K.-J., and Chang, J. S. (2009). Acquiring translation equivalences of multiword expressions by normalized correlation frequencies. In *Proceedings of EMNLP*.

Besançon, R., De Chalendar, G., Ferret, O., Gara, F., Laib, M., Mesnard, O., and Semmar, N. (2010). Lima: A multilingual framework for linguistic analysis and linguistic resources development and evaluation. In *Proceedings of LREC*, Malta.

Bouamor, D., Semmar, N., and Zweigenbaum, P. (2011). Improved statistical machine translation using multi-word expressions. In *Proceedings of MT-LIHMT*, Barcelona, Spain.

Boulaknadel, S., Daille, B., and Driss, A. (2008). A multi-term extraction program for arabic language. In *Proceedings of LREC*, Marrakech, Morocco.

Carpuat, M. and Diab, M. (2010). Task-based evaluation of multiword expressions:a pilot study in statistical machine translation. In *Proceedings of HLT-NAACL*.

Constant, M., Tellier, I., Duchier, D., Dupont, Y., Sigogne, A., Billot, S., et al. (2011). Intégrer des connaissances linguistiques dans un crf: application à l'apprentissage d'un segmenteur-étiqueteur du français. In *Actes de TALN*, Montpellier, France.

Dagan, I. and Church, K. (1994). Termight: Identifying and translating technical terminology. In *Proceedings of the 4th Conference on ANLP*, pages 34–40, Stuttgart, Germany.

Daille, B. (2001). Extraction de collocation à partir de textes. In Maurel, D., editor, *Actes de TALN 2001 (Traitement automatique des langues naturelles)*, Tours. ATALA, Université de Tours.

Harris, Z. (1954). Distributional structure. *Word*.

Jackendoff, R. (1997). The architecture of the language faculty. *MIT Press*.

Koehn, P. (2004). Statistical significance tests for machine translation evaluation. In *Proceedings of EMNLP*.

Koehn, P. (2005). Europarl: A parallel corpus for statistical machine translation. In *Proceedings of MT-SUMMIT*.

Koehn, P., Och, F., and Marcu, D. (2003). Statistical phrase-based translation. In *Proceedings of the Human Language Technology Conference of the North American Chapter of the Association for Computational Linguistics*, pages 115–124, Edmonton, Canada.

Kupiec, J. (1993). An algorithm for finding noun phrases correspondences in bilingual corpora. In *Proceedings of the 31st annual Meeting of the Association for Computational Linguistics*, pages 17–22, Columbus, Ohio, USA.

Lambert, P. and Banchs, R. (2005). Data inferred multi-word expressions for statistical machine translation. In *Proceedings of MT SUMMIT*.

Lambert, P. and Banchs, R. (2006). Grouping multi-word expressions according to part-of-speech in statistical machine translation. In *Proceedings of the Workshop on Multi-word Expressions in a multilingual context*.

Lefever, E., Macken, L., and Hoste, V. (2009). Language-independent bilingual terminology extraction from a multilingual parallel corpus. In *Proceedings of the 12th Conference of the European Chapter of the ACL (EACL 2009)*, pages 496–504, Athens, Greece. Association for Computational Linguistics.

Lopez, A. and Resnik, P. (2006). Word-based alignment, phrase based translation:what's the link? In *Proceedings of the association for machine translation in the Americas: visions for the future of machine translation*, pages 90–99.

Luka, N., Seretan, V., and Wehrli, E. (2006). Le problème de collocation en tal. In *Nouveaux cahiers de linguistiques Française*, pages 95–115.

Och, F. (2003). Minimum error rate training in statistical machine translation. In *Proceedings of ACL*.

Okita, T., Guerra, M., Alfredo Graham, Y., and Way, A. (2010). Multi-word expression sensitive word alignment. In *Proceedings of the 4th International Workshop on Cross Lingual Information Access at COLING 2010*, pages 26–34, Beijing.

Papineni, k., Roukos, S., Ward, T., and Zhu, W. J. (2002). Bleu: a method for automatic evaluation of machine translation. In *40th Annual meeting of the Association for Computational Linguistics*.

Ren, Z., Lu, Y., Liu, Q., and Huang, Y. (2009). Improving statistical machine translation using domain bilingual multiword expressions. In *Proceedings of the Workshop on Multiword Expressions : Identification, Interpretation, Disambiguation and Applications*, pages 47–57.

Sag, I., Baldwin, T., Francis Bond, F., Copestake, A., and Flickinger, D. (2002). Multiword expressions:a pain in the neck for nlp. In *CICLing 2002*, Mexico City, Mexico.

Sagot, B., Clément, L., De La Clergerie, É., Boullier, P., et al. (2005). Vers un méta-lexique pour le français: architecture, acquisition, utilisation. In *Actes de TALN*.

Salton, G., Wong, A., and Yang, C. (1975). A vector space model for automatic indexing. In *Communications of the ACM*, pages 61–620.

Seretan, V. and Wehrli, E. (2007). Collocation translation based on sentence alignment and parsing. In Benarmara, F., Hatout, N., Muller, P., and Ozdowska, S., editors, *Actes de TALN 2007 (Traitement automatique des langues naturelles)*, Toulouse. ATALA, IRIT.

Snover, M., Dorr, B., Schwartz, R., Micciulla, L., and Makhoul, J. (2006). A study of translation edit rate with targeted human annotation. In *Proceedings of Association for Machine Translation in the Americas*.

Tufis, I. and Ion, R. (2007). Parallel corpora, alignment technologies and further prospects in multilingual resources and technology infrastructure. In *Proceedings of the 4th International Conference on Speech and Dialogue Systems*, pages 183–195.

Vintar, S. and Fisier, D. (2008). Harvesting multi-word expressions from parallel corpora. In *Proceedings of LREC*, Marrakech, Morocco.

Wu, C. and Chang, S. J. (2004). Bilingual collocation extraction based on syntactic and statistical analyses. In *Computational Linguistics*, pages 1–20.

# Hand-Crafting a Lexical Network With a Knowledge-Based Graph Editor

Nabil GADER[1] Veronika LUX-POGODALLA[2] Alain POLGUÈRE[3]
(1) MVS Publishing Solutions, Sainte-Marguerite, F-88100, FRANCE
(2) CNRS, ATILF, UMR 7118, Nancy, F-54063, FRANCE
(3) Université de Lorraine, ATILF, UMR 7118, Nancy, F-54000, FRANCE
Nabil.Gader@mvs.fr, Veronika.Lux@atilf.fr,
Alain.Polguere@univ-lorraine.fr

ABSTRACT
We present the data structure of a lexical resource—the French Lexical Network (FLN)—, that is being hand-crafted using a knowledge-based lexicographic editor. The FLN is formally a lexical graph whose structuring is mainly supported by the system of paradigmatic and syntagmatic lexical functions of the Meaning-Text linguistic approach. Section 1 offers a general characterization of the FLN. Section 2 describes the database and the lexicographic editor in their present state. Section 3 focuses on the SQL data structure used to encode lexical information in the FLN, with special attention paid to the encoding of lexical function relations. Section 4 considers the feasibility of porting the FLN data to known standards such as the Lexical Markup Framework (LMF). Finally, in section 5, we consider the cognitive relevance of the FLN approach to the modeling of lexicons.

KEYWORDS: lexical database, lexical graph, virtual dictionary, semantic derivation, collocation, lexical function, Explanatory Combinatorial Lexicology/Lexicography, lexicographic editor, French language.

## Introduction

The *French Lexical Network*, hereafter FLN,[1] is a new hand-crafted lexical resource, currently under development, that possesses many distinguishing features, both in terms of content, structure and building process. In this paper, we focus on the FLN's data structure and on the graph editor that has been designed to support the lexicographic task of building the FLN. This work is currently performed at the ATILF CNRS laboratory (Nancy, France) in the context of a broader R&D project called *RELIEF* (Lux-Pogodalla and Polguère, 2011). Though the process of building the FLN is a long-term enterprise and we are at the time of writing only 18 months into this project, the resource's structure is already sufficiently stable, and the resource itself is sufficiently well into development, for us to be able to account for our first results. We believe that the approach taken in designing the FLN is particularly relevant for the linguistics, NLP and cognitive science communities due to (i) its formal nature, (ii) its strong theoretical linguistic background and (iii) its fundamental semantic orientation. All points that will be made clearer below.

[1]In French: *Réseau Lexical du Français* or *RLF*.

## 1 General characterization of the French Lexical Network (FLN)

The FLN belongs to the family of Net-like lexical databases (Fellbaum, 1998; Baker et al., 2003; Ruppenhofer et al., 2010; Spohr, 2012) and possesses at least four distinguishing characteristics.

1. The FLN is a lexical network—i.e., a network of interconnected lexical units—whose structure is mainly organized around a constantly growing set of lexical links, based on the system of so-called *lexical functions* proposed by the Meaning-Text linguistic theory.[2]

2. Though manually performed, the construction of the FLN is done by means and "under the supervision" of a tailor-made lexicographic editor named *Dicet*—developed by MVS Publishing Solutions (Sainte-Marguerite, France)[3]—that allows lexicographers to browse through the lexical network and directly expand and revise it, using linguistic and metalinguistic information. Dicet can therefore be best conceived of as being a knowledge-based lexical graph editor and browser.

3. Lexical information stored in the FLN is entirely formalized, thus allowing for computer processing of the lexical network, for both lexicographic purposes (automatic coherence checking, implementation of analogical lexicographic reasoning, etc.) and natural language processing.

4. Though not a dictionary—it doesn't possess the textual structure of a paper or computerized dictionary—the FLN is designed to have embedded in it sufficient lexicographic information (both in formal and "popularized" form) to be used to automatically generate dictionaries of multiple formats. It is thus the repository of *virtual dictionaries* (Atkins, 1996; Selva et al., 2003; Polguère, 2012a).

This last characteristic is particularly important as it explains why the construction of the FLN is indeed a true lexicographic project. Ultimately, the FLN is meant to be a multi-purpose lexical resource, that should allow for the automatic generation of (i) dictionaries with various macro- and microstructures targetting human users, and (ii) formalized resources for NLP. The fact that computer programs should be able to make use of the FLN sets the target in terms of formalization and "computability." On the other hand, the targeting of a content that is dictionary-grade and suitable for human users—language learners being the prototypical users—sets very high standards in terms of accuracy. This rules out any strategy of automatically compiling the FLN out of already existing linguistic resources such as electronic dictionaries, corpora, etc. (Sagot and Fišer, 2011). The process of building the FLN has to be a full-fledged lexicographic one and involves an organized team of lexicographers.[4]

## 2 Present state of the lexical graph and lexicographic editor

Let us first mention that, according to our terminology, a *lexical entry* in the FLN corresponds to a (potentially) polysemic word, called *vocable*. We name *lexical unit* each well-specified sense of the vocables that constitute the FLN's wordlist. For instance, the French vocable CHANTAGE

[2] See (Milićević, 2006) for a short introduction to the Meaning-Text approach to language study.

[3] MVS is ATILF's private sector partner in the RELIEF project, that has a significant R&D facet. RELIEF targets both the construction of the FLN and its utilization in natural language processing tasks such as fine-grained semantic access to textual information.

[4] At present, 12 members of the team are directly involved in lexicographic tasks.

'blackmail' comprises two senses—i.e. lexical units—in the current state of the FLN: CHANTAGE **I** 'criminal act' and CHANTAGE **II** 'pressure (put on someone).'

Each lexical unit possesses a unique ID (identifier) in the FLN's database. Such is the case for each vocable, the belonging of lexical units to given vocables being modeled as relations between vocable and lexical unit IDs.

Links between lexical units are also implemented as links between lexical unit IDs. This is true in particular for links based on so-called *lexical functions* of the Meaning-Text linguistic approach (Mel'čuk, 1996), that form the bulk of the FLN's structure. For instance, let us return to the case of Fr. CHANTAGE **I**, whose predicative structure is 'blackmail by \$1 on \$2 regarding \$3 to obtain \$4.'[5] The fact that Fr. CIBLE **II.2** 'target' and VICTIME **II** 'victim' are typical names for the second actant (\$2) of CHANTAGE **I** is modeled by the following *lexical function application*, where $\mathbf{S}_2$ is the paradigmatic lexical function that returns typical names for the second actant of a predicative lexical unit:

$\mathbf{S}_2$( *chantage* **I** ) = *cible* **II.2** [*de* ART ~], *victime* **II** [*de* ART ~]

Such lexicographic information about CHANTAGE **I** is structured in the FLN by means of the following lexical subgraph:

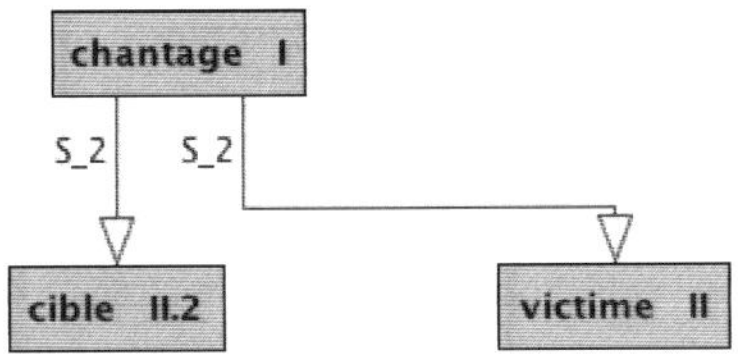


Figure 1: Structure of $\mathbf{S}_2$( *chantage* **I** ) in the FLN

Paradigmatic lexical functions, such as $\mathbf{S}_2$, correspond to semantic relations between lexical units called *semantic derivations* in Meaning-Text linguistics terminology. However, there exist also syntagmatic lexical functions, that correspond to collocational links between lexical units. For instance, the fact that the verbs Fr. CÉDER **IV.1** lit. 'to give in [to someone]', OBÉIR **3** lit. 'to obey' and OBTEMPÉRER lit. 'to comply' are used as collocates of their complement CHANTAGE **I** to express '\$2 does what he/she is expected (by \$1) to do in respect to \$1's blackmail,' is modeled by the following lexical function application, where $\mathbf{Real}_2$ is the syntagmatic lexical function that returns "verbs of realization" that take the second actant of a predicative noun as subject and the noun itself as first complement:

$\mathbf{Real}_2$( *chantage* **I** ) = *céder* **IV.1** [*à* ART ~], *obéir* **3** [*à* ART ~], *obtempérer* [*à* ART ~]

In total, the set of lexical function links that gravitates around a given lexical unit can be quite significant. This is illustrated in Figure 2 below, that displays all lexical function links of which

[5] \$1, \$2, \$3,... are local variables (in the computational sense) that function locally in each individual lexical unit description. They ensure the proper numbering and naming of actant slots and are used in place of the traditional $X$, $Y$, Z, ... variables.

CHANTAGE I is currently the source or the target.[6] Notice that this lexical unit represents a mild case in terms of lexical function connections: many links leaving from and leading to CHANTAGE I are yet to be encoded and it is easy to find lexical units that are much bigger "lexical crossroads" than this particular one.

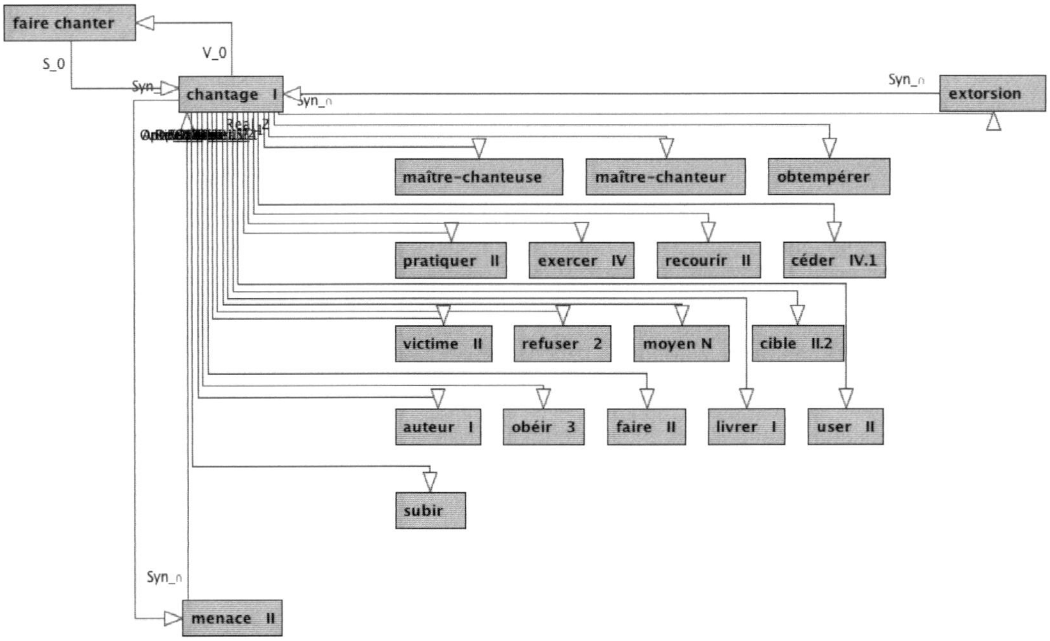


Figure 2: All lexical function links leaving from or leading to CHANTAGE I in the FLN

As one can see, the bulk of the FLN's informational content and structuring lies in the set of lexical units (grouped under given polysemic vocables) and the set of lexical function links that connect lexical units together. Based on the formal characteristics of the resource, the best way to evaluate the FLN's state of development is to count:

1. the number of lexical entities—mainly, vocables ($V$) and lexical units ($LU$)—it contains, such as for standard dictionaries where the number of entries and senses are often used as coverage measurement;
2. the polysemy rate ($LU/V$), that tells us how many lexical units (senses), in average, are grouped under each vocable;
3. the number of lexical function links ($LFL$) between lexical units;
4. the connectivity rate $LFL/LU$, that tells us how many lexical function (in or out) links are connecting, in average, a lexical unit to the rest of the FLN graph.[7]

[6]For lack of space we are forced to select a display that doesn't allow for the legibility of all arc labels. All lexical graphs used here have been automatically generated from the FLN database and displayed by means of the yEd graph editor (http://www.yworks.com/en/products_yed_about.html).

[7]Expressed in mathematical terms (graph theory), the connectivity rate is the average degree of lexical nodes in the FLN graph whose edges are lexical function relations.

Here are the statistics at the time of writing:

| | |
|---|---|
| Vocables, i.e. entries $[= V]$ | : 10363 |
| Lexical units, i.e. senses $[= LU]$ | : 13767 |
| Polysemy rate $[= LU/V]$ | : 1.33 |
| Lexical function links $LU_1 \rightarrow LU_2$ $[= LFL]$ | : 17353 |
| Connectivity rate $[= LFL/LU]$ | : 1.26 |

As the first two numbers show, the FLN is already far from being a sample or prototype of a lexical resource in regard to how many entries and senses it contains. In actual fact, we do consider that we have already reached our target in the RELIEF project in terms of wordlist size. We initially estimated the minimal number of entries to be around 10,000, with no fixed upper limit. However, adding an entry to the RLF wordlist is not a difficult task once a core wordlist for French has been identified. What matters from now on is the growth of information that is to be attached to each vocable: identification of its polysemy through creation of senses associated to it and description of linguistic properties of each senses—essentially, through weaving of lexical function links.

The polysemy rate is a particularly good indicator of how advanced the description of each vocable is. Each time a vocable is actually studied and described, its sense structure is analyzed and described by adding new senses to the database. A good polysemy rate for a fully mature database would be between 2.5 and 3. For the sake of comparison, the French *Petit Robert* reference dictionary—a very detailed dictionary in respect to the polysemic structuring of entries—possesses a polysemy rate of 5. The rate of 1.33 that we currently achieve indicates that the FLN has not reach its full maturity yet, but is already an "adolescent" lexical database on its way to adulthood.

> Let us emphasize the fact that statistics given here are based on the complete database, not on lexical units that have actually been methodically studied. All rates are therefore "diluted" by the mass of targeted units that are participating in holding the graph together but are still unexplored locations in the global RLF topography.

Together with the polysemy rate, the connectivity rate is an important indicator of how fleshy and informative each entry is. Figure 3 below indicates the evolution of statistics on connectivity since the moment the hardcoding of lexical function relations has been launched.

Notice that, at the moment of its birth, the FLN was nothing but a "fully non-connected" graph: a set of individual nodes (lexical units) with no lexical connection to other nodes. This initial set of 3,734 nodes was automatically injected into the RLF database from a manually constructed *priming wordlist*—see (Lux-Pogodalla and Polguère, 2011; Polguère and Sikora, ToAp) for details on the FLN's growth process.

As for the FLN microstructure, lexical units—*headwords*—articles are made up of seven lexicographic zones:

1. `GC` for grammatical characteristics (part of speech, noun gender, specific inflectional behavior, etc.);
2. `DF` for definition;

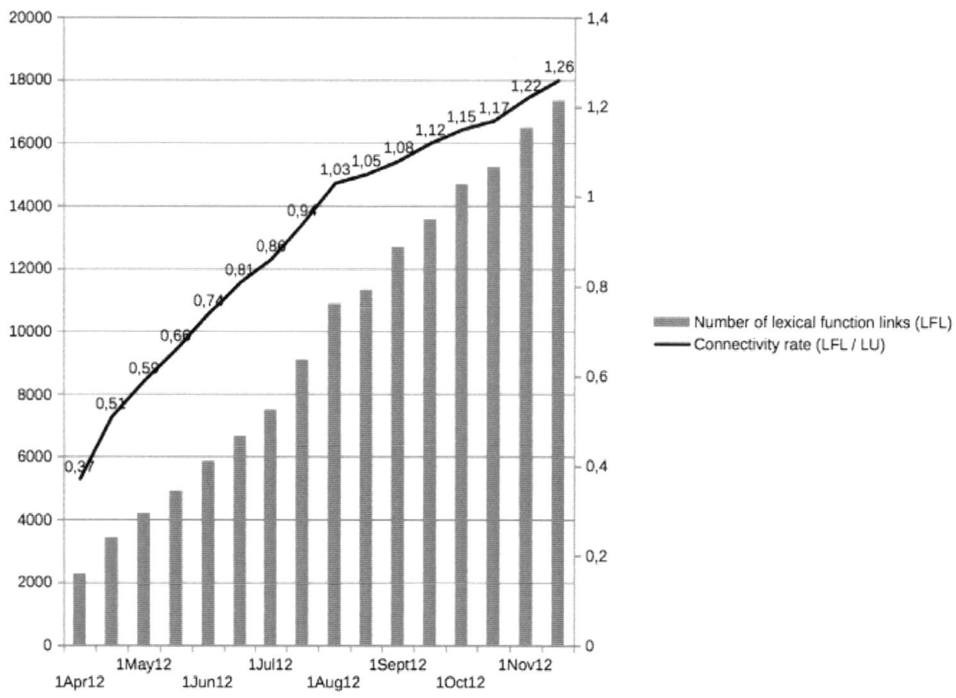


Figure 3: Evolution of lexical connectivity in the FLN

3. `NB` for *Nota Bene* about the headword description;
4. `GP` for the headword's government pattern, i.e. the description of its syntactic valency (Mel'čuk, 2004a,b; Milićević, 2009);
5. `LF` for lexical function relations originating from the headword (headword as argument of lexical function applications);
6. `EX` for lexicographic exemples;
7. `PH` for pointers to so-called *full phrasemes*, i.e. idioms, that are formally made up of a lexemic headword—e.g. BULLET points to BITE THE BULLET.

All lexicographic zones are currently being dealt with by lexicographers. However, only the `GC` (grammatical characteristics) and `LF` (lexical functions) zones are fully formalized and supervised by the Dicet editor at the time of writing. The other zones are for the time being completed as simple text fields and the `EX` (lexicographic examples) zone is presently under formalization and about to be completed at the time of writing.

By saying that a given zone is supervised by the Dicet editor, we mean that:

- Dicet possesses knowledge about the information that has to be provided in the zone;
- embedded in Dicet, are special lexicographic tools that allow for the entering of information under complete supervision of the editor.

In this approach to lexicography, lexicographers do not *write* articles; rather, they *build* them by putting together all microscopic lexical rules that are associated with each lexical unit. The encoded information is used by the editor for computing a textual presentation in what is called an *article-view* of the headword's description. At no time does the lexicographer type a lexicographic text in an implemented zone (except in its `Comments` field). Figure 4 below shows an association between the sub-window of the `LF` zone that is used to pull lexical function links from the headword—at the bottom, right above the `Comments` zone—and the corresponding article-view—on top—that displays the encoded information in textual (dictionary-like) form. The headword used in this figure is CHANTAGE **I**, whose position in a lexical function subgraph of the FLN has been described above (see Figure 2).

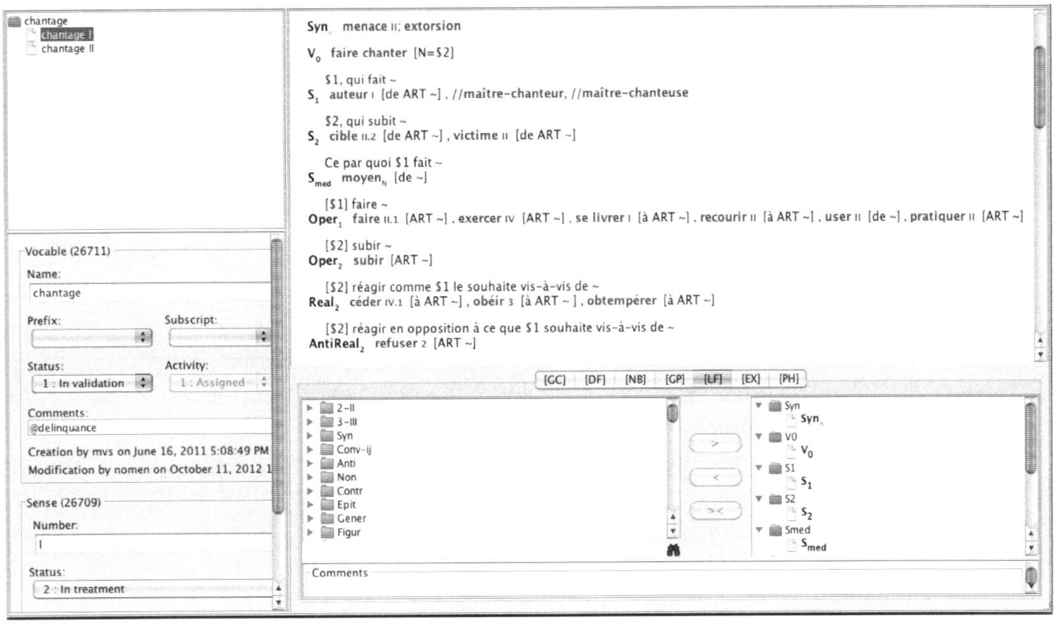


Figure 4: Correspondance between lexical function lexicographic tools and the article-view

Names of targets of lexical function links in the article-view are clickable textual items that give direct access to the edition of the corresponding lexical units (opening of new editing windows). For lack of space, we cannot delve further into the functioning of the Dicet editor. But we will have the opportunity to provide more information on its functionalities when presenting the FLN's computational model (next section).

The designing and programming of the Dicet editor represents a significant investment in terms of time and effort; before undertaking it, we reviewed existing softwares without being able to find anything that came close to what we were looking for: a lexicographic editor supporting graph weaving of lexical function links. It is also important to highlight the fact that Dicet was not built from scratch. It is a customization of resources that were already available from the MVS partner of the project, among its publishing solutions: primarily, the *Dixit* publishing tool.[8] Dicet is indeed a lexicographically-boosted knowledge-based version of Dixit, recoded in Java for portability purposes. Dicet is also part of a suite integrating workflow, user rights

[8] `http://www.mvs.fr/pdf/MVS_Dixit.pdf`

management and controlled connection to an SQL database, while most existing lexicographic editors seem to work on XML databases— for example, IDM DPS (Lannoy, 2010) and the Dictionary Editor and Browser (DEB) (Horák et al., 2006).

In spite of its distinctive features, Dicet shares features with tools such as TLex (Joffe and de Schryver, 2012) or the above-mentioned DEB. In particular, just as TLex supports "smart cross-references" (Joffe and de Schryver, 2012, pp. 25–27 and pp. 68–69), Dicet allows easy creation and maintenance of links between lexical units, a major concern given our lexicographic model. However, beyond lexicographic editing, Dicet was designed to support a completely new approach to building lexical resources. Because we developed our own tool, we were totally free to explore and implement new ways of performing lexicographic activity (cf. section 5 below).

## 3 Data model: a relational SQL database

The FLN's data model is an SQL database which, at the time of writing, comprises 46 separate SQL tables; presenting all of them here is of course out of the question. As very limited space is available to us, we will concentrate on lexical functions. Notice that a significant number of publications on formal and computational modeling of lexical functions are already available, for instance (Kahane and Polguère, 2001; Iordanskaja et al., 1992; Lareau et al., 2012); we will consider solely the FLN's approach to the problem.

In total, 16 SQL tables are used in the FLN's database for the storage of lexical function-related information. Part of these tables are used for modeling lexical functions per se, e.g. $\mathbf{S}_2$, as individual lexical entities; this information could be exported as a stand-alone model of the linguistic system of lexical functions (cf. section 4). Figure 5 below shows the interface that allows lexicographers to manage the lexical function knowledge base embedded in the FLN. In this figure, one can see the database record that defines the $\mathbf{S}_2$ lexical function. It contains the three following types of information, from top to bottom.

1. Classification: $\mathbf{S}_2$ is a simple standard paradigmatic lexical function of the "$\mathbf{S}_2$" family, that comprises also $\mathbf{S}_{2\supset}$, $\mathbf{S}_{2\cap}$, $\mathbf{S}_2^{\mathbf{usual}}$, etc.
2. Formula structure: the lexical function formula $\boldsymbol{S}_2$ is constructed by assembling two atomic formal elements—the name central component $\boldsymbol{S}$ and the subscript $_2$. As one can see, names of lexical functions are broken down into atomic building blocks[9], thus allowing for future automatic compilation of standard lexical function encodings into more "computable" formulas, such as those proposed in (Kahane and Polguère, 2001).
3. Popularization: $\mathbf{S}_2$ is at present associated with three popularization formulas (from the popularization formula database).

In the remainder of this section, we focus on the SQL modeling of lexical function *applications*— e.g. $\mathbf{S}_2$( *chantage* **I** )—rather than lexical function themselves. This modeling is supported by 4 SQL tables, shown in Figure 6 below. This subpart of the database can be seen as storing actual lexical function relations among lexical units. As said earlier, such data represents the crucial element of lexical structuring in the FLN.

The content of each of the 4 SQL tables in Figure 6 can be described as follows.

[9]For instance, the complex lexical function formula $\boldsymbol{Magn}^{quant}\boldsymbol{+A}_1$ is defined in the FLN database as an assembling of 5 atomic elements: $\boldsymbol{Magn}$, $^{quant}$, $+$, $\boldsymbol{A}$ and $_1$.

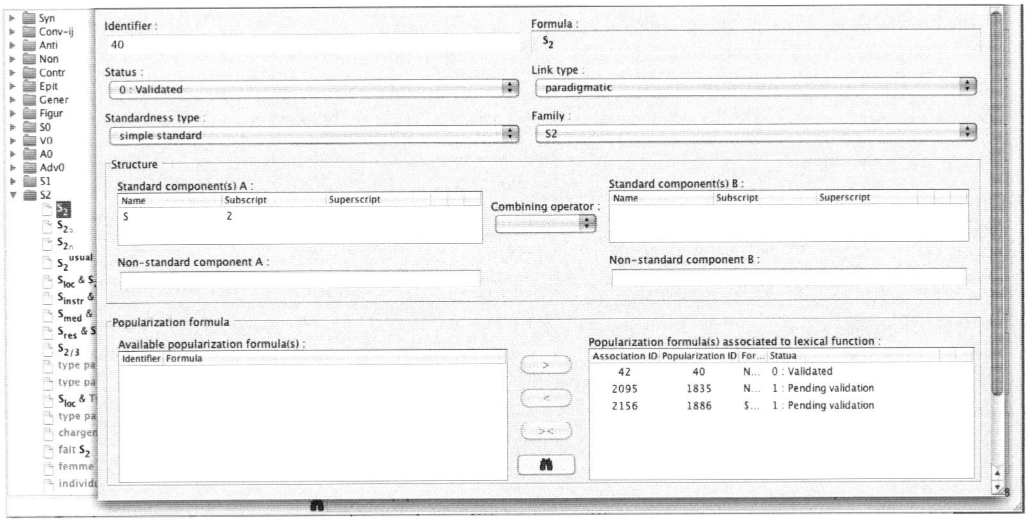


Figure 5: Interface for managing the FLN lexical function knowledge base: definition of $\mathbf{S_2}$

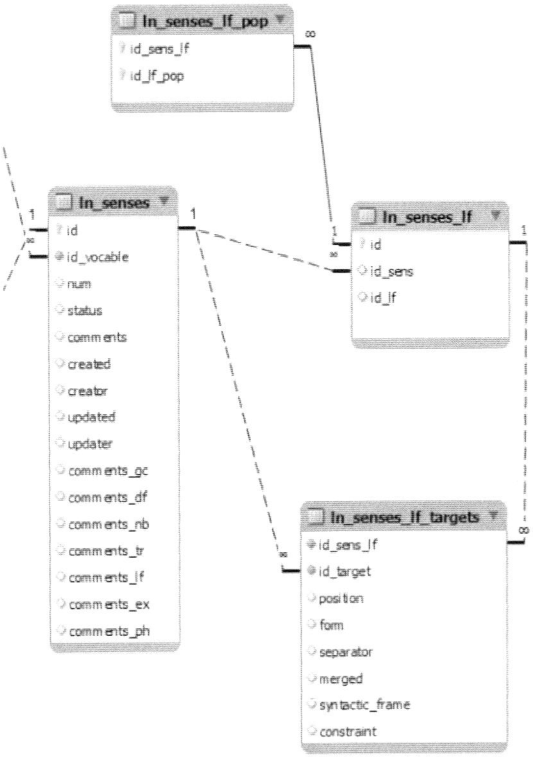


Figure 6: SQL tables handling lexical function applications in the FLN

1. Table **ln_senses** describes each lexical unit (sense), using 16 different fields. A lexical unit, identified by a unique identifier (`id`), is formally linked to the vocable it belongs to (based on `id_vocable`) and is characterized by a lexicographic number (ex. **I.1**) if its vocable is polysemic.[10] To sum up, the `ln_senses` table is used to store basic information about lexical units such as CHANTAGE **I**, CIBLE **II.2**, VICTIME **II**, CÉDER **IV.1**, OBÉIR **3**, OBTEMPÉRER, etc.

2. Table **ln_senses_lf** describes the application of a lexical function **LF** (whose unique identifier is `id_lf` ) to a lexical unit L (whose unique identifier is `id_sens`). Each application of a lexical function to a lexical unit **LF**(L) has a unique identifier (`id` in table `ln_senses_lf`).

3. This identifier is used under the name `id_sens_lf` in the **ln_senses_lf_pop** table, that handles the association between individual lexical function applications and the associated popularization formula. For example, the table `ln_senses_lf` is used to store:

   - the application of the lexical function $\mathbf{S_2}$ to the lexical unit CHANTAGE **I**, application to which the table `ln_senses_lf_pop` associates the popularization formula `[$2] qui subit` ~ (= '[$2] who undergoes ~').[11]
   - the application of the lexical function $\mathbf{Real_2}$ to the lexical unit CHANTAGE **I**, application to which the table `ln_senses_lf_pop` associates the popularization formula `[$2] réagir comme $1 le souhaite vis-à-vis de` ~ (= '[$2] to react as expected by $1 regarding ~').

4. Each target L' of a lexical function application **LF**(L) is specified in the **ln_senses_lf_targets** table, using lexical function identifiers. But the `ln_senses_lf_targets` table also contains:

   - information necessary to logically order all **LF**(L)'s targets (field `position`) when they are enumerated in an article-view;
   - information about target separators (field `separator` whose value can be "`,` ", "`;` " or "<");
   - information about the complementation frame of each target (field `syntactic_frame`);
   - etc.

   In short, this table stores all additional linguistic information that is necessary to compute what is displayed in the article-view for the lexical function zone (see the article-view in Figure 4 above).

[10] Some fields, whose names begin by `comment_`, are used for the storage of "freely" entered information, i.e. information for which Dicet does not yet implement a full formalization (`comments_gc` stands for *comments on grammatical characteristics*, `comments_df` stands for *comments on definition*, etc.). Some other fields are for the management of the lexicographic work. E.g. `status` has a value indicating if the description of the lexical unit is "completed," "being validated," "under description" or "unworked;" `created` contains the creation date; `creator` contains the login of the sense's creator; etc.

[11] The "~" symbol is used throughout a lexicographic article to refer to this article's headword.

When weaving lexical function relations among lexical units, lexicographers work under the supervision of the Dicet editor. Figure 7 shows the interface they use to feed the `ln_senses_lf_targets` table with all the necessary information.

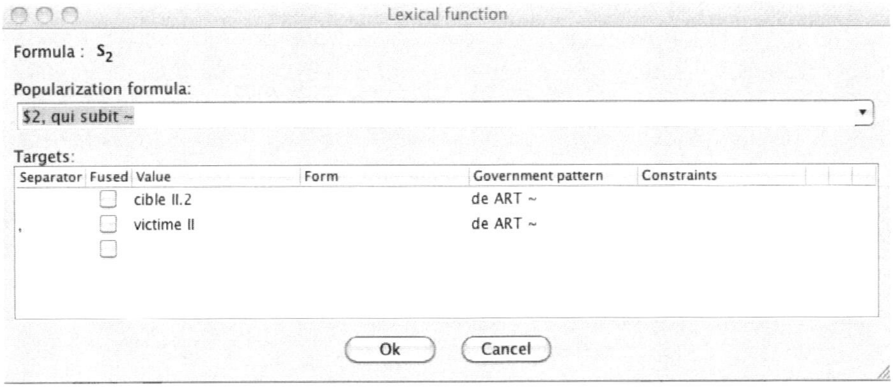


Figure 7: Part of the Dicet interface for pulling lexical function links in the FLN

Because our lexicographic model is implemented as SQL tables and the FLN itself is stored in a relational database, we benefit from the well-established technology of relational database management systems (quick access to data, secure data storage, management of users rights, etc.).

As illustrated in this section, the Dicet editor is a powerful interface. Dicet helps lexicographers to enter data that is compliant to our lexicographic principles. Simultaneously, Dicet computes article-views of lexicographic data that is instantly available to lexicographers as a retroaction they can use in order to check and validate their description. In short, Dicet ensures compliance with a fine-grained formal model while giving lexicographers the clear feeling that they are, afterall, performing a task that is equivalent to "writing" lexicographic articles.

## 4 Compatibility with standards for lexical data structures

It is nowadays unconceivable to target the public distribution of a lexical resource such as the FLN without taking into consideration the compatibility of its computational modeling of linguistic information (i.e., data structure) with available standards. In this section, we present the outcome of some preliminary reflections on this topic.

As explained above, the FLN is implemented as a relational SQL database. This database provides XML (and HTML) data exports, which means that it is conformant with a general well-known data model and a general format standard. We wish to explore the compatibility of FLN's data with a more specialized standard: the *Lexical Markup Framework*—hereafter, LMF—, which is the ISO standard for NLP-compatible lexical databases and dictionaries (ISO, 2008; Francopoulo et al., 2006). LMF Core Package and extensions are defined with the Unified Modeling Language (UML), so that the normative content of LMF is expressed as sets of UML classes with associations among classes. Attribute-value pairs used to adorn the UML classes are not directly provided by LMF. Rather, LMF recomands to use Data Category specifications in accordance with the ISO 12620 standard (ISO, 2009).

To start with, we have checked if the FLN is in accordance with LMF general principles expressed in the LMF core package. The `Lexical Entry` class from the LMF Core Package, which is just “a container for managing the Form and Sense classes” (ISO, 2008, p. 18) perfectly matches the FLN vocable entity, which we model as a grouping of lexical units. More importantly, in both LMF and the FLN, the basic unit for lexicographic description is a `Sense` (= lexical unit in the FLN).

To go further, since the FLN provides a large range of properties for each lexical unit, we would have to select several LMF extensions in addition to the LMF core package. We chose to focus on the encoding of lexical function applications—whose central role in structuring the FLN has been extensively discussed above—and examine how it can be compiled into LMF format.

The LMF NLP semantics extension includes a `SenseRelation` class, defined as “a multipurpose class that can be used to represent *antonymy*, *generic/specific* or *part of* relationship” (ISO, 2008, p. 41), which seems to fit our needs. The code sample below illustrates the use of this class to model the two lexical function applications $\mathbf{S}_2$( *chantage* I ) and $\mathbf{Real}_2$( *chantage* I ), that have been examined in section 2.

```
<LexicalEntry>
    <feat att="partOfSpeech" val="nom"/>
    <Lemma>
        <feat att="writtenForm" val="chantage"/>
    </Lemma>
    <Sense xml:id="chantage:I">
        <SenseRelation targets="#cible:II.2 #victime:II">
            <feat att="lexicalFunction" val="S_2"/>
            <feat att="popularizedFormat" val="[$2] subir ~"/>
        </SenseRelation>
        <SenseRelation targets="#céder:IV.1 #obéir:3 #obtempérer">
            <feat att="lexicalFunction" val="Real_2"/>
            <feat att="popularizedFormat" val="[$2] réagir
                  comme $1 le souhaite vis-à-vis de ~"/>
        </SenseRelation>
    </Sense>
</LexicalEntry>
<LexicalEntry>
    <feat att="partOfSpeech" val="nom"/>
    <Lemma>
        <feat att="writtenForm" val="cible"/>
    </Lemma>
    <Sense xml:id="cible:I"/>
    <Sense xml:id="cible:II.1"/>
    <Sense xml:id="cible:II.2"/>
</LexicalEntry>
<!-- Lexical entry omitted for "victime" -->
<LexicalEntry>
    <feat att="partOfSpeech" val="verbe"/>
    <Lemma>
        <feat att="writtenForm" val="céder"/>
    </Lemma>
    <Sense xml:id="céder:I"/>
    <Sense xml:id="céder:II"/>
    <Sense xml:id="céder:III"/>
    <Sense xml:id="céder:IV.1"/>
    <Sense xml:id="céder:IV.2"/>
</LexicalEntry>
<!-- Lexical entries omitted for "obéir" and "obtempérer" -->
```

The above code is based on the LMF `SenseRelation` class as it is, using only one additional feature to encode the associated popularization formula. For an actual compilation of the FLN into LMF, we will probably need to define a new class, say `LexicalFunctionRelation`, as a specialization of the `SenseRelation` class.

Additionally, this example clearly shows that the XML version of the LMF model, used here, is not rich enough. In particular, the `targets` attribute of the `SenseRelation` element allows us to link a lexical unit to a list of lexical units, using a given lexical function, while, as shown in section 3, we need a data structure that is far more complex than a list, together with additional information attached to links pointing to targeted lexical units.[12] We need a true LMF equivalent of our `ln_senses_lf_targets` SQL table.

From our preliminary exploration of the problem of the FLN's compatibility with existing standards, we draw the following conclusions.

- The FLN is in accordance with the few high-level good-practice principles provided by LMF.
- Since the FLN has a very precisely defined structure, we need to add more specificity to LMF classes in order to get a tighter LMF model.
- If an LMF compatible distribution of the FLN is indeed implemented, several linguistic resources used in the FLN should be converted into Data Category Registries, following the ISO 12620 standard (ISO, 2009). For example, in order to define the attributes and values used to adorn the `LexicalFunction` class, one probably has to build a Data Category Registry dedicated to lexical functions. This could be automatically generated from a subset of the FLN SQL tables, in which a description of all FLN's lexical functions is provided.
- Finally, let's mention that we consider exploring in the future other standards for lexical resources, in particular the Text Encoding Initiative (TEI), that includes two relevant chapters: *Dictionaries* and *Graphs, networks and trees.*

## 5 On the cognitive relevance of the FLN approach

In order to conclude, we wish to reflect on the cognitive relevance of the FLN approach to the modeling of lexical information. Indeed, our motivations for designing such a project—in terms of lexical model and lexicographic methodology—do not originate from computational considerations. The need to implement, fully formalize and make computer-tracktable our lexical model is a non-negotiable constraint, an essential parameter in our approach. However, our first and foremost goal is to build a lexical resource that complies before all not to encoding standards, but to lexicological ones! The FLN design and modus operandi is the outcome of an extremely long process of experimentation with lexicological models and of lexicographic practice: from earlier "theoretical dictionaries" called *Explanatory Combinatorial Dictionaries* (Mel'čuk and Žolkovskij, 1984; Mel'čuk, I. *et al.*, 1999), to the work on the *DiCo* lexical database (Polguère, 2000; Mel'čuk and Polguère, 2006), the layman-oriented pedagogical *Lexique Actif du Français*[13] (Mel'čuk and Polguère, 2007; Polguère, 2007) and the first proposal for a graph-based version of Explanatory Combinatorial lexical databases called *lexical systems* (Polguère,

[12] Cf. Figure 7, section 3, the set of parameters represented by columns to be filled in the Dicet window.
[13] Lit. 'Active French Lexicon.'

2009). All this has matured into a project that, we hope, goes beyond the very specific problem of building a French lexical resource.[14]

As was mentioned at the beginning of this paper (section 1), the constraint of being able to use the FLN as a resource for such a linguistically demanding context of application as language learning (and teaching) imposes on us to consider a lexical model that has relevance to the processes of acquiring and using lexical knowledge. There are at least two aspects of the FLN that we believe make it compatible with this goal.

Firstly, the FLN is a rich, non-hierarchical lexical graph, that is more in line with the plausible structure of "actual" lexical knowledge (Aitchison, 2003) than textual models of the dictionary type.

Secondly, the Dicet editor has a crucial importance in our approach in that it not only helps entering and retrieving formally coherent information, but it also implements a new "lexicographic gesture." We are convinced that this gesture is intrinsically compatible with language speaker's navigation in the lexicon in the context of language learning and use (Wolter, 2006; Zock and Schwab, 2011). We cannot enter here into the detail of this last aspect of our work; it is dealt with in A. Polguère's oral presentation at CogALex III (Polguère, 2012b) and will be developed in later publications. Suffice it to say here that FLN's lexicographers build the lexical model in a non-linear way, through gradual and sometimes aleatory weaving of lexical links. This process of building lexicographic information—that follows semantic, combinatorial and formal relations between lexical units—presents strong analogies with plausible wading of the speaker through the structure of lexical knowledge.

## Acknowledgments

The RELIEF project is supported by a grant from the Agence de Mobilisation Économique de Lorraine (AMEL) and Fonds Européen de Développement Régional (FEDER). We wish to thank our colleague Bertrand Gaiffe for his precious guidance on LMF and CogALex III reviewers for their extremely sound and useful comments on a preliminary version of this paper.

## References

Aitchison, J. (2003). *Words in the Mind: An Introduction to the Mental Lexicon.* Blackwell, Oxford UK, 3rd edition.

Atkins, B. T. S. (1996). Bilingual Dictionaries: Past, Present and Future. In Gellerstam, M., Järborg, J., Malmgren, S.-G., Norén, K., Rogström, L., and Papmehl, C. R., editors, *Euralex'96 Proceedings*, pages 515–590, Gothenburg. Gothenburg University, Department of Swedish.

Baker, C. F., Fillmore, C. J., and Cronin, B. (2003). The Structure of the FrameNet Database. *International Journal of Lexicography*, 16(3):281–296.

Fellbaum, C., editor (1998). *WordNet: An Electronic Lexical Database.* The MIT Press, Cambridge MA.

Francopoulo, G., George, M., Calzolari, N., Monachini, M., Bel, N., Pet, M., and Soria, C. (2006). Lexical Markup Framework (LMF). In *Proceedings of International Conference on Language Resources and Evaluation – LREC 2006*, Genova.

[14]Note that the FLN approach is presently being used, in exploratory satellite projects based on the same data structure and lexicographic editor, for the modeling of the Korean and Spanish lexicons.

Horák, A., Pala, K., Rambousek, A., and Rychlý, P. (2006). New Clients for Dictionary Writing on the DEB Platform. In de Schryver, G.-M., editor, *DWS 2006: Proceedings of the Fourth International Workshop on Dictionary Writing Systems*, pages 17–23, Turin.

Iordanskaja, L., Kim, M., and Polguère, A. (1992). Some Procedural Problems in the Implementation of Lexical Functions. In Wanner, K. H. . L., editor, *Proceedings of the International Workshop on The Meaning-Text Theory*, Arbeitspapiere der GMD 671, pages 197–205, Darmstadt (Allemagne). GMD-MBH.

ISO (2008). Language Resource management – Lexical markup framework (LMF). ISO/TC 37/SC 4 N453. N330 Rev. 16.

ISO (2009). Terminology and other language and content resources – Specification of data categories and management of a Data Category Registry for language resources. ISO/TC37/SC3 ISO 12620. Stage : 60.60 (2009-12-10).

Joffe, D. and de Schryver, G.-M. (2012). TLex Suite User Guide (version 7.0.1). Technical report, TshwaneDJe Human Language Technology.

Kahane, S. and Polguère, A. (2001). Formal Foundation of Lexical Functions. In *Proceedings of "COLLOCATION: Computational Extraction, Analysis and Exploitation"*, 39th Annual Meeting and 10th Conference of the European Chapter of the Association for Computational Linguistics, pages 8–15, Toulouse.

Lannoy, V. (2010). The IDM Free Online Platform for Dictionary Publishers. In *Proceedings of the XIVth Euralex International Congress*, pages 389–401, Leeuwarden.

Lareau, F., Dras, M., Börschinger, B., and Turpin, M. (2012). Implementing Lexical Functions in XLE. In Butt, M. and King, T. H., editors, *Proceedings of the LFG12 Conference*, Stanford. CSLI.

Lux-Pogodalla, V. and Polguère, A. (2011). Construction of a French Lexical Network: Methodological Issues. In *Proceedings of the First InternationalWorkshop on Lexical Resources, WoLeR 2011. An ESSLLI 2011 Workshop*, pages 54–61, Ljubljana, Slovenia.

Mel'čuk, I. (1996). Lexical Functions: A Tool for the Description of Lexical Relations in the Lexicon. In Wanner, L., editor, *Lexical Functions in Lexicography and Natural Language Processing*, volume 31 of *Language Companion Series*, pages 37–102. John Benjamins, Amsterdam/Philadelphia.

Mel'čuk, I. (2004a). Actants in semantics and syntax I: actants in semantics. *Linguistics*, 42(1):1–66.

Mel'čuk, I. (2004b). Actants in semantics and syntax II: actants in syntax. *Linguistics*, 42(2):247–291.

Mel'čuk, I. and Polguère, A. (2006). Dérivations sémantiques et collocations dans le DiCo/LAF. *Langue française*, 150:66–83.

Mel'čuk, I. and Polguère, A. (2007). *Lexique actif du français. L'apprentissage du vocabulaire fondé sur 20 000 dérivations sémantiques et collocations du français*. Champs linguistiques. De Boeck & Larcier, Brussels.

Mel'čuk, I. and Žolkovskij, A. (1984). *Explanatory Combinatorial Dictionary of Modern Russian.* Wiener Slawistischer Almanach, Vienna.

Mel'čuk, I. *et al.* (1984, 1988, 1992, 1999). *Dictionnaire explicatif et combinatoire du français contemporain. Recherches lexico-sémantiques. Volumes I–IV.* Les Presses de l'Université de Montréal, Montreal.

Milićević, J. (2006). A Short Guide to the Meaning-Text Linguistic Theory. *Journal of Koralex,* 8:187–233.

Milićević, J. (2009). Schéma de régime : le pont entre le lexique et la grammaire. *Langages,* 176:94–116.

Polguère, A. (2000). Towards a theoretically-motivated general public dictionary of semantic derivations and collocations for French. In *Proceedings of EURALEX'2000,* pages 517–527, Stuttgart.

Polguère, A. (2007). Lessons from the *Lexique actif du français.* In Gerdes, K., Reuther, T., and Wanner, L., editors, *Meaning-Text Theory 2007. Proceedings of the Third International Conference on the Meaning Text Theory, Klagenfurt, May 20–24, 2007,* Wiener Slawistischer Almanach Sonderband 69, pages 397–405, München–Wien.

Polguère, A. (2009). Lexical systems: graph models of natural language lexicons. *Language Resources and Evaluation,* 43(1):41–55.

Polguère, A. (2012a). Lexicographie des dictionnaires virtuels. In Apresjan, Y., Boguslavsky, I., L'Homme, M.-C., Iomdin, L., Milićević, J., Polguère, A., and Wanner, L., editors, *Meanings, Texts, and Other Exciting Things. A Festschrift to Commemorate the 80$^{th}$ Anniversary of Professor Igor Alexandrovič Mel'čuk,* Studia Philologica, pages 509–523. Jazyki slavjanskoj kultury Publishers, Moscow.

Polguère, A. (forthcoming 2012b). Like a Lexicographer Weaving Her Lexical Network. In *Proceedings of the Third Workshop on Cognitive Aspects of the Lexicon (CogALex III).* Summary of invited talk.

Polguère, A. and Sikora, D. (to appear ToAp). Modèle lexicographique de croissance du vocabulaire fondé sur un processus aléatoire, mais systématique. In Masseron, C., Garcia-Debanc, C., and Ronveaux, C., editors, *Enseigner le lexique. Pratiques sociales, objets à enseigner et pratiques d'enseignement,* volume 5. AiRDF.

Ruppenhofer, J., Ellsworth, M., Petruck, M. R. L., Johnson, C. R., and Scheffczyk, J. (2010). *FrameNet II: Extended Theory and Practice.* International Computer Science Institute, Berkeley CA.

Sagot, B. and Fišer, D. (2011). Extending wordnets by learning from multiple resources. In *Proceedings of LTC 2011,* Poznań.

Selva, T., Verlinde, S., and Binon, J. (2003). Vers une deuxième génération de dictionnaires électroniques. *Traitement Automatique des Langues (TAL),* 44(2):177–197.

Spohr, D. (2012). *Towards a Multifunctional Lexical Resource. Design and Implementation of a Graph-based Lexicon Model.* De Gruyter, Berlin/Boston.

Wolter, B. (2006). Lexical Network Structures and L2 Vocabulary Acquisition: The Role of L1 Lexical/Conceptual Knowledge. *Applied Linguistics*, 27(4):741–747.

Zock, M. and Schwab, D. (2011). Storage does not Guarantee Access: The Problem of Organizing and Accessing Words in a Speaker's Lexicon. *Journal of Cognitive Science*, 12:233–259.

# A Procedural DTD Project for Dictionary Entry Parsing Described with Parameterized Grammars

*Neculai CURTEANU*[1] *Alex MORUZ*[1,2]
(1) INSTITUTE of COMPUTER SCIENCE, ROMANIAN ACADEMY, IAŞI Branch;
(2) FACULTY of COMPUTER SCIENCE, UNIV. "AL. I. CUZA", IAŞI, ROMANIA
ncurteanu@yahoo.com, mmoruz@info.uaic.ro

ABSTRACT

The present paper continues the successful parsing experiments with the method of *Segmentation-Cohesion-Dependency* (SCD) *configurations*, a breadth-first, formal grammar-free, and optimal approach to dictionary entry parsing, proposed in the previous CogALex Workshops and applied to the following *five* very large thesaurus-dictionaries: **DLR** (The Romanian Thesaurus – new format), **DAR** (The Romanian Thesaurus – old format), **TLF** (Le Trésor de la Langue Française), **DWB** (Deutsches Wörterbuch – GRIMM), and **GWB** (Göthe-Wörterbuch). In this work we report new results: **(a)** The lexicographic modeling and parsing experiments of the *sixth* large **DMLRL** (Dictionary of Modern Literary Russian Language); **(b)** Outlining the *Enumeration Closing Condition* (ECC) for solving the recursive calls between sense marker classes situated on different nodes of a sense dependency hypergraph (SCD-configuration, *i.e.* parsing level); **(c)** The central result we report here is the project of a new, *procedural* DTD (Document Type Description) for dictionaries, based on the formalization of the SCD parsing method, providing *parameterized grammars* to describe the dependency hypergraphs that correspond to the main parsing levels in a dictionary entry. Here we give two parameterized grammars for **DLR**, as a small sample from a larger package of combined grammars for the above mentioned dictionaries. This package is constructed as the "least common multiple" of the parameterized grammars written for the parsed dictionaries; it represents the DTD description of a general *parser* for large dictionary entries, and thoroughly extends the current DTD in the XCES TEI P5 standard.

KEYWORDS: SCD dictionary parsing method; procedural DTD for dictionary entry parsing.

## 1 Lexicographic Modeling of DMLRL

A pre-processing parsing stage can be added to the SCD (*Segmentation-Cohesion-Dependency*) *configurations* for **DMLRL** *homonymic entries*, which are discriminated by indexing each of the homonyms with Arabic numerals followed by dot, all in *Arial font*, *Regular* and *Bold* format. These indexes are positioned in front of each homonym-word lemma, enumerating increasingly all the homonyms of the same word-lemma. An example of *four* homonymic entries of the word "**БЫЧОК**" is present in (DMLRL, :860-861), exposed in (Curteanu et al., 2012a :45).

The *first SCD configuration* has to recognize the *lexicographic segments* of a **DMLRL** entry. **DMLRL** comprises (at least) five types of lexicographic packages / segments (Curteanu et al., 2012a): **(1)** a *morpho-lexical* package / segment; **(2)** the *sense description* segment; **(3)** a ***TildaDef*** *package* or *segment of definitions*; **(4)** the *morpho-syntactic variant* segment; and **(5)** the *etymology* segment of the word-lemma. The morpho-lexical definition package is obligatorily present at the beginning of each entry, immediately after the word-lemma. The morpho-lexical package may occur also at the sense lower-levels of the entry sense tree. The ***TildaDef*** package can be attributed not only to any (sub)sense description level of the entry but also to the root-sense (zero-level sense hierarchy), when this package / segment begins at *New_Paragraph*.

The *primary sense* markers in **DMLRL** pointed out so far by the lexicographic analysis are: Latin capital numerals followed by a dot (**I.**, **II.**, **III.**,... etc.), in bold (*LatCapNumb_Mark*), and Arabic numerals followed by a dot (**1.**, **2.**, **3.**,... etc.), in bold (*ArabNumb_Mark*). The markers of these classes are positioned at the beginning of the text row, in fact, at *New_Paragraph* (*NewPrg*) marker, except for the *first sense markers* (**I.**, **1.**), which usually do not occur at *NewPrg*.

The sense markers of the class denoting Latin capital numerals followed by a dot (**I.**, **II.**, **III.**,...etc. or simply, *LatCapLet_Enum*) represent the top of the sense hierarchy in **DMLRL**. These markers establish the lexicographic limits for the *most general senses* of the word-lemma. They are the lexical-semantic equivalent of the sense marker class containing bolded Latin capital letters **A.**, **B.**, etc. (abbreviated as *LatCapLet_Enum*) in **DLR** (Curteanu et al., 2008).

The sense marker class of *Arabic numerals* followed by dot (**1.**, **2.**, **3.**,... etc.), in bold (*ArabNumb_Enum*), stands for the second level of primary sense representation in **DMLRL**. The place of these two sense marker classes is displayed within the left side hypergraph of Fig. 1. The sense marker classes *LatCapNumb_Enum* and *ArabNumb_Enum* are considered as **DMLRL** *primary senses*, similarly to **DLR-DAR** lexicographic modeling (Curteanu et al., 2010).

We placed the *two-oblique-bars* ”//” sense marker, which is specific to **DMLRL**, on the *third level* of the hierarchical dependency structure of **DMLRL** senses. At the same time, the sense marker ”//” is considered to be the first element of the two-markers set {//, ◊} denoting the *secondary senses* in **DMLRL**. The sense marked by ”//” is in lexical-semantics subordination to (or subsumed by) any other primary sense marked by an element in the marker classes {*LatCapNumb_Enum*, *ArabNumb_Enum*}, when they exist in the entry text. Otherwise (when a primary super-ordinated sense is missing), the secondary sense marker ”//” may occur immediately under the topmost level of the **DMLRL** sense hierarchy. The marker ”//” is embodied explicitly into the entry text, even for the case when this sense level is unique.

We notice that *autonomous* definitions in the //-marked subsenses to the primary senses can be refined by the so-called *DictExem*, *i.e. examples-to-definitions* given by **DMLRL** authors. Usually, *DictExems* are separated from *DefExems* that follows through the **DMLRL**-specific marker ”□” called *traverse*. By analogy with the **DLR** hypergraph of sense dependencies, we associate the **DMLRL** ”//” marker with the **DLR** ”♦” sense marker: they are both secondary sense markers and subsume the similar secondary sense marker denoted in both dictionaries by the *empty-diamond* ”◊” (DMLRL, 1994), (Curteanu et al., 2012a, 2010).

The problem of literal enumeration in **DMLRL** is a challenging problem because one may find entry samples that display a recursion between the *literal enumeration* and the *secondary senses* “//” and ”◊” (at least these markers), a typical sample of this situation being the entry **БЫ** (DMLRL, :844). The same type of recursion can occur actually between primary, secondary, and atomic senses, on one hand, and literal enumeration senses, on the other hand. The solution of reducing these recursions to a finite number of cycles should be the consistent control of the monotonic and sound closing of the literal enumeration development on higher or lower levels of the **DMLRL** pre-established hypergraphs of sense marker class dependencies (Fig. 1 below) (Curteanu et al., 2012a, 2012c).

The reverse situation, of the sense levels that could refine the *literal enumeration* sense description is illustrated by the thick-tail arrows, oriented upwards and intersecting the thin-tail arrows, in the first dependency hypergraph, SCD-config2 parsing level (Fig. 1).

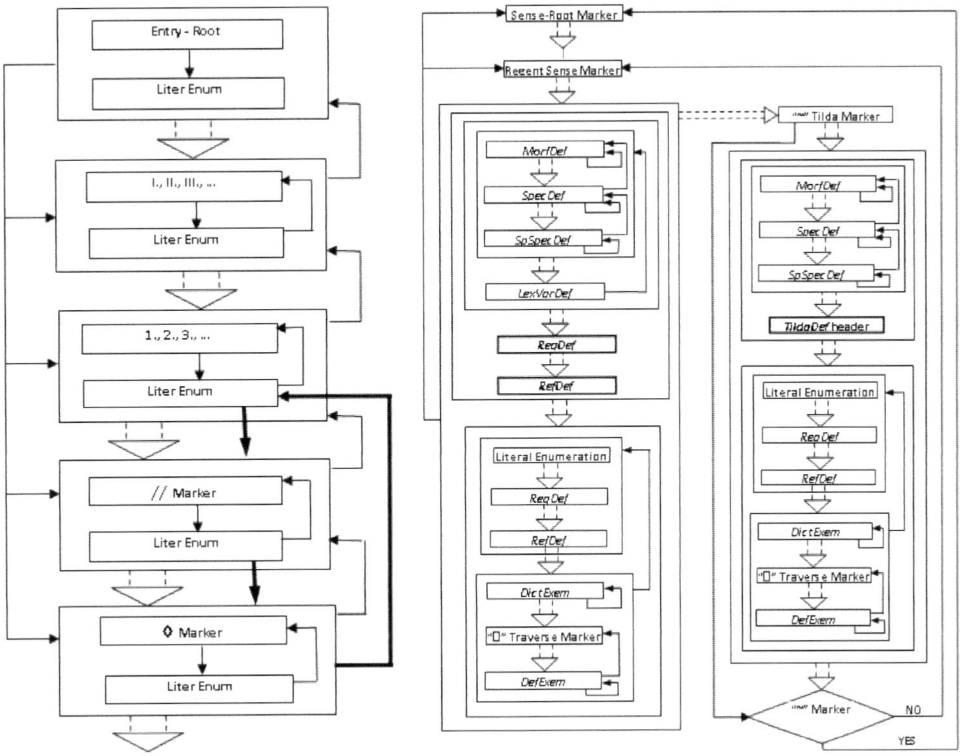


FIGURE 1 – The first dependency hypergraph (SCD-config2 of primary and secondary senses) calling the second dependency hypergraph (SCD-config3 of atomic senses) in **DMLRL**

The lower-level parsing (SCD-config3) is represented in the right side hypergraph of Fig. 1, for the *atomic* sense / definition markers in **DMLRL**. This hypergraph is *interconnected* with the higher-sense parsing level represented by the left side (*i.e.* SCD-config2) hypergraph in Fig. 1. This SCD-config2 hypergraph gives the dependency relationships among the higher-order sense marker classes, handing down from the root-sense, through primary and secondary senses, to the lower and atomic senses / definitions. When structurally accomplished, **DMLRL** lower-level senses are raising up, called by higher-level sense markers, until the structure of the entry sense tree is completed.

## 2 The *Enumeration Closing Condition*: A Solution to Preserve the Soundness of Sense Structure Definitions

The *Enumeration Closing Condition* (ECC) represents a deterministic, computational constraint devoted to check the sound termination (*i.e.* in a deterministic, finite number of steps) of the literal or numeral enumeration marker list, when higher-level sense markers break into the list. When this happens, contextual look-ahead verifications are needed to obtain the correct closing of the enumeration list. More precisely, ECC means that whether after a certain (let us say, *current*) *letter* or *numeral* in the sense enumeration marker list occur higher-level sense markers (on the dependency hypergraph), then one should look forward in the sense marker sequence until the *next* letter or numeral of the same enumeration type occurs. If such an item does exist and follows *monotonously* (*i.e.* in lexicographic ordering) the current one in the enumeration list, then the enumeration should continue. Otherwise, thus if the (letter or numeral) item does not exist or it begins another enumeration, of the same or higher dependency level as the current one, then the ECC holds and the literal enumeration must be closed. For instance, in the Romanian **DLR**, with the filled and empty diamonds ♦, ◊ as secondary sense markers, the enumeration list **a) b) c)** ◊ ♦ ◊ ◊♦ ◊ **d)...** should continue, while the marker sequence **a) b) c)** ◊ ♦ ◊ ◊♦ ◊ **a)...** should close the first literal enumeration (Curteanu et al., 2012a, 2012c). The same is true if non-enumerable sense markers (such as ♦, ◊ in **DLR**) are replaced by another enumeration of sense markers, be it of another numeral or literal type. Two different enumerations, a standard, *literal* one, and a *numeral* one coming from transforming the *New_Paragraphs* into sense markers, are illustrated by the following special entries bearing recursive-calls: "**CAL**" in **DAR**, "**LUMÍNĂ**" in **DLR**, "**БЫ**" in **DMLRL** (DMLRL :844) (Curteanu et al., 2012c, 2012a).

Parsing with SCD configurations, we discovered the special role that the *New_Paragraph* (*NewPrg*) typographic marker is playing in the disambiguation process, either for the lexicographic segment recognition or to ECC verification. For an efficient use of *NewPrg*(*s*) as lexicographic markers, in a preprocessing phase for parsing a dictionary entry, we decided to transform *all* the *NewPrg*(*s*) occurring in the entry into *Latin small numerals* (*LatSmaNumb*) as lexicographic segment markers or sense enumeration markers.

## 3 Parsing Experiments with DMLRL Entries on the SCD-config2 Level

We outline here the parsing results on the six thesauri: **DLR**, completely parsed (175,000 entries; 15,000 pages; 37 volumes) at 98.01% accuracy, **DAR** completely parsed (25,000 entries, 3000 pages, 5 volumes), but no gold standard was available for automatic evaluation, while for **TLF**, **DWB**, **GWB**, and **DMLRL**, around 50 significant (including very large) entries have been parsed with very sound outcomes but not gold standard available for the parsing evaluation. Also, using ECC, we solved the following two difficult parsing problems, met not only in **DMLRL**, but also in **DLR**, **DAR** (as specified above), and other thesauri: (*a*) sense dependencies of the SCD *second configuration* (left side hypergraph in Fig. 1), and (*b*) the mutual calling between literal enumeration and secondary senses. For 50 **DMLRL** entries (of all sizes, including very large ones), the parser provided a really sound parsing percentage, at this level (Curteanu et al., 2012b).

The special entry **БЫ** (DMLRL, :844) contains the marker subsequence "3. a) ◊ ◊ // ◊ ◊ б) ◊ ◊ ◊ в) г) ◊ ◊", which shows (in the partial excerpt below) the occurrence of **DMLRL** secondary senses under the literal enumeration, whose sound parsing is based on ECC to hold (Curteanu et al. (2012a, 2012c).

**БЫ** (сокращенно **Б**), *частица.* В сочетании с глаголами в форме прошедшего времени образует сослагательное наклонение. **1.** Употр. для обозначения предположительной ...

… … … … … … … … … … … … … … … … … … … … … … … … … … … … … … … … … … …

**3.** Обозначает различные оттенки желаемости действия; **а)** Собственно желаемость. *Учился бы сын. Были бы дети здоровы.* ◊ Если бы, когда бы, хоть бы и т. п. О, *если бы когда-нибудь Сбылась поэта сновиденья!* Пушк. Посл. к Юдину. [Николка:] *Хоть бы дивизион наш был скорее готов.* Булгаков, Дни Турб. ◊ С неопр. ф. глаг. *Полететь бы пташечке К синю морю; Убежать бы молодцу в лес дремучий.* Дельв. Пела, пела пташечка.. [Настя:] *Ах, тетенька, голубок! Вот бы поймать!* А. Остр.

Не было ни гроша...— *Жара, дедушка Лодыжкин .. Нет никакого терпения! Искупаться бы!* Купр. Бел. пудель. / / Употр. для выражения опасения по поводу какого-л. нежелательного действия (с отрицанием). *Не заболел бы он.* ◊ С неопр. ф. глаг., имеющей перед собой отрицание. — *Гляди, — говорю, — бабочка, не кусать бы тебе локтя! Так-таки оно все на мое вышло.* Леск. Воительница. ◊ Только бы (б) не.... **б)** Пожелание. *Условие я бы предпочел не подписывать.* Л. Толст. Письмо А. Ф. Марксу, 27 марта 1899. ◊ С неопр. ф. глаг. *Поохотиться бы по-настоящему, на коня бы денег добыть, — мечтал старик.* Г. Марков, Строговы. ◊ В сочетании с предикативными наречиями со знач. долженствования, необходимости, возможности. ... ... ◊ Только бы (б), лишь бы, Употр. со знач. желательности действия. [ Скалозуб:] *Мне только бы досталось в генералы.* Гриб. Горе от ума. **в)** Желание-просьба, совет или предложение (обычно при мест. 2л.). [Марина:] *И чего засуетился? Сидел бы:* Чех. Дядя Ваня.

The beginning of the parsing output shows the correct assignment of sense dependencies:


```
<entry>
 <list>БЫ 1. ◊ ◊ ◊ ◊ ◊ 2. 3. а) ◊ ◊ // ◊ ◊ б) ◊ ◊ ◊ в) г) ◊ ◊ n-23</list>
 <sense value="БЫ" class="0">
  <definition> (сокращенно <b>Б</b>), частица. В сочетании с глаголами в форме прошедшего времени образует сослагательное наклонение. </definition>
   <sense value="1." class="4">
... ... ... ... ... ... ... ... ... ... ... ... ... ... ... ... ... ... ... ... ... ... ... ... ... ... ... ... ... ... ... ... ... ... ...
   <sense value="3." class="4">
    <definition> Обозначает различные оттенки желаемости действия; </definition>
    <sense value="а)" class="5">
     <definition> Собственно желаемость. Учился бы сын. Были бы дети здоровы. </definition>
     <sense value="◊" class="8">
      <definition> Если <spaced> б ы</spaced>, когда <spaced> б ы</spaced>, хоть <spaced> б ы</spaced><spaced> и</spaced> т. п. О, если бы когда-нибудь Сбылась поэта сновиденья! Пушк. Посл. к Юдину. [Николка:] Хоть бы дивизион наш был скорее готов. Булгаков, Дни Турб. </definition>
     </sense>
     <sense value="◊" class="8">
      <definition> С неопр. ф. глаг. Полететь бы пташечке К синю морю; Убежать бы молодцу в лес дремучий. Дельв. Пела, пела пташечка.. ... ... </definition>
     </sense>
     <sense value="//" class="6">
      <definition> Употр. для выражения опасения по поводу ... ... ... </definition>
      <sense value="◊" class="8">
       <definition> С неопр. ф. глаг., имеющей перед собой отрицание. <b>- </b>Гляди, - говорю, - бабочка, не кусать бы тебе локтя! Так-таки оно все на мое вышло. Леск. Воительница. </definition>
       </sense>
... ... ... ... ... ... ... ... ... ... ... ... ... ... ... ... ... ... ... ... ... ... ... ... ... ... ... ... ... ... ... ... ... ... ...
     </sense>
    </sense>
    <sense value="б)" class="5">
     <definition> Пожелание. Условие я бы предпочел не подписывать. Л. Толст. Письмо А. Ф. Марксу, 27 марта 1899. </definition>
     <sense value="◊" class="8">
      <definition> С неопр. ф. глаг. Поохотиться бы по-настоящему, на коня бы денег добыть, - мечтал старик. Г. Марков, Строговы. </definition>
     </sense>
     <sense value="◊" class="8">
... ... ... ... ... ... ... ... ... ... ... ... ... ... ... ... ... ... ... ... ... ... ... ... ... ... ... ... ... ... ... ... ... ... ...
```

```
<sense value="в)" class="5">
  <definition> Желание-просьба, совет или предложение.... ... ... ... </definition>
</sense>
<sense value="г)" class="5">
  <definition> Желаемость целесообразного и полезного действия. </definition>
  <sense value="◊" class="8">
… … … … … … … … … … … … … … … … … … … … … … … … … … … … … … … … … … … …
```

## 4 The Parameterized Grammar of Dependency Hypergraph for the Second Parsing Level (SCD-config2) of DLR

In the course of modeling the SCD configurations for the 6 large dictionaries discussed previously, *i.e.* **DLR**, **DAR**, **TLF**, **DWB**, **GWB**, and **DMLRL** (Curteanu et al., 2008, 2010, 2012a, 2012b), we attempted to use the XCES TEI P5 (2007) dictionary standard for *encoding* the SCD *parsing method*. While, at the basic level, this encoding is sufficient, a detailed description of the sense marker classes and their dependency hypergraphs was not possible. We have therefore examined ways to extend the dictionary encoding standard towards the "*least common multiple*" for the representation of lexicographic structures and dependencies of the dictionaries we have parsed. Since this extension is carried out incrementally, the addition of further information, possibly absent from these dictionaries but present in others, is straightforward. Since the XML format can be described with a DTD, which is, at heart, a grammar representation, we have proposed the extensions given below as *parameterized grammars* for the task at hand.

For the sake of simplicity and ease of understanding, we propose the creation of three grammar types, one for each of the SCD configurations used for parsing. The current form of the SCD-config1 grammar for lexicographic segments is given below. The rules are split into groups, according to the reason for their presence in the grammar: general rules, which are applied to all dictionaries, rules added to represent **DLR** structures, rules added to represent **DAR** structures, etc. (the order of the added rules is that of analyzing the dictionaries). If a rule is already present, it is not added again, as the desired result is a seamless package for the SCD-config1 of all the six dictionaries. We use the attribute type for the *Body_sense* variable in order to link the segment marker type to the actual rule for expanding the body of a segment (the link between SCD-config1 and SCD-config2, as the SCD-config2 is *specific* to each segment it belongs to). In this grammar we also show how we can reuse large parts of the existing XCES TEI P5 dictionary encoding standard. The sense marker class dependency hypergraph of SCD-config2 is (Curteanu et al.; 2010, p. 41):

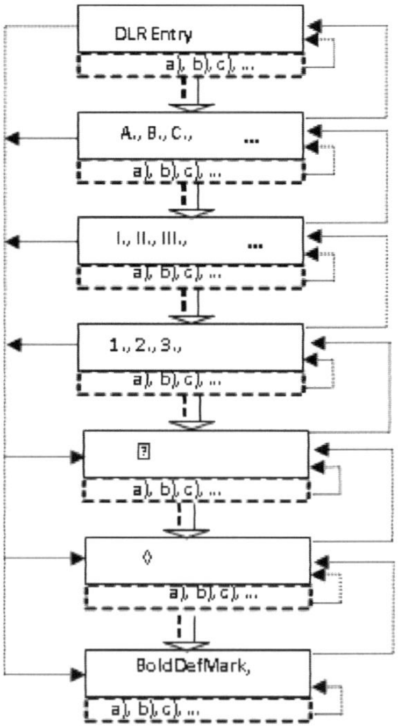


**General**
Entry → Root_sense Seg S
S → Seg S
S → ""
Seg → Mrk Root_sense Body_sense Tail_sense, type(Body_sense) = type(Mrk)
Mrk → ""

Root_sense → ""
Body_sense → ""
Tail_sense → ""

**DLR**
Mrk → newPrg, type(newPrg) = senseSeg
Mrk → newPrgDash, type(newPrgDash) = morphSeg
Root_sense → MorfDef
Body_sense → entry, if(type(Body_sense) = senseSeg)
Body_sense → MorphologicalPart, if(type(Body_sense) = morphSeg)
MorphologicalPart → Gram Etym
Gram → Gram TEI P5
Etym → Etym TEI P5

We propose the following parameterized grammar to describe the above dependency hypergraph functioning (*i.e.* SCD-Config2 parsing level for **DLR**). The rules are grouped in packages according to the direction of generation: *descending rules* go towards less general senses (*e.g.* **A.** to **I.**), *ascending rules* return to superior senses (*e.g.* **I.** to **A.**), describing the closing condition, while *splitting rules* are calls to the enumeration partitioning. The *enumeration* procedure is given in the *enumeration package*, as, although enumeration items are subsenses of their parents, they must meet certain restrictions described in the production rule attributes.

The attributes used are *parent* and *item*. The *parent* of a node is the sense from which that node is generated, and the *item* of an element is its position in the list of sister elements. In order to jump over sense levels, as most dictionaries do (*e.g.* **A.** to **1.**), we have used a *dummy node* for each skipped level, as the grammar is built so that it cannot generate a lower sense level without the superior level (this is a correctness restriction). The dummy nodes derivate to the empty string and are not itemized (the *item attribute* is not incremented for them).

entry → newPrg e LatCapLet; parent(LatCapLet) = e; item(LatCapLet) = 0
entry → e

LatCapLet → LatCapLet_Mrk LatCapNum; parent(LatCapLet_Mrk) = parent(LatCapLet);
  item(LatCapLet_Mrk) = item(LatCapLet) + 1; parent(LatCapNum) = LatCapLet_Mrk;
  item(LatCapNum) = 0
LatCapLet → LatCapLet_Dummy LatCapNum; parent(LatCapLet_Dummy) = parent(LatCapLet);
  item(LatCapLet_Dummy) = item(LatCapLet); parent(LatCapNum) = LatCapLet_Dummy;
  item(LatCapNum) = 0
LatCapLet → LatCapLet_Mrk; parent(LatCapLet_Mrk) = parent(LatCapLet);
  item(LatCapLet_Mrk) = item(LatCapLet) + 1

**==descending==**
LatCapNum → LatCapNum_Mrk ArabNum; parent(LatCapNum_Mrk) = parent(LatCapNum);
  item(LatCapNum_Mrk) = item(LatCapNum) + 1; parent(ArabNum) = LatCapNum_Mrk;
  item(ArabNum) = 0
LatCapNum → LatCapNum_Dummy ArabNum; parent(LatCapNum_Dummy) = parent(LatCapNum);
  item(LatCapNum_Dummy) = item(LatCapNum); parent(ArabNum) = LatCapNum_Dummy;
  item(ArabNum) = 0
LatCapNum → LatCapNum_Mrk; parent(LatCapNum_Mrk) = parent(LatCapNum);
  item(LatCapNum_Mrk) = item(LatCapNum) + 1
**==asending==c**

LatCapNum → LatCapLet; parent(LatCapLet) = parent(parent(LatCapNum));
item(LatCapLet) = item(parent(LatCapNum))

**==descending==**
ArabNum → ArabNum_Mrk RombP; parent(ArabNum_Mrk) = parent(ArabNum); item(ArabNum_Mrk) = item(ArabNum) + 1; parent(RombP) = ArabNum_Mrk; item(rombP) = 0
ArabNum → ArabNum_Dummy RombP; parent(ArabNum_Dummy) = parent(ArabNum); item(ArabNum_Dummy) = item(ArabNum); parent(RombP) = ArabNum_Mrk; item(rombP) = 0
ArabNum → ArabNum_Mrk; parent(ArabNum_Mrk) = parent(ArabNum); item(ArabNum_Mrk) = item(ArabNum) + 1;
**==ascending==**
ArabNum → LatCapLet; parent(LatCapLet) = parent(parent (ArabNum)); item(LatCapLet) = item(parent(ArabNum))

**==splitting==**
ArabNum → ArabNum_Mrk LatSmaLet; parent(ArabNum_Mrk) = parent(ArabNum); item(ArabNum_Mrk) = item(ArabNum) + 1; parent(LatSmaLet) = ArabNum_Mrk; item(LatSmaLet) = 0
ArabNum → ArabNum_Dummy RombP; parent(ArabNum_Dummy) = parent(ArabNum); item(ArabNum_Dummy) = item(ArabNum); parent(LatSmaLet) = ArabNum_Mrk; item(LatSmaLet) = 0

**==descending==**
RombP → ♦ RombG; parent(♦) = parent(rombP); item(♦) = item(RombP) + 1; parent(RombG) = ♦; item(RombG) = 0
RombP → RombP_Dummy RombG; parent(RombP_Dummy) = parent(rombP); item(RombP_Dummy) = item(RombP); parent(RombG) = RombP_Dummy; item(RombG) = 0
RombP → ♦; parent(♦) = parent(rombP); item(♦) = item(RombP) + 1
**==ascending==**
RombP → ArabNum; parent(ArabNum) = parent(parent(RombP)); item(ArabNum) = item(parent(RombP))

**==splitting==**
RombP → ♦ LatSmaLet; parent(♦) = parent(rombP); item(♦) = item(RombP) + 1; parent(LatSmaLet) = ♦; item(LatSmaLet) = 0
RombP → RombP_Dummy LatSmaLet; parent(RombP_Dummy) = parent(rombP); item(RombP_Dummy) = item(RombP); parent(LatSmaLet) = RombP_Dummy; item(LatSmaLet) = 0

**==descending==**
RombG → ◊ Atom; parent(◊) = parent(rombG); item(◊) = item(RombG) + 1; parent(Atom) = ◊; item(Atom) = 0
RombG → ◊; parent(◊) = parent(rombG); item(◊) = item(RombG) + 1
**==ascending==**
RombG → RombP; parent(RombP) = parent(parent(RombG)); item(RombP) = item(parent(RombG))

**==splitting==**
RombG → ◊ LatSmaLet; parent(◊) = parent(rombG); item(◊) = item(RombG) + 1; parent(LatSmaLet) = ◊; item(LatSmaLet) = 0
RombG → RombG_Dummy LatSmaLet; parent(RombG_Dummy) = parent(rombG); item(RombG_Dummy) = item(RombG); parent(LatSmaLet) = RombG_Dummy; item(LatSmaLet) = 0

**==descending==**
DefAtom → DefAtom_Mrk DefAtom; parent(DefAtom_Mrk) = parent(DefAtom); item(DefAtom_Mrk) = item(DefAtom) + 1; parent(DefAtom) = parent(DefAtomSt); item(DefAtom) = item(DefAtom_Mrk)
DefAtom → DefAtom_Mrk; parent(DefAtom_Mrk) = parent(DefAtom); item(DefAtom_Mrk) = item(DefAtom)+1

**==ascending==**
DefAtom → RombG; parent(RombG) = parent (parent(DefAtom)); item(RombG) = item(parent(DefAtom))
**==splitting==**
DefAtom → DefAtom_Mrk LatSmaLet; parent(DefAtom_Mrk) = parent(DefAtom); item(DefAtom_Mrk) = item(DefAtom) + 1; parent(LatSmaLet) = DefAtom_Mrk; item(LatSmaLet) = 0

**==enumeration==**
**==descending==**
LatSmaLet → LatSmaLet_Mrk RombP, if parent(LatSmaLet) > RombP; parent(LatSmaLet_Mrk) = parent(LatSmaLet); item(LatSmaLet_Mrk) = item(LatSmaLet) + 1; parent(RombP) = LatSmaLet_Mrk; item(RombP) = 0;
LatSmaLet → LatSmaLet_Mrk RombP, if parent(LatSmaLet) > RombG; parent(LatSmaLet_Mrk) = parent(LatSmaLet); item(LatSmaLet_Mrk) = item(LatSmaLet) + 1; parent(RombG) = LatSmaLet_Mrk; item(RombG) = 0;
LatSmaLet → LatSmaLet_Mrk LatSmaLet; parent(LatSmaLet_Mrk) = parent(LatSmaLet); item(LatSmaLet_Mrk) = item(LatSmaLet) + 1
**==ascending==**
LatSmaLet → ArabNum, if parent(parent(LatSmaLet)) > ArabNum; parent(ArabNum) = parent(parent(LatSmaLet)); item(ArabNum) = item(parent(LatSmaLet))
LatSmaLet → RombP, if parent(parent(LatSmaLet)) > RombP; parent(RombP) = parent(parent(LatSmaLet)); item(RombP) = item(parent(LatSmaLet))
LatSmaLet → RombG, if parent(parent(LatSmaLet)) > RombG; parent(RombG) = parent(parent(LatSmaLet)); item(RombG) = item(parent(LatSmaLet))
LatSmaLet → DefAtom, if parent(parent(LatSmaLet)) > DefAtom; parent(DefAtom) = parent(parent(LatSmaLet)); item(DefAtom) = item(parent(LatSmaLet))

We highlight the following particular and interesting new lexicographic units during the SCD lexicographic modeling: the intricate recognition and organization of **DWB** segments; the recursive "**Rem.**", "**Dér.**" (and other) segments in **TLF**; the "**TildaDef**" segment / package in **DMLRL**, with similar syntactic behavior as the "**Nest**" segment / package in **DAR**; the sense / definition inheritance "long-dash" marker and rules in **TLF** and **GWB**; the *dictionary authors' examples* in **DLR** and **DMLRL** (the latter, specially marked); the *indexed examples-to-definitions* package, specially marked and met only in **TLF**; various species of "*sigles*" (*i.e.* text source references) etc. While many lexicographic structures are similar or identical in their syntactic or semantic behavior over several dictionaries, the above mentioned examples should be integrated carefully within their appropriate SCD configuration, *i.e.* dependency hypergraph, described by corresponding parameterized grammars within the unitary procedural DTD.

# 5 Conclusion

The current DTD for dictionaries in the standard XCES TEI P5 (2007) represents dictionary entry data types, described with context-free grammars. For the recursive sense dependencies embodied into the dependency hypergraph of a parsing level, the challenge was to provide a formal tool for procedural description, and we delivered the parameterized grammars that describe the functioning of the first and second SCD-configurations (*i.e.* parsing levels) for **DLR**. This is the first phase of the newly proposed, procedural DTD, and there is still a lot of work to accomplish the project of such a general, procedural DTD. We will describe the dependency hypergraphs of SCD configurations for the *six* largest dictionaries we have already parsed (**DLR** completely, the other ones, partially) and augment the parameterized grammars on each level of SCD configuration, such that to obtain a *least common multiple* description for *all* the *six* considered dictionaries. The procedural DTD does not overlap the currently existing DTD for dictionaries in the TEI P5 standard, but effectively extends it from the detailed, static description of dictionary entry data types, to the procedural, hierarchically organized of *all* the component lexicographic structures, SCD-modeled, in the largest dictionaries.

We provided here the parameterized grammars for the first two SCD configurations of **DLR**, and achieved only one atomic sense dependency hypergraph (for **DMLRL**) from the six dictionaries involved. There are necessary (at least) 18 (6 dictionaries x 3 SCD-configurations) grammars, combined into their three *least common multiple* grammars on the synthesized *three* parsing levels of SCD configurations. Any new dictionary parsing experiments could possibly bring (or not!) novelties, incrementally integrated into the final version of the new procedural DTD for dictionaries, made up of (at least) three packages of parameterized grammars.

These are the dimensions of the project (which may also be called Document Structural Description – DSD, as the procedural completion to the current DTD for dictionaries). This project constitutes the formal (and incremental) description framework of a *general parser* for large thesaurus-dictionaries, proved to be *optimal*, *portable*, and *robust* (Curteanu *et al.*; 2010).

## References


Curteanu, N., Moruz, A., Trandabăţ, D. (2008): *Extracting Sense Trees from the Romanian Thesaurus by Sense Segmentation & Dependency Parsing*, Proceedings of CogAlex-I Workshop, COLING-2008, Manchester, UK, pp. 55-63, http://aclweb.org/anthology/W/W08/W08-1908.pdf

Curteanu, N., Trandabăţ, D., Moruz, A. (2010): *An Optimal and Portable Parsing Method for Romanian, French, and German Large Dictionaries*, Proceedings of COGALEX-II Workshop, COLING-2010, Beijing, China, pp. 38-47, http://www.aclweb.org/anthology-new/W/W10/W10-3407.pdf

Curteanu, Neculai, Svetlana Cojocaru, Eugenia Burcă (2012a): *Parsing the Dictionary of Modern Literary Russian Language with the Method of SCD Configurations. The Lexicographic Modeling*. Comp. Science Journal of Moldova, Academy of Sciences of Moldova, Vol. 20, No.1(58), pp. 42-81, http://www.math.md/files/csjm/v20-n1/v20-n1-(pp42-82).pdf

Curteanu, Neculai, Svetlana Cojocaru, Alex Moruz (2012b): *Lexicographic Modeling and Parsing Experiments for the Dictionary of Modern Literary Russian Language*, ConsILR-2012 Proceedings, Bucharest, The Editorial House of "Al. I. Cuza" University, Iaşi, pp. 189-198.

Curteanu, Neculai, Alex Moruz (2012c): *Toward the Soundness of Sense Structure Definitions in Thesaurus-Dictionaries. Parsing Problems and Solutions*. Computer Science Journal of Moldova, Academy of Sciences of Moldova, Vol. 20, No.3 (60), pp. 275-303, http://www.math.md/files/csjm/v20-n3/v20-n3-(pp275-303).pdf.

DWB (2010): Das Woerterbuch-Netz (2010): http://germazope.uni-trier.de/Projects/WBB/woerterbuecher/

DMLRL (1994): Dictionary of Modern Literary Russian Language (20 volumes, 1994): Словарь современного русского литературного языка. В 20 томах. Издательство: М.: Русский язык; Издание 2-е, перераб. и доп. 864 страниц; 1991-1994 г. ISBN: 5-200-01068-3 (in Russian).

TLF (2010): Le Trésor de la Langue Française informatisé (2010) : http://atilf.atilf.fr/tlf.htm

XCES TEI Standard, Variant P5, (2007): http://www.tei-c.org/Guidelines/P5/

# Multilingual Universal Word Explanation Generation from UNL Ontology

*Khan Md. Anwarus Salam*[1,3] *Hiroshi Uchida*[1,2] *Tetsuro Nishino*[3]
(1) UNDL Foundation, Tokyo, Japan.
(2) United Nation University, Tokyo, Japan.
(3) The University of Electro-Communications, Tokyo, Japan.
salamkhan@uec.ac.jp, uchida@undl.org, nishino@uec.ac.jp

ABSTRACT

To develop a common language, it is essential to have enough vocabulary to express all the concepts contained in all the world languages. Those vocabularies can only be developed by native speakers and should be defined by formal ways. Considering the situation, at this moment Universal Networking Language (UNL) is the best solution as the common language, and Universal Words (UWs) are the most promising candidates to represent all the world concepts in different languages. However, UWs itself are formal and not always to be understandable for human. To ensure every language speakers can create the correct UWs dictionary entry, we need to provide the explanation of UWs in different natural languages for humans. As there are millions of UWs, it is very expensive to manually build the UWs explanation in all natural languages. To solve this problem, this research proposes the way to auto generate the UWs explanation in UNL, using the property inheritance based on UW System. Using UNL DeConverter from that UNL the system can generate the explanation in more than 40 languages.

KEYWORDS : UNL; Ontology; Word Semantics; NLP;

## 1 Introduction

To break the language barrier we need to have an artificial common language. For developing such a common language, it is essential to have enough vocabulary to express all the concepts contained in all the world languages. Because, human can understand the dictionary entries by reading the explanation (or meaning) of concepts in natural language. However, those concept dictionaries in different languages can only be developed by native speakers. Those universal concepts should be defined by formal ways.

Considering the situation, at this moment Universal Networking Language (UNL) is the best solution and Universal Words (UWs) are the most promising candidates. UNL represents natural language sentences as a semantic network with hyper nodes. In this semantic network, nodes represent concepts and arcs represent relations between concepts. These concepts are referred as UWs. UWs themselves are formal but not always to be understandable by human. As human should provide the dictionary entries in different language, it is essential to have UWs explanation in different natural language. As there are millions of UWs, it is very expensive to manually build all the UWs explanation in all natural languages.

UNL Ontology is a semantic network with hyper nodes. It contains UW System which describes the hierarchy of the UWs in lattice structure, all possible semantic co-occurrence relations between each UWs and UWs definition in UNL. With the property inheritance based on UW System, possible relations between UWs can be deductively inferred from their upper UWs and this inference mechanism reduces the number of binary relation descriptions of the UNL Ontology. In the topmost level UWs are divided into four categories: adverbial concept, attributive concept, nominal concept and predicative concept.

Since UNL Ontology provides the semantic background of each UWs, the goal of this research is to auto generate the UWs meaning from UNL Ontology. Current UNL ontology contains around 1466598 unique concepts or UWs. So the goal of this research is to auto generate the natural language explanation for all these UWs. UNL ontology is developed in general domain.

Beside UNL Ontology there are other popular lexical resources available in general domain like WordNet (Miller, 1995), EDR dictionary etc. However, from other general ontologies currently it is not possible to auto generate the explanation for the concepts in different languages. To generate such explanation automatically, this research has been inspired from the unique architectural design of UNL (Uchida et. al. 1999). As the UNL systems are successfully implemented and became available online recently, it is possible to utilize UNL architecture now. The original idea of auto generating the explanation for different concepts in different languages is very new. There is no other existing ontology available which attempted to auto generate the explanation in different languages from the ontology itself.

This research proposes the way to auto generate the UWs explanation in UNL from the semantic background provided by UNL Ontology. The system first discover a graph the SemanticWordMap, which contains all direct and deductively inferred relations for one particular UW from the UNL Ontology. Using UNL DeConverter from that UNL the system can generate the explanation in more than 40 languages. This auto generated explanation will help the human to understand the UWs meaning to provide their corresponding dictionary entries. So beside the general users, this system is useful for the UWs dictionary builders and the editors.

With the property inheritance based on UW System, the system converts SemanticWordMap relations into UNL graph using rule-based approach. Finally from this UNL graph, UNL DeConverter generates the UWs meaning in different natural languages.

# 2 BACKGROUND

## 2.1 Universal Networking Language (UNL)

UNL initiative was originally launched in 1996 as a project of the Institute of Advanced Studies of the United Nations University (UNU/IAS)[1]. UNL was first introduced to public in 1999 (Uchida et. al. 1999). In 2001, the United Nation University set up the UNDL Foundation[2], to be responsible for the development and management of the UNL project. In 2005, a new technical manual of UNL was published (Uchida et. al. 2005), which defined UNL as an information and knowledge representation language for computer. UNL has all the components to represent knowledge described in natural languages. UWs constitute the vocabulary of UNL and each concept of natural languages has unique UW. A UW of UNL is defined in the following format:

*<uw> =:: <headword>[<constraint list>]*

Here, headword of a UW is an English expression which can be a word, a compound word, a phrase or a sentence. UWs are the basic elements for constructing one UNL expression of a

[1]http://www.ias.unu.edu/
[2]http://www.undl.org/

sentence or a compound concept. So keys to the information in UNL database are UW. UWs are inter-linked with other UWs using "relations" to form the UNL expressions of sentences. These relations specify the role of each word in a sentence. Using "attributes" it can express the subjectivity of author. Currently, UWs are available for many languages such as Arabic, Bengali, Chinese, English, French, Indonesian, Italian, Japanese, Mongolian, Russian, Spanish, and so forth.

Each UWs are interlinked with each other through the UW System in the UNL Ontology. Master definitions for UWs describe all relations that a UW can hold. A minimum set of relations is used as constraints of UW for the purpose to make a UW distinguishable from sibling UWs.

## 2.2 UNL Ontology

UNL Ontology is a lattice structure where UWs are inter-connected through relations including hierarchical relations such as icl (a-kind-of) and iof (an-instance-of). UNL Ontology includes possible relations between UWs, UWs definition and UNL system hierarchy. In the UNL Ontology, all possible semantic co-occurrence relations, such as 'agt', 'obj', etc, between UWs are defined based on the UW System. Every possible semantic co-occurrence relation is defined between the two most general UWs in the hierarchy of the UW System that can have the relation. With the property inheritance characteristic of the UW System, possible relations between lower UWs are deductively inferred from their upper UWs and this inference mechanism reduces the number of binary relation descriptions of the UNL Ontology. In the topmost level UWs are divided into 4 categories adverbial concept, attributive concept, nominal concept and predicative concept.

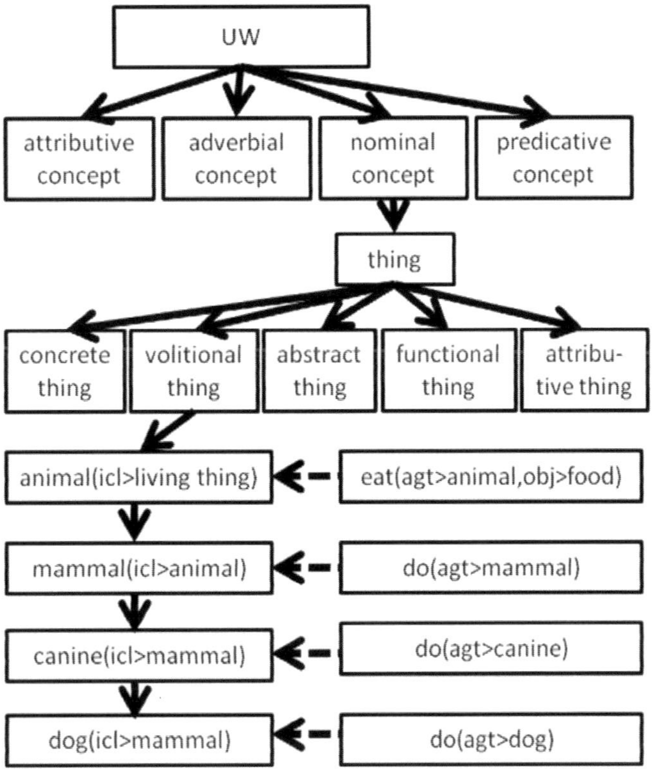


FIGURE 1 – UWs hierarchy in UNL Ontology.

Figure 1 shows the topmost level of partial UNL Ontology where the black directed lines represent "icl" relation and dotted directed lines represent "agt" relations. In Figure 1 we only expanded partial "nominal concept" until "dog(icl>mammal)" to give a brief overview of the UNL Ontology. In UNL Ontology each UWs have incoming and outgoing relations with other UWs, which define the semantic background. For example in Figure 1 "animal(icl>living thing)" has two incoming relations, "agt" from "eat(agt>animal,obj>food)", and "icl" from "volitional thing". "animal(icl>living thing)" has only one outgoing relation "icl" to "mammal(icl>animal)". As possible relations between lower UWs are deductively inferred from their upper UWs, we can infer that "mammal(icl>animal)", "canine(icl>mammal)" and "dog (icl>mammal)" also has an incoming relation "agt" from "eat(agt>animal,obj>food)".

### 2.3 UNL Explorer

UNL Explorer[3] is a web based application, which combines all the components of UNL system to be accessible online. UNL Explorer users can translate the documents in various languages such as UNL, English, Japanese and Arabic etc. UNL Society members can add or edit information using UNL Explorer. It allows users to view the UNL Ontology which contains UWs hierarchy (a lattice structure) in a plain tree form. It can also display incoming and outgoing relationships for each UW.

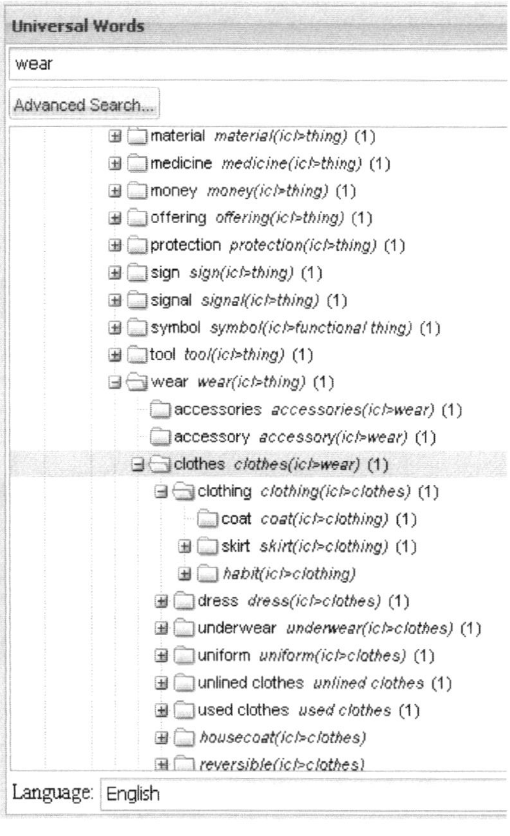


FIGURE 2 – UW search result for "wear" from UNL Ontology

UNL Explorer provides UNL Enconverter for natural language to UNL conversion. It also provides UNL Deconverter for UNL to natural language conversion. Both UNL EnConverter and Deconverter support different languages such as Chinese, English, Japanese and so forth. UNL

[3]http://www.undl.org/unlexp/

Explorer users can browse UNL Ontology from the Universal Words frame in the left side. Figure 2 shows sample UNL Ontology search result for the word "wear".

UNL Explorer also provides an advanced search facility. Users can check incoming and outgoing relationships using this facility. Both UNL Ontology search mechanism is accessible for computer program using UNL Explorer API. However, to use this API, user need to be a UNL society member by signing an agreement with UNDL Foundation.

## 3 Multilingual Explanation Generation

The system framework for the multilingual explanation generation of the UWs is illustrated in Figure 3. The input of this system is one UW and the output of the system is the meaning of that UW in natural language such as English. For the given UW, the system first discover a SemanticWordMap, which contains all direct and deductively inferred relations for one particular UW from the UNL Ontology. So input of this step is one UW and output of this step is the WordMap graph. In next step we convert the WordMap graph into UNL using conversion rules. This conversion rules can generate "From UWs only" and "From UNL Ontology", based on user's requirement. So input of this step is the WordMap graph and Output is the UNL expression. In the final step we describe in natural language by converting the UNL expression using UNL DeConverter, provided by UNL Explorer.

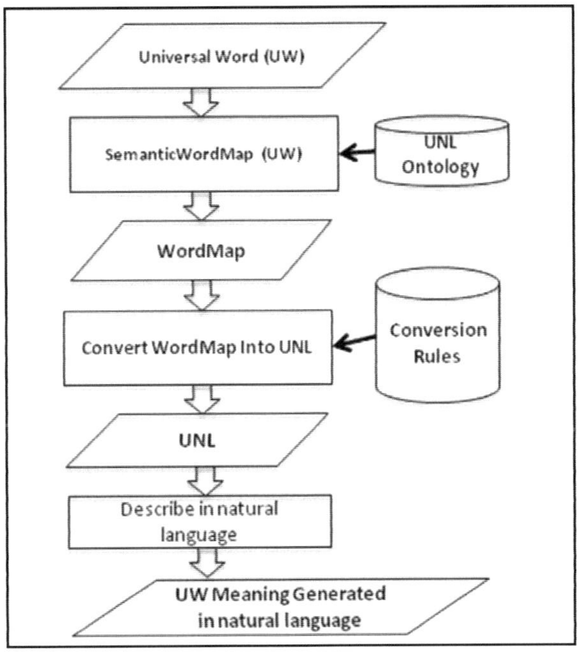


FIGURE 3 - System framework for multilingual explanation generation for UWs

### 3.1 SemanticWordMap

To discover inferred relationships, the system first discovers the SemanticWordMap (Salam et. el. 2011), which contains all direct and deductively inferred relations for one particular UW from the UNL Ontology. Edges of this graph are the relations of UNL Ontology. In UNL Ontology each relation is connected from "fromUW" to "toUW". Starting from a given UW we discover the SemanticWordMap graph which includes deductively inferred relationships. A maximum search depth is established to limit the size of the graph.

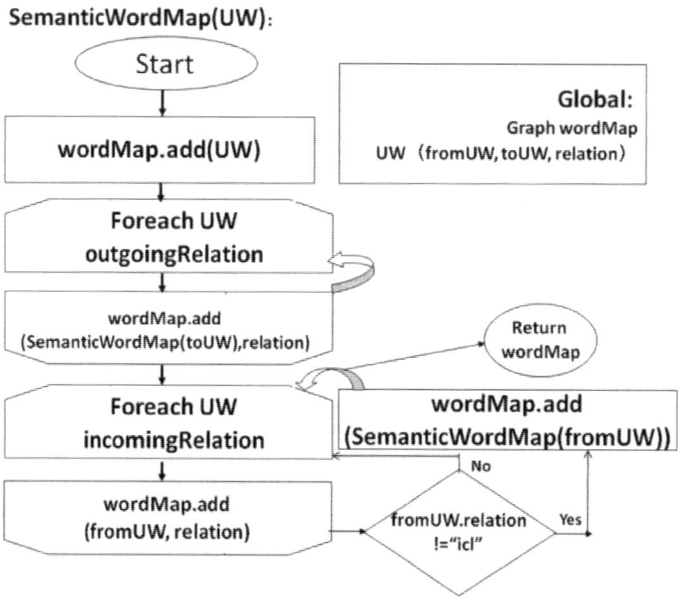


FIGURE 4- SemanticWordMap algorithm

To discover the SemanticWordMap graph from UNL Ontology user has to give a particular UW. First the algorithm adds that UW into the wordMap graph. For each outgoing relation from that UW, it add toUW into the wordMap and then recursively call SemanticWordMap(toUW) to discover the relations from toUW. Then for each incoming relationship it adds the fromUW with relation into the wordMap graph. If the relationship is not "icl", it adds the expanded graph by recursively calling SemanticWordMap(fromUW). As UNL Ontology contains a huge number of UWs and relationships, we have a heuristic approach to limit the SemanticWordMap graph to produce meaningful and specific information. So the algorithm keep discovering the graph until it reach maximum search depth or if it reach the topmost UW. Finally it returns the wordMap graph which contains all the UW relations.

For example, Figure 5 shows the partial SemanticWordMap for dog(icl>mammal). The output of this first step is the SemanticWordMap discovered from UNL Ontology. Here dotted arrows represent "agt" relations and black arrows are "icl" relations.

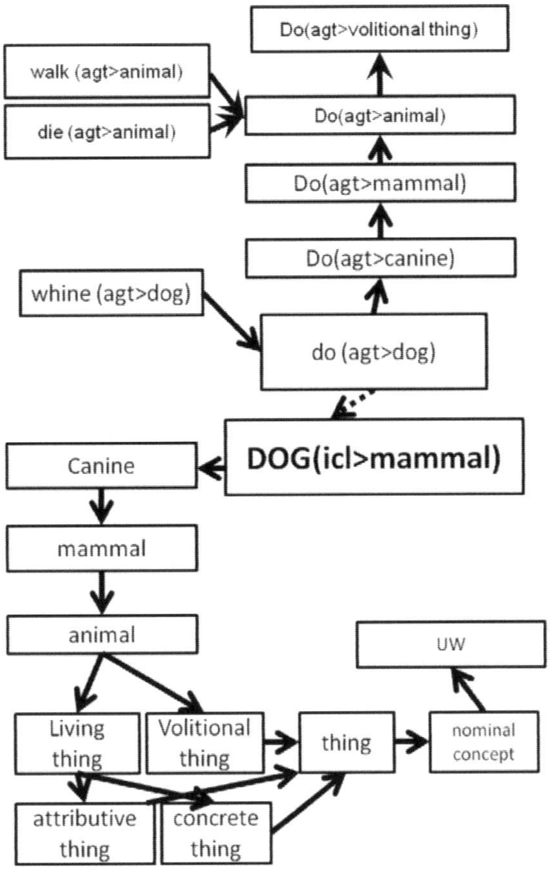


FIGURE 5- Partial SemanticWordMap for dog(icl>mammal)

## 3.2 Convert SemanticWordMap Into UNL

In this step we convert SemanticWordMap relations into UNL using some generalized rules. We first categorize the UWs into several categories such as "do", "is-a", "occur" and "be". In general "do" categories represent actions, "is-a" represent features, "occur" represents changes and "be" represents status. Due to the property inheritance characteristic of the UNL Ontology, possible relations between lower UWs are deductively inferred from their upper UWs. Using SemanticWordMap we deductively infer the relationship with dog(icl>mammal). For example from Figure 3 we can say that UWs walk(agt>animal) and die(agt>animal) are related with dog(icl>mammal) as well.

TABLE I. CATEGORIZED RELATIONS FOR DOG(ICL>MAMMAL)

| **UW** | **Categorized from SemanticWordMap** | |
|---|---|---|
| | ***UW Categories*** | ***Description*** |
| DOG (icl>mammal) | do | whine, walk, die…. |
| | Is-a | canine, mammal, animal, .. |

Table I shows the categorized relations from SemanticWordMap for the UW dog(icl>mammal), and the generated description categorized into several UW relationship types. Steven Pinker pointed out that there are specified connections between verbs and object types in (Pinker, 2007). In this direction, we have manually identified such rules. After categorization we can convert the relations into UNL expression using different rules for each category. All these rules are currently designed by human.

After categorization we can convert the relations into UNL expression using different rules for each category. For example Figure 6 shows UWs relation derived from SemanticWordMap. To convert these category UWs relations into UNL, we use the following "Rule 1":

*(Rule 1: do) If (isaKindof(UW2,"do")) agt(UW3:08.@entry.@ability,UW1:00.@topic)*

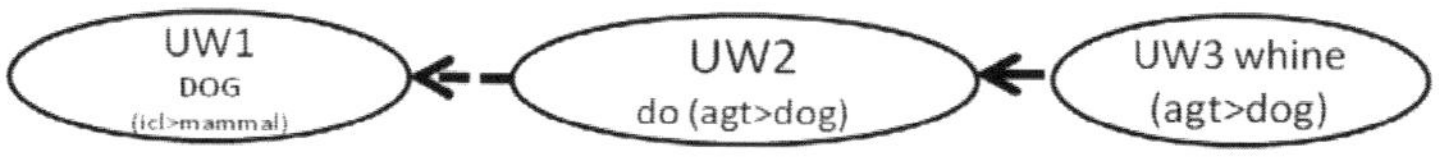


FIGURE 6: *do relations derived from SemanticWordMap*

Rule 1 check whether UW2 is related with "do" by using "*isaKindof* (UW2,"do"). For example if isaKindof("do (agt>dog)","do") = TRUE, then the generated UNL is: *agt(whine(agt>dog):08.@entry.@ability,dog(icl>mammal):00.@topic)*

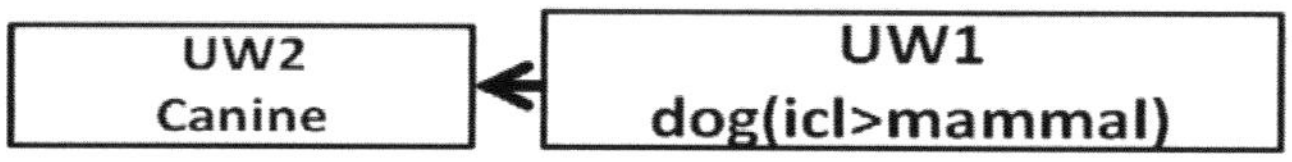


FIGURE 7: icl relations derived from SemanticWordMap

Figure 7 shows "icl" relation derived from SemanticWordMap. To convert this UWs into UNL we use following "Rule 2":

*(Rule 2: is-a) If (isaKindof(UW1,UW2)) icl(uw1:09, uw2:0F)*

Rule 2 check whether UW1 has "icl" relationship by using "*isaKindof* (UW1,UW2). For example isaKindof("dog (icl>mammal)","canine*(icl>mammal)*") = TRUE, so the generated UNL is: *icl(dog(icl>mammal):09, canine(icl>mammal): 0F)*

The above mechanism works for UWs under "nominal concepts". For other types of UWs such as "attributive concepts" we need to use different set of rules. For the UW write(agt>person,obj>report), we can get the partial SemanticWordMap as shown in Figure 7.

From Figure 8 using from UWs only we can get UNL expression for "Person write a report". However in the meaning of the UW we should not use that concept. Instead we can use immediate higher UW concept. So in this case instead of "write" we can use "produce". By replacing person with someone we can get the UNL expression for "Someone produce a report". In this way, using different rules the system can convert SemanticWordMap relations into UNL.

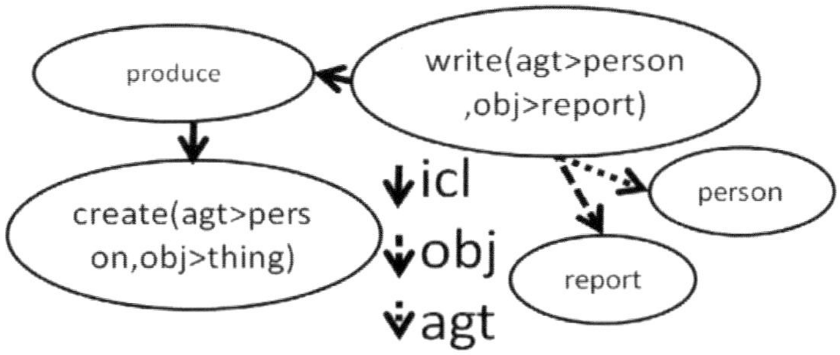


FIGURE 8: UNL Relations from UWs only

## 3.3 Describe in natural language

Finally, we used UNL DeConverter to convert the UNL expressions into natural languages. UNL DeConverter is a language independent generator that provides a framework for syntactic and morphological generation as well as co-occurrence-based word selection for natural collocation. It can deconvert UNL expressions into a variety of native languages, using a number of linguistic data such as Word Dictionary, Grammatical Rules and Co-occurrence Dictionary of each language. We used UNL DeConverter to convert the UNL into several natural languages such as English, Japanese etc.

## 3.4 Implementation in UNL Explorer

Finally the explanation can be expressed in different natural languages such as in English, Japanese or other languages using UNL DeConverter. Determining this kind of relationship can be very useful for knowledge engineering. For experiment we implemented the proposed method in UNL Explorer. Our implementation could successfully produce 1466598 UWs explanation in UNL. Table II shows some sample UWs explanation generated by the proposed method. Here, we only reported sample explanations in English and Japanese, together with the UNL expression.

TABLE II. SAMPLE UWS MEANINGS AUTO GENERATED USING OUR PROPOSED MECHANISM

| **Universal Word** | **Explanation Generated from UNL Ontology in Different Languages** | | |
|---|---|---|---|
| | ***English*** | ***Japanese*** | ***UNL*** |
| write(agt>person,obj>report) | Someone produce a report | 誰かが報告書を作成する | agt(produce(icl>manufacture(agt>thing,obj>thing)):08.@entry, someone:00.@topic) obj(produce(icl>manufacture(agt>thing,obj>thing)):08, report(icl>account) :0I) |
| Dog (icl>mammal) | Dog is a canine, mammal and animal. Dog can eat, whine, walk and die. | 犬は犬、哺乳類や動物です。犬は、食べて駄々をこねる、歩いて、死ぬことができます。 | aoj(:01.@entry,dog(icl>mammal):00) and:01(animal(icl>living thing):0S.@entry, mammal(icl>animal):0H) and:01(mammal(icl>animal):0H,canine(icl>tooth):09.@indef) |

Using UNL expressions and UNL DeConverter it is possible to generate the explanation in more than 40 languages as well. However, the quality of the explanation depends on the quality of that language DeConverter. Therefore precision of the system highly relies on UNL DeConverter and the semantic background provided by UNL Ontology. As the users of this system are the editors of UNL Ontology, it helps them to improve the quality of manually built UNL ontology. The UNL dictionary builders can also differentiate the UWs from the natural language explanation without understanding the UNL language.

## Conclusion

In this research we proposed the way to auto generate the meaning of each UWs using UNL Ontology. However, UNL Ontology by nature is a growing resource with millions of UWs. As UWs are not always understandable by human, the explanatory sentences are needed to develop necessary UWs for every language. For explaining UWs meaning it is necessary to auto generate from the same representation. Using our proposed solution computer can auto generate the meaning of UWs in more than 40 natural languages.

## References


George A. Miller. 1995. WordNet: A Lexical Database for English. Communications of the ACM Vol. 38, No. 11: 39-41.

H. Uchida, M. Zhu, and T. Della Senta. "The Universal Networking Language", 2nd ed. UNDL Foundation, 2005.

H. Uchida, M. Zhu, T. Della Senta. "A gift for a millenium". Tokyo: IAS/UNU. 1999..

Khan Md. Anwarus Salam, Hiroshi Uchida and Tetsuro Nishino. "How to Develop Universal Vocabularies Using Automatic Generation of the Meaning of Each Word", 7th International Conference on Natural Language Processing and Knowledge Engineering (NLPKE'11), Tokushima, Japan. ISBN: 978-1-61284-729-0. Page 243 – 246. 2011.

Steven Pinker. The Stuff of Thought: Language As a Window Into Human Nature. USA. 2007.

# Towards Merging Common and Technical Lexicon Wordnets

*Raquel AMARO*[1] *Sara MENDES*[1,2]

(1) Center of Linguistics of the University of Lisbon,
Av. Professor Gama Pinto 2, 1649-003 Lisbon, Portugal

(2) Universitat Pompeu Fabra
Roc Boronat, 138, Barcelona, Spain

{ramaro,sara.mendes}@clul.ul.pt

ABSTRACT

The growing amount of available information and the growing importance given to the access to technical information enhance the potential role of NLP applications in enabling users to deal with information for a variety of knowledge domains. In this process, lexical resources are crucial.

Using and comparing already existent wordnets for common and technical lexica, we set up a basis for integrating these resources without losing their specific information and properties. We demonstrate their compatibility and discuss strategies to overcome the issues arrising in their merging, namely aspects concerning conceptual variation, subnet and synset merging, and the incorporation of technical and non-technical information in definitions.

As we are using models of the lexicon that mirror the organization of the mental lexicon, the accomplishment of this goal can provide insights on the type of relations holding between common lexical items and terms. Also, the results of integrating such resources can contribute to the better intercommunication between experts and non-experts, and provide a useful resource for NLP, particularly for tools simultaneously serving specialist and non-specialist publics.

KEYWORDS : wordnet, technical lexicon, common lexicon, merging.

## 1 Introduction

Since its appearance, Princeton WordNet (Miller *et al.*, 1990; Fellbaum, 1998) has been the main database used in NLP research and applications. With a strong psychological motivation, relational models of the lexicon have played a leading role in machine lexical knowledge representation. WordNet potential as a resource for NLP has also been explored in tasks typically associated to domain-specific information, such as systems for information extraction and document indexing, retrieval and preservation, and applications for technical domains such as Law (Peters *et al.*, 2006), Medicine (Elhadad & Sutaria, 2007) or Urbanism (Lacasta *et al.*, 2008). Although manifesting a number of shortcomings (Bodenreider *et al.*, 2003; Bodenreider & Burgun, 2002; Burgun & Bodenreider, 2001; Magnini & Strapparava, 2001), which reflect the lack of domain expertise of lexicographers developing it and the fact that it was not originally built for domain-specific applications (Smith & Fellbaum, 2004), WordNet potential to model technical lexica is made apparent by research showing that concept-based resources (ontologies, thesauri and wordnets) have great usability in teaching

(Mudraya, 2006; Fuentes, 2001; Robinson, 1989; Hutchinson & Waters, 1981) or improving mutual understanding between specialist and non-specialist publics (Elhadad & Sutaria, 2007).

The globalization of most activities, alongside technology development, produced significant changes both in the relation between specialist and non-specialist publics and in different aspects of terminology. Recent studies on the use of computer-based tools for technical domains point to a mismatch between technical lexical information incorporated in such tools and non-expert discourse employed by lay users (Slaughter, 2002; Tse & Soergel, 2003; McCray & Tse, 2003). Moreover, while the use of terms by professionals is expected to be subject to control by standardization efforts, the highly contextually dependent usage of terms by lay persons is much more difficult to capture. All these factors make the combination of common and specialized language resources more and more crucial. The importance of encoding domain-specific information in the WordNet model has also been remarked in the last years. In this context, there has been a considerable amount of research dedicated to the integration of domain-specific information into generic synsets (Magnini *et al.*, 2002; Vossen, 2001; Magnini & Cavaglià, 2000) or to the determination of the relevance of common lexicon synsets with respect to specific domains (Buitelaar & Sacaleanu, 2001). In parallel, there have been several efforts to develop dedicated wordnets for technical domains, such as Medicine (Buitelaar & Sacaleanu, 2002; Smith & Fellbaum, 2004), Geography (Giunchiglia *et al.*, 2009), or the Maritime domain (Roventini & Marinelli, 2004).

Research on integrating specialist taxonomies and common lexicon taxonomies (Pedersen *et al.*, 2010) has also been developed, as well as on merging domain-specific lexical resources with WordNet (Bosch, n/d). Following from this research, in this paper we compare a common lexicon wordnet with wordnets for ten technical domains built for Portuguese, setting up the bases for integrating both resources without losing specific information and properties. We expect the merging of technical and common lexica to raise several challenges, particularly regarding mismatches in sense differentiation and the encoding of relevant conceptual relations in models that reflect the organization of the mental lexicon. Accomplishing our goal will set the grounds for providing a useful resource to the research community, particularly to researchers working with domain-specific NLP tools simultaneously serving specialist and non-specialist publics.

## 2 Comparing common and technical lexicon wordnets

The work depicted in this paper is framed by research on wordnets developed for technical domains and on the characteristics of terms and specialized language, as well as on the interface between common and technical lexicon. We use two existing resources, a common lexicon wordnet – WordNet.PT[1] – and ten domain-specific wordnets for different technical domains – LexTec[2], and compare them with regard to different aspects, namely the amount of variants per synset, the type of relations used and the density of the network of relations. Both resources have been independently encoded and revised manually within the general framework of EuroWordNet. WordNet.PT (WN.PT) currently has about 18,000 lexical entries, covering all the main part-of-speech (PoS). We consider a subset of the database (15,000 lexical units) which covers the most salient daily life communication topics (food, clothing, sports, education, geography, transportation, etc.). LexTec covers more than 8,000 lexical units from all the main PoS and was built following the same development strategies

[1] WordNet.PT (Marrafa 2001, 2002), available online at http://www.clul.ul.pt/clg/wordnetpt/index.html.

[2] LexTec (Marrafa *et al.* 2009), available online at http://www.instituto-camoes.pt/lextec/.

and relations used in WN.PT. LexTec is balanced between ten different domains: Banking, Commerce, Economy and Business Management, Energy, Environment, Insurance, International Trade Law, Telecommunications, and Tourism.

We expect this comparison to allow us to identify contrasts and similarities between common and technical lexicon, which not only can be contrasted to previous work but also can be used for designing sound strategies for integrating both resources without losing their specific information and properties. This is not a trivial task, particularly since the common lexicon tends to reflect and integrate popular lexicalizations in specific domains. The taxonomies reflecting popular lexicalizations have been argued to be significantly less elaborate at both the upper and lower levels than in the corresponding technical lexica (Medin & Aran, 1999). Also, popular terms tend to cover a larger range of referent types than technical terms, i.e. to be less precise, while others may cover only part of the extension of their technical counterparts. The information in Table 1 allows for identifying similarities and differences between technical and common lexica regarding phenomena such as PoS distribution and synonymy.

| | | N | V | Adj. | PN | Average |
|---|---|---|---|---|---|---|
| WN.PT | lexical entries (%) | 74.3% | 8.4% | 8.5% | 8.9% | |
| | synsets (%) | 73.6% | 8.5% | 9.3% | 8.7% | |
| | average variant/synset | 1.28 | 1.26 | 1.16 | 1.30 | **1.27** |
| LexTec | lexical entries (%) | 77.1% | 3.6% | 3.3% | 16.0% | |
| | synsets (%) | 77.5% | 5.2% | 5.0% | 12,4% | |
| | average variant/synset | 1.71 | 1.18 | 1.14 | 2.21 | **1.71** |

TABLE 1 – PoS distribution and density in terms of synonymy relations of WN.PT and LexTec

In terms of PoS distribution, the larger percentage of nominal nodes in LexTec (77.5% of nouns and 12.4% of proper nouns), and consequent smaller percentage of the other PoS, is consistent with what is generally assumed, specifically that the description of a given domain is mainly constituted by nominal expressions (Cabré, 1998: 36). However, when it comes to the ratio between variants and synsets, technical lexica would be expected to have a lower ratio, since the "form and content of terms tends towards an unambiguous relationship" (Cabré, 1998: 116). Despite the precision characteristic of specialized discourse, the existence of synonymy in terminology has long been acknowledged (Daille *et al.*, 1996; Freixa, 2002; Cabré, 2008; Montiel-Ponsoda *et al.*, 2011, Aguado-de-Cea & Montiel-Ponsoda, 2012). Moreover, the integration of English terms in the terminology of other languages, sometimes co-existing with variants in these languages, is also to be considered. Table 1 confirms this and makes apparent that synonymy is a distinctive feature of the technical lexicon with regard to the common lexicon. To verify whether these characteristics apply generally and equally to different domains, we looked into the numbers regarding individual domains (Table 2).

Table 2 presents the PoS distribution and the density of synonymy relations for 6 technical wordnets. These regard specifically chosen domains: Banking; Environment; Energy; Telecommunications; Construction; and Tourism. The first four are more classical knowledge domains, rich in terminology. Construction was selected as it includes terms from Civil Engineering, Architecture, but also lexicalizations of traditional construction methods and materials. As to Tourism, its selection was motivated by the fact of it being a more recent and interdisciplinary area, including aspects of Social Sciences, Economics and Commerce, but also very familiar to lay publics, as they interact directly and regularly with tourism products.

| | | N | V | Adj. | PN | Average |
|---|---|---|---|---|---|---|
| **Environment** | lexical entries (%) | 66.5% | 3.0% | 7.0% | 23.6% | |
| | synsets (%) | 67.5% | 4.9% | 11.0% | 16.6% | |
| | average variant/synset | 1.75 | 1.07 | 1.13 | 2.53 | 1.78 |
| **Energy** | lexical entries (%) | 78.8% | 2.5% | 3.8% | 14.8% | |
| | synsets (%) | 80.2% | 4.3% | 6.2% | 9.3% | |
| | average variant/synset | 1.77 | 1.01 | 1.10 | 2.87 | 1.80 |
| **Telecom** | lexical entries (%) | 77.9% | 3.8% | 0.9% | 17.4% | |
| | synsets (%) | 82.1% | 3.3% | 1.5% | 13.1% | |
| | average variant/synset | 1.98 | 2.38 | 2.76 | 2.76 | 2.08 |
| **Banking** | lexical entries (%) | 87.5% | 2.0% | 1.1% | 9.4% | |
| | synsets (%) | 87.0% | 3.8% | 2.3% | 7.0% | |
| | average variant/synset | 2.19 | 1.12 | 1.10 | 2.94 | 2.17 |
| **Construction** | lexical entries (%) | 83.2% | 5.1% | 5.2% | 6.5% | |
| | synsets (%) | 83.5% | 6.8% | 6.5% | 3.2% | |
| | average variant/synset | 1.49 | 1.12 | 1.20 | 3.00 | 1.49 |
| **Tourism** | lexical entries (%) | 48.1% | 4.5% | 4.1% | 43.4% | |
| | synsets (%) | 50.9% | 5.5% | 5.2% | 38.3% | |
| | average variant/synset | 1.34 | 1.15 | 1.11 | 1.61 | 1.42 |

TABLE 2 – PoS distribution and synonymy relation density per technical domain

PoS distribution in these individual domains reflects the general tendency of technical lexica: nominal nodes are predominant, although the proportion between nouns and proper nouns can be considerably different, ranging from 87% of common nouns and 7% of proper nouns (Banking) to 51% of common nouns and 38% of proper nouns (Tourism). The ratios of variants per synset also show significant differences, ranging from an average of 2.17 (Banking) to an average of 1.42 (Tourism). Construction and Tourism are the two domains with the lower ratio, hence closer to WN.PT in this regard. These numbers seem to indicate a higher proximity of these technical domains to common lexicon, which is not surprising since non-specialist speakers interact regularly and directly with contents from these domains.

## 2.1 Lexical-conceptual relations and network density

WordNet.PT and LexTec are lexical-conceptual databases built within the same theoretical framework, using the same set of relations (exceptions being MANNER and CAUSE relations, not used in LexTec). In what concerns the relations used, LexTec presents a higher percentage of HYPERONYMY (24.8% VS. 19.4%), INSTANTIATION (8% VS. 4.2%) and CORRELATION (18.7% vs. 9.3%) relations. In contrast, WN.PT has a higher incidence of MERONYMY and HOLONYMY relations (10.4 vs. 6.1% and 10.1% vs. 5.6%, respectively), and IS A CHARACTERISTIC OF/HAS AS A CHARACTERISTIC relation (12.2% vs. 3.9%). Some of these differences are directly related to the PoS distribution in both resources: INSTANTIATION is the relation linking proper nouns to the nominal nodes they instantiate, thus the higher incidence rate of this relation in LexTec. With regard to the IS A CHARACTERISTIC OF/HAS AS A CHARACTERISTIC relation, it establishes a link between nominal nodes and their salient and definitional characteristics, denoted by adjectives (see Mendes (2009)). The higher incidence of this relation in WN.PT is not independent from the higher proportion of adjective nodes in this resource. The higher percentage of CORRELATION relations in LexTec is also expected since "concepts are related to other concepts in the specific field they together constitute" (Cabré, 1998:116). Also, since nominal expressions are more common in technical language, it is more likely for this type of relations to be more relevant in technical wordnets given that there are not many technical verbs mediating the nodes in domain-specific wordnets, as shown in (1).

{absorbency}$_N$ [measure that reflects the relation between the radiation absorbed by a given surface and the radiation that incides on that surface]

CORRELATES WITH

→ {Gray, Gy}$_N$ [absorbency measure unit that corresponds to the radiant energy absorbed by a given mass and that is equivalent to 1 joule by quilogram]

→ {radiation}$_N$

(1)

Also, it is predictable that HYPERONYMY relations have a strong weight on the overall number of relations in technical lexica, since the specification of concepts, expressed in wordnets through HYPERONYMY/HYPONYMY relations, is known to be quite productive in terminology (Daille *et al.*, 1996; Freixa, 2002; Burgun & Bodenreider, 2001; Roventini & Marinelli, 2004; Cabré, 2008; Montiel-Ponsoda *et al.*, 2011; among others). Moreover, it is generally assumed that when a term, for some reason, becomes part of the common lexicon, it usually loses some of its technical meaning, denoting a broader, less specialized concept (Aguado-de-Cea & Montiel-Ponsoda, 2012; Meyer & Mackintosh, 2000). Being so, the less specification of the concepts denoted is bound to be correlated to shallower HYPERONYMY trees.

Finally, there is also a significant difference in terms of the density[3] of these networks: WN.PT presents a density of 4.5; while that of LexTec amounts only to 3.2. However, we feel that no strong claims can be made in this respect based on this data since WN.PT is a single wordnet, which potentiates the number of nodes available for linking, while for technical language we are working with a set of separate wordnets, each corresponding to a given domain and whose individual size is far from being close to that of WN.PT.

## 3 Merging technical and common lexicon wordnets

The merging of technical and common lexica raises several issues. Contrasts concerning sense differentiation and the establishment of the relevant semantic and conceptual relations with other lexical-conceptual units are bound to arise since these derive directly from the meaning of each unit. And yet, merging common and technical lexica is unquestionably linguistically motivated since specialists always maintain the ability to use common lexicon for communicating with non-specialist speakers, or even with other specialists when terminology for new concepts does not exist (Cabré, 1998), thus never entirely replacing common lexicon with specialized language. This way, the study of the issues involved in the merging of technical and common lexica in models mirroring the organization of the mental lexicon, besides contributing to address a growing need in the scientific community and provide it with a useful and differentiated language resource, can also provide some insights on the type of relations existing between these differentiated subsets of the lexicon. In this section, we present a typology of cases we are confronted with when merging two resources with the characteristics described earlier, illustrating each situation with examples from the databases, and focusing on the issues to be accounted for.

[3] Network density is calculated by summing all the relations encoded in the database and dividing them by the number of synsets represented.

## 3.1 Conceptual variations

Sense discrimination covering domain-specific concepts and common lexicon can result in polysemy and semantic overlapping (Sagri *et al.* 2004, Pederson *et al.* 2010, Chen *et al.* 2011). Differences in the ontological nature of the concepts are expected and can range between what we will call compatible, semi-compatible and incompatible conceptual variations.

Compatible conceptual variations correspond to the cases where the concept denoted by technical synsets is more precise and specialized, but otherwise similar to and compatible with the concept denoted by a corresponding common lexicon synset (see (2))[4]:

(2) **WN.PT**: $\{$gasóleo$\}_N$ [liquid fuel, oil derivative, used in diesel engines] (diesel)
HYPONYM OF $\{$combustível$\}_N$ (fuel)
$\{$derivado$\}_N$ (derivative)

**LexTec**: $\{$gasóleo, <u>diesel</u>$_{english}\}_N$ [liquid fuel, composed mainly of hydrocarbons and obtained by oil distillation, brown colored, with an intense smell, denser and less inflammable than gasoline, used in compression combustion engines] (diesel)
HYPONYM OF $\{$combustível$\}_N$ (fuel)
$\{$derivado do petróleo$\}_N$ (oil derivative)

Semi-compatible conceptual variations include cases like that of (3), where concept specialization entails intermediary hyperonyms – expressing technical specification not existing in the common lexicon –, the concept denoted by both technical and common lexicon synsets being nonetheless the same.

(3) **WN.PT**: $\{$ladrilho, mosaico$\}_N$ [flat building material, square or rectangular, typically made of ceramic, used to cover walls and floor] (tile)
HYPONYM OF $\{$material de construção$\}_N$ (building material)

**LexTec**: $\{$ladrilho, mosaico$\}_N$ [covering that consists of one piece, typically a rectangular ceramic plate, that is applied on the floor or on the wall](tile)
HYPONYM OF $\{$revestimento$\}_N$ (covering)
HYPONYM OF $\{$material de construção$\}_N$ (building material)

Incompatible conceptual variations, in (4), refer to cases where the concepts denoted by technical and common lexica, though closely related, are not the same, as made apparent by the hyponymy chain.

(4) **WN.PT**: $\{$sótão$\}_N$ [floor of a building, with a low ceiling, immediately under the roof] (attic, garret, loft)
HYPONYM OF $\{$piso, andar$\}_N$ (floor, level, story)
HYPONYM OF $\{$parcela$\}_N$ (parcel)

**LexTec**: $\{$sótão$\}_N$ [annex situated immediately under the roof of a building, typically considered for storage] (attic)
HYPONYM OF $\{$dependência$\}_N$ (annex)
HYPONYM OF $\{$construção$\}_N$ (construction)
HYPONYM OF $\{$estrutura$\}_N$ (structure)

These three types of possible situations call for different merging strategies. Cases like (2) can be almost straightforwardly merged, involving only the use of labels already available in the WordNet model (see Section 3.3). In the case of semi-compatible conceptual variations,

---

[4] The information in the examples provided is given in the following format: $\{$synset$\}_{POS}$ [gloss] (English translation). Underlined expressions correspond to variants associated to usage information, given in subscript characters, such as registry or origin (in the case of borrowed expressions, for instance).

besides the merging of synsets, it is also necessary to assure an adequate subnet merger to integrate both technical and common lexica relations and nodes without information loss. Finally, in the case of incompatible conceptual variations, it is not possible to perform a direct merging, since the concepts denoted are distinct. Being so, these cases should be treated as any other case of homonymy in wordnets, where each concept denoted corresponds to a separate node in the network, as suggested by Pedersen *et al.* (2010:3184).

However, as illustrated by (4), the relation between common and technical concepts is a very salient relation, which moreover can provide useful information both for NLP applications and human users. Considering the relations available in the WordNet model, the closest candidate to link these synsets would be the NEAR SYNONYMY relation[5], but this relation fails to cover this particular situation. Near synonyms are lexical units that do not pass the tests that motivate their belonging to the same synset: near synonyms are necessarily co-hyponyms, and have a stronger connection with each other than with their other co-hyponyms, which is not the case here. In this case, there are two different denotations (concepts), related to two different ways of conceiving and eventually lexicalizing a referent that can be, more often than not, the same. For instance, to use the example in (4), any utterance in which *sótão* (attic) occurs will refer to the upper part of a building, independently of whether the speaker is using the technical or common lexicon concept. This way, what seems to be at stake here is a shared reference, i.e. some type of co-reference relation, which requires a further and deeper study of this phenomenon and its properties.

## 3.2 Subnet variation and merging

One of the difficulties expected in the process of merging technical and common lexicon wordnets concerns the differences in the networks of relations established between compatible and semi-compatible synsets, which derive from conceptual variation. The example below illustrates this situation considering the synset {combustível} (fuel) and its relations in WN.PT (in black) and in LexTec (in orange)[6].

The graphical representation presented in Figure 1 illustrates the adaptations necessary, namely the overlapping, duplication and marking of the compatible synsets in both databases, as described in the literature (Roventini & Marinelli, 2004; Roventini *et al.*, 2000; Magnini & Speranza, 2001), to assure the visualization of each net individually. Roventini & Marinelli (2004) present a strategy to connect the databases through plug-in relations, considering that all upward relations (hyperonymy) from a given plugged-in node are taken from the common lexicon wordnet, while all other relations are taken from the technical one (Roventini & Marinelli, 2004: 196). This strategy does not prevent information loss, though.

To assure that all the relations in WN.PT and LexTec are considered, all relations are added, including those involving semi-compatible synsets (like $\{combustível\}_N$ (fuel) and $\{gás\ natural\}_N$ (natural gas)) and horizontal relations (such as ROLE relations) originally only present in one of the subnets. This strategy goes along the lines of the work of Bosch (n/d), although this author defends a partial merging that protects technical acceptions over general ones. In the strategy put forth in this work we do not argue for a proeminence of one resource

[5] We refer here to NEAR SYNOMYNY relation as defined in Vossen (2002:19). Near synonyms with different PoS are linked in EuroWordNet by the xpos_NEAR_SYNONYMY relation.
[6] The complete network of relations for these synsets in WN.PT and LexTec are available in http://www.clul.ul.pt/clg/wordnetpt/index.html and in http://www.instituto-camoes.pt/lextec/, respectively.

over the other, but rather outline a method for combining both resources maintaining their characteristics and properties and avoiding information loss. When overlapping, the relations and respective target nodes are analyzed regarding conceptual variation, in a new iteration of the process described above. In what concerns subtypes of relations (such as subspecified ROLE *vs.* ROLE PATIENT, for instance) finer-grained relations replace general ones. To maintain the possibility of separating the subnets merged, technical nodes have to be labeled, as well as individual lexicalizations in each synset, distinguishing lexical items pertaining to technical language, as described in the next section.

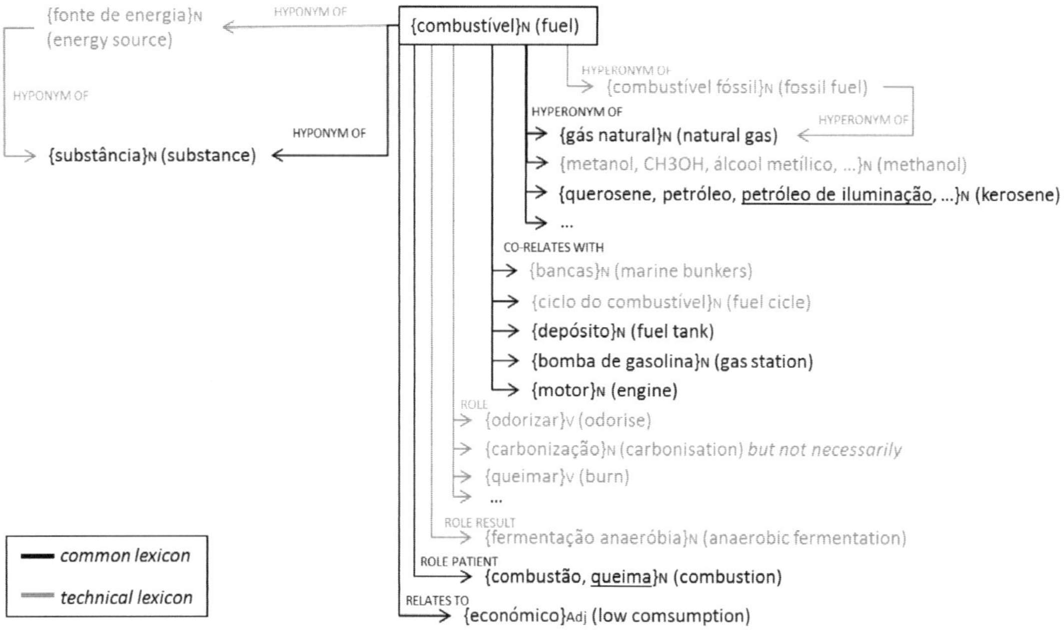


FIGURE 1 - merged network of relations for {combustível} (fuel)

## 3.3 Synset merging

The merging of compatible and semi-compatible synsets, besides requiring the insertion of intermediary hyperonyms when necessary, can also involve the treatment and encoding of lexical units in each set of synonyms. In the type of merging targeted in our work, lexical units can pertain both to common and technical lexica, and this information has to be overtly stated. EuroWordNet, the framework within which the resources considered in this paper have been developed, already allows for the tagging of technical lexical units through usage labels (Vossen 2002:106). This way, in merged synsets – which are part of both common lexicon and technical subnets – all lexical units have to be individually marked, as exemplified in (5), where *C* stands for common lexicon and *E* stands for the technical domain of Energy.

(5) a. {combustível$_{C,E}$}$_N$ (fuel)
b. {querosene$_{C,E}$, petróleo$_C$, petróleo de iluminação$_E$, petróleo iluminante$_E$}$_N$ (kerosene)
c. {combustão$_{C,E}$, queima$_E$}$_V$ (combustion)

The marking of the different lexical units requires only the definition of usage labels to include all the technical domains considered, as well as the common lexicon. With regard to making decisions involving the use of specific lexical units in common and technical contexts, this calls for corpora analyses and experts' advice, as discussed in Burgun & Bodenreider (2001), Magnini *et al.* (2002) or Smith & Fellbaum (2004), among others.

## 3.4 Incorporating common and technical information in definitions

Wordnets are characterized by having synsets as their basic unit and by the fact that the meaning of each unit is determined by its relations in the network. This way, in wordnets, definitions or glosses constitute additional information used to aid human users, to provide examples of use or complementary information considered useful, especially when nodes are not available for linking. Even though not part of the WordNet model, definitions can provide helpful information in many situations, both to human users and to NLP tools. Considering this, in this section we focus on strategies to incorporate common and technical information in definitions avoiding potential incongruities and leaving open the possibility of using either subnet (common or technical) individually, in a process that can be developed automatically (Chen *et al.*, 2011).

Our basic methodology consists in considering the lexical-conceptual relations encoded in wordnets to build definitions. Beginning with the common lexicon subnet, the definition starts by stating the hyperonym and then all the horizontal relations which correspond to definitional properties of the concept. Non-definitional relations are disregarded, namely hyponymy relations and all relations marked as reversed. CO-RELATES WITH relations are typically accessory (i.e. not essential to the definition of the meaning of the lexical unit), although sometimes they provide relevant information, as illustrated in (6). The same procedure is applied with regard to the technical subnet. This methodology results in some level of repetition, as shown in the example below, which can be avoided by controlling the information in common in the first and second part of the definition and omitting it from the second part. The parts regarding the common and technical lexicon are separated by semi-colons and, following the previous color scheme, technical information is presented in orange. For purposes of explanation, redundant information is presented in brackets:

(6) a. **WN.PT definitional relations for {tile}$_N$:** IS HYPONYM OF {building material}$_N$, HAS AS A CHARACTERISTIC {flat}$_{Adj}$ and {glazed}$_{Adj}$, CO-RELATES WITH {wall}$_N$ and {floor}$_N$, IS INVOLVED IN {tile}$_V$

b. **LexTec definitional relations for {tile}$_N$:** IS HYPONYM OF {covering}$_N$, CO-RELATES WITH {wall}$_N$ and {fixative mortar}$_N$, IS INVOLVED IN {pave}$_V$, {paving}$_N$, {lay}$_V$, {laying}$_N$, {tile}$_V$ and {untile}$_V$

c. **definition:** flat and glazed building material used to cover walls and floor; constitutes a covering that is paved, layed or tiled (to walls and floor) with fixative mortar

This two-part definition can function for both subnets individually: in the case where redundant information is maintained, it is just a matter of presenting the first or the second part of the definition for an individual visualization of the common or the technical subnet, respectively; where redundant information is avoided, the first part of the definition is presented for common lexicon subnet visualization and the whole definition is presented for technical lexicon subnet visualization. In our perspective, it is preferable to maintain the redundant information, since on the one hand the individual visualization of technical subnets becomes more coherent, and on the other the visualization of both parts of the definition simultaneously can help to obviate the conceptual variations between common and technical lexica.

## 4 Final remarks and future work

Following from previous research on relational models of the lexicon and on the interface between common and specialized languages, this paper presents a comparison of existing wordnets for common and technical lexica for Portuguese, focusing on their contrasts and similarities, to set the basis for a merging that preserves the specific information and properties of these resources. We discuss strategies to overcome the issues to be accounted for in the merging of these particular lexica, namely in what concerns conceptual variation, subnet and synset merging and the incorporation of technical and non-technical information in the definitions associated to each node.

As pinpointed throughout the paper, several issues deserve nonetheless further attention and constitute topics for future work. In particular, concerning semi-compatible synsets, the number of intermediary hyperonyms allowed while preserving a compatible conceptual variation between common and technical synsets, directly related to the study of the depth of hyperonymy trees in both lexica, needs to be addressed and motivated. Also, research on possible co-reference relations between incompatible yet related synsets requires further work, possibly applying strategies of corpora analysis, and expert and non-expert users surveys, as suggested by Smith & Fellbaum (2004). The validation of the usage of specific lexical units in common and technical lexica is a related issue, which can be addressed using this kind of approaches. Finally, and based on the strategies defined and presented in this paper, future work naturally comprises the implementation of methods for collecting and merging synsets from both resources automatically or semi-automatically, based on approaches like the ones put forth, for instance, by Vossen (2001), Buitelaar & Sacaleanu (2002) or Tse & Soergel (2003), this way assuring a cost-efficient feasibility of the merging.

## Acknowledgments

The work presented here has been supported by Fundação para a Ciência e a Tecnologia post-doctoral fellowships SFRH/BPD/75904/2011 and SFRH/BPD/79900/2011. The authors also whish to thank the remarks of the anonymous reviewers that contrubuted to the final version of this paper.

## References


Aguado-de-Cea, G. & Montiel-Ponsoda, E. (2012). Term variants in ontologies. In *Proceedings of the 30th International Conference of AESLA*, April, Spain (pp. 19-31).

Bodenreider, O. & Burgun, A. (2002). Characterizing the definitions of anatomical concepts in WordNet and specialized sources. In *Proceedings of the First Global WordNet Conference*, Mysore, India (pp. 223-230).

Bodenreider, O., Burgun, A. & Mitchell, J.A. (2003) Evaluation of WordNet as a source of lay knowledge for molecular biology and genetic diseases: a feasibility study. In *Studies in Health Technology and Informatics*, 95, 379-384.

Pedersen, B., Nimb, S. & Braasch, A. (2010), Merging specialist taxonomies and folk taxonomies in wordnets - a case study of plants, animals and foods in the Danish wordnet. In *Proceedings of the International Conference on Language Resources and Evaluation, LREC 2010*, Valletta, Malta (pp. 223-230).

Buitelaar, P. & Sacaleanu, B. (2001). Ranking and selecting synsets by domain relevance. In *Proceedings of the NAACL 2001 Workshop on WordNet and Other Lexical Resources,* Pittsburgh, Pennsylvania.

Buitelaar, P. & Sacaleanu, B. (2002). Extending synsets with medical terms. In *Proceedings of First Global WordNet Conference,* Mysore, India.

Burgun, A. & Bodenreider, O. (2001). Comparing terms, concepts and semantic classes in WordNet and the Unified Medical Language System. In *Proceedings of the NAACL 2001 Workshop on WordNet and Other Lexical Resources,* Pittsburgh, Pensylvania (pp. 77-82).

Cabré, M. T. (2008). El principio de poliedricidad: la articulación de lo discursivo, lo cognitivo y lo lingüístico en Terminología. In *IBÉRICA* 16, 9-36.

Cabré, T. (1998). *Terminology. Theory, methods and applications*, Amsterdam: John Benjamins Publishing.

Chen, R.-C., Bau, C.-T. & Yeh, C.J. (2011) Merging domain ontologies based on the WordNet system and Fuzzy Formal Concept Analysis techniques. In *Applied Soft Computing*, 11(2), March 2011.

Daille, B., Habert, B., Jacquemin, C. & Royauté, J. (1996). Empirical observation of term variations and principles for theirdescription. In *Terminology* 3 (2), 197-257.

Elhadad, N. & Sutaria, K. (2007). Mining a Lexicon of Technical Terms and Lay Equivalents. In *ACL BioNLP Workshop Proceedings*, Prague, Czech Republic (pp. 49-56).

Fellbaum, C. (1998) (Ed.). *WordNet: an electronical lexical database*. Cambridge: The MIT Press.

Freixa, J. (2002). *La variació terminològica: anàlisi de la variació denominativa en textos de diferent grau d'especialització de l'àrea de medi ambient*. Doctoral dissertation, Universitat Pompeu Fabra, Barcelona.

Fuentes, A. C. (2001). Lexical Behaviour in Academic and Technical Corpora: Implications for ESP Development. In *Language Learning & Tecnhology*, vol.5, nº 3, 106-129.

Giunchiglia, F., Maltese, V., Farazi, F. & Dutta, B. (2009). *GeoWordNet: a resource for geo-spatial applications.* Technical Report #DISI-09-071: http://eprints.biblio.unitn.it/1777/1/071.pdf.

Hutchinson, T. & Waters, A. (1981). Performance and competence in ESP. In *Applied Linguistics* 2/1.

Lacasta, J., Nogueras-Isso, J., Zarazaga-Soria, P. & Muro-Medrano, R. (2008). Generating an urban domain ontology through the merging of cross-domain lexical ontologies. In *Conceptual Models for Urban Practitioners*, Bologna: Società Editrice Esculapio, pp. 69-84.

Magnini, B. & Cavaglià, G. (2000). Integrating subject field codes into WordNet. In *Proceedings of the Second International Conference on Language Resources and Evaluation (LREC-2000),* Athens, Greece.

Magnini, B. & Speranza, M. (2001). Integrating Generic and Specialized Wordnets. In *Proceedings of Recent Advances in Natural Language Processing*, RANLP-2001, Tzigov Chark, Bulgaria (pp. 149-153).

Magnini, B. & Strapparava, C. (2001). Using WordNet to improve user modelling in a web document recommender system. In *Proceedings of the NAACL 2001 Workshop on WordNet and Other Lexical Resources,* Pittsburgh, Pennsylvania.

Magnini, B., Strapparava, C., Pezzulo, G. & Gliozzo, A. (2002). Comparing Ontology-Based and Corpus-Based Domain Annotations in WordNet. In *Proceedings of First Global WordNet Conference,* Mysore, India (pp. 146-154).

Marrafa, P. (2002): "The Portuguese WordNet: General Architecture and Semantic Internal Relations", *DELTA*.

Marrafa, P. (2001): *WordNet do Português - Uma base de dados de conhecimento linguístico*, Instituto Camões.

Marrafa, P., R. Amaro, R. P. Chaves, S. Lourosa & S. Mendes (2009), *LexTec – Léxico Técnico do Português: Ambiente, Banca, Comércio, Construção, Energia, Seguros, Turismo, Telecomunicações, Direito Comercial Internacional e Economia e Gestão de Empresas*, Instituto Camões.

McCray, A.T. & Tse, T. (2003). Understanding search failures in consumer health information systems. In *Proceedings of the American Medical Informatics Symposium* (pp. 430-434).

Medin, D.L. & Adran, S. (1999) (Eds.). *Folkbiology*. Cambridge: The MIT Press.

Mendes, S. (2009) *Syntax and Semantics of Adjectives in Portuguese: analysis and modelling*, PhD thesis, Universidade de Lisboa.

Meyer, I. & Mackintosh, K. (2000). L'étirement du sens terminologique: aperçu du phénomène de la déterminologisation. In H. Béjoint & P. Thoiron (Eds.). *Le Sens en terminologie,* Lyon, France: Presses de l'Université Lumière Lyon 2.

Miller, G.A., Beckwith, R., Fellbaum, C., Gross, D. & Miller, K.J. (1990). Introduction to WordNet: An online lexical database. *International Journal of Lexicography, 3*(4), 235-44.

Montiel-Ponsoda, E., Aguado-de-Cea, G. & McCrae, J. (2011). Representing term variation in lemon. In *WS 2 Workshop Extended Abstracts, 9th International Conference on Terminology and Artificial Intelligence (TIA 2011)*, Paris, France (pp. 47–50).

Mudraya, O. (2006). Engineering English: A lexical frequency instructional model. In *English for Specific Purposes* 25, Elsevier, 235-256.

Peters, W., Sagri, M., Tiscornia D. & Castagnoli, S. (2006). The LOIS Project. In *Proceedings of Linguistic Resources Evaluation Conference (*LREC'06), Genova, Italy (pp. 23-27).

Robinson, P.J. (1989). A rich view of lexical competence. In *ELT Journal*, vol. 43/3, Oxford University Press, 274-282.

Roventini, A., Alonge, A., Calzolari, N., Magnini, B., Bertagna, F. (2000). ItalWordNet: a large semantic database for Italian. In *Proceedings of the 2nd International Conference on Language Resources and Evaluation* (LREC'00), Athens, Greece.

Roventini, A. & Marinelli, R. (2004). Extending the Italian WordNet with the Specialized Language of the Maritime Domain. In P. Sojka, K. Pala, P. Smrz, C. Fellbaum & P. Vossen (Eds.). *Proceedings of the Global WordNet Conference 2004 (GWC 2004)*, (pp. 193-198). Brno: Masaryk University.

Sagri, M.T., Tiscornia, D. & Bertagna, F. (2004). Jur-WordNet. In P. Sojka, K. Pala, P. Smrz, C. Fellbaum & P. Vossen (Eds.). *Proceedings of the Global WordNet Conference 2004 (GWC 2004)*, Brno: Masaryk University (pp. 305-310).

Slaughter, L. (2002). *Semantic relationships in health consumer questions and physicians' answers: a basis for representing medical knowledge and for concept exploration interfaces.* Doctoral dissertation, University of Maryland at College Park.

Smith, B. & Fellbaum, C. (2004). Medical WordNet: a New Methodology for the Construction and Validation of Information Resources for Consumer Health. In *Proceedings of COLING 2004*, Geneva, Switzerland.

Tse, T. & Soergel, D. (2003). Procedures for mapping vocabularies from non-professional discourse. A case study: 'consumer medical vocabulary'. In *Proceedings of the Annual Meeting of the American Society for Information.*

van den Bosch, A. (no date), *Merging domain thesauri with a generic Wordnet: A case study with the Dutch Army Museum*, http://www.rnaproject.org/whitepapers.aspx

Vossen, P. (2001). Extending, trimming and fusing wordnet for technical documents. In *Proceedings of the NAACL 2001 Workshop on WordNet and Other Lexical Resources,* Pittsburgh, Pennsylvania.

Vossen, P. (2002) (Ed.). *EuroWordNet General Document*, EuroWordNet Project LE2-4003 & LE4-8328 report, University of Amsterdam, http://vossen.info/docs/2002/EWNGeneral.pdf.

# Building Multilingual Lexical Resources Using Wordnets: Structure, Design and Implementation

*Shikhar Kr. Sarma*[1] *Dibyajyoti Sarmah*[1]
*Biswajit Brahma*[1] *Mayashree Mahanta*[1] *Himadri Bharali*[1] *Utpal Saikia*[1]
(1) Department of Information Technology,
Institute of Science & Technology, Gauhati University, Guwahati – 14 Assam, India
{sks001, dibyasarmah, bswjtbrahma, mayashreemahanta, himadri0001, utpal.sk}@gmail.com

Abstract

The present paper deals with the design and implementation of multilingual lexical resources of Assamese and Bodo Language with the help of Hindi Wordnet. Here, we present the multilingual dictionaries (for Hindi, Assamese and Bodo), synset based word search for Assamese-Hindi and Bodo-Hindi language. These words, of course, will have to go through some pre-processing before finally being uploaded to a database. The user-interface is being developed for specific language (Assamese, Bodo and Hindi language).

KEYWORDS: Lexical Resources, Concept Based Dictionary, Multilingual Dictionary Database, Web-based Interface

## 1 Introduction

In recent years, mono and multilingual lexical resources, Wordnet and other lexical resources are in high demand. Wordnet is a very recent and rich multilingual lexical resource which is being used in MT (Machine Translation), cross-lingual search, information extraction etc. Among the Indian language Wordnet, the Hindi Wordnet[1] was the first one to come into existence from 2000 onwards. It was inspired by the English Wordnet[2] which contains nouns, verbs, adjectives and adverbs organized into synonym sets, each representing one underlying lexical concept (Fellbaum, 1998). Different relations like hypernymy, hyponymy etc. link the synonym sets to each other. Soon, other Indian language Wordnet started getting created. The Wordnet for Assamese and Bodo have followed the Hindi Wordnet.
The present model tries to represent the lexical elements and their multilingual counterparts efficiently and economically. The present frameworks are derived inspiration from the Hindi Wordnet.

## 2 A case study: Introduction of Assamese language and Bodo language

Assamese language is the mainly spoken in the state of Assam. According to the VIII schedule of Indian Constitution, Assamese is recognized as the regional language. It becomes the official language of Assam. It is also used as a medium of communication in many north-eastern states specially Arunachal Pradesh and Nagaland and also in outside the north-eastern regions such as Bhutan and Bangladesh. Apart from these, a large number of Assamese speaking people settled in different parts of India and outside India like U.K. and U.S. due to various reasons. The

[1] http://www.cfilt.iitb.ac.in/wordnet/webhwn/
[2] http://wordnet.princeton.edu/

tentative number of Assamese speaker in the state of Assam and neighboring states of north-east India is 1.4 million and across India is approximately 14.3 million.
Bodo language became the scheduled language in the year 2003. It is spoken in the northern part of the Brahmaputra valley of Assam and also in the southern part of the valley. A small section of Bodo speakers are also found in the border areas like Meghalaya, Nagaland, North Bengal, Nepal and Bhutan adjoining Assam. According to the census 1991, there are approximately 11, 84, 569 Bodo speakers. However, the Bodo language has its written record from the last part of the 19th century. In the year 1963, it was introduced in the primary level of education in Assam and presently, it becomes the medium of instruction up to 10th standard in the state of Assam. The script of the Bodo is Devanagiri.
UNICODE compliant font sets, keyboard drivers, corpus, word-processors, spelling checkers, CLDR (Common Locale Data Repository) etc. are being developed with Government of India initiative very recently. Work has also started simultaneously for developing the Assamese and Bodo Wordnet as part of the North East Indo Wordnet development, which will ultimately be linked to the composite Indo Wordnet [Sarma, 2010].

## 3 The Multilingual Lexical Resources

A lexical resource (LR) is a database consisting of one or several dictionaries. Depending on the type of languages that are addressed, the LR may be qualified as monolingual, bilingual or multilingual. For bilingual and multilingual LRs, the words may be connected or not connected, from a language to another. When connected, the equivalence from a language to another, is performed through a bilingual link (for bilingual LRs) or through multilingual notations (for Multilingual LRs).
Following is the linked synset in Assamese and Bodo Wordnet

| Assamese Linked Synset | Bodo Linked Synset |
|---|---|
| 14958 | 15785 |

TABLE 1 – Synset of Assamese and Bodo Wordnet

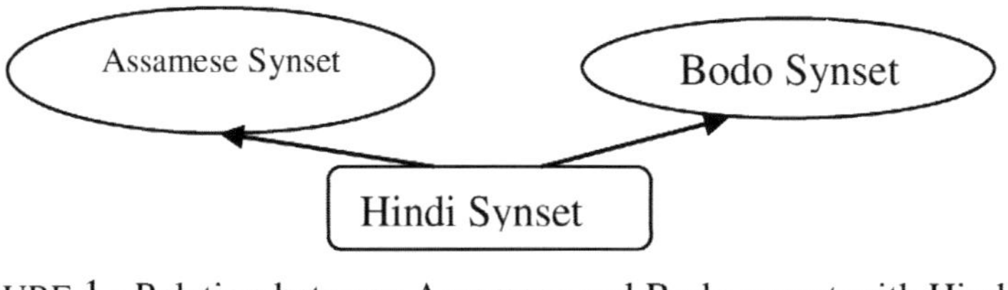


FIGURE 1– Relation between Assamese and Bodo synset with Hindi

Here we define the source language to target language flow diagram. For creating the target language synset, we derive help from Hindi Wordnet. For building the Multilingual (Assamese, Bodo and Hindi) lexical resources we used root Wordnet Hindi for Assamese and Bodo language and mapping words by compare with Hindi.

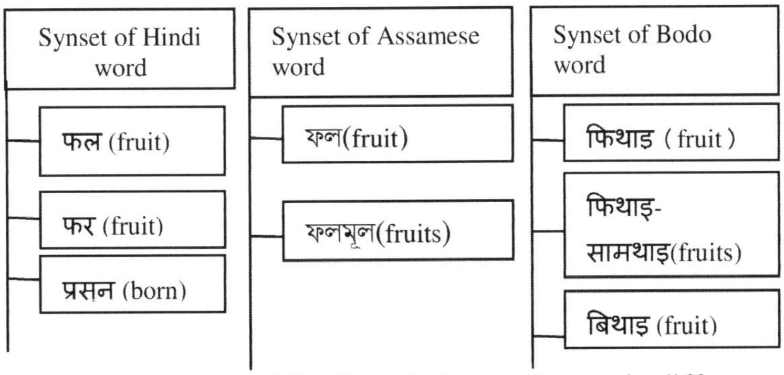


FIGURE 2 –Synset of English 'fruit' word sense in different

There are three words (फल, फर, प्रसून) in Hindi which form the Hindi synset, two words (ফল, ফলমূল) in Assamese from Assamese synset for the same concept and another three words (फिथाइ, फिथाइ-सामथाइ, बिथाइ) in Bodo from Bodo synset, as illustrated in FIGURE 2.

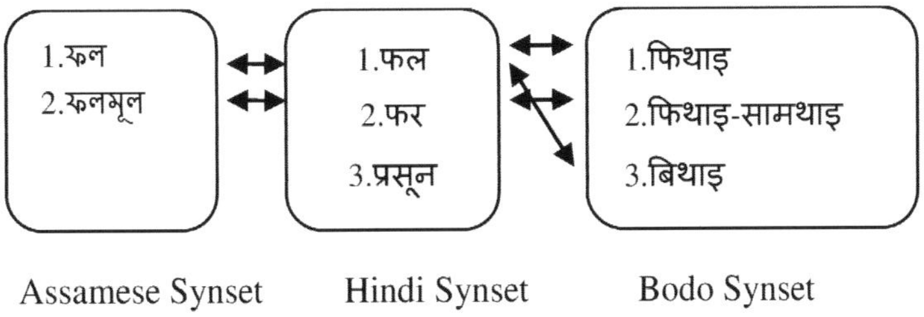


FIGURE 3 –Mapping with root synset (Hindi Synset)

In FIGURE 3 we show the mapping with Assamese and Bodo with root synset Hindi. Here the फल (fruit) word is mapping with Assamese word ফল (phal:fruit) and Bodo word फिथाइ (fithai:Fruit). In the same way फर (phar:fruit) word is related with ফলমূল (phalmul:fruits) (Assamese synset) and फिथाइ-सामथाइ (fithai-samthai:fruits) (Bodo synset). But there is no equivalent Assamese word for Hindi प्रसून word. So, we cannot map this प्रसून with Assamese synset.

## 4 Challenges in Lexical Resources

### Morphological Characteristics (Assamese Language)

Assamese is very rich in morphological features[3]. Some of them are outlined below

1. There is no inflection for number and gender in Assamese. There are two kinds of numbers, viz., singular and plural. Linguistically, Gender is of two types – Masculine and Feminine. But traditionally Common and Neuter gender are also used.
2. Relational nouns or kinship terms are inflected for person and case.
3. Derivation is done by various processes – prefixation, suffixation, zero modification, compounding and change of consonant and vowel phoneme.

[3] Golock C Goswami. 1983. Structure of Assamese, Gauhati University, Assam

4. There are two types of affixes in Assamese language – Prefix and suffix. But there is no infix found in the language.
5. Assamese language contains six types of case markings, Nominative, Accusative, Instrumental, Dative, Ablative and Locative.
6. In negation, the negative 'n-' is prefixed to the verb and morphophonemic changes are also common in the language.

Syntactic Characteristics

a) The basic sentence structure in Assamese language is Subject + Object + Verb (SOV). But it may vary according to the context or mood of the speaker
b) Depending on the form, the sentence in the language is of three kinds – Simple, Complex and Compound.
c) Semantically, sentences in Assamese are classed into – Declarative, Interrogative, Exclamatory, Imperative. In fact, Intonation plays a significant role in determining the sentence type.

Bodo Morpho-syntactic features

a) Sentence pattern of the Bodo is Subject + Object + Verb (SOV) pattern.
b) The language does not follow the concord relation which is the agreement of verb and person.
c) There is no change of verb according to the person and number. In each sentence the verb does not possess change of its character regarding person and number where it is singular or plural form in the sentence.

## 5 Challenges of Lexical Resources

The linkage task has to do a fine balance between maintaining accuracy and providing maximum linkages. While trying to do this for the linkage between the Hindi, Assamese and Bodo Wordnet, several challenges were encountered. The specific such problems were faced are the synset denoting the following:

a) It is often the case that a concept is expressed through a synthetic expression in one language, but through a single word expression in the other language.eg. For Bodo language a single word express a whole sentence.
For example,

[4]HC: एक प्रकार के छोटे जंतु जिनके मुँह में, विशेषकर कुतरने में सहायक, छोटे और पैने दाँत होते हैं

[5]ET: Relatively small gnawing animals having a single pair of constantly growing incisor teeth specialized for gnawing.

[6]HS: कृंतक जन्तु (rodent, gnawer, gnawing_animal)

[7]BS: गोफार_हाथाय_गोनां_जुनार (gwfar-hathai-gwnang-junar: sharped teeth animal)

In this example Hindi Synset कृंतक जन्तु word meaning is like as गोफार_हाथाय_गोनां_जुनार in Bodo Wordnet. This word is a combination of four parts.

[4] HC-Hindi Concept
[5] ET-English Translation
[6]HS-Hindi Synset
[7] BS-Bodo Synset

b) Sometime there is no equivalent concept in target language. For example, the Hindi concept like साधु बन जाना (to become a monk) is not found any equivalent term in the target language Assamese.

Some cultural terms may be missed out from the target languages as these are not available in the Hindi Wordnet. It prevents the true representation of the target language in digital world. For example: the terms relating to festival like বিহু (Bihu) in Assamese and बैसागु (Boisagu) in Bodo are not found in the Hindi Wordnet.

In source language and target language, we have found words with same structure with different meanings in different time. For instance, धुरन्धर (dhurandhar) in Hindi means 'renowned one', but in Assamese ধুৰন্ধৰ (dhurandhar) refers to 'a scoundrel'.

# 6 Multilingual Lexical Database for Computational Framework

Design of multilingual database by help of root Wordnet (Hindi Wordnet) is shown in below. First we create our target language synset from Hindi Wordnet by using multilingual tool. After creating our own language we put that file in our database. In FIGURE 4 we show the DFD (Data Flow Diagram) of multilingual lexical resources.

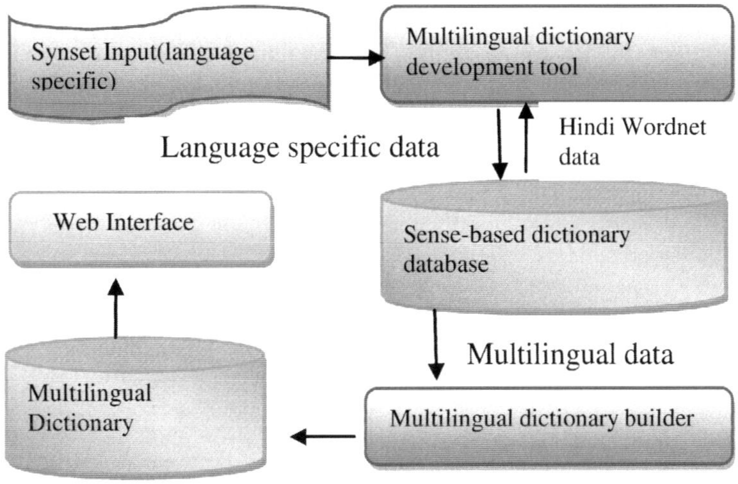


FIGURE 4 – DFD of Multilingual Dictionary creation

# 7 Multilingual Lexical Database for Computational Framework

The Multilingual tool, used by lexicographers for manually linking the two Wordnet, was developed at CFILT, IIT Bombay.

The offline multilingual tool takes as input a source file containing the number of query synset N, where N stands for total number of synset that are to be linked and N lines in following format:

- Synset ID
- POS category
- Concept
- EXAMPLE
- SYNSET

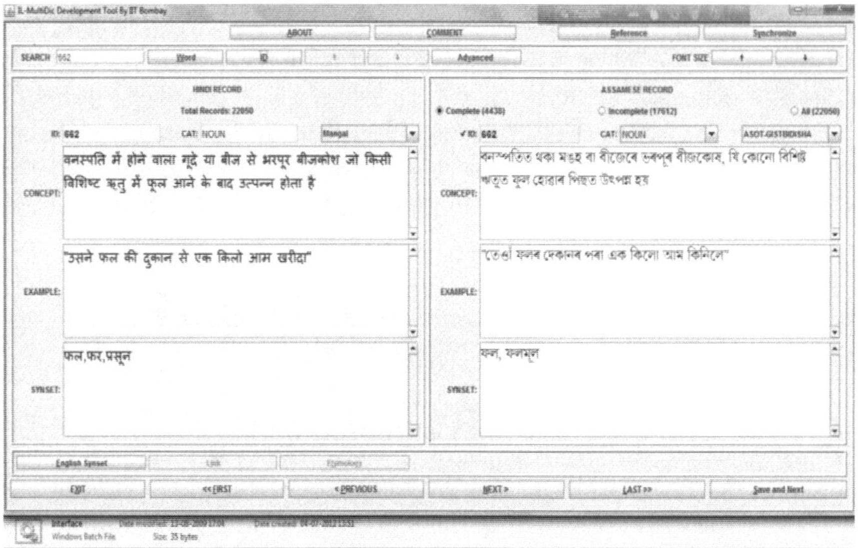


FIGURE 5 –Multilingual Tool (for Assamese language)

In this tool, the synset (synset ID, POS category, Concept, example and synonyms) is displayed in the source synset panel at the top of the tool. Similar information is displayed in the candidate synset panel below it, for each of the N candidate synset. The candidates are displayed in decreasing order of their confidence score. Facility for searching synset in both source and target languages with respect to a word or synset ID is also provided in the tool.

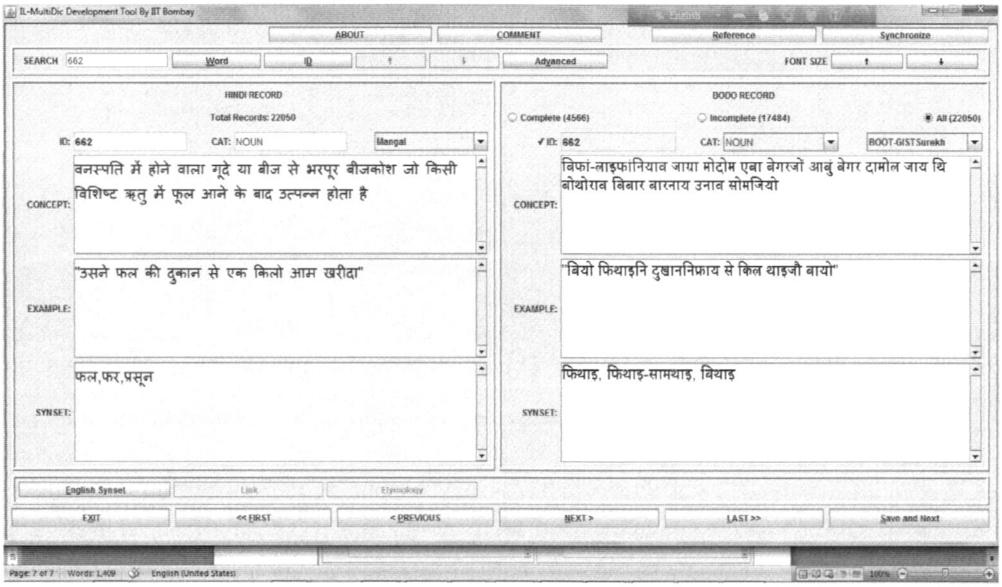


FIGURE 6 –Multilingual Tool (for Bodo language)

We have taken help from the Indo Wordnet website, when we did not find equivalent concept in our target languages. For example, Synset ID, POS (Part Of Speech), Concept, Example, Synset, Hyponymy etc. for respective languages.

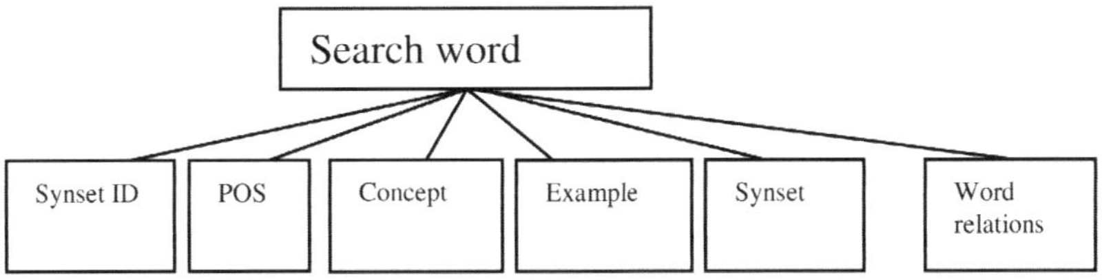


FIGURE 7– Word Structure of Hierarchical order

## 8 User Interface of lexical resources

A. Bilingual link (Assamese-Hindi synset based translation).
B. Bilingual link (Bodo- Hindi synset based translation).
C. Multilingual dictionary (Assamese-Bodo-Hindi).

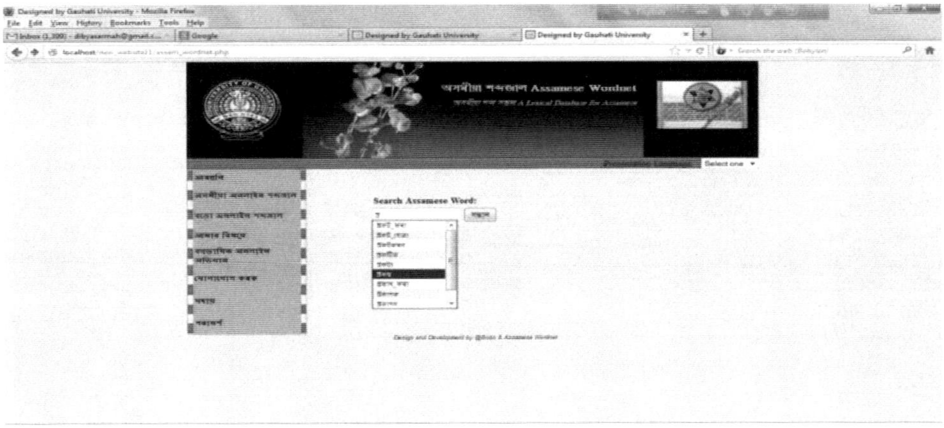

FIGURE 7–Searching a word (User Interface)

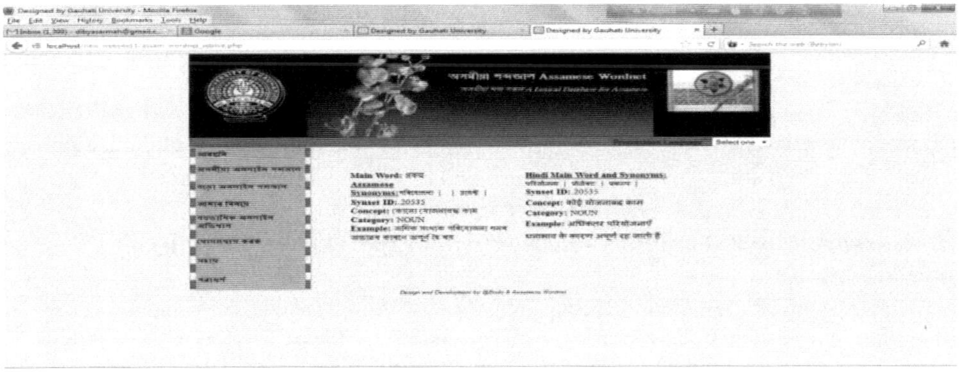

FIGURE 8–Synset based word search (Assamese-Hindi)

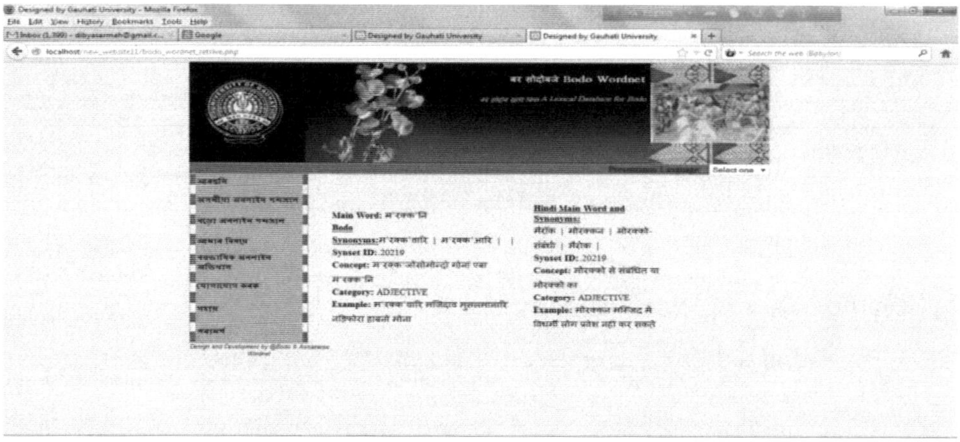

FIGURE 9–Synset based Word search(Bodo-Hindi)

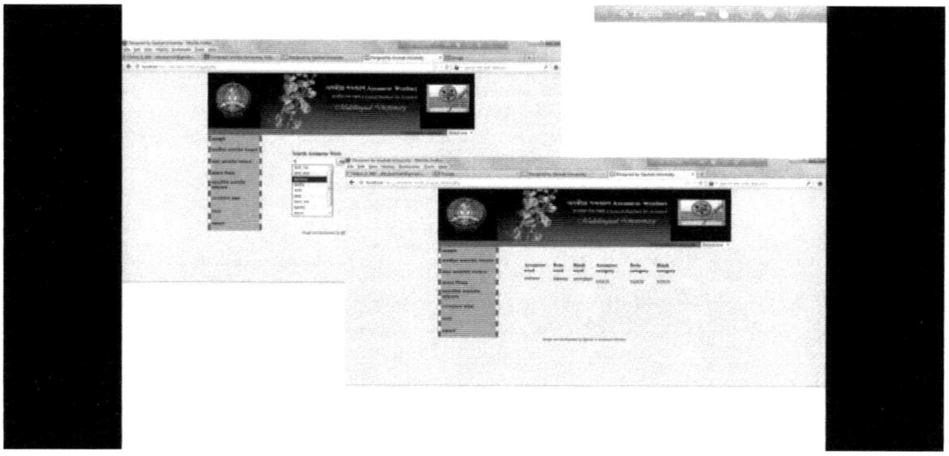

FIGURE 10–Interface of Multilingual Dictionary (Assamese-Bodo-Hindi)

## 9 Conclusions

In this paper, we present a discussion on the structure, design and implementation of the multilingual lexical resources for Assamese and Bodo Wordnet which is done by mapping with the Hindi Wordnet. Besides, the present paper also highlights the challenges faced in creating the Wordnet in Assamese as well as in Bodo such as script issue, cultural terms, similar structure but different meaning etc.

In future, attempts should be taken to create Wordnet for other north-eastern languages as well as other Indic languages which would not only preserve the language but also standardize the language in digital world. This kind of research would help the user for easy browsing of any language data in digital format.

## Acknowledgment

The works have been done during the NE Wordnet development project. The authors acknowledge support from DIT, Ministry of Communication & IT, Govt. of India, & Indwordnet team, IIT Bombay.

## References

Awasthi, S. and (Smt.) I. Awasthi. 2000. Chambers English-Hindi Dictionary (ed.). Allied Publisher Limited, New Delhi, India.

Fellbaum, C. 1998. Wordnet: An Electronic Lexical Database. The MIT Press.

Kamil, Bulke. 1997. An English-Hindi Dictionary (ed.). S. Chand & Co, New Delhi, India.

Khapra, Mitesh, Sapan Shah, Piyush Kedia and Pushpak Bhattacharyya. 2009. Projecting Parameters for Multilingual Word Sense Disambiguation. Empirical Methods in Natural Language Processing (EMNLP09), Singapore.

Narayan Dipak, Debasri Chakrabarti, Prabhakar Pande and P. Bhattacharyya.2002.An Experience in Building the Indo WordNet-a WordNet for Hindi, First International Conference on Global WordNet, Mysore, India.

Ramanand J.. Akshay Ukey, Brahm Kiran Singh, Pushpak Bhattacharyya. 2007. Mapping and Structural Analysis of Multi-lingual Wordnets. IEEE Data Engineering Bulletin, 30(1).

Sarma, Shikhar Kr., Moromi Gogoi, Rakesh Medhi and Utpal Saikia, 2010. Foundation and Structure of Developing an Assamese Wordnet, Global Wordnet Conference, IIT Bombay.

Sarma, Shikhar Kr.,Moromi Gogoi, Biswajit Brahma, Mane Bala Ramchiary,2010. A Wordnet for Bodo Language: Structure and Development.

Sinha Manish,Mahesh Kumar Reddy and Pushpak Bhattacharyya.2006.An Approach towards Construction and Application of Multilingual Indo-WordNet, 3rd Global WordNet Conference (GWC 06), Jeju Island, Korea.

# A New Semantic Lexicon and Similarity Measure in Bangla

*Manjira Sinha, Abhik Jana, Tirthankar Dasgupta, Anupam Basu*
Indian Institute of Technology Kharagpur
{manjira87, abhikjana1, iamtirthankar, anupambas}@gmail.com

ABSTRACT

The *Mental Lexicon* (ML) refers to the organization of lexical entries of a language in the human mind.A clear knowledge of the structure of ML will help us to understand how the human brain processes language. The knowledge of semantic association among the words in ML is essential to many applications. Although, there are works on the representation of lexical entries based on their semantic association in the form of a lexicon in English and other languages, such works of Bangla is in a nascent stage. In this paper, we have proposed a distinct lexical organization based on semantic association between Bangla words which can be accessed efficiently by different applications. We have developed a novel approach of measuring the semantic similarity between words and verified it against user study. Further, a GUI has been designed for easy and efficient access.

KEYWORDS : Bangla Lexicon, Synset, Semantic Similarity, Hierarchical Graph

## 1 Introduction

The *lexicon* of a language is a collection of lexical entries consisting of information regarding words and expressions, comprising both *form* and *meaning* (Levelt,). *Form* refers to the orthography, phonology and morphology of the lexical item and *Meaning* refers to its syntactic and semantic information.

The term *Mental Lexicon* refers to the organization and interaction of lexical entries of a language in the human mind. Depending on the definition of *word*, an adult knows and uses around 40000 to 150000 words. Yet, it has been estimated that an adult can recognize a *word* in her native language in less than 200ms and can reject a non-word in less than 500ms (Aitchison, 2012; Muller, 2008; Seashore and Eckerson, 1940). Therefore, the storage and retrieval mechanisms of the brain have to be efficient enough to facilitate such super-fast access. Words in the mental lexicon are assumed to be associated at various levels of linguistic features such as, *orthography, phonology, morphology* and *semantics*. Although a vast amount of research is going on the mental lexicon, the precise natures of the relations are yet to be explored. The knowledge of semantic association among the words in mental lexicon is essential to many areas such as, developing pedagogical strategies, categorization, semantic web, natural language processing applications like, document clustering, word sense disambiguation, machine translation, information retrieval, text comprehension, and question-answering systems, where the perception of the target user group plays an important role.. However, as we cannot 'look into the mind' to know the exact structure of the mental lexicon, we try to simulate its behaviour with the help of external models.

The rich repertoire of literature on the structure, organization and representation of lexical entries includes simple organization schemes like Dictionary and Thesaurus to more complex ones like

WordNet (Fellbaum, 2010) and ConceptNet (Liu and Singh, 2004) and also methods to measurethe degree of semantic similarity among the lexemes.

Bangla is an Indo-Aryan language having about 193 million native and about 230 million total speakers. Despite being so popular, very few attempts have (Roy and Muqtadir, 2008; Das and Bandyopadhyay, 2010) been made to build a semantically organized lexicon of substantial size in Bangla. Hence, we propose a distinct lexical organization.

The objective of this work is to design and develop a Bangla lexicon based on semantic similarity among Bangla words, which is suitable of automatic access mechanismsand can be used further in various applications like as mentioned above. The design is based on the *Samsad Samarthasabdokosh* (Mukhopadhyay, 2005). The lexicon is hierarchically organized and divided according to the categories or domains represented by different segments. The categories are further divided into sub-categories. The words are grouped into clusters along with their synonyms. Weighted edges between different types of words related to same or different concepts or categories exist, denoting the semantic distance between them. We have also developed a Graphical User Interface on top of the lexicon, which can be used for efficient and easy access. This is an on-going project with an aim of creating an organization containing 50,000 words.

The organization of the paper is as follows: section 2 contains the related works; we have also pointed out some of the differences of our proposed structure with WordNet in section 2; section 3 explains the construction of the lexicon and the GUI; section 4, describes the proposed approach of predicting semantic similarity between words; in section 5 we have discussed the user study; conclusions and future thoughts have been included in the last section.

## 2 Related work

A number of works have been done semantic relation based representations include simple organizational schemes like Dictionary and Thesaurus to more complex ones like WordNet (Fellbaum, 2010) and ConceptNet (Liu and Singh, 2004) and others (Ruppenhofer et al., 2010).Words in WordNet are organized around semantic groupings called *synsets*. Each synset consists of a list of synonymous word forms and semantic pointers that describe relationships among the synsets.However, WordNet suffers from several limitations(Boyd-Graber et al., 2006).ConceptNet is a semantic network containing different types of *concepts* and relationships among them. Here, concepts are represented by words or short phrases and relationships can be of many kinds such as, *MotivatedByGoal*, *UsedFor*, *can cross*.

According to the most recent reference to a Bangla WordNet (Roy and Muqtadir, 2008), the structure is based on Bangla to English bi-lingual dictionaries and in strict alignment (only the synonym equivalents are used) with the Princeton WordNet for English. It contains around 639 synsets and 1,455 words[1]. The assumptions that have been taken are: Bangla and English have significant amount of linguistic similarities and Bangla word senses can be clearly justified by a Bangla-English-Bangla dictionary.

Our proposed lexical representation is different from WordNet in many respects. Some of the important differences being:

---

[1]http://bn.asianwordnet.org/

- No cross parts of speech links are there in the WordNet. That means no link between an entity and its attributes.
- Several lexical and semantic relations are not included in the WordNet such as "actor"([book]-[writer]), "instrument"([knife]-[cut]), but these are perceived as related by human cognition. In our framework these types of relations are, for example under the node [book], [writer] is there in [noun-adjective] type of cluster. [Knife], [cut] are also under same node [weapon] but in different clusters. These kinds of relations can be helpful in word sense disambiguation applications.
- Relational links are qualitative rather than quantitative in WordNet.. In our system we have given weight on different type of links keeping in mind the semantic closeness of the nodes they connect. Moreover, in our structure, there exists a path between each possible word pair.

Our proposed semantic similarity based lexical organization is not a substitution of WordNet; rather it tries to address some of the aspects which are still not incorporated in the WordNet framework. It is useful especially in case of a resource poor language like Bangla.

### 2.1 Work on measuring semantic similarity among words

There exist many approaches to measure semantic similarity between words; some of them are discussed here. Tversky's feature based similarity model (Tversky, 1977), is among the early works in this field. Some scholars (Rada et al., 1989; Kim and Kim, 1990; Lee et al., 1993) have proposed the conceptual distance approach that uses edge weights, between adjacent nodes in a graph as an estimator of semantic similarity. Resnick (Resnik, 1993a; Resnik, 1993b) have proposed the information theoretic approach to measure semantic similarity between two words. Richardson et. al. (1994) has proposed an edge-weight based scheme for Hierarchical Conceptual Graphs (HCG) to measure semantic similarity between words. Efforts (Jiang and Conrath, 1997) have been made to combine both the information content based approach and the graph based approach of predicting semantic similarity. In addition, strategies of using multiple information sources to collect semantic information have also been adopted (Li et al., 2003). Wang and Hirst (2011) have criticized the traditional notions of the depth and density in a lexical taxonomy. However, almost all of the attempts described above have been taken in English based on the representation of WordNet. Das and Bandopadhaya (2010) have proposed a SemanticNet in Bangla, where the relations are based on human pragmatics.

## 3 Construction of the Proposed Lexicon

We have taken the *Samsad Samarthasabdokosh*by Ashok Mukhopadhyay(2005) as the basis for our proposed lexical representation in Bangla. The book contains 757 main words distributed in 30 different sections. Each section addresses a particular domain such as universe-nature-earth, life-living being-body etc. The main words have their corresponding synonyms and similar or related words. Different groups of words that are associated with a single main word are organized together. Relevant information such as Part-Of-Speech (POS) corresponding to every word and antonyms for adjectives are also mentioned. Two types of cross-references are present: one relates two main words or a single word which is simultaneously synonymous to two different main words and the other denotes multiple occurrences of the same. We have termed them as primary link and secondary link respectively. We have also analysed Bangla corpuses:

complete novel and story collection of Rabindranath Tagore, Bankimchandra Chattaopadhayay[2], collection of Bangla blogs over the internet, Bangla corpus by CIIL[3]Mysore and Anandabazar news corpus[4] and have prepared a list of around 4 lakh distinct words in Bangla with their corpus frequencies.

In order to build-up a semantic relation based lexical representation Bangla; we have constructed a hierarchical conceptual graph based on the above mentioned book. We have also individually processed and stored the distinct general words in the book along with their respective details. Our storage and organization of the database facilitate computational processing of the information and efficient searching to retrieve the details associated with any word. Therefore, it will be a useful resource and tool to other psycholinguistic and NLP studies in Bangla. Given a word, its frequency over the five mentioned corpuses, its association with different categories or sub-categories are collected at a single place so that a user can navigate through the storages with low cognitive load. We have also rated the various types of connections among different levels of the graph and developed a mechanism for predicting semantic similarity measures between words in the proposed lexicon. It supports queries like DETAILS(X) (here X can be any type of node of the hierarchy) and SIMILARITY (WORD1, WORD2). The details of the organizational methodology are described below.

The 30 different sections have been considered as 30 root categories. Each category is a collection of concepts, e.g. ইন্দ্রিয়–অনুভূতি/sense-perception. 757 main words have been organized under the root categories as sub-categories, which are actually concepts, e.g. গন্ধ/smell.The words (mainly nouns, adjectives, verbal nouns and verbal adjectives) have been distributed into separate clusters attached to the sub-categories and they form the leaves of the hierarchy. There is a common root node as antecedent to all the categories. Corresponding to each sub-category, there are two types of clusters: one contains the exact synonyms and the clusters of the other type contain related words or attributes. The words belonging to the same cluster are synonymous. Every category, sub-category and cluster has distinct identification numbers.

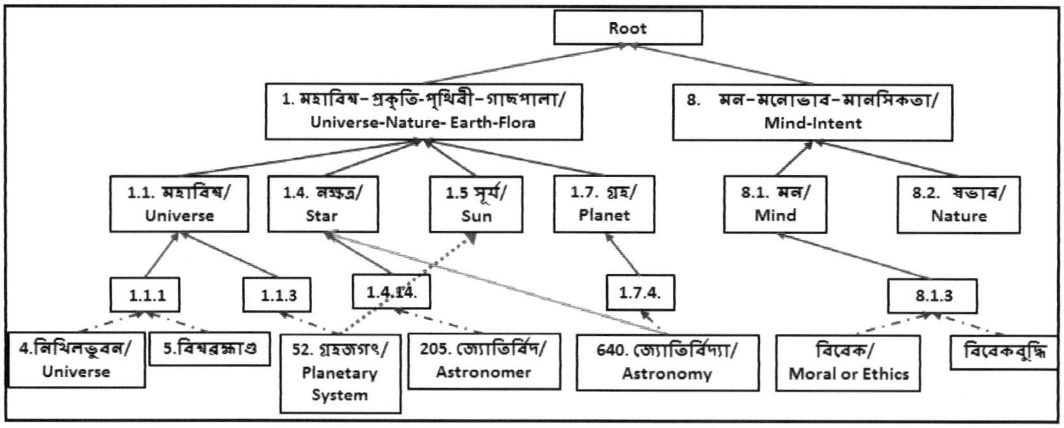

FIGURE 1- Partial view of our proposed lexicon

[2] http://www.nltr.org/
[3]http://www.ciil.org/

In figure 1, the category id of মহাবিশ্ব–প্রকৃতি–পৃথিবী–গাছপালা/ universe-nature-earth-flora is 1, মহাবিশ্ব/ universe has sub-category id 1.1 meaning it is the 1st sub-category of category 1 and নিখিলভুবন/ universe cluster id 1.1.1 as it belongs to the synonym cluster of 1.1. The member relations of words with their clusters have been shown in dashed lines and the round dotted line and the compound line indicate primary link and secondary link respectively.

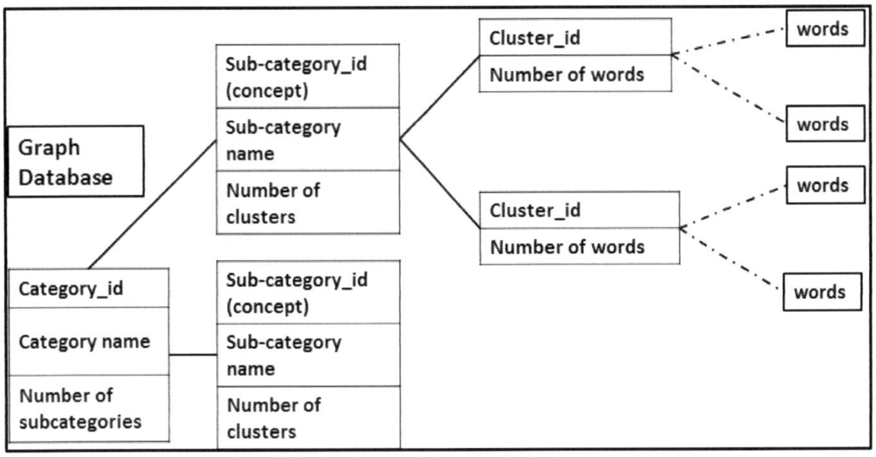


FIGURE 2-Simplified view of the underlying storage structure

Every word has been assigned an information array with 15 fields. They are:

- Serial_no: denotes the serial number of a word in the database
- Part-Of-Speech (POS)
- Corpus frequency
- Cluster_number: number of the cluster of the word
- SC_no.: number of the sub-category under which the word belongs
- SSC_no: number of the sub-sub-category of a word (applicable to few words)
- C_id: number of the category under which the word resides
- P_link: pointer to the cluster id under the sub-category specified by the primary link
- S_link: pointer to the cluster id under the sub-category specified by the secondary link
- Antonym: cluster id of the antonym(s) of the word
- Myth: a flag to indicate any mythical relation to the word
- Details: Serial no. of all the words in the collection denoted by the present word (if it is a collective noun)
- G_word: a pointer to the general word denoting the collection in which the present word belongs
- Verb: a flag to indicate whether the word can be also used as a verb or not.
- To_verb: contains the word which can be appended to the present word to make it possible to be used as a verb.

The fields from 1 to 4 and 5 are available for every word; rests of the fields have values, if available or they have been assigned null. Words belonging to multiple clusters have more than one 14-field information vector associated with them. Refer to the examples below for details:

<table>
<tr><td>Word</td><td>বাঁধ/dam</td><td>স্বর্গ/heav en</td><td>চতুর্দশভুবন/f ourteen worlds</td><td>সমুদ্রযাত্রা/se atravel</td><td>আত্মঘাতী/sucidal</td><td colspan="2">গ্রহগজগ□/plan etary system</td></tr>
<tr><td>Serial_no</td><td>1659</td><td>67</td><td>69</td><td>1440</td><td>6032</td><td colspan="2">52</td></tr>
<tr><td>Pos</td><td>বিশেষ্য [noun]</td><td>বিশেষ্য</td><td>বিশেষ্য</td><td>বিশেষ্য</td><td>বিশেষণ[adjective]</td><td colspan="2">বিশেষ্য</td></tr>
<tr><td>Corpus frequency</td><td>185</td><td>442</td><td>-</td><td>27</td><td>1069</td><td>-</td><td>-</td></tr>
<tr><td>Cluster_no</td><td>7</td><td>7</td><td>7</td><td>8</td><td>56</td><td>3</td><td>4</td></tr>
<tr><td>Sc_no</td><td>17</td><td>1</td><td>1</td><td>14</td><td>9</td><td>1</td><td>7</td></tr>
<tr><td>C_no</td><td>1</td><td>1</td><td>1</td><td>1</td><td>2</td><td>1</td><td>1</td></tr>
<tr><td>P_link</td><td>null</td><td>23.22.1</td><td>null</td><td>null</td><td>null</td><td colspan="2">1.5.2</td></tr>
<tr><td>S_link</td><td>1.47.22</td><td>null</td><td>null</td><td>null</td><td>null</td><td colspan="2">null</td></tr>
<tr><td>Antonym</td><td>null</td><td>null</td><td>null</td><td>null</td><td>2.58.58</td><td colspan="2">null</td></tr>
<tr><td>Myth</td><td>null</td><td>1</td><td>1</td><td>null</td><td>null</td><td colspan="2">null</td></tr>
<tr><td>Details</td><td>null</td><td>null</td><td>71,72</td><td>null</td><td>null</td><td colspan="2">null</td></tr>
<tr><td>G_word</td><td>null</td><td>null</td><td>null</td><td>null</td><td>null</td><td colspan="2">null</td></tr>
<tr><td>Verb</td><td>null</td><td>null</td><td>null</td><td>null</td><td>null</td><td colspan="2">null</td></tr>
<tr><td>M_to _verb</td><td>null</td><td>null</td><td>null</td><td>(ক)</td><td>null</td><td colspan="2">null</td></tr>
</table>

TABLE 1- organization of word database

### 3.1 Graphical User Interface

We have also developed a Graphical User Interface based on the lexical representation described above. It can perform two jobs. First, it can be used to find the details about a particular word or category present in the database. A user can provide input in two different ways: directly typing the word or selecting from the list of words of different parts of speeches. For the ease of typing Bangla, we have also provided a Bangla virtual keyboard associated with the GUI. Given a word, the system outputs all the available fields associated with the word. It also provides the name and link of the corresponding sub-category and category so that the user can view details about just by clicking on them. If a word belongs to more than one cluster or part-of speech, the GUI shows all the associated clusters and sub-concepts, concepts. User can also navigate to the sub-concept(s) associated by primary link or secondary link with the help of the GUI. Second, given two words as input the GUI also calculates the degree of semantic similarity between them along with their corresponding positions in the lexical representation. The method of obtaining the semantic similarity or relatedness measure has been described in the next section.

## 4 Semantic Similarity Measure between Bangla Words

As we have discussed in the above sections, along with relating words semantically, the mental lexicon also assigns a degree of similarity between them. Here, we have proposed a simple graph based semantic similarity measure on our proposed lexicon. We have also verified it with user feedbacks. In our proposed lexicon, the nodes from the top to bottom represent generalized to more specialized concepts. Therefore, the semantic distance or edge weights decrease as one moves down the hierarchy. There are 8 types of direct link in the organization:

| Sr. No. | Type of link | Link weight ( c is a constant whose value can be adjusted according to the need) |
|---|---|---|
| 1. | **member relation**: between a word and its cluster | $c$ |
| 2. | between a cluster and its sub-category | $\frac{c}{2}+\frac{c}{x}$ |
| 3. | between a cluster and its sub-sub-category (if present) | $\frac{c}{2}+0.5*\frac{c}{x}$ |
| 4. | **is-a** relation: between a sub-sub-category and its sub-category (if present) | $c+\frac{c}{x}$ |
| 5. | **is-a** relation: between a sub-category and its root category. | $c+\frac{2c}{x}$ |
| 6. | between a category and the root. | $c+\frac{3c}{x}$ |
| 7. | **primary_link**: between a word and a sub-category (according to the representation, this distance is greater than a member relation but lesser than the total path length between word and its sub-category) | $c+\frac{c}{2}$ |
| 8. | **secondary_link**: between a word and a sub-category (this distance is greater than the distance between a sub-category and its category) | $2c+\frac{2c}{x}$ |

TABLE 2- Edge-weight distributions

We have assumed that the all the nodes at a particular level are equal in weight. The semantic distance between any pair of words $(w_i, w_j)$ is measured by the shortest path distance between them:

$$similarity\ score(w_i, w_j) = x \Big/ \sum_{i \in shortest\ path(w_i, w_j)} (edge_i - weight) \quad \text{..... (1)}$$

Here, $x$ is a constant signifying the scale of measurement. We have taken $c = 0.5$ and $x = 10$ , so that a pair of synonyms has a score of 10 out of 10.Therefore, from table 2and equation (1), the semantic similarity values between different types of word pairs are as shown in table 3.

In order to verify whether the proposed approach to measure semantic similarity or relatedness between a pair of words can actually represent the degree of similarity as perceived by human cognition, we have carried out a user survey. The details of the study have been described in the next section.

| Case | Score (in a scale of 10) |
|---|---|
| both the words are in same cluster (synonym) | $x/2*c = 10$ |
| both the words are in same sub-category $(S_i)$, but in different clusters | $x/(c + 2(c/2 + c/x) + c) = 6.25$ |
| both the words are in same category $(C_i)$, but different sub-categorys | $x/2\left(c + \left(\frac{c}{2} + c/x\right) + (c + 2c/x)\right) = 3.57$ |
| both the words are from different categorys | $x/2\left(c + \left(\frac{c}{2} + c/x\right) + (c + 2c/x + (c + 3c/x))\right) = 2.5$ |
| both the words are from different sub-categorys, but connected through primary_link | $x/\left(\frac{3c}{2} + \left(\frac{c}{2} + c/x\right) + c\right) = 6.45$ |
| both the words are from different sub-categorys, but connected by secondary_link | $x/\left((2c + 2c/x) + \left(\frac{c}{2} + c/x\right) + c\right) = 5.26$ |
| **Antonym** is a special type of relation | -1 |

TABLE 3-Similarity scores

## 5 User Study

**Participants:** 25 native speakers of Bangla participated in the experiment with age between 23 years to 36 years. All of them hold a graduate degree in their respective fields and 10 have a post graduate degree.

**Experiment data selection and procedure:** 50 word pairs were selected from the lexical representation. The word pairs were chosen from the six different categories of relations described in table 4 above, except antonyms. Each user was asked to assign a score from 1 to 10 to each of the 50 word pairs based on their degree of semantic relatedness: 1 for the lowest or no connectivity and 10 for the highest connectivity or synonyms.

### 5.1 Result and Discussions

Perceiving semantic similarity or relatedness between a pair of words or concepts denoted by them depends on the cognitive skill, domain or language knowledge and background of the user. Corresponding to each of the six types of words taken for user study, we have calculated both median and mean of user ratings. Mean has been used because of its popularity and common use, but as mean is very sensitive to outlier or extreme values median has also been taken into account. The table 4 below shows the outcomes of the user validation:

| Category | 1 | 2 | 3 | 4 | 5 | 6 |
|---|---|---|---|---|---|---|
| **Median_user rating** | 8.5 | 6 | 3.59 | 1 | 7 | 5.5 |
| **Mean_user rating** | 8.6 | 5.89 | 2.38 | 1.25 | 6.34 | 4.94 |
| **Predicted similarity score** | 10 | 6.25 | 3.57 | 2.5 | 6.45 | 5.26 |

TABLE 4-User score versus predicted score

The figure 3 below demonstrates the results graphically, it can be easily seen that the user ratings and our proposed measure are very close to each other. One interesting point to be noted here is that the overall mean and median of user ratings for category 1 is less than 10. This means synonyms are not always perceived as exactly similar to each other. Spearman's rank correlation[5] of the predicted semantic similarity measure with the median values of user scores corresponding to each of the 50 word pairs is 0.8. To depict the subjectivity of user's perception, we have plotted the median values against our proposed scores (refer to figure 4).

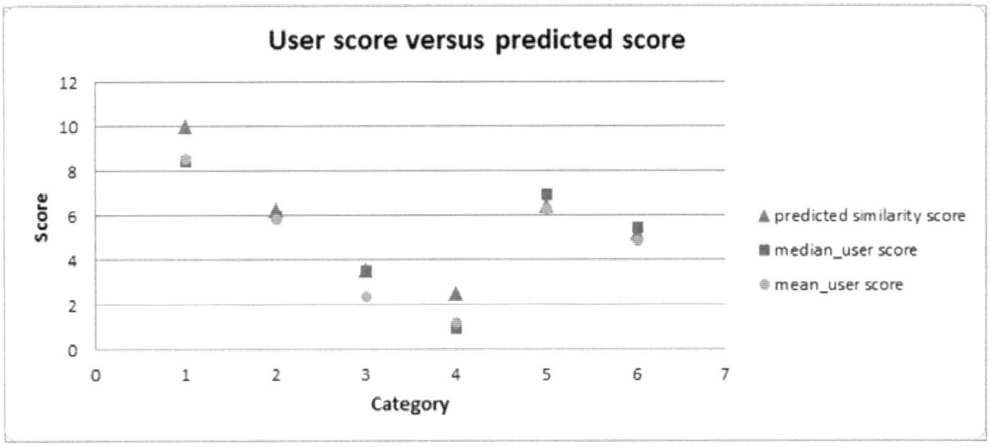


FIGURE 3-Performance analysis of user rating versus predicted measure ´

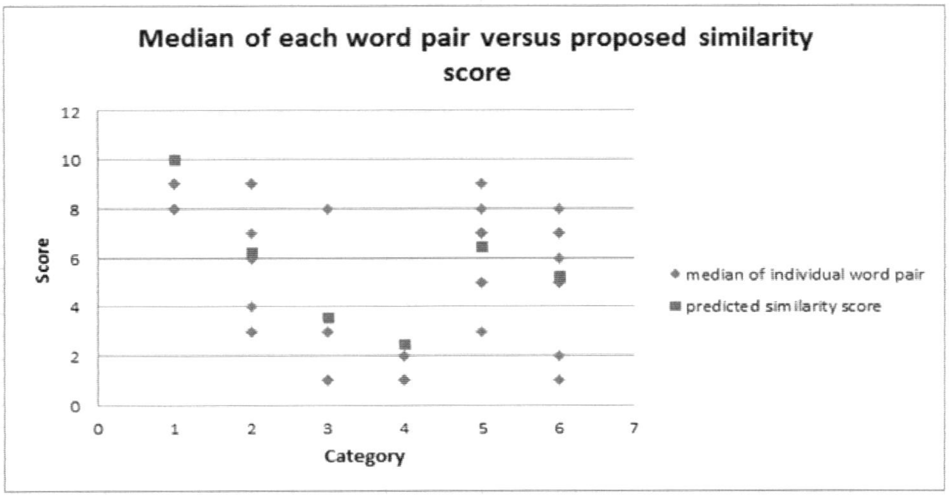


FIGURE 4- Comparison of ratings of individual pairs with proposed score

[5]http://en.wikipedia.org/wiki/Spearman's_rank_correlation_coefficient

Figure 4 shows few outliers in the dataset that have median values far from the group mean and median (type 1). Another type (type 2) of word pair is of interest as they have significant difference (greater than 1) between mean and median values, which implies that user ratings contain some extreme values. The pairs belonging to each type are:

| C | word pair | Type |
|---|---|---|
| 1 | দুর্গা--ভগবতী | 2 |
| 2 | রুচি/interests—রমণীয়/beautiful | 2 |
| 3 | বন্যা/flood—পর্বত/mountain | 2 |
| 5 | গ্রহজগ□/planetary system—সৌরলোক/solar system | 2 |
| 5 | কৃষিজমি/farm land—ফসল/crop | 2 |
| 2 | নগ্নতা/naked—বিবস্ত্র/undresses | 1 |
| | | |

| C | word pair | Type |
|---|---|---|
| 2 | আলাদা/different—বিভেদ/discriminate | 1 |
| 5 | গমন/go, travel—যাওয়া/departure | 1 |
| 5 | শিলাবৃষ্টি/hail -বরফপড়া/snowfall | 1 |
| 6 | ভরাকোটাল/hightide—জলপ্লাবন/flood | 1 |
| 3 | সাফল্য/success—খ্যাতি/fame | 1, 2 |
| 6 | হিমশৈল/iceberg—নুড়ি/pebbles | 1, 2 |
| 6 | ক্রমশ--মন্থরতা | 1, 2 |

TABLE 5- List of type 1 and type 2 words. "C" implies Category.

As can be seen from the above table, word-pairs like (দুর্গা—ভগবতী) demands a certain level of knowledge about the mythology to be perceived as synonyms, therefore, the user scores corresponding to this kind of word pairs also vary from person to person. Again, the similarity for the word pairs (গ্রহজগ□/planetary system—সৌরলোক/solar system) and (কৃষিজমি/farm land–ফসল/crops) depend on how a user connects the two concepts in her cognition. The type 1 word pairs such as (নগ্নতা/naked—বিবস্ত্র/undressed) (শিলাবৃষ্টি/hail–বরফপড়া/snowfall) and (সাফল্য/success—খ্যাতি/fame) have been marked as synonyms or highly similar by the users. These phenomena demonstrate the confusion in distinguishing synonyms and very closely related concepts or words, especially those which are used alternatively in frequent situations. Three pairs belong to both types signifying they have been perceived as very close by most of the users and at the same time have got extreme values from the rest.

## Conclusion and perspective

In this paper, we have proposed a hierarchically organized semantic lexicon in Bangla and also a graph based edge-weighting approach to measure the semantic similarity between two words. The similarity measures have been verified using user studies. We have included the frequency of each word over five Bangla corpuses in our lexical structure and also working on associating more details to words such as, their pronunciations, distribution in spoken corpus, word frequency history over time etc. Our proposed lexical structure contains only relations based on semantic association; we plan to extend the work to incorporate other kinds of relationships such as orthography, phonology and morphology to represent the human cognition more accurately.

## Acknowledgements

We are thankful to Society for Natural Language Technology Research Kolkata for helping us to develop the lexical resource. We are also thankful to those subjects who spend their time to manually evaluate our semantic similarity measure.

## References


Aitchison, J. (2012). *Words in the mind: An introduction to the mental lexicon*. Wiley-Blackwell.

Boyd-Graber, J., Fellbaum, C., Osherson, D., and Schapire, R. (2006). Adding dense, weighted connections to wordnet. In *Proceedings of the Third International WordNet Conference*, pages 29–36.

Das, A. and Bandyopadhyay, S. (2010). Semanticnet-perception of human pragmatics. In *Proceedings of the 2nd Workshop on Cognitive Aspects of the Lexicon*, pages 2–11, Beijing, China. Coling 2010 Organizing Committee.

Fellbaum, C. (2010). Wordnet.*Theory and Applications of Ontology: Computer Applications*, pages 231–243.

Jiang, J. and Conrath, D. (1997). Semantic similarity based on corpus statistics and lexical taxonomy. *arXiv preprint cmp-lg/9709008*.

Kim, Y. and Kim, J. (1990). A model of knowledge based information retrieval with hierarchical concept graph. *Journal of Documentation*, 46(2):113–136.

Lee, J., Kim, M., and Lee, Y. (1993). Information retrieval based on conceptual distance in is-a hierarchies. *Journal of documentation*, 49(2):188–207.

Levelt, W. (1989). Speaking: from intention to articulationmit press. *Cambridge, MA*.

Li, Y., Bandar, Z., and McLean, D. (2003).An approach for measuring semantic similarity between words using multiple information sources.*Knowledge and Data Engineering, IEEE Transactions on*, 15(4):871–882.

Liu, H. and Singh, P. (2004).Conceptnet—a practical commonsense reasoning tool-kit.*BT technology journal*, 22(4):211–226.

Mukhopadhyay, A. (2005). *SamsadSamarthasabdokosh*. SahityaSamsad, 12 edition.

Müller, S. (2008).*The mental lexicon*. GRIN Verlag.

Rada, R., Mili, H., Bicknell, E., and Blettner, M. (1989).Development and application of a metric on semantic nets.*Systems, Man and Cybernetics, IEEE Transactions on*, 19(1):17–30.

Resnik, P. (1993a). Selection and information: a class-based approach to lexical relationships. *IRCS Technical Reports Series*, page 200.

Resnik, P. (1993b). Semantic classes and syntactic ambiguity. In *Proc. of ARPA Workshop on Human Language Technology*, pages 278–283.

Richardson, R., Smeaton, A., and Murphy, J. (1994).Using wordnet as a knowledge base for measuring semantic similarity between words.Technical report, Technical Report Working Paper CA-1294, School of Computer Applications, Dublin City University.

Roy, M. and Muqtadir, M. (2008).*Semi-automatic building of wordnet for Bangla*.PhD thesis, School of Engineering and Computer Science (SECS), BRAC University.

Ruppenhofer, J., Ellsworth, M., Petruck, M., Johnson, C., and Scheffczyk, J. (2010).Framenet ii: Extended theory and practice, available online at h ttp.*framenet. icsi. berkeley. edu*.

Seashore, R. and Eckerson, L. (1940). The measurement of individual differences in general english vocabularies. *Journal of Educational Psychology; Journal of Educational Psychology*, 31(1):14.

Tversky, A. (1977). Features of similarity.*Psychological review*, 84(4):327.

Wang, T. and Hirst, G. (2011).Refining the notions of depth and density in wordnet-based semantic similarity measures. In *Proceedings of the Conference on Empirical Methods in Natural Language Processing*, EMNLP '11, pages 1003–1011, Stroudsburg, PA, USA. Association for Computational Linguistics.

# Where's the Meeting that was Cancelled?
# Existential Implications of Transitive Verbs

*Patricia Amaral*[1] *Valeria de Paiva*[2] *Cleo Condoravdi*[3] *Annie Zaenen*[3]
(1)Department of Romance Languages, University of North Carolina at Chapel Hill, USA
(2)School of Computer Science, University of Birmingham, UK
(3)CSLI, Stanford University, USA
pamaral@unc.edu, valeria.depaiva@gmail.com, cleoc@csli.stanford.ed,
azaenen@csli.stanford.edu

ABSTRACT
This paper describes a preliminary classification of transitive verbs in terms of the implications of existence (or non-existence) associated with their direct object nominal arguments. The classification was built to underlie the lexical marking of verbs in the lexical resources that the automated system BRIDGE developed at Xerox PARC used for textual inference. Similar classifications are required for other logic-based textual inference systems, but very little is written about the issue.

KEYWORDS: textual inference, lexical resources, transitive verbs.

## 1 Motivation

A computational system cannot be said to understand natural language if it cannot draw some rather direct inferences from a text. Central among them are inferences about the existence or non-existence of the entities and eventualities referred to. In this paper we look at two types of referentially opaque transitive verbs: verbs that are inherently negative and thus imply non-existence, and verbs with what we could call time-dependent opacity.

In our discussion we make the simplifying assumption that the reader/the system considers the speaker trustworthy so that anything that the speaker is committed to as being true (or false) by virtue of the linguistic expression used, is treated as true (or false). Our notion of speaker commitment covers both entailments and presuppositions/implicatures (see (Karttunen and Zaenen, 2005) for a short discussion and (Potts, 2005) for an extensive motivation.)

The detection of existential implications is an essential part of computing textual inferences, as conceived, for instance, in the RTE (Recognizing Textual Entailment) Pascal challenge (Dagan et al., 2006). A simplified example is given in (1).

(1) Ed built a spacious hut. There was a spacious hut. YES

Our inquiry and classification extends (Nairn et al., 2006), which looks at implicative verbs with clausal complements. The relation between the two problems can be seen by comparing the implications of the verb 'prevent' construed with a clausal complement or a nominal (event-denoting) complement:

(2) Ed prevented Mary from leaving. Mary left. NO

(3) Ed prevented an accident. There was an accident. NO

The work reported here, as the one in (Nairn et al., 2006) and elsewhere, takes the view that *inferential* aspects are one of the main challenges that lexicographers interested in cognitive features of the lexicon need to address.

The treatment proposed in (Nairn et al., 2006) aims at capturing the author's commitment to the truth or falsity of the complement clause of the verb. This classification is based both on the semantics of the complement-taking verb and on the syntactic type of the clause (e.g. factive *forget that* vs. implicative *forget to*). In the case of nominal complements, different factors need to be taken into consideration to determine the speaker's commitment to the existence or non-existence of the denotation of the complement of the verb. These include:

- syntactic alternations of the verb,
- the aspectual class of the verb phrase,
- whether the nominal complement is event-denoting or not,
- the aspectual properties of the nominal complement if it is event-denoting
- the tense and aspect of the verb.

A final factor is the (in)definiteness of the direct object. Definite NPs tend to presuppose the existence of their referents. We will try to control for this by constructing examples with indefinite NPs. Further complications will be discussed in the relevant sections.

## 2 Constraints on the classification

The classification was conceived to be used in conjunction with the representations produced by the automated system BRIDGE (Bobrow et al., 2007a),(Bobrow et al., 2007b). An important feature of these representations is the *(un)instantiability* of *concepts,* which corresponds to a claim of (non-)existence of an entity or occurrence of an event denoted by the concept. For instance, the sentence "Negotiations prevented a strike" involves events of the type "negotiation", "strike" and "preventing". Intuitively, the negotiations (whatever they may be) are presented as having occurred in the real world and so is the preventing event. In our representation, the terms corresponding to the words "negotiations" and "prevented" are instantiated in the top context, which corresponds to what the author of the sentence considers as true. But the term corresponding to "strike" should only be instantiable in the prevent-context; in the top context the term should be declared uninstantiable. See (Condoravdi et al., 2001), (Crouch et al., 2003) for motivation and details. The use of contexts, which correspond logically to partial possible worlds, allows us to represent further aspects of the situation prevented (for instance, how long that strike would have been or how bitter, etc.) without running into contradictions.

The BRIDGE system, by default, treats the nominal arguments of verbs as carrying existential commitments at least in the context of the predication. This is obviously inadequate for the phenomena that we discuss in this paper and in section 5 we will propose an extension of the system that allows us to treat these phenomena more adequately.

## 3 Criteria for the classification

The main criterion adopted in the classification of the verb classes is whether the verb meaning indicates or does not indicate that the referent of the direct object existed before the eventuality denoted by the verb took place (pre-state) or not and whether the referent of the direct object exists after this eventuality (post-state). We focus on verbs that affect the existence of its object; for example, *annul* meets this description, but *touch* does not; only in the former case is the change with respect to the existence of the referent of the direct object part of the meaning of the verb. This difference in the implications that we intend to capture is exemplified in the contrast between (4) and (5):[1]

(4) Ed touched a teapot.
Pre-state: There was a teapot. YES
Post-state: There is a teapot. YES

(5) The judge has annulled Ed's marriage.
Pre-state: Ed was married. YES
Post-state: Ed is married. NO

We will call verbs that indicate a change in the existence of the referent of their nominal complement, existential change verbs. In this paper we focus on this type of verbs and leave aside verbs that do not encode pre- and post–states (or with pre- and post–states that are the same). We present the different types of existential change verbs in the next section. In section 5, we discuss the representation of information about existence in our system.

## 4 Existential change verbs

In this class we identified eight sub-classes. They can be subdivided broadly into verbs of causation (the first five subclasses) and aspectual verbs (the last three subclasses).

### 4.1 *Cause*-type verbs

In this subsection we look at verbs whose nominal complement is headed by a noun that denotes an eventuality. Examples are *cause*, *provoke*, *force*, *produce*, *bring about*, *induce*. They share the following implications: (i) In positive environments: the predicate entails the occurrence of an eventuality/situation as a post-state, (ii) the caused eventuality/situation does not exist in the pre-state, (iii) in negative environments it is unknown whether the caused eventuality/situation has taken place. This indeterminacy is due to the indeterminacy of the scope of the negation. This pattern of inferences is exemplified in (6) and (7):

(6) The decree caused trouble.
pre-state: There was trouble. NO
post-state: There was trouble. YES

[1] This representation of the lexical meaning of verbs abstracts away from many factors that may intervene in a factual situation. For instance, (5) may be used in a case where Ed has gotten married again.

(7) The decree didn't cause trouble.
pre-state: There was trouble. UNKNOWN
post-state: There was a trouble. UNKNOWN

Similarly, in (8), under normal circumstances, the speaker is committed to the non-occurrence of the revolution before the decree and to its occurrence after the decree.

(8) The decree caused a revolution.
pre-state: There was a revolution before the decree. NO
post-state: There was a revolution after the decree. YES

When the progressive is used we find some cases of the "Imperfective Paradox"((Dowty, 1979)), whereas in others there seems not to be such effect. Compare (9) and (10):

(9) The decree was causing trouble when it was revoked.

(10) The decree was causing a revolution when it was revoked.

Whereas in the first example we conclude that there was trouble (i.e., the decree has caused some trouble), in the second we conclude that a revolution was avoided. We hypothesize that this is due to the nature of the eventuality that the nominal refers to. It is well-known that eventualities can be 'homogeneous' (states and processes) or not (accomplishments and achievements). 'Trouble' is homogeneous: a little bit of trouble is trouble but 'revolution' is not: for instance, the beginning of a revolution is not a revolution.

*Cause*–type verbs can also be used to express a change of degree rather that a change from non-existence to existence as exemplified in (11).

(11) The medicine induced an increase in blood pressure.
pre-state: There was an increase of blood pressure. NO
post-state: There was an increase in blood pressure. YES

Here the event that occurs is not the coming into existence of blood pressure but the increase in it. That is, of course, as expected: here the caused eventuality is the increase.

## 4.2 Verbs of creation

Closely related to the previous class are verbs of creation. They are different in that their complement refers to an object (physical or not) and not to an eventuality. This class includes verbs like *build, bake* (as in 'bake a cake'), *write, coin, compose, compute*(as in 'compute a solution'), *concoct, construct* (see Create verbs 24.4 and 24.1 in (Levin, 1993)) with the following cluster of implications: (i) in positive environments, there is a speaker's commitment to the non-existence of the object before the event (entailment), and (ii) a commitment to the existence of the object after the event in the simple past tense, (iii) in negative environments, it is unknown whether the object exists, all we know is that the referent of the subject of the sentence did not bring it into existence.

(12) John built a house.
There is a house.YES

(13) John didn't build a house.
There is a house. UNKNOWN

The effect of the "Imperfective Paradox", however, is much stronger with these verbs than with the previous class: in positive environments, the use of the progressive form changes the speaker's commitment as to the existence of the object. Therefore, we need a conditional marking in the rules, i.e. if the verb occurs in the simple past, the speaker is committed to the existence of the object, and if the verb occurs in the progressive, the speaker is committed to the non-existence of the object.

(14) John is building a house.
There is a house. NO

Verbs like *draw*, *picture*,*sculpt* etc. behave like verbs of creation when their nominal complement denotes the material or eventive result (*draw a picture, sing a song*). But they belong in the class of intensional verbs when their nominal complement denotes the content of the act: because what you draw may or may not exist in the real world (e.g. *draw a unicorn*).

## 4.3 Verbs of destruction

Verbs like *destroy*, *extinguish*, *terminate*, *annul*, *invalidate*, *nullify*, *break off*, *annihilate*, *demolish*, *undo*, *wreck*, *resolve*, share the following cluster of implications: In positive environments, (i) the speaker is committed to the existence of the object before the event (entailment) and (ii) the speaker is committed to the non-existence of the object after the event (entailment), and (iii) in negative environments, there is no commitment as to the existence of the object, but in common usage the speaker seems to be committed to the existence of the object (plausible, not strict inference). This is exemplified below:

(15) The firefighters extinguished a fire.
pre-state: There was a fire. YES
post-state: There is a fire. NO

(16) The firefighters didn't extinguish a fire.
pre-state: There was a fire. UNKNOWN
post-state: The fire continues. UNKNOWN
(The firefighters didn't extinguish the fire, but the rain did.)

The following two classes of verbs differ from the previous ones in that there is a modal component to their meaning; the nominal complement of the verb may denote either an eventuality that is true in the actual world or whose existence is restricted to a possible world other than the actual world.[2]

[2]Speakers' commitments of existence (or non-existence) allowed by the verbs presented in sections 4.4 and 4.5 may receive a morphological marking.

## 4.4 *Avoid*-type verbs

Verbs like *avoid, elude, escape*, whose meaning can roughly be paraphrased as 'manage not to experience something evaluated as bad', share the following cluster of implications when the nominal denotes an eventuality: In positive environments, (i) the speaker is committed to the potential occurrence of the eventuality denoted by the nominal complement before the event, and (ii) these verbs allow for both a wide and a narrow scope interpretation: in the wide scope interpretation, the speaker is committed to the occurrence of the eventuality after the event, and in the narrow scope interpretation, the speaker is committed to the non-occurrence of the eventuality after the event. (iii) In negative environments, the speaker is committed to the occurrence of the eventuality after the event.

This is exemplified below for *avoid*:
**Narrow scope reading**:

(17) So here's some good news about how hundreds of workers avoided a layoff and didn't lose the jobs to downsizing ...

pre-state: There was a potential layoff. YES
post-state: There was a layoff. NO

**Wide scope reading**:

(18) We landed in Lima only to find that yet again we had narrowly avoided an earthquake (Tokyo all over again). This one was a massive quake of around 7-8 on the richter scale ...

pre-state: There was a potential earthquake. YES
post-state: There was an earthquake. YES

Note that we are concerned here with the inferences that are licensed by the lexical meaning of *avoid*. What has changed between the pre–state and the post–state is precisely the speaker's commitment as to the existence of the eventuality denoted by the nominal complement of the verb in the post–state: the non-occurrence of the eventuality in (17) and its occurrence in (18). When the nominal dependent denotes an object rather than an event, the object is assumed to exist in the pre- and in the post–state (wide scope reading):

(19) We avoided a tree.
pre-state: There was a tree. YES
post-state: There was a tree. YES.

When the nominal complement's direct denotation is an object, by semantic coercion the complement is interpreted as denoting an eventuality:

(20) We avoided a tree.
We avoided hitting a tree.
We avoided the ball.
We avoided being hit by the ball.

The direct denotation of these objects is assumed to exist before and after the act of avoidance but the eventuality described in the expansions is asserted not to take place.

## 4.5 *Prevent*-type verbs

Verbs like *prevent, avert, block, inhibit, impede, hinder, deter, preclude, forbid, forestall,* and *cancel* (in the sense of 'cause not to','prevent from happening'), *spare* (in the meaning 'refrain from harming') share the following cluster of implications: In positive environments: (i) the speaker is committed to the potential existence of the object before the event, and (ii) the speaker is committed to the non-existence of the object after the event, (iii) there is a causal implication, and (iv) in negative environments, the speaker is committed to the existence of the object (plausible inference, seems to be the common usage). The nominal complement of this class of verbs is event-denoting.

(21) The government prevented an oil spill in the bay.
post-state: There was an oil spill in the bay. NO

(22) And nobody questions him because this mayor of a large American city who didn't prevent a major terrorist attack but seemed emotional in its aftermath has some special insight into the nature of terrorism ...
post-state: There was a major terrorist attack. YES

## 4.6 *Begin*-type verbs

This class includes aspectual verbs like *begin, start, initiate* that denote the beginning of an eventuality. When the referent of the nominal complement is an eventuality, these verbs share the following cluster of implications: (i) in positive environments, there is a speaker's commitment as to the non-occurrence of the eventuality before the event (entailment), and (ii) there is no commitment as to the occurrence of the eventuality after the event; (iii) in negative environments, there is a commitment as to the non-occurrence of the eventuality after the event. We illustrate (i) in (24), 25, and (23)):

(23) Ed and Mary didn't begin a relationship.
pre-state: There was a relationship. NO

(24) Ed and Mary began a relationship.
pre-state: There was a relationship. NO

(25) The queen began a visit to India.
pre-state: There was a visit. NO

The status of (ii) depends on the properties of the eventuality referred to by the nominal complement. We hypothesize that the same distinction as discussed above in subsection 4.1 holds here too: when the eventuality is homogeneous, there is an existence commitment, when it is not, there is no commitment. Compare (26) and (27):

(26) Ed began a trip to Paris.
post-state: Ed made a trip to Paris. UNKNOWN
The queen began a visit to India.
post-state: The queen made a visit to India. UNKNOWN

(27) Ed and Mary began a relationship.
post-state: There was a relationship. YES
A boy playing with matches started a Southern California wildfire.
post-state: There was a wildfire. YES

Adapting test for verbs we can illustrate the difference between the nouns in (26) and (27) as follows:

(28) #They had a relationship in 2 months.
#There was a wildfire in two weeks.
They made a trip to Paris in 2 weeks.
They made a visit to India in two weeks.

As is the case with verbs, homogeneous events do not take temporal modifiers that express the duration, whereas accomplishments do.

When the verbs in this class take a nominal complement which is not event–denoting, as is the case of 'book' in (29), semantic coercion changes the denotation to an eventuality. As has been argued inter alia in (Pustejovsky, 1995), a sentence like (29) is ambiguous (at least) between 'starting to write a book' and 'starting to read a book'. As the combination of the verb and the nominal complement does not tell us which reading we have to choose, and this choice bears on the existential commitment about the object (see (30) and (31)), we mark the implications of (29) as UNKNOWN.

(29) John started a book.
pre-state: There is a book.UNKNOWN
post-state: There is a book. UNKNOWN

(30) John started to write a book.
pre-state: There is a book. NO
post-state: There is a book. UNKNOWN

(31) John started to read a book.
pre-state: There is a book. YES
post-state: There is a book.YES

In negative environments, the entailments are the same regardless of whether the denotation of the complement is an object or an eventuality.

## 4.7 *Continue*-type verbs

Verbs like *continue* and *pursue*, which we don't illustrate here, share the following cluster of implications: (i) the speaker is committed to the occurrence of the eventuality in the pre–state (presupposition), (ii) in positive environments, the speaker is committed to the occurrence of the eventuality in the post–state (entailment), (iii) in negative environments, there is a speaker's commitment as to the non-occurrence of the eventuality in the post–state. As with the previous class the implications depend on the aspectual class of the noun.

## 4.8 *End*-type verbs

Examples of end-type verbs are *end, stop, cease, finish, discontinue, suspend, interupt*. When the direct denotation of their nominal complement isn't an eventuality, its interpretation is coerced to an eventuality reading as is the case with begin and continue-type verbs. The end-type verbs share the following cluster of implications: (i) In positive environments, the speaker is committed to the non-occurrence of the eventuality after the end-event (entailment), and (ii) in negative environments, there is no commitment as to the occurrence of the eventuality, but in common usage the speaker seems to be committed to the occurrence of the eventuality after the end-event (plausible, not strict inference).

Again, these verbs, as well as *interrupt* and *discontinue*, have different entailments depending on the aspectual properties displayed by the nouns that they take as complement. With nouns that denote activities, the speaker is committed to the existence of the activity, whereas this is not the case for nouns denoting accomplishments (or achievements):

(32) Ed interrupted a discussion between the students.
pre-state: The students had been discussing. YES
post-state: There was a discussion between the students. NO

(33) Ed stopped the bleeding.
pre-state: There was a bleeding. YES
post-state: There is bleeding. NO

(34) John stopped the evaluation of the system.
pre-state: There was an evaluation of the system. NO
post-state: The system was evaluated. NO

However, we must further distinguish between two sub-classes within this class of verbs. The verbs *end* and *finish* behave differently from *stop* with accomplishment predicates:

(35) Ed stopped a repair.
post-state: There was a repair. NO

(36) Ed ended/finished a repair.
post-state: There was a repair. YES

But this is not the case for nouns that denote activities or states, where both *end* and *stop* display the same pattern of implications:

(37) The president ended/stopped a war.
post-state: There is a war. NO

With respect to nominals whose primary denotation are objects, the interpretation depends again on the eventuality to which the interpretation of the nominal is plausibly coerced. For example, in (38) what is understood to have stopped is the ticking of the clock. Again *finish* and *end* behave differently.

(38) John stopped a clock.
post-state: There is a clock. YES

(39) Ed didn't finish a dissertation.
post-state: There is a dissertation. NO

It is clear, then, that the entailments of sentences containing aspectual verbs like *start*, *continue*, *end* and *stop*, among others, depend on the aspectual properties of the nouns that they take as complements. For event-denoting nouns that are not deverbal (e.g. crime, accident, earthquake, ceremony, game, violence) little is known about these properties.

## 5 Representing existence information

Representation of the kind of information within the system BRIDGE is mediated by the relevant lexical information being imported into the Unified Lexicon (UL) (Crouch and King, 2005). Similarly to complement taking implicative verbs (Nairn et al., 2006), we expect to mark by hand the new implication signatures discussed, using some frequency criteria. We envisage using the British National Corpus (BNC) frequency list to uncover transitive verbs with these new kinds of implicative behavior. The appropriate lexical markings would then trigger rules constructing representations that encode the corresponding implications. We also envisage leveraging some of the Verbnet semantics information to check our proposed pre and post conditions.

Notions of pre- and post conditions are widely used in logics for verification of programs, in the so-called Hoare logics. These kinds of conditions are also used in AI planning and in formal models of concurrency. However, they have found little use in semantics of natural languages. We propose to use these conditions as a first approximation for the inferential meaning of verbs.

## 6 Conclusion

The present investigation of existential implications of transitive verbs shows that any implementation of logic-based textual inference needs to take into consideration different types of factors: the implicative behavior of a set of transitive verbs as a function of their lexical meaning, tense and aspect of the verbs, aspectual properties of the nominal complements, and definiteness. The combination of these factors as clues for the identification of the commitment of the speaker with respect to the existence of the entity or event denoted by the nominal complement of the verb is a challenge for any Entailment and Contradiction Detection system.

Our attempt to spell out the existential inferences leads to theoretical problems: it shows that we need an ontological classification of the nominal complements in eventuality-denoting and object-denoting, that we need a coercion mechanism for the object-denoting nouns and a distinction between the existential implications for the denoted object and for the denoted coerced eventuality and it forces us to look at the ill-understood aspectual properties of eventuality-denoting nouns whether they are morphologically deverbal or not.

## References

Bobrow, D., Cheslow, B., Condoravdi, C., Karttunen, L., King, T. H., Price, L., Nairn, R., de Paiva, V., L.Price, and Zaenen, A. (2007a). Precision-focused textual inference. *Proceedings of ACL-PASCAL Workshop on Textual Entailment and Paraphrasing*, pages 16–21.

Bobrow, D., Condoravdi, C., Karttunen, L., King, T. H., Price, L., Nairn, R., de Paiva, V., L.Price, and Zaenen, A. (2007b). Parc's bridge and question answering system. *Proceedings of Grammar Engineering Across Frameworks*, pages 26–45.

Condoravdi, C., Crouch, R., van den Berg, M., Everett, J., Stolle, R., Paiva, V., and Bobrow, D. (2001). Preventing existence. In *Proceedings of the Conference on Formal Ontologies in Information Systems (FOIS)*, Ogunquit, Maine.

Crouch, D., Condoravdi, C., de Paiva, V., and Stolle, R. (2003). Entailment, intensionality and text understanding. In *Proceedings of the HLT-NAACL Workshop on Text Meaning*, Edmonton, Canada.

Crouch, D. and King, T. H. (2005). Unifying lexical resources. In *Proceedings of the Workshop on the Identification and Representation of Verb Features and Verb Classes*, Saarbruecken, Germany.

Dagan, I., Glickman, O., and Magnin, B. (2006). The pascal recognising textual entailment challenge. In *Lecture Notes in Computer Science, 3944*, pages 177 – 190.

Dowty, D. (1979). *Word Meaning and Montague Grammar*. Reidel, Dordrecht.

Karttunen, L. and Zaenen, A. (2005). Veridicity. In Katz, G., Pustejovsky, J., and Schilder, F., editors, *Annotating, Extracting and Reasoning about Time and Events*, volume Dagstuhl Seminar Proceedings 05151. Dagstuhl, Germany.

Levin, B. (1993). *English Verb Classes and Alternations: A Preliminary Investigation*. The University of Chicago Press, Chicago.

Nairn, R., Condoravdi, C., and Karttunen, L. (2006). Computing relative polarity for textual inference. In *Proceedings of ICoS-5 (Inference in Computational Semantics)*, Buxton, UK.

Potts, C. (2005). *The Logic of Conventional Implicatures*. Oxford Studies in Theoretical Linguistics. Oxford University Press, Oxford.

Pustejovsky, J. (1995). *The generative Lexicon*. MIT Press.

# SEJFEK — a Lexicon and a Shallow Grammar of Polish Economic Multi-Word Units

*Agata Savary*[1] *Bartosz Zaborowski*[2]
*Aleksandra Krawczyk-Wieczorek*[2] *Filip Makowiecki*[3]
(1) Université François Rabelais Tours, Laboratoire d'informatique, Blois, France
(2) Institute of Computer Science, Polish Academy of Sciences, Warsaw, Poland
(3) University of Warsaw, Poland
agata.savary@univ-tours.fr, bartosz.zaborowski@ipipan.waw.pl,
aleksandra.wieczorek@ipipan.waw.pl, f.makowiecki@gmail.com

## Abstract

We present a large-coverage lexical and grammatical resource of Polish economic terminology. It consists of two alternative modules. One is a grammatical lexicon of about 11,000 terminological multi-word units, where inflectional and syntactic variation, as well as nesting of terms, are described via graph-based rules. The other one is a fully lexicalized shallow grammar, obtained by an automatic conversion of the lexicon, and partly manually validated. Both resources have a good coverage, evaluated on a manually annotated corpus, and are freely available under the Creative Commons BY-SA license.

Keywords: electronic lexicon, shallow grammar, Polish, economic terminology, language resources and tools.

## 1 Introduction

Terminology is one of important application domains of Natural Language Processing (NLP). Information extraction, text classification, automatic summarization, machine translation and other NLP fields can greatly support the exploitation of specialized texts by both experts and a large public. These processes heavily rely on identification and understanding of technical terms which are semantically rich linguistic units.

The basic facts about terms are that: (i) terminology is very productive: new terms are constantly created with the rapid advances of science and technology, (ii) most of them are nominal multi-word units (MWUs), (iii) many multi-word terms contain other, previously forged, terminological MWUs, e.g. *read-only memory* (*ROM*), *programmable ROM*, *erasable programmable ROM*, etc. The long tradition of terminological extraction shows that particularly interesting results can be obtained with hybrid approaches which combine statistical lexical association measures and shallow parsing (Smadja, 1993; Daille, 1996). Prevalent inflectional, syntactic and semantic variability of terminological MWUs calls for fine-grained representation of their linguistic properties (Jacquemin, 2001). Moreover the necessity of "looking inside" terminological MWUs, in order to recognize their nested structures, has been more recently recognized (Alex et al., 2007; Finkel and Manning, 2009).

While some work has been done in automatic processing of terminology for Slavic languages (Koeva, 2007; Mykowiecka et al., 2009), which are morphologically complex, relatively few large-coverage NLP resources exist for automatic processing of terminology in these languages. Our work contributes to bridging this gap. We present *SEJFEK*, an NLP-oriented resource for Polish in the domain of economy. It consists of two alternative modules. One is a grammatical lexicon of about 11,000 terminological MWUs, where inflectional and syntactic variation, as well as nesting of terms, are described via fine-grained rules (cf. Sec. 2). The other one is a fully lexicalized shallow grammar, obtained by an automatic conversion of the lexicon, and manually validated (cf. Sec. 3).

## 2 Grammatical Lexicon of Polish Economic Phraseology

*SEJFEK* (*Słownik Elektroniczny Jednostek Frazeologicznych z EKonomii*)[1] was created as a grammatical lexicon of Polish economic phraseology. In this section we describe the scope of this resource, the data selection process, the formalisms and tools used for the lexicographic work, and the current contents of the lexicon.

### 2.1 Knowledge Sources

Constructing any lexical resource has to start with defining its precise scope. We have carried out some initial studies concerning the question which areas should precisely be considered as belonging to the domain of economy. Micro- and macroeconomy, banking, finance, economic policy, trade and international economics seemed undoubtedly relevant, while marketing, management and employment policy might be seen as borderline with respect to economy. We finally relied on the Resolution of the Central Commission for Degrees and Titles of June 23, 2006[2]. We have selected all domains, except commodity, considered in this official document as parts of economic sciences: economy, finance and management with their subdomains. Linguistically speaking, the terms to be included in the lexicon were to be multi-word nominal units with a reasonably fixed terminological meaning. Both common and proper nouns were considered relevant. Quantitatively speaking, the funding project allowed for the description of about 10,000 entries.

The collection of input material has been done mainly manually. The main lexicographer was an expert in linguistics with a thorough knowledge of economy, which greatly facilitated and enhanced the reliability of both the data selection and its grammatical description. Initially, input data were searched for in the following the Web sources:

- *Encyklopedia Zarządzania* 'Encyclopedia of Management' (`http://mfiles.pl`) constructed within a collaborative Wiki framework and containing (at the beginning of our project) about 4,000 terms. Many of them were simple words and had to be eliminated. Numerous relevant data were manually selected from tables and schemas.
- *Money.pl* (`www.money.pl/slownik`), *Bankier.pl* (`www.bankier.pl/slownik`) and *NBPortal.pl* (`http://www.nbportal.pl/pl/np/slownik`) – targeted but relatively small web lexicons.
- Official portals of Polish finance and political institutions, notably *Narodowy Bank Polski* 'Polish National Bank' (`www.nbp.pl`), *Ministerstwo Finansów* 'Ministry of Finance' (`www.mf.gov.pl`), and *Giełda Papierów Wartościowych w Warszawie* 'Warsaw Stock Exchange' (`www.gpw.pl`). Manual browsing of articles and guides allowed to extract additional terms, as well as some proper names, e.g. the list of companies

[1] `http://zil.ipipan.waw.pl/SEJFEK`
[2] Uchwała Centralnej Komisji do spraw Stopni i Tytułów z 23.06.2003

listed in the Warsaw Stock Exchange, financial and political institutions, economic programs, and the *Polska Klasyfikacja Działalności* 'Polish Classification of Activities'.

- Economic and financial services of major Polish web portals (`onet.pl`, `wp.pl`, `gazeta.pl`, `forsal.pl`). Their texts showed a rather low density of economic terms as they were mainly addressed to non specialists.

An attempt was made to extract candidate terms automatically from corpora with a Polish Web crawler and collocation finder *Kolokacje*[3], which however yielded few valuable results. In view of this experiment we think that automatic terminological extraction might greatly benefit from high quality lexical and grammatical resources, such as those described below.

The list of terms selected from the web was further completed with data from indexes of traditional printed economic lexicons and manuals. Those were chosen from bibliographical lists recommended for students of economy and management at the University of Warsaw and included: (Samuelson and Nordhaus, 2003), (Samuelson and Nordhaus, 1998), (Głuchowski and Szambelańczyk, 1999), (Wernik, 2007), (Michoń, 1991), (Rynarzewski and Zielińska-Głębocka, 2006), (Treder, 2005), (Kuciński, 2009), (Chow, 1995), (Śnieżek, 2004), (Michalski, 2003), (Black, 2008), and (Smullen and Hand, 2008). Some terminology dedicated to European integration was found in (Rzewuska et al., 2001).

## 2.2 Formalism and Tool

After selecting the economic MWUs to be included in the lexicon, their grammatical description was done within *Toposław* (Marciniak et al., 2011), the lexicographic framework initially meant for the development of lexical resources of Polish proper names (Savary et al., 2009). This platform offers a user-friendly graphical interface encompassing three core components: (i) *Morfeusz*, the morphological analyzer and generator of Polish simple words, (ii) *Multiflex* (Savary, 2009), a graph-based generator of inflected forms of multi-word units, (iii) a graph editor stemming from *Unitex* [4], a multilingual corpus processor.

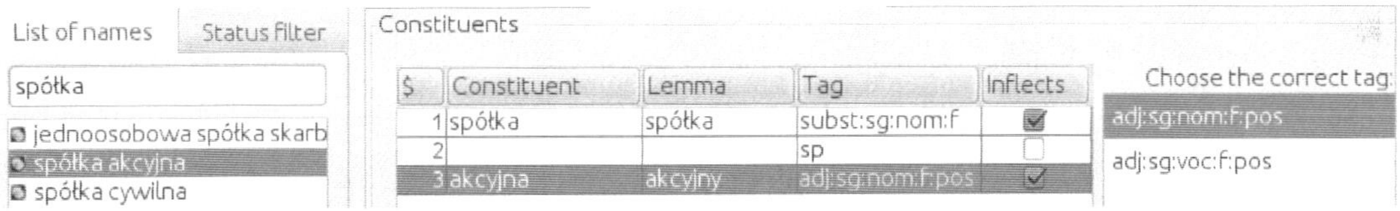


Figure 1: Describing the components of *spółka akcyjna* 'joint-stock company' in Toposław.

The grammatical description of MWUs in Toposław is organized in two steps. Firstly, the internal structure of each term is modeled in that the MWU is divided into numbered tokens, each token is analyzed by Morfeusz and disambiguated manually by the lexicographer. The components which can vary during the inflection of the whole MWU are also marked. Fig. 1 shows the internal structure of *spółka akcyjna* 'joint-stock company'. Three components are delimited: (i) *spółka* 'company' – a substantive (*subst*) in singular (*sg*), nominative (*nom*), feminine (*f*), (ii) a blank space, (iii) *akcyjna* 'joint-stock' – an adjective (*adj*) in singular, ambiguous between nominative and vocative (*voc*), feminine, positive degree (*pos*). The first and the third component can inflect when the whole MWU is inflected.

[3]`http://www.mimuw.edu.pl/polszczyzna/kolokacje/index.htm`
[4]`http://www-igm.univ-mlv.fr/~unitex/`

Secondly, the MWU as a whole is assigned the proper *inflection graph* which describes the generation of its inflected forms and variants. Fig. 2 shows the inflection graph for the MWU analyzed in Fig. 1. The leftmost triangle represents the entry point of the graph, while the encircled square shows its exit. The numbered boxes correspond to constituents of the name (words, spaces, punctuation or sub-compounds). The arrow-laden lines that connect the boxes represent various paths which can be used while generating the inflected forms of a name. Here, the bottom-most path describes the acronymic variant *S.A.* The formulae inside boxes consist of constituents' indexes and equations on morphological constants and variables. These equations impose constraints on the inflection, variation and agreement of constituents. For example, the equations containing constants such as $Init = dot$ and $LetterCase = first\_upper$ mean that only the capitalized initial letter of the current component is taken, followed by a dot. The equations containing variables, $Case = \$c$ and $Number = \$n$, allow the component to inflect for case and number. When these variables reoccur on the same path the respective components must agree, as in the case of component $3 in the upper path of Fig. 2. The formulae appearing below paths determine the features of the inflected forms of the whole compound as a function of the features of its constituents. Here, the form resulting from each path inherits its gender from the first constituent and has the conforming case and number ($Case = \$c; Gen = \$1.Gen; Nb = \$n$).

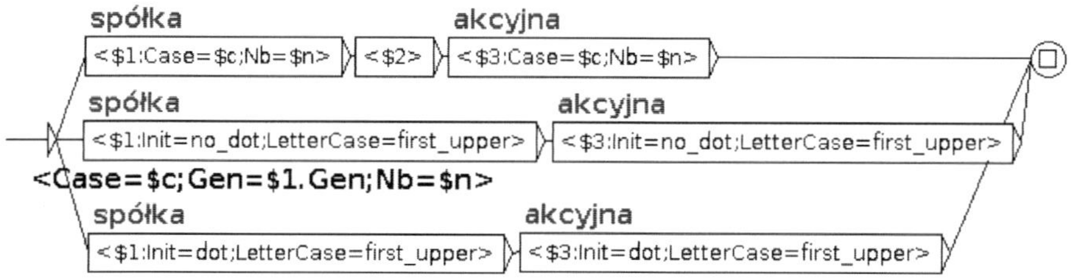


Figure 2: Inflection graph for *spółka akcyjna* 'joint-stock company' in Toposław.

When applying the graph in Fig. 2 to the MWU in Fig. 1 we obtain the set of all inflected forms shown in Tab. 1.

| Inflected forms | Morphological features | Inflected forms | Morphological features |
|---|---|---|---|
| spółka akcyjna SA S.A. | subst:**sg:nom**:f | spółki akcyjne SA S.A. | subst:**pl:nom**:f |
| spółki akcyjnej SA S.A. | subst:**sg:gen**:f | spółek akcyjnych SA S.A. | subst:**pl:gen**:f |
| spółce akcyjnej SA S.A. | subst:**sg:dat**:f | spółkom akcyjnym SA S.A. | subst:**pl:dat**:f |
| spółkę akcyjną SA S.A. | subst:**sg:acc**:f | spółki akcyjne SA S.A. | subst:**pl:acc**:f |
| spółką akcyjną SA S.A. | subst:**sg:inst**:f | spółkami akcyjnymi SA S.A. | subst:**pl:inst**:f |
| spółce akcyjnej SA S.A. | subst:**sg:loc**:f | spółkach akcyjnych SA S.A. | subst:**pl:loc**:f |
| spółko akcyjna SA S.A. | subst:**sg:voc**:f | spółki akcyjne SA S.A. | subst:**pl:voc**:f |

Table 1: Inflected forms of *spółka akcyjna* 'joint-stock company'.

The Multiflex graph formalism allows also to represent embedding of MWUs within other MWUs. Fig. 3 shows the components of a name of a bank, *Bank BPH Spółka Akcyjna*, with the nested MWU discussed above. Note that *Spółka Akcyjna* is analyzed here as a unique multi-word component with number 5. Toposław supports the manual description of embedding by automatically matching the nesting and the nested entries.

Nested structures allow to establish links between different entries of the lexicon, which can be later exploited in semantic processing of texts. Moreover, the inflection graphs are simpler if nesting is taken into account and their number is lower. Fig. 4 shows the graph for the entry in Fig. 3. The upper path corresponds to all inflected forms of the entry (in singular only), with components $1 and $5 agreeing in case, and with the last component taking any of its possible variants (*Spółka Akcyjna*, *S.A.* or *SA*). The lower path describes the elliptical variant *Bank BPH* and its inflection for case. If the sub-term *Spółka Akcyjna* was not delimited as nested then the corresponding graph would have to be much more complex. It would have to explicitly contain all three paths of the graph from Fig. 2.

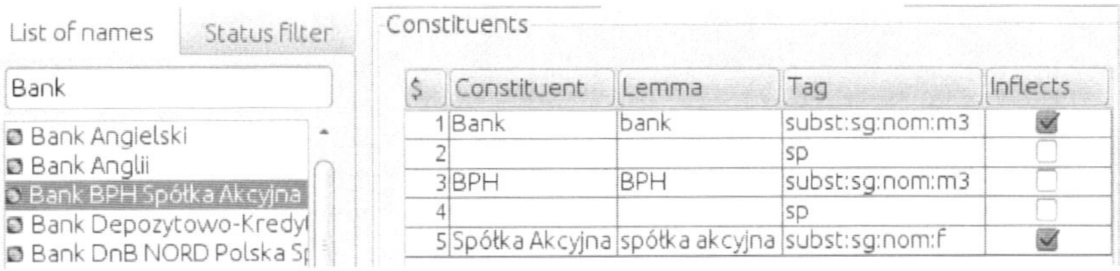


Figure 3: Describing a nested multi-word component in *Bank BPH Spółka Akcyjna* 'BPH Joint-Stock Bank'.

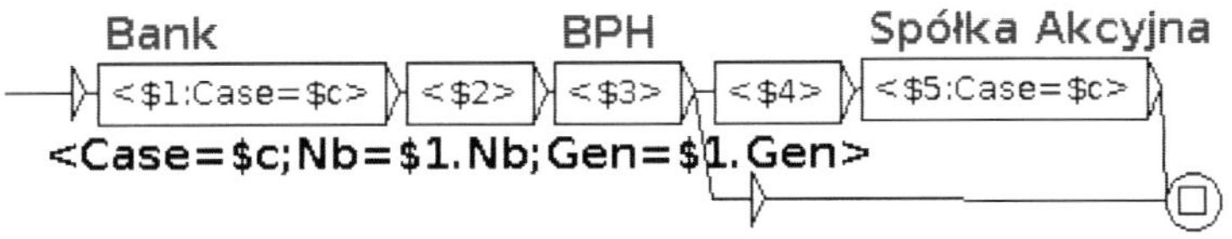


Figure 4: Inflection graph for *Bank BPH Spółka Akcyjna* 'BPH Joint-Stock Bank' with a nested component.

The result of the application of the graph in Fig. 4 to the entry in Fig. 3 is shown in Tab. 2. Note that the nested MWU *Spółka Akcyjna* is a graphical variation (with uppercase initials) of its lemma *spółka akcyjna*. The variation of this kind is automatically reproduced by Multiflex during the inflection process.

| **Inflected forms** | | | | **Morphological features** |
|---|---|---|---|---|
| Bank BPH Spółka Akcyjna | Bank BPH SA | Bank BPH S.A. | Bank BPH | subst:sg:**nom**:m3 |
| Banku BPH Spółki Akcyjnej | Banku BPH SA | Banku BPH S.A. | Banku BPH | subst:sg:**gen**:m3 |
| Bankowi BPH Spółce Akcyjnej | Bankowi BPH SA | Bankowi BPH S.A. | Bankowi BPH | subst:sg:**dat**:m3 |
| Bank BPH Spółkę Akcyjną | Bank BPH SA | Bank BPH S.A. | Bank BPH | subst:sg:**acc**:m3 |
| Bankiem BPH Spółką Akcyjną | Bankiem BPH SA | Bankiem BPH S.A. | Bankiem BPH | subst:sg:**inst**:m3 |
| Banku BPH Spółce Akcyjnej | Banku BPH SA | Banku BPH S.A. | Banku BPH | subst:sg:**loc**:m3 |
| Banku BPH Spółko Akcyjna | Banku BPH SA | Banku BPH S.A. | Banku BPH | subst:sg:**voc**:m3 |

Table 2: Inflected forms of *Bank BPH Spółka Akcyjna* 'BPH Joint-Stock Bank'.

A lexicon in Toposław can be exported to a Multiflex-compatible textual format as shown in Ex. (1)–(2). The final information (inside parentheses) is the inflectional graph's name. Toposław partly constraints this name so as to fit the syntactic structure of the assigned entries. E.g., `NC-O_O` means that the structure is a nominal compound with two inflected (***O****dmienny* in Polish) components, while `NC-O_N_O` suggests two inflected (here: *Bank* and *Spółka Akcyjna*) and one non-inflected (***N****ieodmienny* in Polish, here: *BPH*) component. The remaining part of the graph name is freely chosen by the lexicographer, who may fix his own convention. Here, `nb-inv` suggests that the entry is invariable in number.

(1) spółka(spółka:subst:sg:nom:f) akcyjna(akcyjny:adj:sg:nom:f:pos),subst(NC-O_O-SA)

(2) Bank(bank:subst:sg:nom:m3) BPH(BPH:subst:sg:nom:m3)
{Spółka Akcyjna}(spółka akcyjna:subst:sg:nom:f),subst(NC-O_N_O-nb-inv-SA)

## 2.3 Contents of the Lexicon

Tab. 3 shows the current state of SEJFEK. Complete entries are those whose inflected components are known to Morfeusz, thus the generation of the inflected forms for these entries could be fully performed. Conversely, problematic entries are those containing unknown components, mostly proper names and inflected acronyms (cf. the first dot in Sec. 2.4).

| MWU lemmas | | Inflected forms | Graphs |
|---|---|---|---|
| Complete | Problematic | | |
| 11,211 | 141 | 146,861 | 293 |

Table 3: Contents of the lexicon.

The high number of inflection graphs results from a big variety of syntactic structures typical for technical terms, as well as from their high degree of variability (acronyms, ellipses, word order change, restrictions in number inflection, etc.). Tab. 4 shows statistics of graph assignment. The first 6 lines concern the most frequently assigned graphs, as well as examples of different internal structures of the assigned entries. The agreement structures of type *SubstAdj* and *AdjSubst* as well as the government structures of type $SubstSubst_{gen}$ are the most frequent ones in both nesting and nested terms. For instance *[[czytnik elektroniczny] [kodów kreskowych]]* 'barcode reader (lit. [[electronic reader] of [bar codes]])' has the internal structure of type $Subst(SubstAdj)Subst_{gen}(Subst_{gen}Adj_{gen})$.

Note that embedding of terms is considered on a semantic rather than syntactic basis. For instance the term *teoria powiązań pionowych i poziomych między firmami* 'theory of vertical and horizontal links between firms' can be syntactically parsed into a constituency tree of depth 6. However it has a flat semantic structure in SEJFEK since none of its substrings is an economic term on its own.

## 2.4 Interesting Problems

We give several examples of problems that had to be faced by the lexicographer during morphosyntactic description of terms in SEJFEK:

- **Unknown words** As shown in Section 2.2 the inflection of a MWU consists essentially in combining the proper inflected forms or variants of its components. Consequently, both the morphological analysis and generation is required for the components which vary during the inflection of the whole MWU. Some components were unknown to Morfeusz at the period of the SEJFEK development, notably foreign proper names (*David Hume*, *Davida Hume'a*), foreign common words which inflect in Polish (*Allianz Polska*, *Allianzu Polska*), inflected acronyms (*FAM S.A.*, *FAM-u S.A.*), Polish technical terms (*doktryna libertarianistyczna* 'libertarianist doctrine') and Polish derivation forms (*konkurencja pozacenowa* 'non-price rivalry', *popyt zagregowany* 'aggregate demand'). In order to obtain the correct inflection of the latter cases, problematic derivatives were frequently divided into several known tokens (*poza+cenowa*). Sometimes this division was artificial (*z+agregowany*) and should be eliminated as soon as Morfeusz' dictionary gets sufficiently enlarged.
- **Grammatical homonyms** Some components known to Morfeusz were subject to shift in gender while appearing in economic terms. For instance, the first component in *estymator odporny* 'robust estimator' was analyzed as human masculine noun (*m1*

gender) but it has the human inanimate ($m3$) gender.

- **Unclear inflection paradigm** The lexicographer frequently faced a lack of evidence with respect to the inflection of some proper names, particularly those containing foreign components. For instance *Allianz Polska* might remain unaltered in genitive or might have its first component inflected: *Allianzu Polska.*
- **Productive structures** Some institution names followed a very productive schema, e.g. *Urząd Skarbowy w Białymstoku*, *Urząd Skarbowy w Bydgoszczy*, etc. 'Treasury Office in Białystok/Bydgoszcz/...'. These names were not systematically listed in the lexicon as they would much more conveniently be expressed by regular expressions.

| Graphs | Uppermost syntactic structure: Agreement | Uppermost syntactic structure: Government | Examples | Assigned entries |
|---|---|---|---|---|
| NC-O_O | S Adj<br>Adj S | | *spółka akcyjna*<br>*złoty spadochron, agresywna [zmiana cen]* | 2,573 |
| NC-O_N-nb-inv | | S $S_{gen}$ | *krzywa Beveridge'a, [ryzyko inwestycyjne] obligacji,*<br>*demonetyzacja [zagranicznych [środków płatniczych]]* | 1,482 |
| NC-O_N | | S $S_{gen}$ | *centrum rozliczeń, czynnik [kreacji podaży],*<br>*[kryterium operacyjne] denominacji,*<br>*analiza [polityki [wydatków publicznych]],*<br>*[[czytnik elektroniczny][kodów kreskowych]],*<br>*podstawa [wymiaru [składek [ubezpieczeń społecznych]]]* | 1,320 |
| NC-O_O-nb-inv | S Adj<br>Adj S | | *aktywa niematerialne, [produkt narodowy brutto] realny*<br>*wtórne [ryzyko płynności]* | 1,156 |
| NC-O_N_N-nb-inv | | S $S_{gen}$ $S_{gen}$<br>S Prep $S_{gov}$ | *częstotliwość dokonywania zakupu*<br>*egzekucja z [wynagrodzenia za pracę]*<br>*[poziom dobrobytu] w [skali krajowej]* | 662 |
| NC-O_O-ord | S Adj<br>Adj S | | *dotacja bezpośrednia, [dług ekonomiczny] użytkowy*<br>*lokalne [dobro publiczne]* | 551 |
| Others | | | *teoria powiązań pionowych i poziomych między firmami* | 3,064 |
| Total | | | | 11,352 |

Table 4: Distribution of graphs and variability of internal structures in assigned entries. The following codes are used: nominal compound (*NC*), variable component (*O*), invariable component (*N*), invariability in number (*nb–inv*), variability in order (*ord*), substantive (*S*), substantive in genitive ($S_{gen}$), substantive in a case governed by the preposition ($S_{gov}$), and adjective (*Adj*).

## 3 From Lexicon to Shallow Grammar

A grammatical lexicon such as SEJFEK is currently mainly generation-oriented, i.e. the semantics of inflection graphs was designed in view of automatic generation of all inflected forms and variants of a MWU. The resulting list of over 146,000 forms may be used in particular for matching terms in the process of a MWU-aware morphological analysis of a text, as is the case e.g. in the *Unitex* corpus processor (Paumier, 2008). However this approach, although simple and straightforward, has the disadvantage of not being able to transmit the data about the internal, syntactic or semantic, structure of a recognized MWU to further stages of linguistic processing. Therefore, we wished to experiment with the feasibility of transforming this rich lexical resource into a shallow grammar. The grammatical formalism chosen for this experiment is *Spejd* (Przepiórkowski, 2008; Przepiórkowski and Buczyński, 2007; Zaborowski, 2012).

## 3.1 Spejd Formalism

Spejd's input is a morphologically analyzed text, in which each token possibly gets several morphosyntactic interpretations. While tagging and (partial) parsing are usually done as separate processes, Spejd combines them into one parallel process: it allows to simultaneously disambiguate and build syntactic structures within a single rule. A *Spejd grammar* is a cascade of regular grammars (each of the rules is a separate grammar). A rule falls into 2 parts – a matching part and a list of operations — the former is divided into sections.

The *matching part* specifies a pattern of tokens and/or syntactic structures, as well as their (optional) context. The *Match* section is a regular expression over token specifications. In our case each rule will represent one MWU term, thus regular expressions come down to sequences. A specification of a token consists of constraints on its morphosyntactic features. A constraint contains an attribute name, a comparison operator and a regular expression specifying the desired value. Multiple requirements for a single token are connected with conjunction (&&) which applies at the level of a single interpretation. In our case the most useful comparison operators are ~ and ~~. The former means that there is at least one interpretation of the token which satisfies the constraint. The latter ensures that all its interpretations do alike. For a non ambiguous token both operators are equivalent.

Ex.(3) shows a sample rule whose matching part matches two tokens. The first one is a noun (`pos~"subst"`) and has the lemma *spółka* (`base~"spółka"`, `/i` stands for case-insensitive). The second one must be an adjective and must have the (case-insensitive) lemma *akcyjny* . The capital letters `A` and `B` enable referring to particular tokens from the second part of the rule. The additional sections of the matching part (e.g. a context specification), which are not used here, can be built in a similar way.

(3)
```
Rule  "syntok Spółka Akcyjna"
Match:  A[base~"spółka"/i && pos~subst] B[base~"akcyjny"/i && pos~adj];
Eval:  unify(case gender number, A,B);
       leave(base~~"spółka", A); leave(pos~~"subst", A);
       leave(base~~"akcyjna", B); leave(pos~~"adj", B);
       word(A, , "Spółka Akcyjna");
```

The second part of a rule consist of a *list of operations* preceded by the keyword `Eval`, and executed in the order they appear in the list. Some of them, e.g. *unify*, evaluate to a Boolean value (similarly to predicates in PROLOG). When an operation evaluates to *false*, the execution is broken (like in PROLOG) but the changes made by previous operations are not rolled back (contrary to PROLOG).

In Ex.(3) the *unify* operation checks for agreement in case, gender and number between tokens `A` and `B`. If these tokens have no interpretations with the same values on those attributes, the operation returns false and the execution of the list breaks. Otherwise all combinations of interpretations which violate agreement are removed and the evaluation continues. The *leave* operations remove all those interpretations of tokens `A` and `B` which have lemmas different from *spółka* and *akcyjna* or parts of speech different from `subst` and `adj`, respectively. The last operation (*word*) builds a syntactic word consisting of all matched tokens with morphosyntactic interpretations copied from the token `A` and lemma *"Spółka Akcyjna"*. As a result, the rule matches all 14 inflected forms shown at the first position of each line in Table 1, as well as their capitalized variants.

## 3.2 Conversion Methodology

In the original form, the lexicon is represented by a list of entries annotated by a set of graphs. Since the semantics of graphs is complex and not easily transformable into a grammar, we base our conversion on a textual representation of the lexicon, as in Ex. (1)–(2). It discards the detailed information contained in graphs but simplifies further automatic processing and still allows to perform analysis. In some rare cases this approach led us to problems described in Section 3.3.

### 3.2.1 The conversion algorithm

The main assumptions for the conversion algorithm are the following:

- For each term appearing in the lexicon, the grammar should build a syntactic word.
- The word's morphosyntactic features are derived from its headword.
- The correct recognition of terms should be ensured by unification of inflection features.
- Nested terms should be properly represented as nested syntactic words.

The conversion relies on the term's general structure (shown in the name of its inflection graph, cf. Sec. 2.2). Ex. (4) shows the Spejd rule resulting from converting the lexicon term with structure `O_N_O` from Ex. (2). The matching pattern is created with constraints on the word's: (i) lemma (case-insensitive), POS, and negation value (for participles only) if the component is **inflected** (here: *Bank* and *Spółka Akcyjna*; the latter is a nested term recognized previously by a dedicated rule), (ii) orthographic form (case-insensitive) if it is **uninflected** (here: *BPH*). We have also experimented with allowing a formally uninflected word to be plural in order to cover cases such as *jakość produktu/produktów* 'quality of product(s)'. This property may over-generate, but proves useful for the purpose of analysis.

(4)
```
Rule  "syntok Bank BPH Spółka Akcyjna"
Match:  A[base~"bank"/i && pos~subst] [orth~"BPH"/i]
        B[base~"Spółka Akcyjna"/i && pos~subst];
Eval: unify(case, A,B);
      leave(base~~"bank"/i, A); leave(pos~~"subst", A);
      leave(base~~"spółka akcyjna"/i, B); leave(pos~~"subst", B);
      word(A, , "Bank BPH Spółka Akcyjna");
```

As explained in Sec. 3.1, the *Eval* section of a rule should: (i) ensure the term is correctly recognized, (ii) disambiguate it morphosyntactically, (iii) build a syntactic word. Task (i) is performed for most terms by a naive approach: unification in case, number and gender is required between all inflected components, as in Ex. (3). For some rare exceptions, as in Ex. (4), the unification is limited to the case (cf. Sec. 3.3). Task (ii) is performed by *leave* clauses which conserve for each inflected component only those interpretations whose lemmas and POSs match the morphosyntactic annotation in the lexicon (here: *bank* and *subst* for *Bank*, and *spółka akcyjna* and *subst* for *Spółka Akcyjna*). Task (iii) is done by the 3-argument "copying" version of the *word* action: the morphosyntactic features for the resultant syntactic word are copied from the headword (here: *Bank*) while the resulting lemma is constructed by simple concatenation of component forms (here: *Bank BPH Spółka Akcyjna*). The headword is determined according to the following rules:

- inflected elements take precedence over non-inflected ones,

- nouns (*subst* and *ger*) have a higher priority than adjectives (*adj*, *pact* and *ppas*),
- the case of the headword in the MWU's lemma must be nominal,
- if the above rules select more than one element, the left-most one is selected.

## 3.3 Problems with Conversion

As mentioned above, only the textual export form of the lexicon was used for conversion, which was sufficient in the majority of cases but provoked three main problems. Firstly, and most importantly, the morphosyntactic variants not expressed on the level of a graph's name could not be taken into account. In particular, word order change, elliptical variants and acronyms, as those described by the graph in Fig. 2, are currently not recognized.

Secondly, the general rule of imposing number, case and gender agreement of all inflected components (cf. Sec. 3.2) failed in appositions and coordinations, where several components may agree in case but usually only one of them is the headword. In Ex. (2) *Bank* is in masculine inanimate (*m3*), and *Spółka Akcyjna* in feminine (*f*) but both agree in case. In Ex. (5)[5] the first and the third constituent differ both in gender and in number but they still agree in case. Such cases were manually marked in the lexicon before conversion and the corresponding Spejd rules were tuned so as to perform case unification only, as shown in Ex. (4). We think that an automated procedure might help detect such apposition and coordination cases and restrict agreement to case accordingly. Special care must however be taken if nouns are accompanied by adjectival modifiers. Moreover some appositions may even exclude case agreement of nouns, as in *Allianz Polska*, *Allianzu Polska*, etc.

(5) kapitał(kapitał:subst:**sg**:nom:**m3**) i rezerwy(rezerwa:subst:**pl**:nom:**f**) 'capital and reserves'

(6) *old entry*: funkcja **Cobba-Douglasa(:qub)**,subst(NC-**O**_**N**-nb-inv)
*new entry*: funkcja **Cobba(:qub)-(:interp)Douglasa(:qub)**,subst(NC-**O**_**NNN**-nb-inv)
'Cobb-Douglas function'

(7) *old entry*: Runda **Kennedy'ego**(Kennedy:subst:sg:gen:m1) 'Kennedy Round'
*new entry*: Runda **{Kennedy'ego}**(Kennedy:subst:sg:gen:m1)
*added rule*:
```
Match:  [orth~"kennedy"/i] ns [orth~"'"/i] ns [orth~"ego"/i];
Eval:   word(subst:sg:gen:m1, "kennedy");
```

Thirdly, the tokenization conventions might differ between the lexicon and the grammar. In Morfeusz, in which tokenization is inherent in morphological analysis, some sequences with hyphens or apostrophes, such as *Cobba-Douglasa* or *Kennedy'ego*, were seen as unique tokens because they can be compound names or inflected forms of one-word names. Spejd always divides them into 3 tokens. Thus, entries such as in the first lines in Ex. (6)[6]–(7) could not yield an operational Spejd rule and had to be transformed as shown in the lines below. Additionally, an extra rule for the new nested term *Kennedy'ego* had to be created in Spejd, as shown at the bottom of Ex. 7.

## 3.4 Conversion as a validation

During the automatic lexicon-to-grammar conversion some errors and inconsistencies could be spotted and corrected in the grammar (their correction in the lexicon will be done

[5]For readability reasons only the relevant parts of the lexicon entries are shown in Examples (5)–(7).

[6]The `qub` label is a dummy POS chosen for the obviously nominal names *Cobb* and *Douglas* due to the fact that these names are currently unknown to Morfeusz. Since they never vary in this MWU they do not have to be fully analyzed for the sake of inflection of the MWU.

shortly). Below we give examples of the most frequent errors[7]:

- Failing markup of a nested term, despite the existence of a lexicon entry for the subterm, cf. Ex. (8). These errors concerned about 1,000 entries. If they were not corrected Spejd would completely fail to recognize these terms since it applies shorter rules first. The rule for a nested term such as *działalnością gospodarczą* would fire first, it would create a syntactic word, and its components would no longer be recognizable separately by the larger rule. Such errors were automatically corrected by a naive script which searched for common sequences of single word lemmas through all the terms in lexicon. Some remaining problems were corrected manually.
- Missing base entry for a nested term, cf. Ex. (9). This problem could be solved either by separating the components of the nested term or generating a new rule for it. The latter solution was applied. Since the detailed characteristics of the nested term were not easy to determine in a general case, a simplified ruled was created which only applied to the particular inflected form.
- Redundant plural entries, cf. Ex. (10). Other entries for the same terms, with a lemma in singular, already allowed inflection for number. The redundant entries were eliminated.
- Erroneous morphosyntactic features or lemma of a component due to grammatical syncretism, as in Ex. (11)–(12).
- Inconsistence if the graph name wrt. the entry's structure, cf. Ex. (13).
- Typographical mistakes, cf. Ex. (14).

(8) działalność(działalność:subst:sg:nom:f) gospodarcza(gospodarczy:adj:sg:nom:f:pos)
∗kierowanie **działalnością(działalność:...) gospodarczą(gospodarczy:...)**
kierowanie **{działalnością gospodarczą}(działalność gospodarcza:...)**
'business management'

(9) wyliczanie {agregatów monetarnych}(agregat monetarny:subst:pl:gen:m3)
'monetary aggregate estimation'
∗*missing entry*: agregat(agregat:...) monetarny(monetarny:...)
*added rule*: `Match: [orth "agregatów"/i] [orth "monetarnych"/i];`
`Eval: word(subst:pl:gen:m3, "agregatów monetarnych");`

(10) **zasada**(zasada:subst:**sg**:nom:f) rachunkowości,subst(NC-O_N)
∗**zasady**(zasada:subst:**pl**:nom:f) rachunkowości,subst(NC-O_N-nb-inv)
'accountancy rules'

(11) ∗cechy(cecha:subst:**sg:gen**:f) demograficzno-społeczne pracowników
cechy(cecha:subst:**pl:nom**:f) demograficzno-społeczne pracowników
'demografically-social features of employees'

(12) ∗BIG Bank Gdański(**Gdańsk**:subst:pl:nom:m3)
BIG Bank Gdański(**gdański**:adj:sg:nom:m3) 'BIG Bank of Gdańsk'

(13) ∗krajowa {akcja kredytowa},subst(NC-O_**N**)
krajowa {akcja kredytowa},subst(NC-O_**O**) 'national credit action'

(14) ∗konkurencja poza(poza:qub)**ceno(cena:subst:sg:voc:f)**
konkurencja poza(poza:qub)**cenowa(cenowy:adj:sg:nom:f:pos)** 'non-price competition'

[7] For readability reasons only the relevant parts of the lexicon entries are shown in Examples (8)–(14). Each incorrect entry is preceded by an asterisk (∗).

## 3.5 Contents and Output of the Grammar

The Spejd grammar obtained by the SEJFEK lexicon conversion counts 11,266 rules. As many as 3,205 rules contain nested terms. Only 59 rules required human correction since they limit the unification of inflected components to case agreement only.

(15)
```
<syntok rule="syntok␣Bank␣BPH␣Spółka␣Akcyjna">
    <orth>Bankiem BPH Spółką Akcyjną</orth>
    <lex><base>Bank BPH Spółka Akcyjna</base><ctag>subst:sg:inst:m3</ctag></lex>
    <tok><orth>Bankiem</orth>
        <lex><base>bank</base><ctag>subst:sg:inst:m3</ctag></lex>
    </tok>
    <tok><orth>BPH</orth>
        <lex><base>BPH</base><ctag>subst:sg:nom:m3</ctag></lex>
        <lex><base>BPH</base><ctag>subst:sg:gen:m3</ctag></lex>...
    </tok>
    <syntok rule="syntok␣spółka␣akcyjna"><orth>Spółką Akcyjną</orth>
      <lex><base>spółka akcyjna</base><ctag>subst:sg:inst:f</ctag></lex>
      <tok><orth>Spółką</orth>
          <lex><base>spółka</base><ctag>subst:sg:inst:f</ctag></lex>
      </tok>
      <tok><orth>Akcyjną</orth>
        <lex><base>akcyjny</base><ctag>adj:sg:inst:f:pos</ctag></lex>
        <lex disamb="0"><base>akcyjny</base><ctag>adj:sg:acc:f:pos</ctag></lex>
      </tok></syntok></syntok>
```

Ex. (15) shows a simplified fragment of a Spejd output processed by the rule in Ex. (4). Each ⟨`syntok`⟩ element encodes a syntactic word. Nesting of syntactic words is determined by the ordering of grammar rules in the cascade, which is automatically deduced from lexicon entries. The ⟨`tok`⟩ elements reflect the input tokens. Morphosyntactic interpretations are encoded as ⟨`lex`⟩ elements. Note, that one of them (marked by the `disamb="0"` attribute) has been eliminated here by the *unify* action in Ex. (3) since it violates the case agreement.

# 4 Evaluation

In order to perform an evaluation of both the lexicon and the grammar we have prepared a manually annotated corpus of economic texts. It consists of fragments of the *plWikiEcono* corpus[8] containing Polish Wikipedia articles assigned to Wikipedia categories and subcategories in economy[9]. Because Wikipedia articles are of encyclopedic nature the density of technical terms they contain is very high (in comparison to economic newspapers and magazines or Wikinews). Thus, these texts seem particularly well suited for evaluating targeted lexical and grammatical resources like ours.

| **Wikipedia articles** | **Tokens** | **Compound terms** | | |
|---|---|---|---|---|
| | | **Occurrences** | | **Unique forms** |
| | | **Nouns** | **Adjectives** | |
| 191 | 220,905 | 11,106 | 11 | 6,805 |

Table 5: Statistics of the evaluation corpus consisting of Wikipedia economic articles

The corpus annotation has been performed by one annotator within the GATE platform (Wilcock, 2009). The annotation schema was rather simple: contiguous sequences of words

[8] `http://bach.ipipan.waw.pl/wiki/zil/Korpus%20plWikiEcono`
[9] `http://pl.wikipedia.org/wiki/Kategoria:Ekonomia`

judged as multi-word economic terms were to be tagged as such and their syntactic category was to be indicated. Only two categories proved relevant: *economic compound noun* and *economic compound adjective*. The annotator was neutral with respect to the project, i.e. she had been involved neither in creation of the lexicon, nor in its conversion to grammar. She had a deep linguistic knowledge but only a common knowledge of economy, which may partly bias the quality of the annotation. Tab. 5 resumes the contents of the resulting evaluation corpus.

In order to compare the lexicon approach and the grammar approach we automatically annotated the evaluation corpus by means of both methods. Both of them were applied within the Spejd framework but involving different modules. For the lexicon approach, we used the list of all inflected forms and variants of the lexicon terms. Spejd's dictionary module used this list for straightforward term matching in the corpus. The dictionary module built syntactic words so as to preserve the nesting structure of terms. The grammar approach involved the main (grammar) module of Spejd. It generated similar structures in the output — syntactic words with preserved nesting structure, as shown in Ex. (15) — but using the grammar for searching terms. It additionally performed a partial disambiguation, which was not done in the case of the lexical method.

The evaluation consisted in the comparison of the original annotation of the corpus and the automatically generated annotation produced by each method. Since we searched for multi-word terms, we used not only the standard binary measure (score 1 if the precise term was found, 0 otherwise), but also a weak correctness measure. The latter was based on accuracy of BIO-type (Begin-Inside-Outside) tags in the scope of each term and of its 1-word left and right context. The 11,117 terms present in the evaluation corpus yielded about 47,500 BIO tags extracted in this way (with an average of 4.27 tags per term).

Consider for instance the three-word manually tagged term in the sequence *niedawna [krajowa akcja kredytowa] była* 'recent [national credit action] was', whose corresponding tag sequence is `O-B-I-I-O`. If an automatic annotation yields `O-B-I-O-O`, it gets the score 4/5 (4 out of 5 BIO tags match). Similarly, for `B-I-I-O-O` the score is 1/5. For the exact match (`O-B-I-I-O`) this measure gives 1, which is equal to the standard binary measure.

| method | correctness | weak correctness | false positives |
|---|---|---|---|
| lexicon | 36.32% | 64.66% | 0.12% |
| lexicon (case insensitive) | 41.43% | 68.14% | 0.21% |
| grammar | 42.01% | 68.45% | 0.13% |

Table 6: Evaluation results of the lexicon and the grammar.

The evaluation scores are presented in Tab. 6. Both approaches give very similar results. A notable difference appears only if the inflected lexicon is applied in a case-sensitive manner (the grammar is case-insensitive by default) since it results then in many false negatives e.g. at the beginning of a sentence or in article titles. This difference can be toned down by case-insensitive searching for lexicon terms at the cost of a slightly larger amount of false positives. In any case the percentage of false positives is extremely low. They result mostly from an uncertain terminological status of some MWUs (*państwo członkowskie* 'member state'), from some minor corpus annotation errors (non annotated *prawo poboru* 'rights issue') or from overlapping terms ($[_1$*wartość nominalna* $[_2$*banknotów*$]_1$ *w obiegu*$]_2$

‘nominal value of currency banknotes’). This low number of false positives may be seen as an evidence of a high quality of the corpus annotation. Namely, almost each term which was included in the lexicon by the linguistics/economy expert and which appeared in the corpus was correctly spotted by the lingustics-only expert.

Note that partial matches can be very useful in some applications, e.g. in automatic terminology extraction or corpus pre-annotation prior to human validation. If a term is at least partly recognized the manual correction of its annotation is easy, while it might be totally overlooked otherwise. Over 98% of the manually annotated corpus terms were at least partly recognized both by our lexicon and by our grammar, which is a very good score even if many of them were non exact matches.

## 5 Related Work

SEJFEK is the third grammatical lexicon of Polish multi-word units built under Toposław lexicographic suite, and the first one to have been converted into a shallow grammar. Two other resources are: (i) *SAWA*[10] (Marciniak et al., 2009), a grammatical lexicon of Warsaw urban proper names containing 9,000 names of streets, squares, bus stops, monuments and other objects linked to the communication network in Warsaw, (ii) *SEJF*[11], a grammatical lexicon of Polish phraseology containing over 3,000 nominal, adjectival and adverbial compounds of the Polish general language.

A similar lexicon for Serbian (Krstev et al., 2010), containing general language compounds, was built within another lexicographic framework, *Leximir* comprising a Unitex morphological analyzer and generator module for Serbian, as well as Multiflex. This tool offers interesting facilities for automatic prediction of inflection graphs, based on rule-based mining of both the lexicon entries and the new incoming entries.

Complementary formalisms for inflectional paradigms of Polish MWUs have been presented in (Graliński et al., 2010) and (Broda et al., 2007). Like our grammar, they rely mainly on identifying the MWU's headword and checking its agreement with other components.

*DuELME* (Grégoire, 2010) is a lexicon of Dutch multi-word, notably verbal, expressions (MWE), which may go beyond contiguous text segments. It contains about 5,000 entries. Candidate MWEs are extracted from a corpus by pattern-based methods and filtered by a decision-tree classifier into probable true and false positives. Their variants in the corpus are analyzed in order to detect their unpredictable properties, which are definitional criteria of MWEs. Pre-selected MWE candidates are then validated and described in two steps, similar to those in SEJFEK. Firstly, the lemmas of the lexically fixed components are identified (however, unlike in SEJFEK, the morphological features of these components are stated in external parameters) and some restrictions for the non fixed components are expressed, e.g. animate object, admitted pronominalization, modal verbs going with the head component (*have* or *be*), possible adjectival modifiers, and restriction to negated use only. Secondly, the MWE is assigned a pattern. Patterns are represented as *parameterized equivalence classes* which reflect the syntactic structure of MWEs. A sample class is: *expression headed by a verb, taking a direct object consisting of a fixed determiner and a modifiable noun*, whereas an external parameter states if the object noun is in singular or in plural. Parameters allow to prevent the explosion of the number of classes. The DuELME formalism is meant to be

[10]http://zil.ipipan.waw.pl/SAWA
[11]http://zil.ipipan.waw.pl/SEJF

theory- and implementation-neutral and its applicability to a particular dependency parser has been demonstrated. We think that this description framework is very promising in that it applies to the lexical description of verbal MWEs and offers an abstract formalism, which can potentially be compiled into different parsing frameworks.

Other morphosyntactic frameworks for several European languages have been developed over the past decades. A contrastive study (Savary, 2008) shows that most of them apply one of the two complementary approaches presented in this paper: a MWU lexicon or a lexicalized local grammar. Besides Multiflex, two of these approaches, *lexc* and *FASTR*, were judged as best adapted to inflectional morphology of MWUs.

A finite-state morphology tool *lexc* (Karttunen et al., 1992; Karttunen, 1993) represents compounds by their lemmas, inflection classes and alternation rules yielding inflected forms. Like Spejd, it efficiently implements cascades of rules by a finite-state machinery. It emulates unification operators (crucial in describing agreement and government rules) and it allows the expression of various types of variations in MWUs. To the best of our knowledge, no studies report on a large-scale application of lexc to creating MWU resources.

*FASTR* (Jacquemin, 2001) is a shallow parser dedicated to the recognition, normalization and acquisition of compound terms, developed within a unification-based framework. FASTR's input is a corpus and an initial set of controlled complex terms that are analyzed morphologically and transformed into feature structure rules. *Metarules* can then apply to selected rules in order to model inflectional, syntactic and semantic variants of the controlled terms. As a result FASTR produces a set of links between the initial terms and occurrences of these terms and their variants in the corpus. Large coverage FASTR grammars and metagrammars have been developed for English and French terminology. Representing MWUs as fully lexicalized rules is common for FASTR and Spejd. The notable difference in Spejd is to perform both disambiguation and shallow parsing simultaneously.

Other shallow parsers have been efficiently applied to large-scale processing of Polish MWUs, notably named entities. *SProUT* (Becker et al., 2002) offers: (i) a rich grammar formalism with finite-state operators, unification and cascading, (ii) a very fast gazetteer lookup, (iii) an XML-based output in the form of typed feature structures whose type hierarchy can be defined by the user. It has been used for Polish named entity recognition (Piskorski, 2005) and annotation (Savary and Piskorski, 2011). Unlike in the Spejd grammar presented here, Polish rules in SProUT are generally less lexicalized. This fact reflects the lexical nature of named entities, in which productive structures (cf. Section 2.4) are very frequent.

Another contribution to automatic information extraction from Polish terminological texts has been presented in (Mykowiecka et al., 2009). Here again, a SProUT grammar is used, together with a medical domain ontology, a gazetteer of medical terms, and a domain-specific fine-grained grammar, in order to extract structured data from unstructured natural language mammography reports and hospital records of diabetic patients.

## Conclusions and Perspectives

We have described SEJFEK, a large-coverage lexical and grammatical resource of Polish economic terminology. It consists of two alternative modules. One is a grammatical lexicon of about 11,000 terminological MWUs, where inflectional and syntactic variation, as well as nesting of terms, are described via graph-based rules. The other one is a fully lexicalized shallow grammar of a roughly equal number of rules, obtained by an automatic conversion of the lexicon, and partly manually validated.

SEJFEK is the first NLP-oriented resource for Polish economic terminology and one of the first resources of this kind for Slavic languages. It is freely available[12] under the Creative Commons BY-SA license[13]. It might be used in automatic term extraction, document classification, domain-specific information extraction or question answering, or any application where a reliable inflection-aware identification and conflation of terms and their variants is crucial. As a means of term normalization it might also be useful in professional writing support software, such as *Acrolinx*[14], or in computer-assisted translation tools which allow users to import external terminology, e.g. *SLD Trados Multiterm Desktop*[15].

Both resources show a good and largely comparable coverage, which demonstrates the complementarity of a lexicon and a fully lexicalized grammar. The evaluation results, obtained on a 221,000-token manually annotated economic corpus, show the MWU-per-WMU correctness of over 41% and the token-per-token correctness of more than 68%. About 98% of all corpus terms are at least partly recognized by both the lexicon and the grammar. The main advantage of the lexicon-to-grammar conversion lies in the fact that the entire lexico-syntactic knowledge contained in a lexicon entry can be explicitly expressed in the structured output of the grammar. This result contributes to a better lexicon-grammar interface as far as the treatment of MWUs is concerned.

Since the lexicon-to-grammar conversion does not exploit the internal semantics of lexicon's inflection graphs, it fails to account for some syntactic variants of terms (word order changes, ellipses, acronyms optional inflection, etc.). However its strength lies in the fact that it can operate on roughly annotated input data. Thus, it might be used reversely: (i) it might yield approximate grammar rules in order to match text occurrences of a new term, (ii) these occurrences might help match or develop graphs in Toposław for new lexicon entries.

Other perspectives include: (i) completing Morfeusz' lexicon in order to cover all components appearing in our resource, notably foreign proper names, (ii) editing a proofread version of the resource resulting from the Morfeusz completion and from an analysis of conversion errors, (iii) involving a second annotator, expert in economy or in translation of economic texts, on order to increase the corpus quality, (iv) completing the grammar by partly non-lexicalized rules covering productive patterns, as those mentioned in Sec. 2.4, (v) designing a standard LMF[16] exchange format (possibly both lexicon- and grammar-compatible), (vi) a better automation of graph matching in Toposław inspired by (Krstev et al., 2006), (vii) exploiting the internal structure of graphs during conversion in case a higher-precision grammar is needed.

## Acknowledgments

This work has been carried out within two projects: (i) *Nekst*[17], funded by the European Regional Development Fund and the Polish Ministry of Science and Higher Education, (ii) CESAR[18] - a European project (CIP-ICT-PSP-271022), part of META-NET.

[12]http://zil.ipipan.waw.pl/SEJFEK

[13]http://creativecommons.org/licenses/by-sa/3.0/

[14]http://www.acrolinx.com/terminology_support.html

[15]http://www.translationzone.com/en/translator-products/sdlmultitermdesktop/

[16]http://www.lexicalmarkupframework.org/

[17]http://www.ipipan.waw.pl/nekst/

[18]http://www.meta-net.eu/projects/cesar

-

## References


Alex, B., Haddow, B., and Grover, C. (2007). Recognising nested named entities in biomedical text. In *BioNLP '07: Proceedings of the Workshop on BioNLP 2007*, pages 65–72, Morristown, NJ, USA. Association for Computational Linguistics.

Becker, M., Drożdżyński, W., Krieger, H.-U., Piskorski, J., Schäfer, U., and Xu, F. (2002). SProUT - Shallow Processing with Typed Feature Structures and Unification. In *Proceedings of ICON 2002, Mumbay, India.*

Black, J. (2008). *Słownik ekonomii.* Wydawnictwo Naukowe PWN, Warszawa.

Broda, B., Derwojedowa, M., and Piasecki, M. (2007). Recognition of structured collocations in an inflective language. In *Proceedings of the International Multiconference on Computer Science and Information Technology — 2nd International Symposium Advances in Artificial Intelligence and Applications (AAIA'07)*, pages 237–246.

Chow, G. C. (1995). *Ekonometria.* Wydawnictwo Naukowe PWN, Kraków.

Daille, B. (1996). Study and implementation of combined techniques for automatic extraction of terminology. In Klavans, J. L. and Resnik, P., editors, *The Balancing Act: Combining Symbolic and Statistical Approaches to Language*, pages 49–66. MIT Press, Cambridge.

Finkel, J. R. and Manning, C. D. (2009). Nested Named Entity Recognition. In *Proceedings of EMNLP-2009*, Singapore.

Graliński, F., Savary, A., Czerepowicka, M., and Makowiecki, F. (2010). Computational Lexicography of Multi-Word Units: How Efficient Can It Be? In *Proceedings of the COLING-MWE'10 Workshop, Beijing, China.*

Grégoire, N. (2010). DuELME: a Dutch electronic lexicon of multiword expressions. *Language Resources and Evaluation*, 44(1-2).

Głuchowski, J. and Szambelańczyk, J., editors (1999). *Bankowość. Podręcznik dla studentów.* Wydawnictwo Wyższej Szkoły Bankowej, Poznań.

Jacquemin, C. (2001). *Spotting and Discovering Terms through Natural Language Processing.* MIT Press.

Karttunen, L. (1993). Finite-State Lexicon Compiler. Technical Report ISTL-NLTT2993-04-02, Xerox PARC.

Karttunen, L., Kaplan, R. M., and Zaenen, A. (1992). Two-Level Morphology with Composition. In *Proceedings of the 14 th International Conference on Computational Linguistics (COLING'92), Nantes*, pages 141–148.

Koeva, S. (2007). Multi-word term extraction for bulgarian. In *Proceedings of the Workshop on Balto-Slavonic Natural Language Processing*, pages 59–66, Prague, Czech Republic. Association for Computational Linguistics.

Krstev, C., Stankovic, R., Obradovic, I., Vitas, D., and Utvic, M. (2010). Automatic construction of a morphological dictionary of multi-word units. In *Proceedings of IceTAL 2010*, volume 6233 of *Lecture Notes in Computer Science*, pages 226–237.

Krstev, C., Stanković, R., Vitas, D., and Obradović, I. (2006). WS4LR: A Workstation for Lexical Resources. In *Proceedings of the 5th International Conference on Language Resources and Evaluation (LREC 2006), Genoa, Italy*, pages 1692–1697.

Kuciński, K., editor (2009). *Geografia ekonomiczna*. Szkoła Główna Handlowa, Kraków.

Marciniak, M., Rabiega-Wiśniewska, J., Savary, A., Woliński, M., and Heliasz, C. (2009). Constructing an Electronic Dictionary of Polish Urban Proper Names. In *Recent Advances in Intelligent Information Systems*, pages 233–246. Exit.

Marciniak, M., Savary, A., Sikora, P., and Woliński, M. (2011). Toposław - a lexicographic framework for multi-word units. *Lecture Notes in Computer Science*, 6562:139–150. Springer.

Michalski, E. (2003). *Marketing. Podręcznik akademicki.* Wydawnictwo Naukowe PWN, Warszawa.

Michoń, F., editor (1991). *Ekonomika pracy: zarys problematyki i metod.* Państwowe Wydawnictwo Naukowe, Kraków.

Mykowiecka, A., Marciniak, M., and Kupść, A. (2009). Rule-based information extraction from patients' clinical data. *Journal of Biomedical Informatics*, 42(5):923–936.

Paumier, S. (2008). Unitex 2.1 User Manual.

Piskorski, J. (2005). Named-Entity Recognition for Polish with SProUT. In *LNCS Vol 3490: Proceedings of IMTCI 2004, Warsaw, Poland.*

Przepiórkowski, A. (2008). *Formalizm ♠*, chapter 7. Akademicka Oficyna Wydawnicza EXIT, Warsaw.

Przepiórkowski, A. and Buczyński, A. (2007). ♠: Shallow parsing and disambiguation engine. In *Proceedings of the 3rd Language & Technology Conference*, Poznań.

Rynarzewski, T. and Zielińska-Głębocka, A. (2006). *Międzynarodowe stosunki gospodarcze. Teoria wymiany i polityki handlu międzynarodowego.* Wydawnictwo Naukowe PWN, Warszawa.

Rzewuska, M., Gałkiewicz, A., and Falkenberg, J., editors (2001). *Ekonomia — finanse — pieniądz: glosariusz angielski–francuski–niemiecki–polski.* Urząd Komitetu Integracji Europejskiej, Warszawa.

Samuelson, A. and Nordhaus, W. D. (1998). *Ekonomia*, volume 2. Wydawnictwo Naukowe PWN, Warszawa.

Samuelson, A. and Nordhaus, W. D. (2003). *Ekonomia*, volume 1. Wydawnictwo Naukowe PWN, Warszawa.

Savary, A. (2008). Computational Inflection of Multi-Word Units. A contrastive study of lexical approaches. *Linguistic Issues in Language Technology*, 1(2):1–53.

Savary, A. (2009). Multiflex: a Multilingual Finite-State Tool for Multi-Word Units. *Lecture Notes in Computer Science*, 5642:237–240.

Savary, A. and Piskorski, J. (2011). Language Resources for Named Entity Annotation in the National Corpus of Polish. *Control and Cybernetics*, 40(2):361–391.

Savary, A., Rabiega-Wiśniewska, J., and Woliński, M. (2009). Inflection of Polish Multi-Word Proper Names with Morfeusz and Multiflex. *Lecture Notes in Computer Science*, 5070:111–141.

Smadja, F. (1993). Xtract : An overview. *Computer and the Humanities*, 26:399–413.

Smullen, J. and Hand, N., editors (2008). *Słownik finansów i bankowości.* Wydawnictwo Naukowe PWN, Warszawa.

Treder, H. (2005). *Podstawy handlu zagranicznego.* Wydawnictwo Uniwersytetu Gdańskiego, Gdańsk.

Wernik, A. (2007). *Finanse publiczne. Cele, struktury, uwarunkowania.* Polskie Wydawnictwo Ekonomiczne, Warszawa.

Wilcock, G. (2009). *Introduction to Linguistic Annotation and Text Analytics.* Synthesis Lectures on Human Language Technologies. Morgan & Claypool Publishers.

Zaborowski, B. (2012). *Spejd 1.3.6 - User manual.*

Śnieżek, E., editor (2004). *Wprowadzenie do rachunkowości — podręcznik z przykładami, zadaniami i testami.* Oficyna Ekonomiczna, Kraków.

# The Compreno Semantic Model as an Integral Framework for a Multilingual Lexical Database

*Ekaterina MANICHEVA Maria PETROVA Elena KOZLOVA Tatiana POPOVA*

ABBYY SOFTWARE HOUSE, Otradnaya str. 2b/6, 127273, Moscow, Russia

Ekaterina_M@abbyy.com, Maria_Pet@abbyy.com, Helen_Koz@abbyy.com, Tatiana_P@abbyy.com

ABSTRACT:

The paper presents an integral framework for multilingual lexical databases (henceforth MLLD) based on Compreno technology. It differs from the existing approaches to MLLD in the following aspects: 1) it is based on a universal semantic hierarchy (SH) of thesaurus type filled with language-specific lexicon; 2) the position in the SH generally determines semantic and syntactic model of a word; 3) this model proposes a suite of elaborate tools to determine universal and language-specific semantic and syntactic properties and deals efficiently with problems of cross-lingual lexical, semantic and syntactic asymmetry. Currently, it includes English, Russian, German, French and Chinese and proves to be a compatible MLLD for typologically different languages that can be used as a comprehensive lexical-semantic database for various NLP applications.

KEYWORDS: multilingual lexical database, semantic and syntactic model, cross-lingual asymmetry

## 1. Introduction: Integral Framework for the MLLD

Over the past decade, NLP has witnessed a surge in the development of multilingual lexical databases and tools for cross-lingual tasks such as information retrieval, machine translation and foreign language acquisition.

Most of the large-scale lexical databases that lately evolved into multilingual frameworks for language-specific lexicons have been initially designed as monolingual databases and developed independently without referring to any particular processor or potential NLP applications. In order to integrate typologically different languages into these frameworks, adjust them to certain processors and guarantee their cross-platform applicability communities of developers have carried out a great amount of work to develop tools for cross-platform integration and universal standards for semantic representations. Still these projects encounter a lot of problems of uniformity and consistency across languages, categories and applications.

By contrast, the Comreno semantic model developed by ABBYY was initially designed for multilingual purposes and aimed at machine translation, without being limited to it. The system consists of a language database and includes interrelated modules: morphological, syntactic, semantic and statistical ones. The semantic module is based on a universal semantic hierarchy of thesaurus type which is filled with lexical information. The morphological and the syntactical modules, in turn, are language-specific. This approach proved to be efficient to provide high-quality machine translation for English<->Russian pair (refer to Anisimovich et al., 2012).

At present, we continue working on German, French and Chinese languages. Currently, we have described more than 96000 English, 85000 Russian, 12 000 German, 11 000 French and 8500 Chinese lexical classes. The choice of the languages is mostly determined by the applied tasks of machine translation within corresponding language pairs, though as we have languages here that are typologically different such a choice allows testing the universality of the Compreno model as well.

The format in which the lexical data is implemented has been worked out for this particular system by ABBYY developers. Compreno Parser is available on a fee-for-service basis.

In the following, we briefly present existing multilingual lexical databases (2) and linguistic problems they have to encounter (3); give an overview of Compreno semantic framework (4) and, finally, present in more detail how Compreno MLLD deals with cross-lingual asymmetry and serves as a basis for machine translation (5).

## 2. Snapshot of the Existing Multilingual Lexical Databases

In this section we provide an overview of the most representative wide-scale projects aimed at constructing multilingual lexical resources in terms of their theoretical approaches and potential NLP applications leaving aside other less known MLLDs for the reason of space limits.

### 2.1 EuroWordNet project

The mainstream approach to the construction of wide-scale multilingual resources has been demonstrated by the EuroWordNet (Vossen, 2004) and the following Global WordNet Grid initiative. In these projects the goal is to build a worldwide grid of wordnets by means of an interlingual platform.

EuroWordNet consists of individual databases for seven European languages (Dutch, English, Italian, Spanish, German, French, Czech and Estonian) and is analogous to the original Princeton WordNet for English. EuroWordNet provides a fine-grained formal concept analysis for nouns. However, it comes with a poor database of illustrating examples and lacks information about the syntactic behavior of verbs and nouns.

Besides, in EuroWordNet, each language-specific WordNet is an autonomous language-specific ontology where each language has its own set of concepts and lexical-semantic relations based on the lexicalization patterns of that language. EuroWordNet differentiates between language-specific and language-independent modules. The language-independent modules consist of a top concept ontology and an unstructured Inter-lingua-Index (ILI) that provides mapping across individual WordNet structures and meanings.

### 2.2. PAROLE/SIMPLE lexicons

The initial goal of the LE PAROLE project conducted by the Council of Europe was to produce a head of the harmonized corpora and lexicons for 12 European languages: Catalan, Danish, Dutch,

English, Finnish, French, German, Greek, Italian, Portuguese, Spanish, and Swedish. These efforts resulted in monolingual morphological and syntactic lexicons for these languages, the volume of each lexicon amounting to 20000 entries.

The next step towards cross-lingual usage of these resources was the SIMPLE project, when existing morphological and syntactic data were provided with semantic representations. The SIMPLE lexicons were developed in line with the EAGLES (Experts Advisory Group on Language Engineering Standards) requirements on lexical-semantic representations for NLP tasks. Thus developers tried to bear in mind potential NLP applications; still they did not refer to any particular applications that would use this information. The SIMPLE lexicons cover 10000 word meanings for the above mentioned languages; they are built around the same head ontology and the same set of semantic templates.

Just as EuroWordNet SIMPLE is constructed not as a property-rich ontology but as a hierarchical net of the lexical items that imposes constrains to its NLP applicability: it lacks disambiguating power and the relations between entities are insufficient (Nirenburg, 2004). To ensure an overlap of lexical senses certain EuroWordNet's Base concepts were converted into each language providing linking of the lexical stock.

The theoretical foundations of the semantic description in SIMPLE are based on the extensions of Generative Lexicon theory (Pustejovsky, 1995) that makes it different from EuroWordNet. A SIMPLE lexical entry includes the following semantic information: 1) semantic type, corresponding with the SemU (semantic unit); 2) domain information 3) lexicographic gloss 4) argument structure for predicate 5) selectional restrictions on the arguments 6) event type to characterize the aspectual properties of verbal predicates 7) link of the arguments to the syntactic subcategorization frames, as represented in PAROLE lexicons 8) Qualia Structure 9) information about regular polysemous alternation in which a word sense may enter 10) cross-part-of-speech relation (derivation) 11) synonymy (McShane et al., 2004).

## 2.3. FrameNet and FrameNet-like lexicons

Another large-scale multilingual project is FrameNet (Baker et al, 1998). FrameNet is based on Fillmore's Frame Semantics (Fillmore, 1976). Frame Semantics models the lexical meaning of predicates in terms of *frames*; frames describe a conceptual structure or prototypical situation together with a set of semantic roles, or *frame elements (FEs)* involved in the situation. FrameNet currently contains about 600 frames. FrameNet projects employ the deep syntactic representations provided by large-scale lexical functional grammars as syntactic basis for frame-based meaning assignment. As an additional knowledge source FrameNet uses the public SUMO/MILO ontology whose classes are also aligned with WordNet.

By employing semantic frames as interlingual representations, FrameNet, as opposed to other MLLDs, focuses on organizational units larger than words. Besides, each FrameNet entry contains exhaustive information about its semantic and syntactic combinatorial potential and semantically annotated example from large parallel corpora. Thus FrameNet's database deals effectively with paraphrase patterns across languages.
Currently, there are several autonomous FrameNet and FrameNet-like lexicons for English, German, Danish, French, Swedish, Spanish, Japanese and Chinese languages, all on different stages of completion.

## 3. Challenges for Multilingual Lexical Databases

Construction of MLLDs faces even more complicated problems than those encountered in the creation of monolingual lexical databases (Boas, 2005). Among the main issues developers of the MLLDs have to face are: 1) cross-linguistic polysemy; 2) asymmetry of source and target semantic and syntactic structures; 3) cross-language asymmetry in the delimitation of semantic fields.

- cross-linguistic polysemy

Dictionaries often vary in their organization of word meanings, which makes it difficult to compare definitions across different dictionaries. Besides, most polysemous words are usually the most frequent ones and their meanings are often domain-independent which may make disambiguation impossible. In the case of MLLDs for NLP tasks granularity of sense distinction is a key and controversial both to professional lexicographers and applications (Palmer et. al, 2006).

Cross-linguistic polysemy is even more problematic. It may vary from a complete overlapping of word senses through diverging polysemy to the absence of correspondences among senses across languages (Altenberg and Granger, 2002). Thus, consistent criteria for sense distinction and strategies for cross-lingual sense mappings are crucial for the successful implementation of a MLLD.

- semantic and syntactic asymmetry

In addition to providing information about different meanings of a word, any MLLD should accurately describe deep semantic model of each sense and all its possible surface realizations to ensure correct cross-language mapping.

- cross-language asymmetry in the delimitation of semantic fields

As Talmy (2000) points out, languages differ in the kinds of semantic components they lexicalize. This has a number of important implications for the overall architecture of a MLLD. Some languages might make semantic distinctions that are irrelevant in others. For example, English verbs use particles to show the path of motion (*"run into"*, *"go out"*, *"fall down"*), whereas in Russian and German the path is encoded by affixation, in French – usually by the verb itself and in Chinese by directional modifiers.

Another challenge is posited by culture-specific vocabulary, lexical gaps and their translation equivalents across languages. In this sense, the conception of MLLD development should stem from the Principle of Practical Effability (Nirenburg and Raskin, 2004), which states that what can be expressed in one language can be *somehow* expressed in all languages, be it by a word, phrase, etc. It should also take into account fixed multiword expressions (idioms, terms and collocations) and include a description of how to map such multiword expressions across languages.

Below, we present in more detail the theoretical approaches that Compreno semantic model employs and demonstrate how it treats the problems mentioned above.

## 4. Key features of Compreno Semantic Model

The Compreno linguistic technology has been originally developed for machine translation, but now it is applied for a wider range of NLP applications aimed at semantic analysis.

In the following we will focus on the universal semantic module of the system and show how its mechanisms can be applied to describe a group of typologically different languages (English, Russian, German, French and Chinese).

### 4.1. Semantic Hierarchy

All words in our system are organized in the form of a thesaurus-like hierarchical tree which we call the **semantic hierarchy** (henceforth SH). The tree consists of language-independent branches called **semantic classes (SC)**, which are filled with lexical items of natural languages – **lexical classes (LC)**. Higher semantic classes denote general notions like entities, characteristics or actions, while their children have more specific meanings, so the deeper the class is the more particular notion it expresses:

*ENTITY_LIKE_CLASSES > ENTITY > FOOD > SOUP > KHARCHO > kharcho*

*ENTITY_LIKE_CLASSES > ENTITY > FOOD > food*

Each semantic class can have both semantic and lexical classes as its descendants (fig. 1).

FIGURE 1 - Fragment of the Semantic Hierarchy.

Lexical classes, in turn, contain lexemes with morphological paradigms. Each lexical class can have several lexemes that are **grammatical derivates (GD)**: typical instances are verbs and verbal nouns (like "*translate – translation*") or adjectives and adverbs (like "*beautiful – beautifully*") that differ only in their part of speech type.

The **lexicographic description** of the classes includes the following information: 1) a gloss drawn from a dictionary; 2) compatibility examples; 3) semantic and grammatical restrictions for different surface realizations of the actant valencies; 4) examples of voice transformation (for verbs) and additional restrictions imposed by them, if any; 5) relevant grammatical information; 6) examples of nontrivial translations, set expressions and any other relevant information. For Chinese, we also indicate the transcription, the spelling in Traditional characters, variant spellings and give glosses for all examples. It is essential to provide exhaustive information for the core vocabulary as it serves as basis for the syntactic descriptions and parser. Later on, the work becomes more labor-saving as syntactic and semantic models of LCs are inherited from their ancestors and only local mismatches should be marked.

All words in the hierarchy are attributed with grammatical and semantic values, called **grammemes** and **semantemes** respectively. The usage of grammemes has been minutely examined in Anisimovich et al. 2012, some illustrations will be given below as well. **Semantemes** help to distinguish different lexical items within one semantic class (for other their functions see Anisimovich et al. 2012): i.e., *"beautiful, pretty, handsome"* have a <<PolarityPlus>> semanteme while *"ugly"* takes <<PolarityMinus>>. Semantemes are universal for all languages. We use more than 1100 semantemes in SH. On the contrary, **grammatical** system is unique for every language. So, the number of grammatical categories varies depending on the language. For example, in Russian we set up about 460 categories and 2500 grammemes, 420 / 2400 in English, 240 / 940 in French, 260 / 1300 in German and 60 / 160 in Chinese.

The LC-descendants of one semantic class that have a similar set of semantemes are synonyms. During translation, lexical choice at the synthesis stage usually favors the lexical class with the most similar set of semantemes. Such a choice gets a better evaluation than mismatches between input and output classes.

Words with the same root that differ not only morphologically but also semantically are introduced as **semantic derivates (SD)**: SDs are the descendants of one lexical class that differ in semantemes, for example – "*handsome – unhandsome*".

The possibility to store multiple SDs under one lexical class is especially helpful for words with a big number of SDs. For instance, the verb "*go*" has about 30 SDs like "*go away, go back, go in*", etc., corresponding to such verbs as "*leave, return*" and "*enter*", so we can place all these verbs in one SC, where "*go, leave, return*" and "*enter*" will be different LCs while "*go away, go back, go in*"– the SDs of the LC "*go*". Both LCs "*leave, return, enter*" and the SDs "*go away, go back, go in*" acquire the semantemes <<From>>, <<Back>> and <<To>>, respectively. This ensures their distinction from the neutral "*go*".

Semantic derivates are formed by regular morphological models and express semantic relations which are typical for the derivates formed by these models: "*go away, fly away, swim away*" are all formed with *'away'* particle and express the semantics of leaving the place, or "*go in, come in, fly in*" are formed with the help of *"in"* particle and express the semantics of moving inside.

Such derivates can also differ in the semantic valencies they attach: for instance, valency indicating initial point ("*come [from school]*") is typical for neutral „*come*" but is rather marginal for the "*come in*" derivate.

The derivates are marked with **derivatemes** – fixed combinations of corresponding grammemes and semantemes, which describe both their syntactic and semantic features. For example, the German verb "*laufen*" ("*to run*") has 40 SDs such as "*durchlaufen*" ("*to run through*"), "*zurücklaufen*" ("*to run back*") or "*fortlaufen*" ("*to run away*") with the derivatemes <Durch_EnRouteLandmark>, <ZurückRück_Back> and <Fort_Depart> respectively. These derivatemes, in turn, contain semantemes <<En_Route>>, <<Back>> and <<From>>. At the current stage of the project the system numbers about 120 English derivatemes, 150 Russian derivatemes, 120 German derivatemes and 10 French derivatemes.

The following table provides data on language-specific descendents of the SC TO_RUN with a few illustrating examples:

| | English | Russian | German | French | Chinese |
|---|---|---|---|---|---|
| number of LCs | 9 (run, scatter, jog, lope, etc.) | 3 (бежать, трусить, пробежка) | 2 (laufen, rennen) | 1 (courir) | 2 pǎo (跑, bēnpǎo 奔跑) |
| number of SDs | 37 | 42 | 42 | 2 | N/A |
| number of GDs | 46 | 52 | 44 | 3 | N/A |
| <<Back>> | *run_back* | - | *zurücklaufen* | - | pǎohuí 跑回 |
| <<To>> | - | *прибежать* | - | *accourir* | pǎodào 跑到 |
| <<From>> | *run_away* *whip_off* | *убежать* | *davonlaufen* | - | pǎoqù 跑去 |

TABLE 1 - Language-specific descendents of the SC TO_RUN

N/A in some fields of the table means 'not applicable'. In Chinese a verb with a directional and resultative complement can insert potential marker between a main verb and a complement and a lot of disyllabic verbs can be used nominally; thus we decided to treat Chinese verbs differently. We do not add them to the SH as grammatical derivates, but describe their derivation paradigm as high as possible on ancestor SC. Examples on the derivates are provided in the LC commentary and nominal syntactic usage is marked with grammeme <VerbNoun>.

- cross-language asymmetry in the delimitation of semantic fields

The asymmetry between different languages is neutralized by marking semantic classes with a representativity feature: this feature defines the relation between a given class and its parent.

There are 3 types of representativity: a SC can be **non-representative**, **semi-representative**, or **fully representative**. A non-representative SC is completely cut off from its parent, so the translation equivalent for a source concept will be chosen among the LCs of this semantic class only (that is actually a normal situation, where no language asymmetry occurs). A semi-representative SC allows choosing translation equivalents from the parent SC as well (an option for cases where no direct correspondence in a target language can be found and the optimal equivalent is a hyperonym for the word). Finally, a fully representative semantic class is "transparent", i.e., it allows choosing translation equivalents both in the parent and child semantic classes. For instance, English "*go*" and French "*aller*" mean both "*go on foot or by vehicle*" while in Russian or German different verbs must be used here: correspondingly „*идти*" and "*gehen*" for motion on foot and "*ехать*", "*fahren*" for motion by vehicle. When translating "*go*" and "*aller*" into Russian or German we normally have to choose between these verbs. So we put "go" and "*aller*" in a parent class that has two representative SC-descendents: MOTION_WITHOUT_DEVICES with "*идти, gehen*" and MOTION_ON_DEVICES with „*ехать, fahren'*. The choice between them depends on the semantic valencies expressed at a given sentence, their filling and statistics as well.

We claim that the tree of semantic classes is universal for the classification of all languages. It may certainly still look a bit contrastive. The fact is that we cannot simultaneously fill the hierarchy with a correct representative sample of meanings for both typologically similar and typologically different languages. But our successive description of Russian, English, Chinese, French and German has clearly showed that the structure of semantic classes underwent practically no important changes: cases of language-unique lexicalization lead us to adding low-level semantic classes.

Another problem concerning cross-language asymmetry is a phenomenon of semantic incorporation, so to say: under semantic incorporation we mean here cases like an English verb "*fish*" – "*to catch fish*". Such incorporation is not universal and occurs within words with different meanings in different languages. Thus Russian lacks a verb like "fish", and intransitive usage of "fish" must be translated with two words – "*ловить-catch рыбу-fish*".

To solve this problem we create a SC TO_FISH with English LC "*fish*" and put the whole expression – "*ловить рыбу*" in the Russian part of the class. This verb can attach an [Object] slot as well – "*to fish [for trout]*", but its usage without the [Object] slot is also possible - in "*he is fishing*" the semantic valency of [Object] is not expressed explicitly and is incorporated in the semantic structure of the verb.

- lexical gaps and multiword expressions

SH is a dynamic database that can be revised (mainly on its lower SCs) and supplemented when we add new languages and have to describe culture-specific realities. For example, when describing the Chinese word "旗袍 (qípáo)" which denotes traditional Chinese body-hugging one-piece dress we create a new SC and fill it with corresponding loan-words in other languages – "*ципао*" in Russian, "*qipao*" and "*cheongsam*" in English.

If a language lacks the necessary loan-word and the translation requires the use of several words, we put the whole necessary expression in the SC. For instance, we created SC S_BAHN_RAILWAY for German-specific entity "urban railway". This SC is filled with LC S-Bahn in German, loan-word S-Bahn in English and a multiword expression "*городская железная дорога"* (*"urban railway"*) in Russian as it is the only way to translate this word into Russian.

- language-specific challenges: some examples

Each language can have some peculiarities that require special attention in formal descriptions. Thus, we have elaborated consistent methodological guidelines for each language that take into account language-specific features to guarantee effective semantic and syntactic parsing.

For instance, upon adding German compounds to the SH, we consider whether their translation can be derived from their internal structure. If not, we add them to the SH into existing SCs or create new ones. For instance, the analysis of the compounds "*Geldautomat*" (*"ATM"*) and "*Straßenbahn*" (*"tram"*) is technically possible as there are lexical classes "*Geld*" (*"money"*), "*Automat*" (*"automat"*), "*Straße*" (*"street"*) and "*Bahn*" (*"train"*) in the SH and there are semantic slots that can describe semantic relations between them. However, possible interpretations, e.g. "*der Automat mit Geld*" (*"an automat with money"*) and *"die Bahn auf der Straße"* ("*a train in the street*") do not make any sense since they are not equal to the notions these compounds represent. So we add them to the SH into existing SCs or create new ones.

Possible disadvantage is that adding new languages, like German here, may demand the adding of new SCs to the SH as well, so the number of the universal SCs may grow to provide the necessary translation correlations. But the necessity of adding new SCs doesn't seem to cause any inconvenience for the model in general.

Another example: Chinese has a relatively strict word order and limited freedom to attach dependent constituents to the left or to the right of the head-verb. This often leads to asymmetry in the semantic model of Chinese and the semantic model of the target/source language. Thus, in order to translate a sentence with several dependent constituents attached to the head verb into Chinese we have to resort to one of the following transformations:

- to reduplicate a verb,
- to move a child constituent to another head, usually downwards a syntactic tree,
- to add another coordinated or dependent predication,
- to move a dependent constituent into a topic position.

Thus, it is essential for Chinese to provide 'negative' information in the verb LCs indicating which of semantic slots typical for the SC cannot be attached to the head and what type of transformation will be needed. For more details concerning Chinese-specific challenges and solutions refer to Manicheva et al., (2012).

## 4.2 Compatibility, semantic and syntactic model

Semantic relations between words are described in terms of **semantic slots** that partially correlate with the notions of Tesnière"s valencies (Tesnière, 1976), Fillmore"s cases (Fillmore, 1968), as well as with semantic and thematic roles in later theories. The key difference in the Compreno system is that most theories usually focus on verbal arguments only, underlining the difference between complements and modifiers, while in Compreno project we introduce the semantic slots for all possible semantic dependencies, more than 300 slots in total.

This means there are semantic slots for verbal actants (such as [Agent] in "*[the man] came in*" or [Possessor] in "*[I] have a pen*"), adjectival and adverbial modifiers (such as [Ch_Parameter_Dimensions] in "*[large] drops*" or [Ch_Evaluation] in "*[good] idea*"), circumstantial adjuncts (spatial or temporal, for instance, as [Time] and [Locative] in "*[yesterday] I saw him [in the street]*") and plenty of others.

Semantic slots are language-independent and get surface syntactic realizations (we call them **surface** or **syntactic slots**) in every language ([Agent] usually corresponds to the subject surface slot in an active mood and characteristical slots like the above-mentioned adjectival and adverbial modifiers are often expressed by attributive modifiers).

The semantic hierarchy is organized according to **inheritance** principle: many slots, especially the circumstantial ones like adjuncts or characteristics, are introduced on the upper levels and the child classes inherit them, as such constituents can be governed by almost any heads ("*an [important] person, book, meeting, work*" or "*[last year] she worked there/had this opportunity/was very rich*").

Other constituents, especially the arguments, are introduced on lower levels. For instance, verbs like "*have*" or "*possess*" need a [Possessor] slot while verbs like "*work*" or "*run*" do not have this valency as they have an [Agent]-subject. So the [Possessor] slot is introduced in the necessary semantic class only.

The inheritance principle means that most part of manual work is done on the initial stage of the description, when the core vocabulary is added to the SH, as words placed to the SH later inherit the most part of their semantic and syntactic model.

In different branches semantic slot can have different **status**: usually the **allowed** one, **normal** or **preferred**. For instance, the [Possessor] slot in "*[I] have a pen*" has the preferred status, while the [Possessor] slot in "*[my] pen*" has the normal status.
Each semantic slot can be **filled** with a fixed set of the semantic classes. I.e., [Possessor] is filled with beings, organizations and some territorial units: "*[my/our school's/Russia's] property*", while slots for characteristics are filled with classes containing, for instance, adjectives and adverbs with corresponding semantics ([Ch_Evaluation] is filled with LCs like "*good, bad, excellent*", etc.).

The instantiation of semantic slots can be restricted to semantic classes. For instance, the [Object] slot can be filled with a wide range of vocabulary ("*to have [a cat/good health/an advantage]*"), but some verbs require additional constraints on filling: "*to read [a book]*", but * "*to read [a chair]*". Still, one can find marginal examples like "*I'll eat [my hat] if Kim ate [a motor-bike]*" (Soehn, 2005). For such cases, we define two sets of fillers: the allowed one and the preferred one. Thus, additional restrictions are normally imposed by further constraining the preferred fillers.

There are as well special cases of nontrivial compatibility, when a lexeme in some meaning can be combined with only one or several words. For example, we can say "*broad difference*" in the sense of "*big difference*" but can hardly say "*broad love*" in the same meaning. To describe this type of restricted compatibility A.K. Žolkovskij and I.A. Mel'čuk introduced a mechanism of

**lexical functions (LF)** in their "Meaning-Text Theory" (Žolkovskij, Mel'čuk, 1967 and later papers of the authors).

We have adopted the idea for Compreno system. If the descendants of some semantic class have such narrow compatibility, we declare this class to be a lexical function, mark the semantic slot where the narrowing is necessary, and indicate the fillers of this slot (the LF-arguments) for each LC-descendant of the semantic class. The arguments can be both the dependent or parent constituents. I.e., the SC GROUP_OF_ANIMALS is a LF and includes LCs like "*swarm*" or "*shoal*", the former usually combines with insects, the latter – with fish. Here "*swarm*" and "*shoal*" syntactically govern their LF-arguments ("*swarm [of insects]*", "*shoal [of fish]*") while in the example with "*[broad] difference*" "*broad*" is a dependent constituent.

The mechanism of LF proved to be an indispensable tool to describe classifiers and measure words in Chinese. Classifiers and measure words are used together with numbers to define the quantity of a given object. Different groups of nouns collocate with different classifiers:
yī bǎ yǐzi
一/把/椅子 - One chair (one + m. w. for objects with a handle + chair)

liǎng zhāng zhuōzǐ
两 / 张 / 桌 子 - Two tables (two+ m. w. for objects with flat surface + table)

### 4.3 Sense distinction and disambiguation problem

Sorting out meanings and positioning them in the SH is a controversial issue. On the one hand, we should describe them thoroughly and consistently in terms of the source language. On the other hand we need to correlate meanings with the material in other languages to ensure appropriate translation.

It often happens that dictionaries define several meanings of a word that can be actually added to the same SC in the SH or at least to the neighboring SCs. However, having homonyms that have no clear distinction expressed in mutually exclusive formal terms in closely-related classes is highly problematic. The choice of the necessary homonym becomes a problem and the number of hypotheses at the analysis stage grows. So the general principle of our lexicographic description is to merge homonyms with similar models and use other mechanisms to define the differences in translation (such as collocations, for instance).

Another key NLP problem is disambiguation. In most cases proper description of the semantic model of the word helps to distinguish its different meanings. For instance, we can understand that
(1) *I took to London,*
(2) *I took a book,*
(3) *I took a shower*
have different instances of "take" (from different semantic classes) as in the first sentence "take" has no [Object] slot which is obligatory for its usage in two other meanings, and we know that the example (2) can't have "take" in the meaning we have it in the example (3) as "take" from the third example evidently has rather narrow compatibility, so it is located in a LF-class and has narrow arguments thus.

Still, nothing in the semantic description prevents us from understanding *"take"* in sentence (3) as equal to "take" in sentence (2): indeed, sentences like *"I took the shower in my left hand"* are also possible. Here the statistical mechanism comes into play.

To describe a semantic model of a word and to differentiate its meanings we also use grammemes as well – for example, reflexivity or transitivity grammemes. Consider some French examples: "POSITION_IN_SPACE: trouver" (*"to be situated"*) is used in a reflexive form only and thus has a grammeme <OnlyReflexive> (*"La maison se trouve à Paris"*– *"The house is situated in Paris"*), while "TO_SEEK_FIND : trouver" (*"to find"*) is non-reflexive (*"J'ai trouvé un emploi"* – *"I have found a job"*) or self-reflexive (*"Je me suis trouvé un emploi"*. – *"I have found a job for myself"*).

.

## 5. Compreno MLLD as basis for machine translation

Compreno MLLD serves as a lexical-semantic database for a rule-based MT system. Currently it provides a high quality machine translation for the EN<->RU language pair. It was also tested on a limited text material for GE<->RU and FR<-> RU language pairs. Below we briefly describe the translation process with a special focus on the processing of the semantic model.

When the program translates *"food"* from English to Russian, for example, the following operation is being done: we see the lexeme *"food"* which is in the corresponding English lexical class in the semantic class FOOD, go to the universal level – SC FOOD, and descend back to the necessary lexical class in the Russian language – *"еда"*:
*food => FOOD => еда*

Important convenience is that generally when adding some new language (French, for instance) we do not have to describe French-Russian and French-English translation separately. We just add a necessary lexical class *"nourriture"* in French and thus get all the desired translation pairs (that"s an ideal situation though).

Of course, there is a lot of asymmetry between languages when such a straightforward translation is impossible. Let's consider some examples and illustrate briefly different mechanisms that can help (here we will just show different possibilities of the description without going into details and arguing where each of these mechanisms shall be chosen).

To treat cross-lingual asymmetry effectively, we have elaborated a wide range of universal instruments. Important tools related to the semantic module are 1) **collocations** and 2) **transformational rules**. Basically, both 1 and 2 represent a formalized description with conditions expressed in terms of SCs, LCs, semantemes, grammemes, semantic and/or syntactic slots and are aimed at setting exact correspondences between languages.

**Collocations** are used in more trivial cases, where the transformation of the structure is not very hard (usually to ensure the correct lexical choice or to set correspondences between different semantic models). Some collocations are written manually, other are gathered automatically. For instance:

(1) English construction *"Y-sized X"* must be translated in Russian like *"X размером с Y"* (the Russian variant roughly corresponds to the English *"X like Y in size"*), so we need a transformation of the structure here and add a collocation specifying all the necessary semantic, syntactic and grammar conditions for both languages. The collocation is written on a relatively high level of the SH as at least any entity can correspond to the X. Hence, we get proper translations for *"egg-sized hail"* <-> *"град размером с яйцо"* and etc.

(2) German prepositions like "*angesichts*" (*"in the face of"*), "*gegenüber*" ("*towards*") can correspond to noun phrases in other languages:
German: *Grausamkeit [gegenüber Object_Relation: Tieren],*
English: *cruelty [towards Object_Relation: animals] / cruelty [with Ch_Relation: respect [to Relation_Correlative:animals]],*
Russian: *жестокость [по Ch_Relation: отношению [к Relation_Correlative: животным]]* (a structure equal to the English one *"cruelty [with respect [to animals]"*).
Some collocations are gathered automatically, some are written by linguists.

**Transformational rules** are applied when the transformation is rather complicated, especially when the head of the constituent must be changed, or when dealing with regular cross-lingual asymmetry. Consider some examples:

(1) French expression "*l'ensemble [de x]*" means *"[all] x's"*, i.e. "*l'ensemble [de messages]*" – "*[all] messages*". In French the variable [x] depends on "*ensemble*", while in English "*message*" becomes the head.

(2) In European languages numerals that go between thousand and million are counted by thousands, while in the numeral system of Chinese there is a special word for ten thousands – "万" (wàn), and all the following numerals are derived from it. I.e., "百万" (bǎiwàn) (100 wans) stands for million, "二十五万" (èrshíwǔwàn) (25 wans) stands for 250,000.

Thus we have to add a new SC WAN_NUMBER to SH with a semanteme <<Rank_Wan>>. WAN_NUMBER is a descendent of the SC NUMBER along with other numeral units - TENS, THOUSANDS, etc. As we see, a direct translation through semantic classes is impossible, so we make the transformation with the help of a transformational rule that translates numerals over 9999 from/into Chinese through converting the numerals from one language into another.

## Conclusion

The Compreno technology combines both multilingual lexical database and parser technology. It includes several levels of language description: the morphological, semantic, and syntactic ones, and possesses a wide range of powerful tools to describe lexicon and grammar of typologically different languages and establish correlations between them as well.

The universal and full description of the semantic models of the lexicon together with additional mechanisms like collocations, transformational rules and statistics allows to cope with the problems typical for NLP applications, i.e. the problems of language asymmetry and language polysemy.

The existing description shows that Compreno semantic model can serve as a universal integral framework for multilingual lexical databases and be successfully applied for different NLP tasks such as machine translation, text mining, information retrieval, fact extraction and other problems concerned with semantic analysis.

Furthermore, the English, Russian, German, French and Chinese lexical-semantic dictionaries can be studied from a cognitive perspective, as filling universal semantic hierarchy with language-specific vocabulary gives a vivid representation of the structure of language-specific vocabulary, lexicalization patterns and different conceptualizations of the world.

## References


Altenberg, B. and Granger, S. (2002). Recent trends in cross-linguistic lexical studies. In B. Altenberg and S. Granger (ed.), *Lexis in Contrast*. Amsterdam/Philadelphia: Benjamins, pages 3-50.

Anisimovich K. V., Druzhkin K. Y., Minlos F. R., Petrova M. A., Selegey V. P., Zuev K.A.(2012). Syntactic and semantic parser based on ABBYY Compreno linguistic technologies //Komp'juternaja lingvistika i intellektual'nye tehnologii: Trudy mezhdunarodnoj konferencii. 'Dialog' 2012 [Computational Linguistics and Intellectual Technologies: Proceedings of the International Conference "Dialog 2012"], Bekasovo.

Baker, C. F., Fillmore C. J. and Lowe J. B. (1998). The Berkeley FrameNet Project. In *Proceedings of COLING-ACL '98*, Montréal, Canada.

Boas, H C. (2005). Semantic frames as interlingual representations for multilingual lexical databases. *International Journal of Lexicography*, Volume 18(4), pages 445–478.

Fillmore , C.J. (1968). The case for case. In *Universals in linguistic theory*, Bach, E. and Harms, R. (ed.), pages 1-90, New York.

Fillmore, C. J. (1976). Frame Semantics and the Nature of Language. Annals of the New York Academy of Sciences: Conference on the Origin and Development of Language and Speech, Vol. 280, pages. 20-32.

Manicheva, E. S., Dreyzis, Y. D., Selegey, V.P. Razrabotka leksiko-semanticheskogo slovar'a kitaiskogo yazika dlya mnogoyazichnoy sistemi analyza teksta [Development of Chinese language lexical-semantic dictionary for multilingual NLP system] 2012. Komp'juternaja lingvistika i intellektual'nye tehnologii: Trudy mezhdunarodnoj konferencii. 'Dialog' 2012 [Computational Linguistics and Intellectual Technologies: Proceedings of the International Conference "Dialog 2012"], Bekasovo.

McShane, M., Zabludowski, M., Nirenburg, S. and Beale, S. (2004). OntoSem and SIMPLE: Two multi-lingual world views. In *Proceedings of ACL-2004 Workshop on Text Meaning and*

*Interpretation*, Barcelona, Spain.

Nirenburg, S., McShane, M., Beale, S. (2004). The rationale for building resources expressly for NLP. In *Proceedings of LREC 2004*, Lisbon, Portugal.

Nirenburg, S. and Raskin V. (2004). Ontological Semantics. Cambridge, MA: MIT Press.

Palmer, M., Dang, H. T., Fellbaum C. (2006). Making fine-grained and coarse-grained sense distinctions, both manually and automatically. In *Natural Language Engineering*, Volume 13(2), pages 137-163.

Pustejovsky, J. (1995). The Generative Lexicon. Cambridge, pages 11-21.

Soehn, J.-P. (2005). Selectional Restrictions in HPSG: I'll eat my hat! In Stefan Müller (ed.), In *Proceedings of the HPSG-2005 Conference*, University of Lisbon, Portugal, Stanford: CSLI Publications.

Talmy, L. (2000). Toward a cognitive semantics. Cambridge, MA: MIT Press.

Tesnière L. (1976). Éleménts de syntaxe structural, Paris: Klincksieck, 1976.

Vossen P. (2004). EuroWordNet: a multilingual database of autonomous and language-specific wordnets connected via an Inter-Lingual-Index. In *International Journal of Lexicography*, Volume 17 (2), OUP, pages 161-173.

Žolkovskij, A. I., Mel'čuk, I. A. (1967). O semantičeskom sinteze. Problemy kibernetiki, Volume 19, pages 177–238.

# Author Index